Ulrike Krause

Linking Refugee Protection with Development Assistance

Analyses with a Case Study in Uganda

Die Deutsche Nationalbibliothek lists this publication in the Deutsche Nationalbibliografie; detailed bibliographic data is available in the Internet at http://dnb.d-nb.de.

a.t.: Magdeburg, Univ., Diss., 2012

ISBN 978-3-8487-0262-6

1. Edition 2013

Dedicated to Gerhard H. A. Schlegel

Preface

This book is a revised version of my doctoral thesis about "Development-oriented Refugee Assistance: Sustainable, Efficient and Gender-sensitive? Theoretical and Practical Analyses based on a Case Study of the Rhino Camp in Uganda", submitted to the Otto-von-Guericke University of Magdeburg in 2012.

Several hurdles were encountered during the course of research. Though, I was and am fortunate to have a number of enthusiastic, supportive and understanding people around me whose invaluable assistance and patience made it possible that the last three years I worked on this project came to a happy end. I would like to sincerely thank each one and at the same time apologize for not being able to name everyone.

I am especially grateful to my 'Doktorvater', Prof. Dr. Karl-Peter Fritzsche and my second supervisor, Prof. Dr. Birgit Sauer for their guidance, intellectual insights and valuable comments, encouragement and trust.

My research profited enormously from the former DED Refugee/IDP Programme in Uganda by providing data access, and from all interviewees by offering information. I would like to especially thank Astrid Peter for her constant readiness to professionally support my research endeavor and to personally believe in me. I also thank Safinah Namyalo and Moses Obbo for their continuous support.

The Otto-von-Guericke University of Magdeburg enabled me to conduct research in Uganda by granting the postgraduate scholarship for which I am grateful.

My colleagues and friends of both research and operations contributed to my work by numerous constructive and controversial discussions. I appreciated all of the critical comments and impulses. The work of Alexander Betts has been a great source of information and inspiration for me.

Finally, I wish to thank Andy Gooch for allowing me to use his photo on my front cover, my family and friends for their moral support, motivation, welcomed distractions and patience.

And Lala.

Bad Homburg, January 2013 — Ulrike Krause

Table of Contents

List of Figures

List of Tables

List of Acronyms

1951 Convention	Convention relating to the Status of Refugees
1967 Protocol	Protocol relating to the Status of Refugees
3Rs	Relief, Rehabilitation and Resettlement
4Rs	Repatriation, Reintegration, Rehabilitation and Reconstruction
AGDM	Age, Gender, and Diversity Mainstreaming
CEDAW	Committee on the Elimination of Discrimination against Women
CIREFCA	International Conference on Central American Refugees
CM	Care and Maintenance
DAR	Development Assistance for Refugees-Hosting Areas
DAW	Division for the Advancement of Women of the UN
DAWN	Development Alternatives with Women for a new era
DED	Deutscher Entwicklungsdienst (German Development Service)
DFID	Department for International Development
DLI	Development through Local Integration
DRC	Democratic Republic of Congo
EC	European Commission
ECOSOC	United Nations Economic and Social Council
EU	European Union
ExCom	Executive Committee of UNHCR
GAD	Gender and Development
GDI	Gender-related Development Index
GDP	Gross Domestic Product
GFMD	Global Forum on Migration and Development
HDI	Human Development Index
HIV	Human Immunodeficiency Virus
HPI	Human Poverty Index
ICARA I	first International Conference on Assistance to Refugees in Africa
ICARA II	second International Conference on Assistance to Refugees in Africa
IDP	Internally Displaced Person
ILO	International Labour Organization
IOM	International Organization for Migration
IR	International Relations
KY	Kabaka Yekka
LC	Local Council
LRA	Lord's Resistance Army
LRRD	Linking Relief, Rehabilitation and Development
LS	Local Settlement

MDGs	Millennium Development Goals
MFPED	Ministry of Finance, Planning and Economic Development
NGO	Non-governmental Organization
NRM/A	National Resistance Movement and Army
OPM	Office of Prime Minister
OSAGI	United Nations Office of the Special Advisor on Gender Issues and Advancement of Women
PEAP	Poverty Eradication Action Plan
PRSP	Poverty Reduction Strategy Papers
POP	People-oriented Planning
QIP	Quick Impact Project
RBM	Results-based management
RE	Resettlement
RP	Voluntary Repatriation
RWC	Refugee Welfare Council
SGBV	Sexual and Gender-based Violence
SRS	Self-Reliance Strategy
TDA	Targeted Development Assistance
UN	United Nations
UNDG	United Nations Development Group
UNDP	United Nations Development Programme
UNFPA	United Nations Population Fund
UNHCR	Office of the United Nations High Commissioner for Refugees
UNICEF	United Nations Children's Fund
UNIFEM	United Nations Development Fund for Women
UPC	Uganda Peoples Congress
V.I.P. latrine	Ventilated Improved Pit Latrine
WFP	World Food Programme

Chapter I Introduction

1. Research Subject

Wars and armed conflicts greatly impact on civil society. People are tortured, trafficked, murdered, and driven from their homes. Especially displaced and escaped individuals and collectives add to the long lasting traumatization of the respective societies. Thus, adequate refugee assistance is essential to improve conditions and situations.

To assist refugees, the United Nations (UN) established the United Nations Office of High Commissioner for Refugees (UNHCR) through the adoption of the General Assembly Resolution 319 (IV) on 3 December 1949. Establishing this agency was pivotal in the aftermath of the Second World War which left countless refugees in its wake. Then, UNHCR was mandated to assist those who had become refugees as a result of the Second World War in Europe.

Within the past six decades, UNHCR's mandate changed according to arising needs. It was extended to assist not only refugees, but also Internally Displaced Persons (IDPs), and other groups of disadvantaged people. UNHCR is to provide assistance by means of emergency aid and relief as well as long-term care and maintenance programs. The agency's mission is to build, manage, and maintain refugee camps and settlements, to provide legal protection and advice as well as to supply beneficiaries with shelter, food, safe water, sanitation, and medical care in order to meet their basic needs. UNHCR's regional scope was broadened over the past sixty years and is now capturing the whole world (UNHCR 2007: 21).

Holding the mandate to protect and assist refugees worldwide appears particularly important when taking into account current developments. Most refugees are driven from their homes in the global South and seek safety within the global South. Hence, most refugees flee from one developing country to another developing country. Often, these less or least developed countries suffer from the pressure of incoming refugees on top of existing internal issues. These countries often lack basic infrastructure. The majority of refugees is imprisoned in protracted refugee situations. Long-term encampment, restrictions to their rights and little positive perspectives towards durable solutions complicate their lives and add onto their traumatization.

Preventing protracted refugee situations in the first place is often impossible because once people are forced to flee their countries of origin in need for support, they are rarely able to return immediately or within a short timeframe. Improving their long-term stay in countries of first asylum is a task taken on by

UNHCR. According to the agency, the three durable solutions are voluntary repatriation to the country of origin, resettlement to a third country, and local integration within the country of first asylum (UNHCR 2003b: 9ff). While voluntary repatriation and resettlement basically aim to relocate refugees away from the country of first asylum, local integration refers to the actual stay in the country of first asylum. Finding a way to create a care and maintenance program suitable for the host country and refugees, is desirable for UNHCR. One way to do so, from which the primary beneficiaries of refuge as well as the host country benefit, is development-oriented refugee assistance.

Development-oriented refugee assistance aims to bridge the gap between emergency aid and development. Host countries may suffer from the residence of refugees as natural resources may be used. Internal conflicts may arise due to the national community's feeling of being disadvantaged. They may perceive refugees as the ones receiving aid while they are left out. Development-oriented refugee assistance strives for not only providing aid to refugees, but also to local communities. It is understood to have the potential to improve the long-term stay of refugees in the countries of asylum. Moreover, operations under this scope can also bring about benefits for local communities through regional development initiatives.

It is exactly this strategy of development-oriented refugee assistance which is the central subject of my doctoral research and this book. Development-oriented refugee assistance is found to have numerous potentials for refugees and the hosting nations; it can contribute to an improvement of the long-term stay of refugees in the host countries, while also assisting host countries in carrying out development initiatives. My focus, however, is not the large scope of potentials it may capture. I aim to understand and analyze the programmatic sphere of this type of assistance against the migration-development nexus. How is development-oriented refugee assistance implemented? What is necessary? My attention is therefore clearly centered on the side of program implementation.

My research is guided by the overall question: How can a development-oriented approach to refugee assistance be delivered in a way that is sustainable, efficient and gender-sensitive? By means of my overall research question, I aim to determine what refugee and development assistance actually are and how both concepts of refugee assistance and development have been combined in international programs in the past. I strive for finding out what constitutes development-oriented refugee assistance and what specific features the approach has. Based on my analysis, I explore a case study in-depth. I aim to analyze operationalizations of care and maintenance programs implemented at Rhino Camp in the West Nile region of Uganda within the period of 1997 until 2006.

In Uganda, UNHCR and the Government of Uganda committed themselves to a strategy, which was to improve the original ad-hoc and short-term refugee aid.

One crucial aspect of the strategy was treating development as a central feature. Realizing this simultaneously implies that operations were neither spontaneous nor immediate. Rather, activities were to always ensure that the criterion of sustainability is fulfilled. Moreover, in the framework of such an approach, not only the original beneficiary group, namely refugees, but also national communities were targeted to benefit from activities.

During the defined research timeframe, refugees in Uganda were mainly from neighboring countries such as South Sudan, the Democratic Republic of Congo, Rwanda and Burundi. Mostly South Sudanese refugees were settled at Rhino Camp which constitutes the case study of this research project. Uganda's risk to receive new refugee waves remains high as the volatile regions of Sudan and DRC are continually in a state of conflict. By taking this specific fact in connection with the development status of Uganda into account, the value of integrating a development aspect into refugee aid becomes accentuated. Development-oriented refugee assistance is seen as essential in positively influencing Uganda's growth in spite of a high number of refugees cross the country's borders.

In Uganda's Rhino Camp, a development-oriented approach has been practiced since the mid-1990s. Established in 1992, it is located in the West Nile region and has been managed by the German Development Service (DED)[1] since 1996. Rhino Camp is more than just a mere campground; it is a refugee settlement. In spite of the similarities of basic structures between camps and settlements, the concept of refugee settlements is broader as it incorporates developmental components in all operational sections (health, education, sanitation etc.). The participating actors play significant roles in the planning and implementation processes. UNHCR provides the implementing partners with programmatic concepts and guidelines, while the Office of the Prime Minister (OPM) holds a supervisory function ensuring that operations proceed according to agreements between UNHCR and the Government of Uganda. The actual implementation is carried out by the DED Refugee/IDP Programme in particular.

1 The Government of Germany merged Deutscher Entwicklungsdienst gGmbH (DED, German Development Service) with two other organizations and established the Deutsche Gesellschaft für Internationale Zusammenarbeit GmbH (GIZ). Since the former DED implemented refugee-related operations in Rhino Camp, it will be referred to as DED or DED Refugee/IDP Programme and not GIZ throughout this writing.

2. *Current State of Research*

Development-oriented refugee assistance has hardly been the center of research. The contemporary debate on forced migration and migration studies in research is strongly influenced by the changing political spheres. Especially since the terrorist attacks on September 11th, 2001, 'terrorism' and 'security' became the keywords in the new millennium. While the media pushed a negatively connoted perception further, political communities reacted. The War against Terror was initiated and led by the United States. "As underdevelopment, poor governance and economic inequality were highlighted in the causation of conflict a decade ago [...], so they [the refugees] are now identified with the origins and causes of terrorism" (Harmer/Macrae 2004: 4). Preventing further terrorist acts was made a priority in the agenda of the international community. Humanitarian, relief and development aid initiatives were integrated into security concepts.

The language of security along with global incidences had far reaching impacts on the international perception of displaced persons, refugees and asylum seekers. They were increasingly perceived as causes for insecurity or simply as threats (Harmer/Macrae 2004: 4; Gibney 2002: 40-41). Northern industrialized nations tightened their asylum laws and policies[2] and the northern world prepared to prevent further incidences from happening. Southern refugee hosting spheres received more and more refugees despite their developing state of nation. They lacked the capacity to absorb the high number of refugees and additionally suffered from insecurity. The altering language in refugee discourse implied the perception of refugees as being a 'burden'; refugee situations were not approached as challenges which were to be met and resolved jointly. Refugees were rather seen as burdens or problems which caused further afflictions and difficulties. Based on this North-South divide, the international community continuously raised the question of 'burden-sharing'. According to refugee law, states are obliged "to protect the refugees who reach their territory" (Betts 2008b: 1). Durable solutions for refugees, however, still need to be found.

The above constellation has shaped contemporary debates on forced migration and migration studies in research and politics. Gaim Kibreab and Barbara Harrell-Bond[3] are two pioneers in the field of refugee assistance, which entailed the integration of development as a potential solution even before the language and perception of refugees were altered. In Kibreab's book from 1987 *Refugees and Development in Africa*, the author examines self-reliance strategies and asks

2 Though, migration issues were linked to security in the past (Gibney 2002: 40-41).

3 Also, Robert Gorman was also one of the early trend setters in this research field.

whether programs reached the intended success. He argues that "[to] transform the refugees from a liability to an asset and to enable them to become an important factor in the process of national development, three conditions must exist simultaneously": national economies must improve, refugee policies must be integrated nationally, and refugee policies must encourage refugees to partake in development processes (Kibreab 1987: 278). These aspects are still debated in the academic community (Kibreab 1983, 1987, 1990, 1996, 1999, 2001, 2004; Gorman/Kibreab 1997).

Harrell-Bond has concentrated on forced migration and migration studies throughout her career. In her writing *Imposing Aid: Emergency Assistance to Refugees* (1986), she criticizes relief structures and bureaucracy. She notes that

> [t]he international aid community is unprepared to maintain refugees on relief assistance for a protracted period of time. Thus, refugees must become economically independent. This requires 'planning', but when the planning of refugee settlements is done in isolation by outsiders who lack the benefit of even such basic information as what are the ecological, economic, and social constraints of an area, the results are bound to be problematic (Harrell-Bond 1986: 93).

Up to today, the isolated planning and implementation aspect remains an issue. Hence, there is a critical need for inter-agency and international cooperation and collaboration.

Recent debates in research are predominantly led by Alexander Betts, Gil Loescher and James Milner. In addition, Joanna Macrae, Jeff Crisp and Mark Duffield also strongly contributed to the state of research on the linkage of refugee assistance and development aid.

Alexander Betts focuses on the state level and takes into account the contemporary international efforts such as the Convention Plus or Global Consultations in order to grasp the complexity of political players and means to assist beneficiaries (Betts 2003, 2004, 2005a, 2005b, 2006a, 2008a, 2008b, 2009a, 2009b). His focus is on the North-South relations and the significance of bringing forward cooperation because the status quo reveals that the "North-South burden-sharing [exists] in the absence of a formal, binding institutional framework". This leads to impasses and "the under-provision of refugee protection" (Betts 2008b: 8, 13). In his recent articles on *Development assistance and refugees towards a North-South grand bargain?*, Betts writes about 'targeting development assistance for refugee solutions' (TDA). He elaborated a list of 'political ingredients' needed to achieve successful outcomes when implementing TDA (Betts 2009a). Due to the state-level focus, application on the ground is hardly feasible. He accentuates that "[d]evelopment assistance has the potential to enhance the quality of protection through facilitating self-sufficiency for refugees and/or by opening up the possibility for local integration as a durable solution" (Betts 2009a: 5). He highlights that connecting development and refugee assistance as a durable solution can turn into a win-win situation for the Northern and Southern countries as well as the beneficiaries. He presents necessary factors to implement development-oriented refugee assistance. His central features are protection and security (Betts 2009a: 5-6).

Gil Loescher and James Milner predominantly concentrate on protracted refugee situations. They analyze why long-term encampments exist and how humanitarian assistance can contribute to a beneficiary-oriented solution (Loescher/Milner 2005, 2009; Loescher 2009). Although they concentrate on protracted situations, the link to international cooperation is constantly underlined in order to find solutions. According to them, "[c]omprehensive solutions [...] are the best way to address concerns of Western states, meet the protection needs of refugees, and respond to the concerns of countries of first asylum" (Loescher/Milner 2009: 11). These solutions embrace "to develop a policy agenda that extends beyond conventional boundaries and seeks to integrate the resolution of chronic and recurring regional refugee problems with economic development and security issues" (Loescher/Milner 2005: 170).

Jeff Crisp does policy-oriented research as the Head of the Evaluation and Policy Analysis Unit of UNHCR. He conducted relevant studies on the methods needed to implement refugee protection with development initiatives. By taking former frameworks and current dynamics of forced migration into account, he raises factors, which support failures, and analyzed methods to reach improvements. With a focus on Africa and in particular Sub-Saharan Africa, he addresses the different institutional, financial and conceptual gaps, which occurred when humanitarian assistance was intended to be integrated with development initiatives. Eventually, he stresses the complicated process of bridging the gap between relief and development (Crisp 2001, 2003, 2006).

Joanna Macrae seeks to grasp and explain how to bridge the gap between relief and development. While it is emphasized that insecurity, conflict and violence threaten developmental progress, the "transition from war to peace carries important political and economic opportunities" (Macrae/Zwi/Gilson 1996: abstract). The political continuum embraced 'relief - rehabilitation - development'. While the continuum is often demonstrated as a linear process, "parallel aid transition from relief to development assistance" takes place in reality (Macrae 1999: 1, 17). Despite potential opportunities, political, technical and ethnic factors negatively contribute to attaining goals. Macrae stresses that UNHCR's superior mandate for protection and the level of assistance should not diminish due to "[u]ncritical adoption of developmental and peace-building objectives [...]. Ensuring that reintegration approaches are driven by an analysis of need and grounded in principle, rather than by the interests of donor and recipient governments, will [therefore] be crucial in protecting the rights of returnees" (Macrae 1999: 31; see also Macrae/Bradbury 1998).

Mark Duffield also recognizes the conventional boundaries or rather the linkage between war, peace, security and development, and their impact on international relations. Alongside with the political continuum, he questions the possible positive impact of short-term relief. He discerns that "[r]elief alone, however, will not eradicate permanent emergency in the South" (Duffield 1994: 47). While relief alone may not solve all issues, Duffield predominantly disregards the role of Southern actors within the global constellations (Duffield 2001, 2005, 1994). As Betts notes, Duffield "simply regards the structures of global governance as a function of Northern hegemony which are directly imposed upon, and are purely constraining of the South" (Betts 2006a: 6).

The above research especially focuses on the international community and their (in-)activeness on the linkage of refugee protection and assistance. However, operations in the field of development-oriented refugee assistance have been implemented worldwide. Due to the focus on decision-making level of the political elite, it lacks comprehensiveness.

Research on refugees in Uganda and in particular in the West Nile region was conducted by Tania Kaiser, Christina Bützer, Wiebke Hoenig, Jozef Merkx, Sarah Dryden-Peterson and Lucy Hovil.

Kaiser, Dryden-Peterson and Hovil (Dryden-Peterson/Hovil 2003; Hovil 2001; Kaiser 2002, 2005a, 2005b, 2006) look at South Sudanese refugees in Uganda through field studies in their research. One of the major aspects highlighted in their papers is the restrictive rights of refugees in hosting nations, especially rights of movement. They provide a broad view on the living conditions of refugees in the West Nile region of Uganda. Operational strategies such as local integration and camp methods such as agriculture are examined critically (Kaiser 2006; Dryden-Peterson/Hovil 2003). Their analyses are rather selective and not focused on distinguished and specific long-term timeframes.

In *The Long Way Home,* Bützer focuses on Southern Sudanese refugees in Uganda. She analyzes individual aspirations of repatriation. The development aspect of the assistance while the refugees are forced to remain in the Ugandan settlements is not part of her study. Her emphasis is on the question whether all needs of the refugees are covered highlights specific issues, which the involved parties and agencies are required to work on (Bützer 2007).

Hoenig as well focuses on individual perceptions of refugees in the settlement in *Self-image and the well-being of refugees in Rhino Camp Settlement, Uganda.* Her case study also takes place in Rhino Camp which makes it interesting for me. She tackles the question what their inner, emotional state as a refugee is. She sums up with the statement that "Rhino Camp Settlement is a good example of a participatory refugee project where refugees feel powerful and empowered, and have opportunities to feel competent" (Hoenig 2004: 27). While she recognizes the possible impact of the development orientation, she does not integrate it to a satisfactory extent during her analyzes. In addition, Merkx also analyzes refugee identities in the borderland of Northern Uganda and South Sudan. His papers provide information about historic developments, political constellations, and livelihood conditions (Merkx 2000, 2002).

There is little gender-related research on development-oriented refugee assistance, which concentrates on a particular country. Elizabeth G. Ferris, Vanessa A. Farr and Deborah Mulumba analyze gender issues in the refugee context. In *Abuse of Power: Sexual Exploitation of Refugee Women and Girls*, Ferris emphasizes the extent of Sexual and Gender-based Violence (SGBV) in terms of perpetrators and victims. Although "[g]ender roles often change in refugee camps", traditional power allocations remain. In her conclusion, she points out that despite the amount of initiatives to prevent from incidences, "the fundamental disparity of power and the inadequacy of relief assistance that lead women and children to exchange sex for things that they need to survive" remain. Ferris did not take into account the difference between refugee settlement and camp. Since the concepts differ, SGBV may be observed and treated differently (Ferris 2007: 586, 590).

While Ferris looks at refugees in camps, Farr takes another path by concentrating her article *Notes toward a Gendered Understanding of Mixed-Population Movements and Security Sector Reform after Conflict* on four forms of forced movement. Farr point out that gender concepts change but disparities still play significant roles in all forms. Although she does not indicate the timeframe, which is important for this study — the one of refugees in settlements — she nonetheless stressed an aspect that is of great significance: "invisibility of these [mistreated] women" remains high. Hence, SGBV and gender inequality among refugee communities is something hardly verbalized (Farr 2007: 595).

Mulumba focuses on gender relations, livelihood security and reproductive health among women refugees in Uganda in her research (Mulumba 2005). Although her analyses incorporates condition in Rhino Camp and provide invaluable information about cultural specifics, she concentrates on livelihood and reproductive health. She continuously looks at SGBV, gender role allocations, and women's vulnerability. The regional and thematic focus makes it important for my research. A broader view on assistance including the diverse sectors is missing. Also, while integrating the development aspect into refugee assistance, gender sensitivity may need to go one step further towards striving towards obtaining a comprehensive view on equality issues across the operational sectors. By observing refugee aid only as emergency aid and by focusing on distinct sectors only, perspectives remain too limited and potential areas of failure or success may remain invisible.

Consequently, operations bridging refugee protection and assistance with development initiatives received little attention by the international research communities thus far. As illustrated above, research has concentrated on state level decisions and collaboration, single operational strategies such as local integration and/or rather punctual analyses of operations. Program-driven research on certain operations in the field over longer time periods was not found. Few regional-specific studies were conducted on refugees in Uganda or especially South Sudanese refugees in Rhino Camp in the West Nile region. Although literature has been published on refugees and refugee aid in Uganda, only few publications took into account the development aspect in general and lacked a focus on comprehensive methods. Cross-cutting topics of gender are often left out and the gender perspective is mainly excluded. Most available sources on the topic are descriptive accounts of current conditions with insufficient critical or reflexive analyses. They do not appear to have the intention of improving the poor conditions in the individual cases that they present to readers. Further publications were completed by associates of refugee organizations in which the possibility of biased subjectivity needs to be kept in mind. Additionally, many records are outdated. The criticism exposes that the available literature can only be consulted carefully and to a certain extent.

To sum up the presented state of the art of research on development-oriented refugee assistance in Uganda, great gaps can be identified. Development-oriented refugee assistance in Uganda in depth and in focus of sustainability, efficiency, and gender sensitivity has not been researched so far.

3. Research Relevance and Interest

Development-oriented refugee assistance constitutes a working model to guarantee adequate assistance to refugees and includes development initiatives that local communities benefit from. The model aims to prevent protracted refugee situations with encampment of refugees. In Uganda, this model was planned and implemented on a broad and country-wide scale. The Government of Uganda and UNHCR agreed on basic regulations and targets. The greatest modification from the original to the revised version of refugee aid is the integration of the development aspect. Realizing the development orientation within the refugee context implies that operations are neither spontaneous nor immediate. Rather, activities are intended to be planned with a medium or long-term perspective, targeting sustainable effects to refugees and local communities of the refugee hosting region.

Since this working approach has only been launched in the 1990s in Uganda, it is thus relatively new but implemented with a broad scope in Uganda. Since refugees remained in settlements for almost fifteen years, analyses of operations are crucial to understand the nature of linking refugee aid with development.

Research on development-oriented refugee assistance has predominantly been neglected. As summarized above, research on development-oriented refugee assistance has focused on three main aspects: how state authorities make decisions and collaborate in finding solutions in 'sharing the refugee burden'; in what way single operational strategies such as local integration are implemented; how selective operations are implemented. Moreover, refugee identities have also played a role in research. Program-driven research on operations implemented in one settlement over several years is lacking. Based on the existing literature, questions such as the following could not be answered: how are single activities combined in programs to not only provide refugee protection and assistance, but to also include development aspects? How are gender aspects as cross-cutting issues taken into consideration in program design and implementation? What is the broad scope of development-oriented refugee assistance? What characterizes the programmatic approach on a meta-level?

In my research, I aim to seek answers to these questions. Guided by my overall research question of "How can the development-oriented approach to refugee assistance be delivered in a way that is sustainable, efficient and gender-sensitive?", I seek to conduct program focused research and achieve two main results: 1. Elaborating features for development-oriented refugee assistance, and 2. conducting a case study.

Thus, I aim to analyze previous international development interventions towards connecting refugee assistance and development. Based on that, I strive for identifying factors that feature development-oriented refugee assistance. The features are supposed to support an efficient, sustainable and gender-sensitive implementation of operations. In his writing on *Development assistance and refugees towards a North-South grand bargain?,* Alexander Betts produced lists on "ingredients for political agreement" and "ingredients for practical viability" (Betts 2009a: 13-18). These "ingredients" focus predominantly on the 'high' levels of 'decision-making actors' of Northern donor countries and Southern refugee hosting nations. While these levels are certainly significant, I extend the scope and furthermore integrate the 'low' level, or in other words, the programmatic grassroots level of the distinct beneficiaries. Hence, the "ingredients" form the basis of the ideal-typical features for development-oriented refugee assistance that are to be elaborated.

In order to reach the second result, I conduct a case study on Rhino Camp in Uganda. Long-term commitment to and operations of development-oriented refugee assistance is strived to be examined through the case study in Rhino Camp in Uganda. Each new or revised approach and strategy needs sufficient time for planning and implementation until researchers can analyze practices and performances. Only then, can they examine feasibility and efficiency, and produce representative results. After more than one decade of applying the approach of development-oriented refugee assistance at Rhino Camp, the required time has elapsed. Therefore, this research project reveals great thematic research relevance. During the field work, a presently still processed case is critically analyzed. That way gaps and obstacles can be identified. The focused timeframe of analysis from 1997 until 2006 provides me with the opportunity to examine long-term operations and its potential sustainable impact as well as efficient and gender-sensitive realization. Highlighting the pillars of sustainability, efficiency and gender sensitivity is perceived as significant because development initiatives aim for durable effects. Efficient operations are necessary because most refugees flee from one to another developing country where resources are scarce and should be used considerately. Gender-sensitivity is understood as the guiding pillar. Gender sensitivity in development-oriented refugee assistance is understood to entail a dual imperative: adequate refugee assistance would support the psychological transitional process in promoting equality targets for reaching gender parity, and development aid is based on social processes and can only be performed sustainably and efficiently if, both, men and women are involved. Hence, this research topic provides up-to-date impressions, and thus, satisfies current demands.

The added value of my research project to the academic field is threefold. Firstly, refugee aid and protection is stereotypically still observed as emergency assistance. The connection with development aspects, however, is not new. A study capturing all previous programmatic moves towards development-oriented refugee assistance is, nevertheless, still missing. In my research project, I screen the previous concepts that link refugee aid with development assistance and highlight reasons for failure where possible. Secondly, the current focus of research, development-oriented refugee assistance, is on high-level actors and their power to influence processes. I aim to extend the current focus in order to encompass the integration of the grassroots level when analyzing this type of assistance. This lower level captures programmatic fields; thus, the political, social, and geographical spheres in which development-oriented refugee assistance are being implemented. By incorporating the manner of programming, it receives intense weighting, which is necessary because refugee assistance does not take place between state powers but on the ground. The decisions of state powers are rather only preconditions. Taking this into account, the features comprise situational, timely, and actors' dimensions, and are thus multi-dimensional. Thirdly, development-oriented refugee assistance is not merely a theoretical concept. It is implemented in the real world. In order to grasp to what extend it may be implemented, I aim to study the case of Rhino Camp in Uganda over a period from 1997 until 2006. This way, insights of implementation are gained, which help to draw up comprehensive conclusions.

4. *Research Focus*

4.1. Research Question, Objective and Hypothesis

Based on the above identified gaps in scientific literature, it is necessary to undertake further research. My overall research focus is on development-oriented refugee assistance in theory and practice; i.e. I aim to understand the complexity of programmatic development-oriented refugee assistance. Thus, the migration-development nexus is explored. It is believed that factors of programmatic planning, implementation, and evaluation as well as political decision-making shape this type of assistance. Hence, I pursue the claim to grasp the complexity of the subject and identify features that ensure development orientation in refugee protection and assistance. Moreover, it is also assumed that development-oriented refugee assistance is based on the three pillars of sustainability, efficiency, and gender sensitivity.

The principal question is concentrated on exploring what the new working model is about and to what extent the three chosen pillars — sustainability, efficiency, and gender sensitivity — are respected. Hence, the overall question is: How can the development-oriented approach to refugee assistance be delivered in a way that is sustainable, efficient and gender-sensitive? Relating to this, sub-questions are to be asked: How has the approach of development-oriented refugee assistance been developed over the past years? How is the approach of development-oriented refugee assistance implemented in practice?

The hypothesis is twofold. Development-oriented refugee assistance can only be achieved sustainably, efficiently and in a gender-sensitive manner, when the direct actors (UNHCR, OPM, and DED) cooperate, when transparency is ensured, and an information flow, as well as when beneficiaries are fully integrated in processes. On the operational level, it is assumed that activities of different sectors must be combined and implemented simultaneously in an integrated or cross-sectoral manner.

The overall research aim is to determine what refugee and development assistance is and how both concepts have been and can be combined. Then it is to reveal how development-oriented refugee assistance is constituted and what specific features the approach has. Developing the necessary features constitutes the main objective of this research project. Finally, another objective is to find out how operations are implemented under the umbrella of development-oriented refugee assistance at Rhino Camp in Uganda and whether operations meet the previously elaborated features.

4.2. Research Approach

The approach of this project characterizes a firm theory-practice linkage based on post-modern Feminism of International Relations. It can be categorized in three sections: First of all, through literature and research review, the original operational assistance tactics led by UNHCR are examined. This is necessary to understand that refugee assistance and protection have originally been an ad hoc type of work or rather emergency aid to meet basic needs of refugees. Since gender sensitivity is identified as a central pillar, it is analyzed how gender aspects are included in this common type of refugee protection and assistance. The term and concept of development is to be explored. It is to identify what development assistance is and how the focus has changed over the years, because revisions in the field of development may also influence its integration in refugee aid. These parts are predominantly based on research review and evaluative documentation such as articles by UNHCR or other organizations.

Secondly, efforts to link development and refugee assistance are screened. The idea and concept is not new; it has been realized for decades. It is to determine how they were implemented. This section is mainly anchored in international research publications and evaluative documentation. Documents of UNHCR are predominantly accessed to discover progress and conceptual changes. In addition, to develop and identify features necessary for development-oriented refugee assistance, the operational methods of refugee assistance are screened to identify what is needed to implement the working approach sustainably, efficiently and gender-sensitively.

Thirdly, based on this foundation, it is examined how the approach is practically implemented in Rhino Camp between 1997 and 2006. Besides screening the overall operations, it is analyzed how specific strategies such as the self-reliance strategy were realized. Information for analyses is mainly drawn from research literature and narrative annual reports of the DED Refugee/IDP Programme. In addition, field studies with participatory observation, expert interviews and ero-epic dialogues are used to collect data on the implementation of development-oriented refugee assistance. Through all collected information, the beforehand elaborated features are applied and, by this, it is investigated how sustainable, efficient and gender-sensitive operations were.

Theoretical research is particularly rooted in consulting subject-specific and research literature. Additional data is collected through field studies and applied methods which are explained in detail in the annex.

In order to realize this research approach, I undertook research in Uganda from August 2009 until May 2011. Close contact was maintained with the DED Refugee/IDP Programme personnel, especially the Programme Coordinator, Astrid Peter and the Assistance Programme Coordinator, Safinah Namyalo. For security reasons, field visits were planned and conducted in close cooperation with DED while based in the capital of Uganda, Kampala.

5. Structure

The book is structured in six chapters. Chapter I contains the introduction and reveals basic information about the research subject. Following this, Chapter II is about the definitions of relevant terms and their correlations.

Chapter III discusses the three sections of refugee assistance and protection, refugees and gender, as well as development assistance in broader terms. Refugee assistance and protection is the main subject of the research. Therefore, it needs to be clarified how it has developed and been altered since the Second World War, what mandates and goals UNHCR has, and how it is realized. Refugee assistance and gender is screened to see how gender aspects are included in refugee policies and operations from the early stages of planning and implementation. In the third section, development assistance and its changes is analyzed to grasp what development aims for. Understanding it is crucial to comprehend the connection of refugee assistance and development later on.

Chapter IV addresses refugee assistance and development. It discusses when and how the idea of combining refugee assistance and protection with development initiatives was created. Previous concepts are examined to find out what their status quo of research is. Finally, necessary features for realizing development-oriented refugee assistance are deduced from gathered information.

Chapter V is about the case study and hence the application of development-oriented refugee assistance in Rhino Camp. After looking at the context of Uganda and especially the West Nile region, Uganda's refugee policy is examined. Background data about Rhino Camp, including details on beneficiaries, capacity and structure, are compiled to then analyze the operations and assistance during the past ten years. The chapter closes by examining operations against the features for development-oriented refugee assistance. The previously elaborated features are applied against the operations at Rhino Camp in order to be able to conclude how sustainable, efficient, and gender-sensitive the assistance between 1997 and 2006 was.

Chapter VI contains the conclusion. After summarizing research findings, final references are made to the elaborated features of development-oriented refugee assistance and the case study of the Rhino Camp.

The annex contains information about the applied research approach, thematic containments and limitations faced during the research process.

Chapter II Definitions and Correlations

Development-oriented refugee assistance is understood as a comprehensive frame in which diverse approaches and methods are realized. It is assumed that development-oriented refugee assistance is based on three pillars: sustainability, efficiency and gender sensitivity. Relevant terms will be defined hereafter.

1. Development

The term development is associated with various definitions. Drastically simplified, the linguistic semantics of development captures the process of change and advancement. It refers to a growing or progressing course. It is a synonym for expansion, improvement, and enlargement. Development also stands for an event, occurrence, or stage in a transforming period.

In the context of international development aid, the term refers to growth and modernization of a local, national or regional area. In this context, development has numerous definitions. Ricardo Conteras takes note of the diversity of meanings. He states that "in order to understand the various theories of development, one must place them in a historical context" (Conteras 1999a: 1). He goes back to the thirteenth century to portray the different denotations of development. In his article, he reveals significant keywords such as feudalism, bourgeoisie, capitalism, communism, socialism which characterize the route development undertook. This route is strongly influenced by Western or Eurocentric ideas because the Western world shaped the theory and practice of development. Conteras highlights on several occasions that the term has not always been defined as it is today, as a "continuous improvement of social welfare" (Conteras 1999a: 1). Historically, development progressed passively without elaborating a long-term schedule with outlined goals.

Today's denotation indicates a clear result orientation towards modernizing and industrializing entire states or regions. Nowadays, development of underdeveloped regions is planned. Explicit targets have altered over time. The focus on social aspects substituted the ones on economic growth and infrastructural improvement. Despite the modifying targets, targets per se remain to exist and constitute a distinct trait of the concept.

In the 2004 published resource pack on conflict-sensitive approaches to development, humanitarian assistance and peace building, several non-governmental organizations (NGOs) jointly defined development in broad terms as "[l]ong-term efforts aimed at bringing improvements in the economic, political and social status, environmental stability and the quality of life of all segments of the population" (International Alert et al. 2004: 4). Despite the scope, the target orientation remained.

Joseph Stiglitz, chief economist at the World Bank, says "[d]evelopment represents a transformation of society, a movement from traditional relations, traditional ways of thinking, traditional ways of dealing with health and education, traditional methods of production, to more 'modern' ways" (Stiglitz 1998). William Easterly, a well-known development economist, writes "that economic development is a complicated interplay of markets (with many imperfections), politics, social norms, institutions, and government policies, social services, and microeconomic interventions. Nevertheless, the idea of an aid-financed takeoff into growth has maintained its appeal in the development policy community" (Easterly 2006: 98).

Defining development through numbers such as a Gross Domestic Product (GDP) is commonly used by several international organizations. Yet, it also continues to be of unsatisfying nature. Indexes such as Human Development Index (HDI), Human Poverty Index (HPI), and Gender-related Development Index (GDI) were designed to empirically prove certain levels of development, poverty, or inequality. However, "economic growth as such cannot be automatically associated with a real improvement of present-day and future living conditions" (Diefenbacher/Zieschank 2008: 1).

In 1987, United Nation's World Commission on Environment and Development adds sustainability to the concept of development. In its *Report of the World Commission on Environment and Development: Our Common Future*, commonly known as the Bundtland Report, it defines sustainable development in regard to meeting needs of current and future generations (A/RES/42/187).

In his book *Development as Freedom* (1999), Amartya Sen argues that "[a]n adequate conception of development must go much beyond the accumulation of wealth and the growth of gross national product and other income-related variables" (Sen 1999: 12). He would therefore agree with the urgency of the need of respecting and regarding needs of different generations as stated by World Commission on Environment and Development. Yet, he goes further in defining development as "a process of expanding the real freedoms that people enjoy". Thus, "[d]evelopment requires the removal of major sources of unfreedom [...]" (Sen 1999: 3). Sen reveals "five types of instrumental freedoms: (1) political freedoms, (2) economic facilities, (3) social opportunities, (4) transparency guarantees and (5) protective security" (Sen 1999: 10, 38; cf. 38-40). These five types are both interrelated and objectives of development. He stresses their "joint importance" by announcing that

> [f]reedoms are not only the primary ends of development, they are also among its principal means (Sen 1999: 10; cf. xii).

According to the definition of development presented by Sen as "a process of expanding the real freedoms that people enjoy", I apply the understanding as the guiding idea and working definition with more precise explanations hereafter.

2. *Sustainability*

When sustainability entered development-related discussions, it quickly took over and was used in numerous contexts. Sustainable strategies followed sustainable indicators to achieve sustainable outcomes, which all were anchored in projects taking sustainability into account. In international debates and scientific discussions it "is often stated, albeit ironically, that the only thing that can be said about sustainability that everyone agrees upon is that it is defined and applied in so many different ways" (Polk 2001: 14). Does that mean that sustainability is an air bubble without content, just a trendy word?

No, sustainability is not only a trendy word. Sustainability postulates a moral concern or obligation of the promotion and support of durable and livable global surroundings. "It is an obligation [...] to preserve the capacity to be well off [...]" (Solow 1993: 186-187).

Sustainability targets horizontal and vertical dimensions. The horizontal time dimension captures succeeding generations, while the vertical dimension embraces different societies and their areas of life. Sustainability includes a societal imperative for continuity conditions. It demands to consider and maintain ecological, social, political and economic aspects (Pies/Sass/Frank 2005: 1).

The understanding of sustainability has changed over the past two decades and the aspect of 'sustainable' entered the international agendas. One of the great milestones is the Bundtland Report (Pies/Sass/Frank 2005: 1). It finalizes the integration of sustainability in development debates and assistance. According the Bundtland, sustainable development is defined as

> development that meets the needs of the present without compromising the ability of future generations to meet their own needs. It contains within it two key concepts:
>
> - the concept of 'needs', in particular the essential needs of the world's poor, to which overriding priority should be given; and
> - the idea of limitations imposed by the state of technology and social organization on the environment's ability to meet present and future needs (A/RES/42/187).

Thus, socio-economic and ecological premises exist and aim to protect natural resources, overcoming poverty and the satisfaction of basic needs (A/RES/42/187).

Since then, sustainability remains to be an integral part of development assistance. Not only has the term sustainability per se received moral obligations, sustainable development also entails "moral injunctions" (Kumar/Graf 1998: 144). In the framework of the United Nations Earth Summit in Rio de Janeiro, Brazil of 1992 (A/CONF.151/26) a series of conferences was initiated which focused particularly on sustainable development. Ten years after the first summit took place, a follow-up summit was launched in Johannesburg, South Africa. With revised and new goals and programs, the importance of sustainability was again underlined (A/CONF.199/20).

The civil process of sustainable development implies the connection to a specific sector — development assistance — with durable effects. Polk writes, that "it is the limitations of ecological processes as well as their interactions with social and cultural factors that are foundational to sustainable development" (Polk 2001: 15). She later criticized that many definitions for sustainable development "refer more generally to a prioritization of socioeconomic efficiency with environmental issues being a goal, but not an underlying priority" (Polk 2001: 16).

Bauhardt uses a feminist approach in depicting sustainable development. She says that "sustainability as a normative concept contains the claim for social justice and security of material livelihood" (translated: Bauhardt 2004: 280). Her idea of material livelihood consists not only of natural, but also social resources of contemporary and future generations. Sustainable development strives for a balance between economic, ecologic and social fields. She reveals that gender relations are to be included in the concept of sustainable development due to the impact of gender constellations on the dimensions of economic actions, social relations, and the finiteness of natural resources. Her conclusion is that "the de-hierarchizations of human-nature-relations, as well as social relations are the prerequisite for just operations for humans and nations. Hence, the deconstruction of gender hierarchies is a necessary prerequisite to realize sustainability" (translated: Bauhardt 2004: 280).

Taking the information of the definitions of the Bundtland Report as well as of Polk and Bauhardt into account, my use of the term sustainable development is a type of development assistance that strives for identifying durable solutions that better the lives of current and future generations by intentionally respecting and protecting the limited natural resources, supporting economic growth and promoting just social relations between gender.

3. *Efficiency*

Before defining efficiency in the context of development assistance, it is necessary to generally understand why efficiency and not effectiveness is understood as the second supporting pillar.

Clearly abstracted and simplified, effectiveness or effective operation means to work successfully, produce intended results, and eventually achieve goals. Efficiency or efficient operation implies a well-measured and managed use of resources without any or only little waste. The scope of resources is not limited but rather encompasses all means such as time, capital, human or natural resources, energy etc. Operations are conducted in a way that minimum inputs reach maximum outputs. While effectiveness and efficiency refer to the wide-ranged quality of work, effectiveness concentrates on the outcome by means of its implication and result orientation, and efficiency focuses on the output reached through the suitability and productiveness of a certain performance.

Efficiency was therefore chosen as a pillar for the analyses in order to examine how the inputs or activities of development-oriented refugee assistance contribute to reaching the best or optimal results of refugee protection while integrating local communities as an addition beneficiary group.

It is to ask which concept of efficiency is to be applied in the context of development-oriented refugee assistance. Economic efficiency is often divided in three types: allocative, productive and dynamic efficiency. The three concepts constitute economic measurements offering different approaches and points of action. While efficiency generally aims to optimizing processes, the minimum or maximum problem can be applied. The first one means that subject costs are minimized to reach greater output. The maximizing problem refers to a maximized subject to achieve a given output.

Productive efficiency, based on the abovementioned statement, applies to the minimization problem. It attempts to reach a certain output by means of combining resources in the most economical way. Hence, productive efficiency is only achieved when the producing actor generates the targeted output through the most inexpensive method and therefore uses the least costs possible (Betts 2005c: 8-9; Griffiths/Wall 2004: 82). The measurement of productive efficiency is mainly rooted in Farrell's efficiency frontier approach (Farrell 1957).

> His approach is to compare the performance of actual establishments with the best-practice techniques observed in reality, instead of taking ideal combinations of inputs as the point of reference. He starts out by constructing an envelope including the minimum combinations of necessary inputs for producing one unit of output. Productive [...] efficiency is then measured by comparing observed input coefficient points for an establishment with the input coefficients on the efficiency frontier for the same factor proportions. Productive efficiency may thus be viewed as how closely the establishment attains the lowest possible real cost for the output it produces (Blomström 1986: 98).

Productive efficiency therefore searches for the lowest costs of production to achieve the greatest profit. This type of efficiency can only be realized in perfectly competitive market constellations, because in monopolist structures one or very few firms lead the market and set prices. When competition exists, firms have to combine resources in a way to minimize costs so they can achieve a certain output or profit level.

Also in accordance with Farrell, two schemes are predominantly followed to discover how productively efficient a firm or the respective examined unit is: "within a firm, or firms within a given industry" or in other words "within [...] or among the firms" (Sengupta 1988: 153; cf. Betts 2005c: 11; Blomström 1986: 98ff). The 'within a firm' approach calculates an "efficiency frontier" of a particular firm or unit. The analyses of the units 'among' a particular industry or field rather targets "to estimate an explicit frontier production function" (Sengupta 1988: 153).

The strongly simplified approach of productive efficiency converted to refugee assistance yields the following result: If the least-possible input necessary is used to reach the best output, than a market is productively efficient. The output is represented by the refugee protection and the minimum input combinations are the assistance activities. However, as Betts notes, "methods of protection" and "rights one normatively assumes constitute protection" need to be taken into account and can vastly change results. In addition to the relevance of the various input combinations, the diverse dimensions of costs must be considered. While empirical data may verify that financial costs are lower for refugees in under-developed regions, political and social costs may be higher, especially on long-term basis (Betts 2005c: 9-10).

Allocative efficiency belongs to the abovementioned maximization problem. It emanates from the Pareto optimality, which targets equally distributed welfare among members of a society or collective. The Pareto optimality captures the assumption of allocating resources within a society in a way that does not benefit one person and disadvantages another one (Estrin/Laidler 1995: 438). Allocative efficiency is also based on the Farrell approach (Farrell 1957) and was originally referred to as price efficiency (Kopp 1981: 479). It takes place when used or produced goods generate the greatest value or outcome (Antle/Crissman 1990).

> The theory of efficient allocation through dispersed decision-making in response to a price system revolves around two propositions, which have not always been sufficiently distinguished in the literature. These two propositions are in a relation of logical inverses in that the conclusion of either occurs among the premises of the other (Koopmans 1961: 478).

In other words, allocative efficiency of markets is "the total profit actually earned by all the traders divided by the maximum total profit that could have been earned by all the traders (i.e., the sum of producer and consumer surplus)"

(Gode/Sunder 1993: 131). Allocative efficiency can also be attained in perfectly competitive economies or markets. Knowledge capacity in stakeholders exists to produce the goods and utilities needed and demanded. By doing so, the total profit will be maximized for the entire society (Krouse 1975: 685).

Measurements are therefore conducted through inputs. A firm or unit applies "the selection of an input mix that allocates factors to their highest valued uses" (Kopp 1981: 479-480). Consumption and production must be taken into account in efficiency measurements (Betts 2005c: 14).

The strongly simplified approach of allocative efficiency converted to refugee assistance yields the following result: If allocative efficiency aims to achieve the best results through a composition of chosen inputs while continuing to pursue equal welfare of all individuals, then refugee protection constitutes the best result.[4] Chosen inputs are influenced by states' motivations; while donor nations may make contributions for geo-political interests, refugee hosting countries of first asylum may create a refugee policy which addresses their individual concerns. Nevertheless, the mix of all inputs is supposed to create the most efficient refugee protection while still considering equal welfare. When refugee assistance is development-oriented, the welfare aspect not only targets refugees but also comprises local communities located in the refugee hosting areas.

Both, productive and allocative efficiency[5] are 'static' concepts and too inflexible in order to consider immediate incidences or claims in an appropriate manner. They furthermore "hold constant factors which may change over time" (Betts 2005c: 26). I.e., they are "suppressing the time dimension of economic activities [...]" (Bordoff et al. 2006: 11). Factors particularly comprise the dimensions of costs, which are not only of financial nature but also of social and political one. Hence, it is generally criticized that "[t]he inelasticity of demand [...] suppresses questions of short-run allocative efficiency" (Gilbert/Newbery 1994: 540).

Dynamic efficiency focuses on innovation efficiency instead of cost efficiency as static concepts do. Conditions are continuously reconsidered (Ghemawat/Costa 1993: 59). Since dynamic efficiency overcomes the static approach, it "involves taking a longer term view of economic activity and thus seeking to ensure that the right incentives are maintained for optimal creation of new products over time" (Bordoff et al. 2006: 11). It can thus "be defined as a virtuous circle of increasing productivity, output and wages" (McCartney 2004).

4 Betts reveals another perspective, which is accessible through Betts 2005c: 12-24.

5 See also: Krouse 1975, Estrin/Laidler 1995, Koopmans 1961, Ghemawat/Cosa 1993, Gode/Sunder 1993, Betts 2005c.

The concept is mainly applied in monopolistic and not perfectly competitive contexts. In contrast to situations where diverse economic competition exists, monopolistic constellations may lead to innovative motivation. Produced goods and services can be consumed and invested. By means of investments, capital becomes accumulated. Hence, accrued production factors increase the production potential. In other words, dynamic efficiency aims to use production opportunities in the most optimal way over time. The capital accumulation seeks to reach an optimal income increase. Hence, the monopoly achieves gains (Soretz 2009: 41, 44, 46). This can be explained because "the dynamic gains rising from the continuous technological progress [through innovation incentive] (induced by lower and lower levels of competition in the product market) should be compared with the (static) welfare losses related to a higher (product) market 'monopolization'" (Bucci 1998: 22-23).

In short, dynamic efficiency takes place preferably in monopolistic markets or little competitive market niches, which increases the innovation incentives in order to decrease final costs. An economy is understood to be dynamically efficient, "[i]n situations where the population growth rate exceeds the steady state marginal product of capital, or equivalently the economy is consistently investing more than it is earning in profit" (Abel et al. 1989: 1). In a more simplified picture, "[d]ynamic efficiency is a situation characterised by a virtuous circle of higher productivity, output growth and higher wages rather than having a rigorous mathematical definition" (McCartney 2004).

The strongly simplified approach of dynamic efficiency converted to refugee assistance yields the following result: If dynamic efficiency captures an innovative input to achieve best outputs within monopolies, than the output would be the protection of refugees. The innovative input constitutes an optimal use of resources and a mix of adequate approaches and methods to ensure refugee protection. The input may be influenced by costs. In the refugee context, financial, natural, political and social costs need to be considered. For example, a monopoly state 'invests' in refugee protection and has the motivation or incentive to apply innovate means. As Betts notes, the 'protection-in-the-region-of-origin' may be an innovative mean. Unions of Western nations, such as the EU, revised "asylum and immigration policy. This may ultimately allow EU member states to equalise their cost structures for a 'fixed technology', helping to bring improved long-run allocative efficiency within the EU." Yet, innovative profits "are likely to favour the states that initiate change" (Betts 2005c: 27).

For this research, the dynamic efficiency constitutes the most appropriate concept especially due to the innovative methodological application of development orientation in refugee protection. Although comparably little theorized, I agree with Betts; dynamic efficiency "offer[s] [...] nuanced insights for sustainable refugee protection". The term 'sustainable' is here not only to be grasped in the context of finding durable solutions but also of the respect and apt use of all national resources in the country of first asylum, including natural and human resources. This is because it "broadly refers to the economically efficient usage of scarce resources through time and thus it embraces allocative and productive efficiency in an inter-temporal dimension" (Betts 2005c: 1, 26).

While returning to the above stated understanding of sustainable development, it is necessary to take the interrelated aspect of efficiency into account. While sustainable development refers to the long-term and durable impact of programs and projects, efficiency targets an operation that is carried out in a resource-efficient and -saving manner and seeks to reach maximum results. This coincides and is consistent with the contemporary international objectives of development assistance such as the goal of greater coherency incorporated in the Paris Declaration, as well as the realization of the Millennium Development Goals.

4. *Gender sensitivity*

The chosen pillars — that the analyses concentrate on — are gender sensitivity, sustainability, and efficiency. The different magnitudes of each pillar can be simplified and displayed while comparing them with the structure of a house; gender sensitivity would constitute the guiding center or foundation pillar, and sustainability and efficiency would be vital supporting corner pillars. While all of the pillars are needed to maintain the structure of the house, gender sensitivity is assumed to be the most important one strengthening the foundation of the building. The explanation for pursuing this idea is given hereafter through the interrelated definitions.

4.1. Gender

By means of including gender-sensitive methods in activities of refugee projects, discrimination and inequality are attempted to be tackled and eventually overcome. But what does 'gender' mean and how does UNHCR define it?

In general, gender contrasts to sex. Oakley introduced it to social science.

> 'Sex' is a biological term: 'gender' a psychological and cultural one. Common sense suggests that they are merely two ways of looking at the same division and that someone who belongs to, say, the female sex will automatically belong to the corresponding (feminine) gender. In reality this is not so. To be a man or a woman, a boy or a girl, is as much a function of dress, gesture, occupation, social network and personality as it is of possessing a particular set of genitals (Oakley 1972: 158 quoted in: Moser 1993: 249).

Sex therefore represents the biological, anatomic sexual category of a person. Gender is not biologically limited or pre-structured. It is seen as a social identity, a construct that encompasses features of identities, social and societal relations between women and men. It also captures expected roles, behaviors, hierarchies and attitudes of as well as dynamics between both sexes. These dichotomies always take place in the context of a societal structure such as patriarchate or matriarchate and social constellation such as marriage, family or occupation.

Gender embraces three connected dimensions according to Reiman: firstly, the individual identity which incorporates social norms and specific societal characteristics of women and men; secondly, the symbolism which includes dichotomies and its classifications of status, roles and stereotypes, here particularly dichotomies such as men are strong and brave in contrast to women who are weak, soft, and peaceful; thirdly, structures of relations which entail the (inter-)action of women and men within public and private spheres. The three dimensions influence one another and thereby build a correlated triangle (Reiman 2003: 7-11).

Recognizing gender as a 'socially constructed' product is important in order to understand that it "is learned and changes over time" (Tuyizere 2007: 111-112). Moreover, it develops in due course, is influenced by specific time and regional contexts, and reflects surroundings. Gender is therefore not a constant framework; "it can be changed" and modified (Pettman 1997: 488). Determinants of gender are among others culture, region, hierarchy, religion, and time because they shape gender as social models.

Since gender has become a central analytical category for IR feminists, several explanations and definitions of gender have been elaborated over the past three decades of the growth of IR feminism. Sandra Whitworth, for instance, explains that "[g]ender refers not to women or to men per se, but to the ideological and material relation between them, which historically has been an unequal relationship. Additionally, gender is not given biologically, as a result of the sexual characteristics of either women or men, but is constructed socially" (Whitworth 1989: 265). Mary Caprioli states that gender "captures the complex matrix of social relationships within society" and "gender stratification subsists across class and socio-economic status" (Caprioli 2003: 4). V. Spike Peterson defines it as a „systematic social construction that dichotomizes identities, behaviors, and expectations as masculine and feminine" (Peterson 1992: 194). Cordula Dittmer understands gender as the "ascribed or acquired identity which structured and organized into hierarchy all societal fields in a more or less strong manner, and which assigns the social actors with their societal position" (translated: Dittmer 2007: 6) Finally, J. Ann Tickner defines gender

> as a set of socially constructed characteristics that are typically associated with masculinity and femininity. Characteristics associated with an "ideal type" or "hegemonic" masculinity, such as autonomy, rationality, and power, are generally preferred by both men and women over characteristics such as dependence, emotionality, and weakness, associated with femininity. Importantly, gender is not just about women; it is about

relations between men and women, relations that are generally hierarchical and unequal. Gender hierarchies, including subordinated masculinities, intersect with, and are compounded by, other hierarchies such as class and race (Tickner 2005b: 6, Footnote 18).

All mentioned definitions of gender capture certain aspects which overlap and infer to similar contents. Based on the stated meanings, gender is a social construction which develops historically, comprises dichotomies and relations between women and men, and contains ascribed or acquired identity features.

4.2. Gender Inequality in Theoretical Terms

Due to different understandings of gender, it is clear how broadly discussed the term is per se within the context of IR. Some definitions already refer to the often unequal role allocations and problematic relations between the two sexes and within the gender hierarchies. It is thus indispensable to give further details of the meaning of gender inequality. What does gender inequality refer to?

Gender inequality exists worldwide. It predominantly refers to imbalanced and disparate relations between men and women. However, gender inequality also exists among just one sex. It embraces dynamic hierarchies embedded in societies, cultures, classes, ethnicities, religion, races, tribes; basically all categories of social and collective gatherings. Gender inequality moreover comprises political, economic and social spheres. Thus, factors and determinants of gender inequality are manifested in various dimensions of everyday life.

Simone de Beauvoir accepts that "[t]he division of the sexes is a biological fact" (Beauvoir 1988: 19). However, she argues that a woman is not born a woman; she rather becomes one which is a distinct inference to the social identity of a female individual (Beauvoir in Holland-Cunz 2003: 97). In *All Said and Done*, she stresses that "[a]ll male ideologies are directed at justifying the oppression of women… women are so conditioned by society that they consent to this oppression" (Beauvoir quoted in Blair 1986: 156). Women therefore face a double imperative in terms of natural and biological limitations which are produced through their reproductive functions as well as societal and male-dominated matrixes in which they are captured. The ultimate goal of Simone de Beauvoir is to achieve freedom as of autonomy. She perceives the idea of equality as an ideal of freedom (Holland-Cunz 2003: 97-111). Equal rights and access to opportunities for women and men is thus essential in order to enjoy freedom. Freedom extends the political freedom of movement or speech; it rather also includes aspects such as access to natural resources, education and professions, or participation in decision-making processes on all levels.

Simone de Beauvoir's interdependent connection of equality and freedom concludes to the argument that gender inequality sets boundaries within the freedom of women. Since most societies are patriarchal or male-dominated, they are led and ruled by men. History shows that the brave men were in charge of battles and the soft women were in charge of peaceful homes. Being a fighter, a soldier, a leader was and still is associated with a heroic and masculine image. Men were/are the warriors and women the worriers. This is due to (ascribed) gender roles or rather gender-specific stereotypes: on the one hand, men represent the stronger sex that is able to live independently, in autonomy, and remote from the outside world. On the other hand, women are seen as defenseless, somewhat weak, and vulnerable without an active role in conflicts. This stereotypical perspective displays a clear androcentric identity perception. It differentiates unambiguously between generalized features and abilities of the two sexes: one can achieve something that the other cannot – he can participate in conflicts actively but she can only contribute passively. While these gender-specific stereotypes subsist, they contribute to gender inequality.

Gender inequality is always linked with power constellations. For instance, in the broad field of peace, conflict and security, lives of women and girls are to be protected, rights provided, and needs regarded. Female participation is often little respected. In the informal sector, women work in medical service, organize peace marches, dialogues, and support intercultural tolerance. In the formal sector, they are engaged in developing early warning mechanisms, applying preventive diplomacy, and operating in peace consolidation and global disarmament. However, female participation is still less visible and less accepted (Anderlini 2007: 33-34).

Referring to gender inequality in connection to power constellations should lead to integrating Johan Galtung's theory of structural violence. It indicates that unequal opportunities persist within the social structures of societies. Criteria to determine the differences or inequality are, for example, global wealth, education, distribution of resources, and power allocations (Galtung 1975). Galtung emphasizes the intensity of structural violence by comparing it with (inter-) personal violence.

> When this structural violence is built around a feudal interaction pattern with a tightly integrated topdog group and a highly atomized underdog group, then personal violence is no longer necessary. Personal violence is only for the amateur in dominance; structural violence is the tool of the professional. The amateur who wants to dominate uses guns, the professional uses social structure (Galtung 1975:80 quoted in Caprioli 2003: 4).

According to Caprioli, "[g]ender is an integral aspect of structural and cultural violence, for gender forms the basis of structural inequality in all countries". Despite her recognition of national differences of gender-related inequality, she continues by saying that "women are universally unequal in both the economic and political spheres" (Caprioli 2003: 3-4). Gender roles and identities continuously alter and modify. Nevertheless, "gender is used as a benchmark to determine access and power, and is the rubric under which inequality is justified and maintained" (Caprioli 2003: 4).

Worldwide, activities have been initiated to progress in reaching gender equality. Laws were adjusted and specific projects launched in many countries. However, gaps between de jure and de facto gender equality persist worldwide.

4.3. Gender sensitivity as the Central Pillar

Gender sensitivity is understood as prior to the other two pillars. It is thus the central pillar for two reasons: to use transformation opportunities in the distinct refugee context and to achieve progress in the development context.

1. Gender-sensitive operations are understood to be crucial to use the transformation opportunities in the refugee context: Refugee aid used to be known as ad hoc emergency humanitarian assistance. Refugee waves cannot be planned and occur spontaneously for multiple reasons. Refugees often flee from violent conflicts or natural disasters to seek security and safety in order to survive. Once they reach a hosting country that allows them to stay until solutions are found, several issues and security threats continue to endanger their lives, among others "forgery, aggravated assault, murder, forced prostitution, kidnapping, human trafficking, smuggling, and carrying weapons" (UNHCR 2006d: 39). Humanitarian aid takes places to calm humanitarian crises caused by, e.g., violent conflicts and natural disasters. It is about helping and facilitating victims. "Human and physical resources need to be rapidly mobilised to meet vital needs – for example for shelter, food, water and medical care" (EU 2007).

UNHCR recognizes the importance of integrating the gender perspective as both an opportunity and a challenge. "On the one hand, forced displacement can be a disempowering experience for women. Traditionally responsible for children, older people, and domestic work, women are often overburdened during displacement" (UNHCR 2008a: 39). Women are hardly able to voice their opinions due to their broad exclusion from decision-making processes. Observing the opposite site as an opportunity requires a revised view on refugee women and gender role constellations, which may have changed during conflict. UNHCR notes on the other hand that

> forced displacement and return can be an empowering experience for women. Their experience and the changes in gender roles brought about by displacement may enable them actively to challenge traditional gender roles that hinder their participation in the political, economic, and social realms. Where they have organized, they may be able to claim their right to participate in different aspects of camp or urban life and in return communities (UNHCR 2008a: 40).

In my research, integrating the gender perspective into all operational sectors of refugee assistance is seen as necessary for that very reason: as an opportunity supporting the process of gender equality. Most of the Southern Sudanese refugees in the settlements in the West Nile region of Uganda have experienced violent conflicts or civil war in their country of origin. People were tortured, trafficked, murdered, and driven from their homes. Displaced and escaped individuals and collectives especially, add to the long-lasting traumatization of such societies. When refugees reach the settlements, they have a long journey behind them. They are in a new country, surrounded by unknown natural and social conditions, often live without their husbands or wives or greater family circles, have to head households, make their own decisions, take care of ensuring their survival through receiving different foods, etc. Thus, with their arrival, transitional conditions are caused. These conditions could be used to release the strict hierarchical social structures, the structures that define gender role allocations. Refugee assistance could initiate adequate activities to support a psychological transformation towards women's empowerment and gender equality while considering men. Consequently, in my opinion, the composition of past, pressure and new surrounding produces psychological transformation opportunities, which may lead to progress in gender equality among refugee if adequate activities are launched. Applied activities would fall under the umbrella of integrating the gender perspective. This view has been researched insufficiently so far.

2. Gender-sensitive operations are crucial to achieve progress in the development assistance context: In Uganda, refugee assistance went one step further than merely providing humanitarian aid. When the Government of Uganda and UNHCR signed the agreement on the development orientation in 1996, they implied to not only provide adequate assistance to the original beneficiaries, but also to support Uganda's development and integrate the national society as a further group of beneficiaries.

In 2001, the former Deputy Secretary-General Louise Fréchette spoke on the "Women and Peace" panel at the UN on the occasion of International Women's Day. She underlined the importance of integrating women in all processes and activities to reach the goals of peace and development. She said the following:

> No development strategy is likely to work unless it involves women as central players. Their involvement has immediate benefits for nutrition, for health and for savings and reinvestment at the level of the family, the community, and ultimately the whole country. In other words, empowering women is a development policy that works. It is a long-term investment that yields an exceptionally high return (Fréchette 2001).

Applying the statement of Fréchette infers to the inextricable connection between developmental progress and full female inclusion. Development, growth, peace consolidation, and female inclusion are connected social processes; if refugee assistance receives a development orientation, actions regarding both sexes need to be taken.

The development of a country is dependent on a stable political system. A study of the World Bank proves that "gender inequality increases the likelihood that a state will experience internal conflict" (Caprioli 2003: 14). Hence, if gender equality is pursued or already exists, than this indicates the stability as well as the developmental readiness of a country. Development furthermore means to reach independence, enjoying economic opportunities and social security. In view of that, a prior aspect that is thus strongly connected with development is freedom. Understanding development — in accordance with Sen — through freedom (Sen 1999: 3) indicates that an entire society shall benefit from development and freedom, which consists of both men and women.

Durable or sustainable results are goals of development. While the World Commission on Environment and Development defines sustainable development though progress that meets the needs of present and future generations, I grasp it by adding Amartya Sen's focus on freedom to all members of a society. Hence, my definition of sustainable development is a type of development assistance that strives for identifying durable solutions that betters the lives of current and future generations by intentionally respecting and protecting the limited natural resources, supporting economic growth, regarding cultural factors, and promoting balanced social relations between the genders to reach freedom.

Since my definition of sustainable development integrates the reference of resources and a positive durable advancement throughout the entire respective society, operative manners should be efficient. Efficiency targets to perform activities in a resource-considering mode to reach maximum results. If refugee assistance intends to be development-oriented, actions must respect all resources including natural and human resources. This is only possible if cost and usage elements are factored in and the entire society is involved, which reveals the importance on integrating women.

Gender equality and sensitivity thus obtains a dual imperative in the context of development-oriented refugee assistance: adequate refugee assistance can support the psychological transitional process in promoting equality, and development aid can only be performed sustainably and efficiently if both men and women are involved in the process.

In order to operate while considering gender in the diverse fields including refugee and development assistance, the UN defined how to mainstream the gender perspective.

> Mainstreaming a gender perspective is the process of assessing the implications for women and men of any planned action, including legislation, policies or programmes, in all areas and at all levels. It is a strategy for making women's as well as men's concerns and experiences an integral dimension of the design, implementation, monitoring and evaluation of policies and programmes in all political, economic and societal spheres so that women and men benefit equally and inequality is not perpetuated. The ultimate goal is to achieve gender equality (A/52/3, Chapter IV, Agreed conclusions, 1997/2).

The gender perspective therefore means to observe issues from *one* perspective that constitutes gender relations. It attempts to understand the (in)equity and (in)equality of both sexes in a social, ecological, political, and economical sense. Furthermore, it expects that in revealing obstacles and difficulties the process towards equity and equality will be promoted. The initial step to integrate the gender perspective is to collect and evaluate profound data on gender relations; e.g., on access to resources of female and male refugees or their political participation in refugee camps. The gender perspective and its integration do not intend to reach uniformity between the two sexes. Instead, its goal is to respect and recognize the diversity of gender-related needs.

In the context of this research, gender sensitivity is therefore defined as an integrated part of operations of development-oriented refugee assistance through psychological support to refugees, integration and participation of both sexes of refugee and local communities and therewith provides equal opportunities. Gender-sensitive operations should moreover be a cross-cutting theme.

Based on the above explanative inference, gender sensitivity constitutes the foundation pillar while sustainability and efficiency are corner pillars. They are nevertheless interrelated.

Chapter III Refugee Aid, Gender and Development

This chapter introduces key aspects with historical and current trends of refugee protection and assistance, refugees and gender as well as development aid.

1. International Refugee Regime and UNHCR's Scope of Operations

1.1. Historical Developments within UNHCR

1.1.1. Establishment of UNHCR

While the International Refugee Organization still undertook actions and the General Assembly extended the organization's operational mandate to September 1951 (A/Res/430 (V)), discussions of member states on the possibility and necessity of a new agency targeting the ongoing refugee issue were held. On the 14th of December in 1950, the General Assembly adopted Resolution 428 (V) and therewith the statute of the new international refugee agency called the United Nations Office of the High Commissioner for Refugees (UNHCR).

Similar to the previous two refugee agencies — United Nations Relief and Rehabilitation Administration and the International Refugee Organization — UNHCR was also established as a non-permanent organization. The greatest change of UNHCR was the non-operational working model, which was — at least during the initial period — to be pursued (Goodwin-Gill 2006: 3). UNHCR rather followed the function of a protection agency.

The Statute of UNHCR was agreed on by the member states through General Assembly Resolution 428 (V). It specifies the character of the agency, its mandates, functions, and the definition of refugees. The Convention relating to the Status of Refugees contains several new aspects to the statute. It was adopted on the 28th of July in 1951 by the UN Conference of Plenipotentiaries on the Status of Refugees and Stateless Persons convened under General Assembly Resolution 429 (V) of 14th of December in 1950. The Convention came into force on the 22nd of April, 1954.

1.1.2. The Refugee Definition

In comparison to the Statute, the 1951 Convention defines refugees under a temporarily and geographically limited scope. Article 1, states the revised definition of the term 'refugee':

> As a result of events occurring before 1 January 1951 and owing to well-founded fear of being persecuted for reasons of race, religion, nationality, membership of a particular social group or political opinion, is outside the country of his nationality and is unable or, owing to such fear, is unwilling to avail himself of the protection of that country; or who, not having a nationality and being outside the country of his former habitual residence as a result of such events, is unable or, owing to such fear, is unwilling to return to it.
>
> In the case of a person who has more than one nationality, the term "the country of his nationality" shall mean each of the countries of which he is a national, and a person shall not be deemed to be lacking the protection of the country of his nationality if, without any valid reason based on wellfounded fear, he has not availed himself of the protection of one of the countries of which he is a national (A/Res/429 (V): article 2).

The definition furthermore clarifies that the phrase "events occurring before 1 January 1951" should be understood as "events occurring in Europe before 1 January 1951". By means of these restrictions, the definition of a refugee applies to individuals and not groups, yet is by far not universally applicable. The Convention with its rights shall not apply to any person who suffered from war crimes or any crime against humanity (A/Res/429 (V): article 2).

1.1.3. UNHCR's Focus during the 1950s and 1960s

The scope of the work of this newly established agency grew tremendously and changed from the very beginning throughout the following decades. New geographical areas were included into the mandate, groups of beneficiaries entered the protection function of UNHCR, and working methods were improved and adjusted to the needs.

In the early 1950s, the major assignment of UNHCR was to find solutions for the remaining people within Europe who became refugees following the Second World War. UNHCR undertook resettling initiatives to find new homes for the refugees mostly in the Americas and Oceania. In 1952, the agency cooperated for the first time with NGOs to provide material assistance in the context of care and maintenance activities, and resettlement. Funded by the Ford Foundation, UNHCR could provide protection and NGO assistance (Ferris 2003: 119).

Only four years later, in 1956, UNHCR faced the first massive refugee wave after, and not directly connected to, the Second World War. Nearly 200,000 Hungarian refugees who fled from the Soviet suppression in the Cold War reached Western Europe and in particular Austria and Yugoslavia. Austria requested UNHCR to assist in responding to the refugee influx. UNHCR solved its first major challenge by setting up coordination groups and providing refugees with protection, as well as care and maintenance with funds raised for this emergency. It found permanent solutions, either through resettlement in third countries, or voluntary repatriation (Loescher et al. 2008: 21-22).

During the same timeframe of the late 1950s, UNHCR was confronted with further refugee waves and issues, in particular in Morocco, Tunisia, and China. All these crises were recognized by the UN and its General Assembly which adopted resolutions to verify the provision of protection and assistance (A/RES/1167 (XII); A/RES/1286 (XIII). In General Assembly Resolution 1165 (XII), the member states announce through the General Assembly that they are prolonging UNHCR while "considering the need for international action on behalf of refugees" (A/RES/1165 (XII)). In Resolution 1166 (XII), the General Assembly even emphasizes "that new refugee situations requiring international assistance have arisen to augment the problem since the establishment [...]" (A/RES/1166 (XII)). Therewith, the General Assembly goes one step further by accepting the need of international and not only European assistance.

Based on the already extended mandate and functions of the Office, the General Assembly in 1959, adopted a new approach for the operations named "good office". This was done in order to handle and solve the newly arisen issues relating to refugees worldwide. In General Assembly Resolution 1388 (XIV), the High Commissioner was authorized "to use his good office in the transmission of contributions designed to provide assistance to these refugees" (A/RES/1388 (XIV)). This formula allowed UNHCR to reach and protect refugees who were not typically embraced in the definition stated in the Convention or Statute. Therefore, the operational scope was extended to an international level. It needs to be kept in mind, however, that all international activities carried out by UNHCR were still to be confirmed by the General Assembly or ECOSOC.

In the 1960s, several new refugee waves occurred which UNHCR had to respond to although they were not within the mandate due to geographic restrictions. Due to the ending era of colonialism and numerous violent fights for independence, UNHCR became particularly involved in protection and assistance on the African continent. "Exodus upon exodus from Cambodia, Ethiopia, Laos, Southern Africa, Sudan and Viet Nam increased the number of refugees in only 10 years from 2.5 million to 8 million" (UNHCR 1993: 5). In addition, the Cold War expanded to the developing world to gain power. A great issue of the Office revealed its domination by Western nations and its dependency on donors, which were also from the Western world. While more and more African states reached independence, they became members of the UN and therefore were able to make their voices heard at the General Assembly. In this particular context, it became clear that "the traditional refugee concept and legal definitions that the Office had used in Europe would not apply in the developing countries". Hence, further steps had to be initiated to successfully provide protection and assistance to the refugees and "to expand the Office's global reach" (Loescher et al. 2008: 26; cf. Martin et al. 2005: 34-36).

1.1.4. UNHCR's Protocol relating to the Status of Refugees

As a reaction to the new global challenges, the General Assembly adopted Resolution 2198 (XXI) and therewith the Protocol relating to the Status of Refugees (1967 Protocol). In the Resolution as well as in the beginning of the 1967 Protocol, it was considered "that new refugee situations have arisen since the Convention was adopted and that the refugees concerned may therefore not fall within the scope of the Convention" (A/RES/2198 (XXI)).

The 1967 Protocol constitutes an independent legal instrument, which revises certain aspects of the Convention. A state can therefore agree to the Protocol without being or becoming a party of the Convention. It can also become a party to the Convention with certain provisions.

The 1967 Protocol modernized the international refugee protection through a major aspect: It broadened the refugee definition in article 2 to any person who

> owing to well-founded fear of being persecuted for reasons of race, religion, nationality, membership of a particular social group or political opinion, is outside the country of his nationality and is unable or, owing to such fear, is unwilling to avail himself of the protection of that country; or who, not having a nationality and being outside the country of his former habitual residence as a result of such events, is unable or, owing to such fear, is unwilling to return to it (Protocol 1967: Article 1, 2).

Thus, the geographic and time limitations were omitted. With this improvement, UNHCR received its universal mandate, which was already included in the Statute.

Before the 1967 Protocol was adopted, the General Assembly had to approve each activity that was slightly out of the original scope of UNHCR's mandate and functions. The General Assembly announced its approval through a particular resolution. This encompassed further regional or geographical areas of action, as well as their special persons requiring assistance. By means of altering the definition, the General Assembly recognized the need of a universal understanding of the refugee issue and its internationalization of protection and assistance.

The temporary restriction of UNHCR, however, remained. UNHCR's need for continuing protection and assistance to refugees was verified by a General Assembly resolution every five years. Yet, UNHCR's Convention and its 1967 Protocol "remain the cornerstone of the international legal framework to protect the world's refugees" (UNHCR 2006a: 10).

1.1.5. Changes from the 1970s onwards

After the targeted beneficiaries of UNHCR were redefined, the work of UNHCR proceeded internationally and mainly in developing countries. The 1970s constituted the decade of newly founded organizations, which focus on human rights, human rights violations, and fights for improvements. UNHCR still applied the "good office" formula. For the first time, internal displacement became part of operations. UNHCR's international role was increasingly used for coordinating humanitarian and relief activities of several UN agencies "when the technical and material needs [in a disaster and its area] would exceed the mandate and capacity of any one agency" (Loescher et al. 2008: 30).

In 1976, the General Assembly recognized not only the growing role of UNHCR but also new persons of concern, which UNHCR should take into its protection mandate. It identified "refugees and displaced persons, victims of man-made disasters, requiring urgent humanitarian assistance" (A/2011).

Already during the 1960s and 1970s, the idea of integrating development initiatives in care and maintenance activities within refugee protection and assistance was born. Due to large refugee influxes particularly in developing countries, projects were supposed to target the original beneficiaries as well as the national populace. By the 1980s, 'refugee aid and development' was incorporated in several national programs. It was replaced by the 'returnee aid and development' concept in the 1990s (Crisp 2001, 2003; Betts 2009a).

The 1980s constituted a decade of asylum restrictions. More and more refugee waves appeared all over the world. While the two prior decades were already marked by exoduses, the difference now was that UNHCR and the beneficiaries suffered from limitations and operational challenges. "Economic recessions and the election of conservative governments in many Western states led to [...] increasingly restrictive asylum policies" (Loescher et al. 2008: 30). States feared that incoming refugees would cause further economic obstacles. Thus, the Office was forced to find other solutions. The interim solutions were several long-term care and maintenance programs in connection with diverse side projects which, for the first time in history, connected refugee assistance with development initiatives. The programs were initiated in Central America and Africa. The durable solution came up after most civil wars settled down, which enabled UNHCR to promote and conduct voluntary repatriation activities.

The 1990s, the decade of repatriation, were marked by the end of the Cold War, which strongly influenced world politics with all its activities. Humanitarian needs, however, persisted. Several European countries set up "temporary protection policies in response to movements of large numbers of former Yugoslavian refugees at different times during the 1990s" (Martin et al. 2005: 36). In developing countries, UNHCR applied mainly repatriation to diminish the refugee populations in hosting countries. To do that, the Office established assessment measures on safety. While conflicts in some countries might have been ongoing, UNHCR still encouraged refugees to repatriate because the specific areas of return were rated as safe. This kind of approach was termed "safe return" and belonged to a new policy on repatriation, which UNHCR mainly applied during the 1990s. In connection with the "safe return" model, UNHCR developed and realized "returnee aid and development" projects to promote the area of return. Due to repatriation efforts, more than nine million refugees returned between 1991 and 1996 that was comparably high to the 1.2 million returnees between 1985 and 1990 (Loescher et al. 2008: 47-50).

In addition to that, during the 1990s, UNHCR produced several policies and guidelines to control and overcome threats and violence women and children were facing in day to day life in refugee settlements. Especially to mention is the *Policy on Refugee Women* from 1990.

The new millennium began with the tragedy of the terrorist attacks in New York on September 11th, 2001. In the aftermath, the war on terror was initiated, which deteriorated the conditions for refugees and migrations due to constant and arising suspicion against them. At the same time, UNHCR faced negative criticism regarding its international protection activities, which was why it initiated the so-called Global Consultation on International Protection. NGOs, states, and experts were provided with an instrument to announce aspects which needed improvement. Besides a declaration, the rather important outcome of the Consultation was the Agenda of Protection. The main content comprised six broad goals with explanations of how they were supposed to be implemented (UNHCR 2003c). Since the agenda was not a legally binding instrument, it "did not benefit from universal support [...] and its potential was largely unrealized" (Loescher et al. 2008: 63; cf. Gibney 2002: 40-42; Newland et al. 2002: 4-7).

The year 2003 not only constituted the end of the Global Consultations and the beginning of Convention Plus. It was also the year in which the General Assembly adopted Resolution 58/153 and therewith removed the temporary restriction of UNHCR.

Launching Convention Plus was an attempt to create a forum for states to develop special international agreements that complement the 1951 Convention. The intention was "to improve access to durable solutions through improved north-south responsibility-sharing" by taking development initiatives and activities into account (Betts 2004: 1). Despite efforts, the process "failed to reach its initial aims" (Loescher et al. 2008: 64-65).

Today, UNHCR provides protection and assistance to refugees, IDPs, war-affected populations, asylum-seekers, stateless persons, returnees, and further individuals whose nationality has been disputed (UNHCR 2006a: 17-31). Thus, the targeted group of beneficiaries is extended. Current international discussions particularly embrace the inclusion of development in refugee assistance which reveals the *Global Forum on Migration and Development.* It is based on the *High Level Dialogue on International Migration and Development*[6] in 2006.

1.2. Brief Distinction between Refugee Protection and Assistance

To support refugees, UNHCR is mandated to provide them with protection and to seek permanent solutions. But what does it mean to provide protection? How does UNHCR function while providing protection and assistance? How does it cooperate with implementing and operational partners?[7]

'Normally', states protect their citizens with their respective authorities and national structures. In cases of refugees, they are forced to flee and do not receive the protection they are supposed to have. UNHCR takes over the task to protect refugees and other persons of concern in order to "compensate for this lack of national protection" (Bützer 2007: 46).

UNHCR's protection activities are led by "international law, including international refugee law, international human rights law, and international humanitarian law" (UNHCR 2008a: 23). What it means to realize the protection functions is already stated in the 1951 Convention. Most tasks, which the High Commissioner and his office are supposed to perform, are strongly related to protecting the beneficiaries. The list of duties as stated in the 1951 Convention is of utmost priority. UNHCR cooperates with states in providing protection.

First and foremost, it means to ensure access to their rights. The cooperation with states is necessary to guarantee that states admit asylum-seekers and refugees, register them to prove their status, and thus not to force them to return to the place where their lives are threatened. The non-refoulement principle is a key aspect of international refugee law and important to ensure the survival and adequate protection of the beneficiaries. According to article 12 of the 1951 Convention, the "personal status of a refugee shall be governed by the law of the country of his domicile or, if he has no domicile, by the law of the country of his residence." UNHCR and the government of the hosting state therefore determine who counts as a refugee. In practice, refugees are recognized as "prima facie" group determination or following individual status determinations (UNHCR

6 Further information on the High Level Dialogue and the Global Forum is provided in *Chapter IV Development-oriented refugee assistance*.

7 The mentioned features of protection are by far not complete. They are simply supposed to demonstrate an excerpt of what the protection role of UNHCR entails.

1999a: 13). Either way, official decisions are especially significant for the issuing of documents for the individuals (UNHCR 2006a: 13).

Providing protection also includes seeking durable solutions for all the beneficiaries. UNHCR mainly focuses on local integration, voluntary repatriation to the countries of origin of beneficiaries and resettlement to a third country. "UNHCR assists large scale movements to countries of origin as well as individuals who decide to repatriate" (Martin et al. 2005: 230). The option of resettlement is particularly used for "vulnerable and special cases such as persecuted ethnic minorities, women, and minors". However, the competition is high which "has led to scandalous cases of corruption" (Juma/Kagwanja 2003: 230). The Office, however, strives to identify additional durable solutions which suit the particular situation and country.

Regarding the protection role of UNHCR towards national states, two main elements are to be pointed out. On the one hand, UNHCR monitors states that have signed the 1951 Convention with or without its 1967 Protocol concerning the adequate implementation of the contents. In that context, the Office also advises governments on the integration of these contents. UNHCR is "assisting countries in developing and implementing national laws that protect the rights of refugees, the internally displaced and others of concern to" (UNHCR 2006a: 13). Thereby, the Office examines and ensures basic humanitarian standards.

According to UNHCR's Operational Protection in Camps and Settlements,

> [r]efugee protection encompasses measures to ensure refugees' physical security (preserving the physical safety of refugees), social security (delivery of minimum standards of material assistance) and their legal security (restoring and safeguarding legal rights) (UNHCR 2006d: 39).

Providing protection — therefore and again — entails that human rights of refugees and further persons of concern are granted and respected. "The bulk of the [1951] Convention specifies the social, economic and political rights to be afforded to individuals recognized as refugees" (Loescher et al. 2008: 99). The aforementioned non-refoulement principle belongs to the list of rights. Further rights comprise, e.g., shelter, food, water, medical assistance, primary education, and legal protection and advice. To ensure that rights are respected and that special needs are taken care of, UNHCR often gets involved directly and engages its partners in assistance provided. At this exact point, the undividable connection of refugee protection and refugee assistance becomes obvious.

The original mandate of UNHCR clearly focuses on protection; however, already during the 1950s, the international community came to the conclusion that protection alone will not solve the issues. Despite the conviction that repatriation, resettlement and local integration are durable solutions, at times they cannot be realized as quickly as the Office might wish for. Then, the assistance undertakings are applied. I.e., UNHCR provides material support and care and maintenance in refugee camps and settlements; either on its own or through partners. Although it appears that refugee assistance covers different activities than refugee protection, it is part of the refugee protection mandate. Eventually, assistance also aims to protect vulnerable beneficiaries. Why and when did the change towards integrating the assistance aspect occur? What does it mean to provide assistance to refugees and other persons of concern?[8]

As mentioned before, enormous refugee waves occurred in less or least developed countries already in the 1950s. The General Assembly recognized the need for UNHCR to provide assistance in connection with the protection of beneficiaries. The General Assembly therefore adopted several resolutions. It authorized the extension of the mandate of the High Commissioner and his office in regard to, firstly, undertaking operations outside of the geographical area underlined in the Statute, and secondly, coordinating material assistance. Moreover, the General Assembly also authorized the High Commissioner to look for further funds for emergency assistance in the Resolutions 638 (VII) and 639 (VII). In 1954, the United Nations Refugee Fund was set up and replaced by the Executive Committee in 1957. Its function was to "continue emergency assistance to the most needy cases" in addition to finding durable solutions (UNHCR 2003b: 4). In 1957, the High Commissioner was authorized to develop an annual assistance program, which was to be submitted to and approved by the Executive Committee. Hence, the UN realized only shortly after the establishment of UNHCR that assistance is required to provide adequate support to refugees (UNHCR 2003b: 4-6; Goodwin-Gill 2006: 3).

Providing refugee assistance remains to be a part of protection and seeking durable solutions. According to the Operations Management Handbook, UNHCR distinguishes between five types of assistance:

> a. Emergency (EM): covers activities following an influx of refugees or persons of concern to the High Commissioner, aimed at meeting basic /survival needs quickly. This type of assistance will normally not last more than one year, and will essentially focus on life-saving/life-sustaining measures.
>
> b. Care and Maintenance (CM): covers activities for refugees in relatively stable situations, where survival is no longer threatened, but where the future of the refugee group in terms of a durable solution has not yet been determined. This may include the provision of food, transportation, household utensils and clothing, water, sanitation, health services, shelter and basic education. When feasible, it may also include vocational training or small income-generating activities to prepare refugees for a more productive life and to promote limited self-reliance. This assistance should not exceed a period of two years; however, in many countries these projects have lasted much longer because the

8 The features of refugee assistance are not exhaustive, as mentioned in the context of refugee protection. They show the wide scope of practical refugee assistance.

refugees were granted temporary asylum only, and the attainment of a durable solution has proven impossible.

c. Voluntary Repatriation (RP): covers activities linked to the return home of a refugee group, this being the most desirable solution, as long as the voluntary nature of the repatriation is safe-guarded. Assistance in this category is designed to help refugees overcome practical difficulties in repatriating to their home country. In the country of asylum, it includes preparations for departure and measures to help organize the journey home. Often, tripartite commissions are formed, involving the countries of origin and asylum along with UNHCR. Reception facilities may have to be organized in the home country, as well as assistance in the initial phase of reintegration, e.g. the provision of basic needs and measures for rehabilitation.

d. Local Settlement (LS): where voluntary repatriation is not yet possible, and refugees have the opportunity to legally reside in the host country and to enjoy civil and economic rights comparable to the local population, activities in this category help refugees become selfsupporting in the country of first asylum, and to integrate into the economic and social life of the new community. It requires the full participation of the refugees themselves, and the agreement of the host country. Measures to meet the refugees' needs must also take into account the living standards of the local population.

e. Resettlement (RE): where no other durable solution is feasible, activities in this category enable refugees to resettle in a new country. This is usually applied when refugees are admitted only temporarily to a country of asylum, on condition of permanent resettlement elsewhere. It may also be the only answer if local integration is impossible for ethnic, political or economic reasons, or in cases where the security of the refugees is at risk. Family reunion is another major reason for resettlement. Assistance may include measures to secure places, and arrangements for both travel and prior to departure – exit formalities, medical screening, counselling, language training and other measures designed to facilitate integration in the new country of asylum (UNHCR 2003b: 38-39).

UNHCR undertakes these actions in cooperation with governments of hosting countries, countries of origin, and third countries, depending on the kind of activity. UNHCR works with implementing and operational partners. Partners can be international organizations, NGOs or further institutions. Operational partners complement UNHCR's work through the respective mandates of the organizations. For instance, WFP and UNHCR signed a Memorandum of Understanding in 2002 to cooperate in refugee assistance on a global basis. That way, operational duplications can be avoided and synergies generated. Implementing partners realize activities delegated and funded by UNHCR. Responsibilities are defined in sub-agreements which include a budget proposal, work plan, and project description. Implementing partners are required to regularly report their progress. For example, DED is an implementing partner of UNHCR in Uganda (UNHCR 2003b: 28-34).[9]

9 Hereafter, I will mainly refer to refugee assistance, meaning to capture protection as well.

2. *Gender Sensitivity in the Context of the Refugee Regime*

2.1. Gender from the Angle of the UN and UNHCR

UNHCR, in accordance with the UN system, does not equate the term gender with women and their advancement or empowerment. The feminist research has had a great impact on practical and global politics in terms of highlighting the issue of inequality and thus taking the analytic category of gender into account while operating in the broad field of politics. For example, in 1997 the UN established the Office of the Special Advisor on Gender Issues and Advancement of Women (OSAGI)[10] in order to support the UN in decision making concerning gender-related questions (UN OSAGI 2009).[11]

UN's General Assembly explains and defined the term gender in its *1999 World Survey on the Role of Women in Development* broadly, yet clearly:

> Gender is defined as the social meanings given to biological sex differences. It is an ideological and cultural construct, but is also reproduced within the realm of material practices; in turn it influences the outcomes of such practices. It affects the distribution of resources, wealth, work, decision-making and political power, and enjoyment of rights and entitlements within the family as well as public life. Despite variations across cultures and over time, gender relations throughout the world entail asymmetry of power between men and women as a pervasive trait. Thus, gender is a social stratifier, and in this sense it is similar to other stratifiers such as race, class, ethnicity, sexuality, and age. It helps us understand the social construction of gender identities and the unequal structure of power that underlies the relationship between the sexes (A/54/227: 7).

UNHCR and its operations work with the above provided definition. The Executive Committee of UNHCR produced a separate and more precise definition that focuses on the refugee context. The Executive Committee stresses that "it should be noted that UNHCR recognizes that "gender" is not synonymous with addressing the needs of one particular segment of the population, such as women. Nor is it about setting up discrete projects for women" (EC/49/SC/CRP.22: 1).

10 OSAGI is now part of UN Women.

11 The UN accepted the need for further actions in the gender sector to progress in working towards gender equality. In order to address gender and women's issues more effectively, the member states through the General Assembly adopted Resolution 63/311 on the 14th of September in 2009 (A/RES/63/311) while recalling the previous Resolution 62/208 on the triennial comprehensive policy review of operational activities for development and Resolution 62/277 on system-wide coherence. The General Assembly therewith decided on the establishment of a new United Nations agency on gender and women's (rights) issues. By means of that, the UN tackles the gaps in internal coherence.

In UNHCR's guidelines on *Sexual and Gender-Based Violence against Refugees, Returnees and Internally Displaced Persons*, both sex and gender are defined.

> The term sex refers to the biological characteristics of males and females. These characteristics are congenital and their differences are limited to physiological reproductive functions.
>
> Gender is the term used to denote the social characteristics assigned to men and women. These social characteristics are constructed on the basis of different factors, such as age, religion, national, ethnic and social origin. They differ both within and between cultures and define identities, status, roles, responsibilities and power relations among the members of any society or culture. Gender is learned through socialisation. It is not static or innate, but evolves to respond to changes in the social, political and cultural environment (UNHCR 2003a: 11).

UNHCR therefore observes differences between sex and gender as well as IR feminists do. UNHCR moreover stresses the fact that "[g]ender is learned, and therefore changeable" (UNHCR 2003a: 11). Thus, the social construction of gender is accepted by UNHCR.

According to the definition of gender, UNHCR does not grasp the meaning of gender equality in terms of

> women and men will become the same but that women's and men's rights, responsibilities and opportunities will not depend on whether they are born male or female. Gender equality implies that the interests, needs and priorities of both women and men are taken into consideration – recognizing the diversity of different groups of women and men. Gender equality is not a 'women's issue' but should concern and fully engage men as well as women (UNHCR 2008a: 12).

In UNHCR's Handout No. 3 of Module 1 of the guidelines on *Ensuring Gender Sensitivity in the Context of Refugee Status Determination and Resettlement*, the understanding of gender roles is clarified. It is stated that

> [g]ender roles are learned behaviours in a given society/community or other social group, that condition which activities, tasks and responsibilities are perceived as male and female. Gender roles are affected by age, class, ethnicity, religion or other ideologies, and by the geographical, economic and political environment (UNHCR 2005a: 132).

The Executive Committee emphasizes furthermore that

> [g]ender affects girls and boys, women and men, elderly women and men as well as disabled women and men. Moreover, gender must be considered when developing policy, protection responses, programmes, community services responses, public information campaigns and durable solutions, as well as any area of technical assistance.
>
> Using a gender equality perspective implies understanding each of these areas with their varying implications for women and men of all ages, and any inequitable relationships that may arise or be reinforced through UNHCR's interventions (EC/49/SC/CRP.22: 1-2).

Nevertheless, UNHCR does recognize that "gender-related barriers exclude women from full participation in society". Therefore, projects and activities have to reflect on the issues to ensure “that activities benefit both women and men” (EC/GC/02/8: 3, 1).

Targeting gender issues in the humanitarian field and in the context of refugee protection and assistance integrates fighting against gender-based violence. UNHCR is aware of the differences between gender-based violence and violence against women. It thus announces that

> gender-based violence is used to distinguish common violence from violence that targets individuals or groups of individuals on the basis of their gender. Gender-based violence has been defined by the CEDAW Committee as violence that is directed at a person on the basis of gender or sex. It includes acts that inflict physical, mental or sexual harm or suffering, threat of such acts, coercion and other deprivations of liberty.
>
> The term violence against women refers to any act of gender-based violence that results in, or is likely to result in, physical, sexual and psychological harm to women and girls, whether occurring in private or in public. Violence against women is a form of gender-based violence and includes sexual violence (UNHCR 2003a: 10).

In addition to gender-based violence and violence against women, UNHCR furthermore defines how it comprehends sexual violence, including exploitation and abuse, sex and gender-based violence, and domestic violence.[12]

> Sexual violence, including exploitation and abuse, refers to any act, attempt or threat of a sexual nature that results, or is likely to result, in physical, psychological and emotional harm. Sexual violence is a form of gender-based violence. [...]
>
> Sexual and gender-based violence is largely rooted in unequal power relations. These perpetuate and condone violence within the family, the community and the State. The distinction made between public and private spheres should not serve as an excuse for not addressing domestic violence as a form of SGBV. The exclusion of women and girls from the public arena only increases their vulnerability to violence within the family. Domestic violence reinforces gender-based discrimination and keeps women subordinate to men (UNHCR 2003a: 10-11).

Based on these definitions, it is clear that UNHCR observes differences within the context of threats against women and men. While taking both into consideration by offering the adequate protection, UNHCR is aware that women face further compulsions in all spheres, from private to public. Hence, guidelines and mechanisms were developed to tackle threats in appropriate manners.

12 In addition to those definitions, UNHCR also offers explanations of the meanings of further relevant terms (UNHCR 2003c: 8-15).

2.2. Gender-sensitive Refugee Assistance

Based on UNHCR's operational definition of gender, it is to be examined how it aims to overcome these issues and what gender-sensitive work means.

2.2.1. Refugees, Threats, and Gender?

As already illustrated in theoretical terms, gender inequality is both influenced and shaped by social structures and has an impact on societies. Refugees flee from violent conflicts or other disasters in search of security in another country. However, during the search or even after being allowed to remain in a country until solutions are identified, they face diverse threats.

> Threats to the security of refugees may take a number of forms: Theft, assault, domestic violence, forced marriage, cattle rustling, vandalism, child abuse, rape and other sexual assault, arson, fraud, forgery, aggravated assault, murder, forced prostitution, kidnapping, human trafficking, smuggling, and carrying weapons. Security threats can rise to the level of war crimes or crimes against humanity, to include: targeted or serial rape; exploitation; enslavement; and torture; war crimes (UNHCR 2006d: 39).

These threats encompass a wide range. Both sexes can be affected by them. Nevertheless, many of them are connected to violence or oppression against the sex that is seen as more vulnerable, women. Forced prostitution, sexual assault, and rape only constitute three of many possible threats women and children face within the refugee framework.

UNHCR recognizes that "women and girls everywhere still face greater obstacles claiming and enjoying their rights than do men and boys" (UNHCR 2008a: i). During the different phases — during the conflict, the flight, while in the country of asylum, during repatriation, and reintegration — various threats may occur. UNHCR's Executive Committee also recognizes particular threats and acknowledges in its Conclusion on Women and Girls at Risk of 2006,

> while forcibly displaced men and boys also face protection problems, women and girls can be exposed to particular protection problems related to their gender, their cultural and socio-economic position, and their legal status, which mean they may be less likely than men and boys to be able to exercise their rights and therefore that specific action in favour of women and girls may be necessary to ensure they can enjoy protection and assistance on an equal basis with men and boys [...] (A/AC.96/1035).

In addition, the Executive Committee points out distinct risk factors threatening lives and security conditions of women and girls in the refugee context. It stresses that factors can occur as a consequence of violent conflicts, the flight, or during settlement. In particular, women and girls are exposed to sexual and gender-based violence (SGBV), but also other types of physical and non-physical violence such as

> inadequate or unequal access to and enjoyment of assistance and services; lack of access to livelihoods; lack of understanding of women's and men's roles, responsibilities and needs in relation to reproductive healthcare, and lack of understanding of the consequences of SGBV on women's and girls' health; the position of women and girls in the displaced or host community which can result in their marginalization and in discrimination against them; legal systems, which do not adequately uphold the rights of women and girls under international human rights law, including those relating to property; those informal justice practices which violate the human rights of women and girls; asylum systems which are not sensitive to the needs and claims of female asylum-seekers; and mechanisms for delivering protection which do not adequately monitor and reinforce women's and girls' rights (A/AC.96/1035).

Ferris presumably agrees with the listed threats and risk factors. In *Abuse of Power: Sexual Exploitation of Refugee Women and Girls*, she emphasizes the extent of SGBV in terms of perpetrators and refugee victims located in refugee camps. Although "[g]ender roles often change in refugee camps", traditional power allocations remain in gender-related terms. Her findings show "that not only was sexual exploitation widespread, it was also perpetrated by aid workers, peacekeepers, and community leaders. Humanitarian workers traded food and relief items for sexual favors". Her conclusion points out that despite the amount of initiatives to prevent from incidences, "the fundamental disparity of power and the inadequacy of relief assistance that lead women and children to exchange sex for things that they need to survive" remain (Ferris 2007: 586, 585, 590).

While Ferris looked at refugees in camps, Farr focuses on four forms of forced movements in her article *Notes toward a Gendered Understanding of Mixed-Population Movements and Security Sector Reform after Conflict*. She points out that gender concepts change, but disparities still play significant roles in all forms. Moreover, she emphasizes that "invisibility of these [mistreated] women" remains high (Farr 2007: 595). By treating SGBV and gender-related violence and inequality among refugee communities as something 'unspoken', issues cannot be targeted or solved by actors.

UNHCR recognized the numerous and diverse issues and threats refugee women and girls are confronted with. In addition to threats, gender issues and violence are predominantly perceived as "taboo topics in public or private conversations" with beneficiaries, which is why a sensitive approach to handle obstacles is crucial. In order to respect the idea that "[g]ender equality is [...] a human right" (UNCHR 2008a: 16, 12), UNHCR produced several policies and guidelines to develop adequate prevention, control, and response mechanisms in order to overcome the threats and undertake satisfactory operations.

2.2.2. Gender-related Policies and Guidelines

The operations of UNHCR are based on a great amount of legal documents, policies, and guidelines. All aspects of operations are covered in order to work effectively and to provide adequate protection. Thus, UNHCR also produced guiding principles to aim the course of action of gender-related issues in the right direction. Hereafter, gender-specific documents of the UN system and UNHCR per se are listed.[13] The ones of particular importance are briefly described afterwards.[14]

UNHCR provides a comprehensive list of legal documents on gender and gender equality that are relevant for the agency's operations on the website of RefWorld:

- Resolution 1820 (2008) [on women and peace and security], Adopted by the Security Council at its 5916th meeting, 19 June 2008
- Resolution 2005/31 on Mainstreaming a Gender Perspective Into All Policies and Programmes in the United Nations System, Adopted by the UN Economic and Social Council at its 39th plenary meeting, 26 July 2005
- Protocol to Prevent, Suppress and Punish Trafficking in Persons, Especially Women and Children, Supplementing the United Nations Convention against Transnational Organized Crime, 15 November 2000
- Resolution 1325 (2000) [on women and peace and security], Adopted by the UN Security Council at its 4213th meeting, S/RES/1325 (2000), 31 October 2000
- Agreed Conclusions 1997/2, Adopted by the UN Economic and Social Council on 18 July 1997, and as contained in A/52/3/Rev.1, "Report of the Economic and Social Council for 1997"
- Declaration on the Elimination of Violence against Women, General Assembly Resolution A/RES/48/104, 20 December 1993
- Convention on the Elimination of All Forms of Discrimination against Women, 18 December 1979, and its Optional Protocol to the Convention on the Elimination of All Forms of Discrimination Against Women (6 October 1999)
- Declaration on the Elimination of Discrimination against Women, General Assembly Resolution A/RES/2263, 7 November 1967
- Convention on Consent to Marriage, Minimum Age for Marriage and Registration of Marriages, 7 November 1962
- Convention for the Suppression of the Traffic in Persons and of the Exploitation of the Prostitution of Others, 2 December 1949 (UNHCR RefWorld 2009)

13 All listed documents, policies, and background papers relevant in the refugee context can be accessed via UNHCR's online platform *RefWorld* (UNHCR 2009d).

14 Due to the great amount of relevant documents on gender topics in the context of refugee assistance, it is feasible that not all of them are briefly described. It was nevertheless crucial to indicate a complete list. Key documents for this study are described hereafter.

Along with the above listed documents, specific policy papers of UNHCR on gender and women's issues are listed below:

- UNHCR Handbook for the Protection of Women and Girls, UNHCR, First edition, January 2008
- Secretary-General's Bulletin: Special Measures for Protection from Sexual Exploitation and Sexual Abuse, ST/SGB/2003/13, 9 October 2003
- Sexual and Gender-Based Violence against Refugees, Returnees and Internally Displaced Persons. Guidelines for Prevention and Response, May 2003
- Guidelines on International Protection No. 1: Gender-Related Persecution Within the Context of Article 1A(2) of the 1951 Convention and/or its 1967 Protocol Relating to the Status of Refugees, HCR/GIP/02/01, 7 May 2002
- UNHCR's Commitments to Refugee Women, 12 December 2001
- UNHCR Policy on Harmful Traditional Practices (Annexes) , 19 December 1997
- UNHCR Policy on Refugee Women, 20 August 1990 (UNHCR RefWorld 2009)

In addition, relevant documents of UNHCR's Executive Committee and Standing Committee are listed below:

- At many occasions, UNHCR's Executive Committee has dealt with issues relating to gender equality and women.
- Report on the High Commissioner's Five Commitments to Refugee Women, EC/55/SC/CRP.17, 13 June 2005
- Refugee Women and Mainstreaming a Gender Equality Perspective, EC/51/SC/CRP.17, 30 May 2001
- Progress Report on Refugee Women, SC/1998/INF.1, 25 May 1998
- Progress Report on Refugee Women and UNHCR's Framework for Implementation of the Beijing Platform for Action, EC/47/SC/CRP.45, 15 August 1997
- Executive Committee Conclusion No. 105 (LVI) - 2006 on Women and Girls at Risk, 6 October 2006 (in French)
- Executive Committee Conclusion No. 60 (XL) - 1989 on Refugee Women, 13 October 1989 (in French)
- Executive Committee Conclusions relating to age, gender and diversity mainstreaming
- Executive Committee Conclusions relating to sexual violence
- Executive Committee Conclusions relating to women (UNHCR RefWorld 2009)

After listing these relevant documents[15], the most important ones for this study are to be briefly explained: UNHCR developed a *Policy on Refugee Women* in 1990, the *Guidelines on the Protection of Refugee Women* in 1991, the *Sexual Violence against Refugees: Guidelines on Prevention and Response* in 1995, and *UNHCR's Commitments to Refugee Women* in 2001. The *Policy on Refugee*

15 UNHCR states clearly which groups of beneficiaries are targeted with policies and guidelines. In regard to specific gender-related activities, UNHCR predominantly points out that they aim at gender and women. Through that, the special emphasis on women is more intense than on men and is clearly stated without equalizing 'gender' with 'women'.

Women of 1990 outlines basic principles on gender mainstreaming and integration efforts as well as organizational goals. It stresses objectives such as providing protection, respecting special needs, identifying suitable and durable solutions, promoting women's participation in operations, and building capacities. While the *Guidelines on the Protection of Refugee Women* emphasize the particular need of protecting refugee women through generated tools, the *Sexual Violence against Refugees: Guidelines on Prevention and Response* concentrates on SGBV. It defines sexual violence with causes and effects. Along with naming legal aspects, it outlines preventive and practical measures to respond to events of sexual violence. It furthermore gives information on female genital mutilation and how staff traumas are to be handled.

UNHCR's Five Commitments to Refugee Women of 2001 go one step further and underline the five specific self-set obligations of UNHCR towards refugee women. Known by the exact same term — "Five Commitments to Refugee Women" — they focus on women's empowerment and apply equally to IDPs. The commitments are to promote women's and girls' membership and participation in decision-making processes, include their needs in registration and documentation, tackle SGBV, facilitate their participation in food distribution, and provide sanitary materials to women and girls of concern.

Those documents build the foundation of UNHCR's commitment to gender-related obstacles. They are also the basis for UNHCR's partners, which are involved in refugee assistance.

After an Inter-Agency Lessons Learned Conference on Prevention and Response to Sexual and Gender-Based Violence in refugee situations took place and produced several recommendations, UNHCR revised the *Guidelines for the Prevention of and Response to Sexual and Gender-based violence against Refugees, Returnees and Internally Displaced Persons* in 2003.[16] It updates the guidelines of 1995, explains types, causes and consequences of SGBV. It conceptualizes guiding principles and gives options on how to prevent and respond to SGBV incidences. Furthermore, the handbook highlights the importance of monitoring and evaluating events of SGBV in order to react to them in an adequate manner.

In 2002, UNHCR produced *Guidelines on Gender–Related Persecution.* They outline the manner of analyzing gender-related persecution in refugee status

16 UNHCR created a Policy on Refugee Women in 1990, the Guidelines on the Protection of Refugee Women in 1991, and UNHCR's Commitments to Refugee Women in 2001. UNHCR generated a paper on Sexual Violence against Refugees: Guidelines on Prevention and Response in 1995.

determination processes while concentrating on particular issues such as Female Genital Mutilation and domestic violence. The *Agenda for Protection* of 2003 embraces an action and activity program which seeks to improve and optimize the protection of refugees and asylum-seekers worldwide. It contains not only a wide scope of recommendations to further operations on protection of refugees and other persons of concern, but also specific recommendations for protection needs of refugee women.

In 2005, UNHCR developed a resource package with three training modules on *Ensuring Gender Sensitivity in the context of Refugee Status Determination and Resettlement*. They contain "readily-usable, user-friendly materials to encourage UNHCR offices, relevant authorities, legal advisory services and NGOs to mainstreaming gender aspects into all training activities related refugee status determination and asylum system development" (UNHCR 2005a: 2).

The latest relevant document was published in 2008. UNHCR engendered the *Handbook for the Protection of Women and Girls*. It reveals up-to-date information on the impact of displacement on women and girls, and states principles and practices for gender equality. After stressing diverse aspects to identify, prevent, and respond to risks and threats that women and girls are confronted with, the handbook exposes protection tools and security solutions to exercise rights and to ensure protection. The handbook furthermore gives an overview of the international and regional legal framework related to women and girls. Besides highlighting human rights, humanitarian and refugee law, it also stresses bi-lateral and multi-lateral conclusions, resolutions and declarations.

Besides the documents produced by UNHCR, two resolutions of UN's Security Council are of significance in the context of gender issues and refugee assistance: *the Resolutions 1325 (2000)* and *1820 (2008)* both *on Women, Peace and Security*. Both resolutions recognize the significant status women obtain within peace and conflict processes. While women used to be seen primarily as victims or might have acted in the background by assisting men at the front, they are nowadays involved in the informal, as well as the formal sector. Thus, the resolutions reveal the important double role women have in peace and conflict: victims and actors. As refugee women flee from conflicts and seek security, they require special security for their protection. They belong to the persons of concern mentioned in the resolutions. The resolutions focus on furthering female participation in the field of peace and conflict. Besides "reaffirming the important role of women in the prevention and resolution of conflicts and in peace-building," they also express "concern that civilians, particularly women and children, account for the vast majority of those adversely affected by armed conflict, including as refugees and internally displaced persons, and increasingly are targeted by combatants and armed elements" (S/RES/1325: 1).

In addition to these specific guidelines and policies on the subject, UNHCR integrates gender, particular gender-related aspects, in handbooks on other topics such as protection, operational management, registration, resettlement, etc.[17] By doing so, the Office ensures the integration of the gender perspective and consideration of the special needs of women and children within all operational sectors. Also, by emphasizing it in handbooks, policies, and guidelines, UNHCR's partners build awareness. They learn to respect and implement gender sensitive activities. Through that, UNHCR ensures to spread knowledge on the topic among staff and eventually also among beneficiaries. These circumstances of stating knowledge in documents, informing partners and therefore supporting transparency on the topic are a best case scenario. Further initiatives need to be respected to actually achieve gender-sensitive refugee assistance.

2.2.3. Gender-sensitive Operations in Refugee Assistance

It has been explained how UNHCR defines gender, which threats against both sexes and in particular against women and girls occur in the refugee context, and what guidelines and policies were produced to tackle these threats. The question that remains is how UNHCR attempts to embark upon the threats. How does UNHCR provide adequate protection and assistance to refugee women to ensure their security? Which methods, procedures, and tools did the agency develop to deal with issues and carry out activities in a gender-sensitive manner? Finally, how does UNHCR define gender-sensitive operations?

In a statement of the Global Consultations on International Protection, it was recognized that "[d]etailed guidelines on protecting refugee women exist, but until they are systematically implemented, refugee women will remain at risk of violence and abuse" (EC/GC/02/8: 2). It is therefore important to notice that the *1990 Policy on Refugee Women* states that

> [i]t is the intention of UNHCR to integrate the resource and needs of refugee women in all aspects of programme planning and implementation. This does not mean that separate women's projects are to be initiated or added on to existing general programme activities (UNHCR 1990: 5).

17 See also: UNHCR 2003b: 14ff; UNHCR 2008d: 24; UNHCR 2001c: 32; UNHCR 2006a: 61ff; UNHCR 2003e: 12f; UNHCR 2007c: 34ff; UNHCR 2004a: 14f, 79ff, 107ff; UNHCR 2004b: 26, 38.

In 1999, the Senior Management Committee of UNHCR approved a strategy that focuses on mainstreaming the gender equality perspective. The strategy's core elements comprise among others the following:

- Adoption of a gender equality policy statement;
- Incorporating a gender perspective in all programming and reporting activities;
- Regular review of progress (EC/49/SC/CRP.22: 2).

Hence, UNHCR targets to mainstream the gender perspective into refugee assistance in a holistic manner rather than through individually framed undertakings (A/AC.96/1035). The refugee definitions are therefore understood and interpreted while diverse gender dimensions are incorporated, in order to ensure the integration of gender-related claims[18] in refugee protection and assistance (HCR/GIP/02/01: 1-2).

Particularly while observing women at risk, the Office differentiates between the spheres of action: prevention and response. Prevention activities are developed and established in order to preclude threats beforehand and ensure safety and security of the whole beneficiary society. Prevention activities encompass a broad field in connection with the identification, assessment, and monitoring of possible and gender-related threats. In addition to gender awareness trainings of staff (EC/51/SC/SRP.17), UNHCR focuses, among others, on developing data by sex and age, conducting monitoring conditions through individuals working in the field, integrating the gender perspective into early warning mechanisms, performing situational analyses and participatory assessments. UNHCR also aims at gender-balanced recruitments, capacity building and awareness of issues, prevention and responses on the local level, and strengthened justice systems in the hosting countries. Moreover, it seeks to involve women with participatory tools through the attainment of which women are to advance in leadership and decision-making positions to ensure the

18 The refugee definition includes gender-related claims in recognition of the refugee status. Alice Edwards highlights the "progress in relation to the recognition of gender-related claims to refugee status over the last decade". She furthermore says that "[c]ase law has recognized a wide range of valid claims, including sexual violence, domestic violence, punishment and discrimination for transgression of social mores, sexual orientation, female genital mutilation, and trafficking [...]" (Edwards 2003: 51, 52). This goes along with the statement of the *Global Consultations on International Protection* in 2002: "The refugee definition, itself, allows for an array of valid gender-based asylum claims, including fear of female genital mutilation, severe forms of domestic violence, and fear of reprisals or retaliation from trafficking rings in the case of a trafficked woman's being returned to her home country. In addition, most countries recognize non-state actors of persecution, including husbands or partners who violate a woman's human rights, where the State is unable or unwilling to protect against persecution" (EC/GC/02/8: 5).

integration of women's voices (A/AC.96/1035). Due to the list of diverse prevention activities, UNHCR intends to strengthen all levels from the ground to decision-making, to impede gender-related threats, to ensure adequate protection, to further women's participation, and to promote women's equal status to men.

Response activities and mechanisms are closely linked to prevention endeavors. A clear line between prevention and response can often not be drawn. While some incidences might have already taken place, which must be responded to, other threats or occurrences have yet to be prevented and overcome. Already during the asylum seeking process of refugees, the connection of prevention and response activities becomes clear. UNHCR reflects on gender-related claims through, for instance, involving female interviewers to interview female asylum seekers. They try to be interviewed separately from men. This is to respond to oppressed stemming from traditional role allocations. It also aims to prevent hectoring or intimidation by male interviewers and to receive uninfluenced information from the interviewee (HCR/GIP/02/01: 8-10). UNHCR's response strategies for women at risk involve close cooperation with governments and partners at all times. It seeks to respond to threats against women at risk as quickly as possible. To do that, UNHCR monitors situations, provides information material, ensures access to justice and further facilities (e.g., education and health services), and provides psycho-social care. Furthermore, resettlement initiatives, voluntary repatriation, and special evacuation schemes belong to particular long-term responses to ensure safety and security (A/AC.96/1035).

Working gender-sensitively implies furthermore the consideration of the Five Commitments to Refugee Women. In planning and implementation procedures of refugee assistance, standards and indicators are to be created in a way that result-based management targets the entire beneficiary populace. That also means to take into account that women require special assistance, e.g., on a very basic level, sanitary material. Among many other activities, UNHCR therefore aims to involve women in camp management committees and distributions of food and non-food items, providing trainings and information material to build awareness on SGBV and other gender-related issues (EC/55/SC/CRP.17: 1-9).

During the Global Consultations on International Protection in 2002 the following additional advice was given to UNHCR, governments, and partners to apply refugee law and procedures in a gender-sensitive manner:

- Refugee women should be given legal advice, access to the refugee status determination process, and information about the process in a manner and language they can understand;
- Women asylum-seekers should be interviewed separately, without the presence of male family members, so that they have an opportunity to present their case, based on the clear understanding that they may have a valid claim in their own right;

- Claimants should be informed of the choice to have interviewers and interpreters of the same sex as themselves. These should be provided automatically in the case of women claimants. Immigration officials and decision-makers should be trained in gender-sensitive interviewing techniques and interpretations of the refugee definition; other relevant officials in contact with refugees should also receive gender-sensitive training;
- States, UNHCR and other actors should include information in country of origin reports on the general situation facing women and, in particular, on gender-related persecution (EC/GC/02/8: 5-6).

Prevention and response activities are therefore integrated in planning and implementation processes of refugee assistance. As explained above, UNHCR promotes integrating the needs of women by means of several approaches and methods. UNHCR understands that

> [w]hile working from a gender perspective is not necessarily equivalent to working on projects for women, this may be required in order to remove barriers to access to and control of assistance experienced by refugee women. However, focusing on refugee women in isolation rarely results in long-term change. Instead, transforming unequal power relations between women and men requires analysing these relations and involving both women and men (EC/49/SC/CRP.22: 1-2).

Hence, pursuing gender-sensitive work within refugee assistance for UNHCR means to involve both sexes and to transform traditional power relations. The above statement already indicates that analysis efforts must be performed in order to understand and renovate power relations. Integrating the gender perspective and eventually operating in a gender-sensitive manner requires satisfactory tools, which suit the humanitarian character of refugee protection and assistance. In 1999, the Executive Committee highlights that "the Country Reporting and Operations Plan (CROP) [contains] programming and reporting mechanisms [that ensure to] mainstream a gender equality process, that Funding Appeals are gender-sensitive, as well as guidelines, checklists and manuals included in the Knowledge and Information Management System" (EC/49/SC/CRP.22: 2). The Executive Committee continues by underlining that

> [e]ven in countries where the challenges are great, women are being encouraged to participate in decision-making and trained to take over the management of activities for themselves. Recognizing that accesses to learning and to financial independence are steps towards empowerment, countries have included income-generation, skills training, literacy, credit schemes and education in their programmes (EC/49/SC/CRP.22: 2).

However, these are actions performed and supported by UNHCR. Which tools does UNHCR apply for gender-sensitive operations?

Tools to ensure gender-sensitive operations target analysis, planning, monitoring, and evaluation efforts. Four tools are to be named: rights-based approach, community-based approach, age, gender, and diversity mainstreaming, and people-oriented planning.

The rights-based approach is a tool applied as a conceptual framework that systematically focuses on respecting and implementing human rights. To grasp the difference between a needs-based and a rights-based approach, UNHCR designed a brief table with key terms clarifying the difference and particularity of the rights-based approach (UNHCR 2008a: 17).

Table 1. Needs-based and rights-based approach.

Needs-based Approach	Rights-based Approach
Deserving	Claim and entitlement
No one has definite obligations	Clear obligations
Receiving – beneficiaries	Active participation – partners
Some are left out	Equal rights for all
Charitable and voluntary	Mandatory, legal obligation and accountability
Addresses symptoms	Addresses causes

According to the table 1, the rights-based approach stresses the fact that human rights are universal and can be claimed. The rights-based approach was introduced in 1997 when the United Nations' Secretary General launched the reform *Renewing the United Nations.* He emphasized that human rights should cut across the four main areas of Peace and Security, Economic and Social Affairs, Development Cooperation, and Humanitarian Affairs. His program thus aims for a system wide collaboration of all UN agencies to respect, promote, and integrate international human rights into policies, activities, and programs (A/51/950; Goodwin-Gill 2006: 4-5).

According to Goonesekere, by applying the rights-based approach in development and humanitarian aid, the aim is to create an "environment in which human rights can be enjoyed […] [and] an environment which can prevent the many conflicts based on poverty, discrimination and exclusion". She notes that

> the advantage of a human rights-based approach to development and governance including the realisation of gender equality, is that it encourages an inherently holistic vision of outcomes. It encourages people-centred and sustainable development approaches to planning and decision making, on the assumption that respect for individual human rights, dignity and gender equality must be the foundation of any civil, political, social and economic agenda (Goonesekere 1998).

UNHCR also expand the boundaries of the rights-based approach as a conceptual framework because it is rooted in "the principles of participation and empowering individuals and communities to promote change and respect for rights." Integrating such factors are "essential aspects of a rights-based approach" (UNCHR 2008b: 16). It conveys to responsibilities and obligations. "[H]uman rights determine the relationship between individuals and groups with valid claims (rights-holders) and State and non-state actors with correlative obligations (duty-bearers)" (UNHCR 2006d: 17). UNHCR and states thus provide rights as 'duty bearers' to beneficiaries as 'rights' holders' which precisely refers to the protection mandate of UNHCR.

The community-based approach and its application is clearly described in UNHCR's manual *A Community-based Approach in UNHCR Operations* (2008b). The manual explains that this approach is a tool that outlines how to perform activities in cooperation with persons of concern and with partners. It is not limited to a specific sector in or stage of operations but can be applied throughout all levels of programs. The approach "recognizes the resilience, capacities, skills and resources of persons of concern, builds on these to deliver protection and solutions, and supports the community's own goals." Moreover, it requires analysis, understanding, respect, and consideration of "political context, the receiving population, gender roles, community dynamics, and protection risks, concerns and priorities" (UNHCR 2008b: 14-15).

Both the community-based approach and the rights-based approach are jointly applied by UNHCR. Both approaches constitute integral components of each other's concepts due to common principles and objectives. The advanced dual approach entails "policies, programmes and activities be based on international legal standards, and that members and leaders of the community consider their roles as both rights-holders and duty-bearers" (UNHCR 2008b: 17). It targets to respect cultures, but also to overcome and transform cultural and traditional practices that creates obstacles to progressing gender equality by revealing that human rights are universal (UNHCR 2008a: 28-29). In practice, UNHCR therefore cooperates with community members, states, and partners to provide rights and empower individuals.

Age, Gender, and Diversity Mainstreaming (AGDM) was adopted in 2004 after UNHCR started to apply the gender perspective in 1999 (UNHCR 2008a: 15). AGDM was established to target progress of gender equality, to promote the respect for human rights, and to ensure the protection of all beneficiaries with no regard to ethic, social, or religious statuses. It is a strategic analysis tool to comprise the differentiated proportions of a refugee populace. Specific data is collected which makes it easier to grasp conditions of and for refugees and to conduct assessments of the implications of risks (UNHCR 2006d: 14). Through this, an adequate protection and assistance strategy can be designed. The analysis becomes an integral part of "protection strategies and programme designs" and implemented in cooperation with "staff members and government and operational partners" (A/AC.96/1024: 16).

By applying AGDM, UNHCR aims to consolidate and institutionalize the process of protecting and assisting women and men, boys and girls through the creation of suitable programming instructions, standards and indicators. It promotes a multi-functional team approach that helps to encompass experience and skills at diverse levels. While using results-based management and participatory assessments, UNHCR focuses on the best results rather than short-term needs by integrating concerns and capacities in an efficient manner. The "persons of concern [are thus put] at the heart of operational planning" (UNHCR 2008a: 34).[19]

People-oriented Planning (POP) was introduced by UNHCR in 1992 with the manual *A Framework for People-oriented Planning in Refugee Situations taking Account of Women, Men and Children*. The method was developed as a follow-up to the *Policy on Refugee Women* from 1990. It aims to provide a "framework for analyzing the socio-cultural and economic factors in a refugee society which can influence the success of planned activities" (UNHCR 1992: 1).

POP is a mechanism that focuses on raising awareness of gender analysis and issues in refugee contexts. The POP framework targets to "conduct population and gender analysis in refugee situations and to facilitate the planning and implementation of programmes using a beneficiary-based approach" (UNHCR 2001: 19). This planning method facilitates to comprehend and examine "needs, talents and resources of every group of refugees, returnees and displaced persons (including women and men) during the various stages of flight and return, in order to help them maximize their potential" (UN 2002: 122). To apply POP, gender and age mainstreaming employs a situation analysis approach that concentrates on particular conditions. The situation analysis approach is conducted with methods of data collection and analysis based on refugee participation. Due to dialogues, a beneficiary-based approach with objectives on rights and needs is ensured. Thus, it "will help highlight the respective roles, responsibilities and needs of refugee men and women" (UNHCR 2003b: 16).

Consequently, based on the above tools, gender-sensitive operations are designed and performed. Operations are assessed, planned, implemented, and evaluated with respect to the targeted refugee population. By means of integrating the needs of both sexes instead of the linear focus on women, it is to assume that UNHCR targets to qualitatively tackle inequality issues through the revision of obsolete images and ideas of gender roles. These role images produce the oppressed status of women. As a result, the consciousness of both sexes is supposed to be enhanced towards equality.

19 See also: UNHCR 2008: 34 ff; UNHCR 2006d: 14ff, 107ff; UNHCR 2008b: 19f.

3. *Development of Development Aid*

3.1. Historical Developments

If refugee assistance is to be linked with development aims, the concept of development needs to be explained. What is development? When did it start and when is it supposed to end? Where does it take place? Who 'does' development? What are the overall goals?

The concept of development aid is a Western one; created, established, and implemented by Westerns actors. "Modernization, Westernization, and especially Industrialization are [...] terms people have used when discussing economic development" (Conteras 1999a: 1). It is generally acknowledged and agreed on among the research community that development aid was initiated in the 1940s. By accepting the 1940s as the starting point, development is understood as a process in which sovereign states, bi-lateral or multilateral organizations support other sovereign states in order for them to achieve economic growth. In particular in the first decades, development aid was applied to assist developing countries in becoming modern industrial societies (Fischer et al. 2007: 17); the keywords thus were modernization and industrialization.

Even before the 1940s, development initiatives took place. In the late 19th and early 20th century, the United States and Britain were involved in providing assistance, only to name two examples. In 1896, the United States provided food assistance to countries in need; "the US Department of Agriculture, sidestepping the Congressional veto on relief actions, began shipping out cereal surpluses through its Foreign Agriculture Service with the avowed intention of developing new markets for US cereals, and presidential prerogative was used to provide relief operations for earthquake victims in Martinique (1902) and Sicily (1908)" (Singer/Wood/Jennings 1987: 17). In 1929, Britain undertook economic reconstruction initiatives. It observed the African colonies "as having potential for agricultural development, East Africa was a major target. Cabinet discussed a development program for Kenya as early as 1923. The Colonial Development Act of 1929 (the first of several) made provisions for the funding of development projects in African colonies, but their usefulness was limited by low funding" (The National Archives 2009).

3.1.1. Early Developments after the Second World War

In spite of early attempts to provide international development aid to the countries rated as underdeveloped, the boom of development aid only started after the Second World War ended in 1945. In July 1944, the Bretton Woods

Conference — officially named the United Nations Monetary and Financial Conference — took place in New Hampshire, USA. With over seven hundred delegates from forty four countries, the purpose of the conference was to identify ways to handle the aftermaths of the Second World War, to aid European recovery, and to create a "framework for a global system financial and monetary management" (Moyo 2009: 10). The most important accomplishments of the twenty two days conference were the establishment of the International Monetary Fund, the International Trade Organization (today's World Trade Organization), and the International Bank for Reconstruction and Development, which is now part of the World Bank. These organizations received economic and financial responsibilities to sustain global markets (Bessis 2003: 635; Kolland 2007: 83-85).

In June 1947, the Marshall Plan was proposed. It was a rescue package of US$ 20 billion provided by the United States of America to support the recovery of war-torn Western Europe. The plan targeted the reconstruction of infrastructure and physical capital to speed up the rebuilding and stabilizing economic systems, to bolster democracies, and to repel communism. The overall aim was to restore a functioning global economy. The massive economic support was to strengthen the bond between western European states and the United States. At the same time, it resulted in a greater dissociation to communist countries. According to Marshall, it aimed at fighting hunger, poverty and chaos (Fischer et al. 2007: 14-17; Friedrich 1991: 31).

In his inauguration speech on the 20th of January in 1949, the re-elected president of the United States, Harry S. Truman, unambiguously stressed issues of economic underdevelopment and its consequences. He suggested that the American way of globalization in cooperation with other nations should be the strategy used to overcome poverty. Among others, he accentuated the following:

> More than half the people of the world are living in conditions approaching misery. Their food is inadequate. They are victims of disease. Their economic life is primitive and stagnant. Their poverty is a handicap and a threat both to them and to more prosperous areas. For the first time in history, humanity possesses the knowledge and skill to relieve the suffering of these people. The United States is pre-eminent among nations in the development of industrial and scientific techniques. The material resources which we can afford to use for assistance of other peoples are limited. But our imponderable resources in technical knowledge are constantly growing and are inexhaustible. I believe that we should make available to peace-loving peoples the benefits of our store of technical knowledge in order to help them realize their aspirations for a better life. And, in cooperation with other nations, we should foster capital investment in areas needing development. Our aim should be to help the free peoples of the world, through their own efforts, to produce more food, more clothing, more materials for housing, and more mechanical power to lighten their burdens. We invite other countries to pool their technological resources in this undertaking. Their contributions will be warmly welcomed. This should be a cooperative enterprise in which all nations work together through the United Nations and its specialized agencies whenever practicable. It must be a worldwide

> effort for the achievement of peace, plenty, and freedom. With the cooperation of business, private capital, agriculture, and labor in this country, this program can greatly increase the industrial activity in other nations and can raise substantially their standards of living (Truman 1949).

"Truman broke the ground" (Easterly 2006: 24). He made clear that the poor countries should imitate systems from the West, particularly from the United States, in order to catch up to and eventually reach modernization. This equals striving for economic growth and industrialization (Fischer et al. 2007: 17).

3.1.2. Changes from the 1950s until the 1990s

After the 1940s, alongside with the Bretton Woods Conference, the Marshall Plan and the Inauguration Speech of Truman, scholars and economists assumed that it was possible to plan development and economic growth (Kolland 2007: 83). After the post-Second World War phase of reconstruction, the regional focus soon moved from Europe towards underdeveloped countries in Asia, South America and Africa. The shining example of Western Europe's quick recovery and economic growth was supposed to be transferred to these distant regions. Development was seen as a universal concept (Blanco 1999:1).

The 1950s and 1960s constitute a time in which Western powers lost distinct power over their colonies due to independence movements. By means of aiding the now-independent yet underdeveloped countries, the former colonial masters attempted to withhold powers. Development assistance was furthermore a tool of the 'capitalism versus communism contest' of the Cold War to maintain geo-political interests (Moyo 2009: 12-14).

Development activities were conducted through a great range of newly established national and international development organizations, some of which were part of the UN system (Easterly 2007: 25). The 1950s and 1960s also comprised the golden era of economic development of "those developing countries that had the most advanced economic and political institutions were the major beneficiaries from the strong growth-impetus imparted by trade with developed countries" (Adelman/Morris 1997).

During these two decades, the aid focus was on economic growth and financial assistance; in the 1950s, programs focused on internal factors and thus the overcoming of interior obstacles.

During the 1950s, it was "widely assumed that poor countries lacked the financial capital to spur development" (Moyo 2009: 13). In order to close the gap, rather than merely taking economic and financial aspects into account, modernization theories were developed. They were mainly created by American economists, political and social scientists; "all adopted a multi-indicator theory of development including transformations of production structures as well as social, cultural, and political modernization" (Adelman 1999: 4). The theories assumed that the national state constitutes a framework for development and growth takes place in stages. Walt Whitman Rostow exemplifies in his book *The Stages of Economic Growth* (1960) how progress is achieved. It states that "countries could emerge out of stagnation into self-sustained growth thanks to an aid-financed increase in investment" (Easterly, Sachs 2006: 98). Parsons explains development and underdevelopment through pattern variables in his work *The Social System* (1951). Based on the model of balance, change and alteration within one sector also generated modification within further sectors. Pattern variables thus define interplay between an individual which makes decisions and the structures which embrace the individual. The pattern variables constitute the point of departure for Hoselitz to describe the development of societies within a continuum in *The Progress of Underdeveloped Areas* (1952) (Kolland 2007: 85-89). Additionally, a widely and well-known strategy is the Big Push. It was born in the 1940s and is based on the idea of quickly ending the poverty tragedy by the "doubling of foreign aid, to about $100 billion a year, then nearly doubling again by 2015." Underdeveloped countries could fill their financial gaps with foreign aid, leave the poverty cycle, and initiate economic growth on self-dependent basis (Easterly/Sachs 2006: 97).

By assuming that economics and growth can be planned, nations were required to have sufficient capital and profound economic analyses to enjoy the result of constant and balanced growth. Development plans were outlined with a focus on the increase of agricultural productivity and employment of and for industrialization (Kolland 2007: 83). The formula 'development = economic growth = industrialization' advanced above assumption and represented the development optimism of the 1950s (Fischer et al. 2007: 18).

In the 1960s, researchers moved from the modernization theories to the dependence theories which now observed external factors as reasons for underdevelopment. Overcoming colonialism and integrating into the world market was considered the way forward. The term dependence explains the unbalanced relations between different economies. If a socio-economic development of a country is depending on external factors, then the dependence theories apply. The asymmetric dependence structure predominantly integrates positive effects for the industrialized part and negative ones for the developing country (Kolland 2007: 92-98).

Thus, already in the 1960s, it was realized "that economic development was not as universal as the founders had supposed. The gap between the rich and the poor in developing countries grew extensively" (Blanco 1999: 1). External factors apart from internal ones, such as national capital, were taken into account. Now, in the period after colonialism, the need for integrating the underdeveloped countries in the global market were the solution to reach growth

(Kolland 2007: 92-98). Infrastructural (re-)construction was understood as the starting point to initiated economic growth. Industrialization was still the main goal of development and infrastructure was supposed to be the foundation to facilitate the process to reach progress. Until the mid-1980s, industrial projects and "large-scale infrastructure and engineers made up a significant proportion of development bank or agency staff" (Barnes 2004: 1).

The 1970s were marked by the realization that economic growth has not been achieved to the planned extent. Poverty grew and several countries were threatened by political and social imbalances. Hence, led by the World Bank, scholars and policy planners switched to strategies which initially targeted meeting basic material and immaterial needs, such as shelter, food, clothing, health care, and education. Human rights and participation in social lives became key terms. The basic needs strategy and anti-poverty theory drew along a transformation from the top-down to the bottom-up approach (Fischer et al. 2007: 38; Moser 1993: 66-70). In addition, in the 1970s the need for the integration of the particular needs of women[20] was raised. "Low-income women were identified as one particular 'target group' to be assisted in escaping absolute deprivation" (Moser 1993: 67).

Hence, the 1970s constitute the decade of fighting against poverty and for basic human needs. Keywords like equality, participation, democracy, cultural difference, natural resources, and liberty entered the dictionary of international development aid. After taking technical expertise and assistance into account, life standards and quality were to be regarded and advanced through international aid (Fischer et al. 2007: 24-27). Along with this, human capital instead of physical capital was supposed to be built and maintained through better access to health facilities, education, and political participation. It was perceived as essential in order to tackle underdevelopment. The proportion of social services grew over 50 per cent. Projects predominantly focused on "agriculture and rural development, social services (including housing, education and health), mass inoculation programmes, adult literacy campaigns, as well as food for the malnourished" (Moyo 2009: 16).

The decade of the 1980s is commonly known as 'the lost age of development' (Fischer et al. 2007: 46; DeLong 2001; Ünay 2006: 2; Carrasco 1999a: Chant/McIlwaine 2009: 42). The economic crises initiated by oil embargos

20 Among others, in her book Women's Role in Economic Development (1970), the economist Boserup stresses factors that were left out up to this point, yet were required to be taken into account in order to reach economic growth (Moser 1993: 67; Marchand/Parpart 1995: 31-33).

began in the previous decade. Prices tripled worldwide and created tremendous obstacles for developing countries, particularly with regard to oil imports. Commercial Banks offered loans, which appeared to be cheap money, yet they had high interest rates. Developing nations were interested in these loans and received them. After the global recession started in the early 1980s, the loans came to a halt. Timely payments could not be made and interest rates grew along with global rates. In the mid-1980s, the World Bank proposed a case-by-case solution with structural adjustment programs in developing countries. Since this solution failed, the Brady Initiative was proposed in 1989. This debt reduction strategy "shifted the focus of the strategy from increased lending to voluntary, market-based debt reduction (reduction of outstanding principal) and debt service reduction (reduction of interest payments) in exchange for continued economic reform by debtor countries" (Carrasco 1999a: 4). After the strategy was combined with economic reforms and capital flows, the crisis was overcome in the early 1990s (DeLong: 2001; Carrasco 1999a: 2-5).

Due to the debt crisis throughout the 1980s, development programs were scaled down. While most economic planning stemmed from governments, their plans were then seen as the "prime obstacle to growth" (Moyo 2009: 20). The developmental optimism of the 1950s turned into development pessimism in the 1970s, but found its climax in the 1980s. In research, neo-liberalism and arising Think Tank institutions are characteristic for the decade (Fischer et al. 2007: 38-39). "The neo-classical economic development theorists emphasize that international trade can provide a substitute for low domestic aggregate demand" (Adelman 1999: 10). While continuously following the basic needs strategy and anti-poverty theory, economists aim to find the path to economic growth through the integration of developing countries into the global trade market (Carrasco 1999a). Bilateral agreements arose in addition to the aid provided by multilateral institutions. Stabilization and structural adjustment programs were theoretically observed as the way forward. Programs therefore focused on stabilizing economies to survive the debt crisis. The stabilization concept aimed at overcoming the imbalances of national fiscal positions and import-export ratios. By the mid-1980s, programs switched their policies to structural adjustment plans. Liberalizing trade and controlling prices were principal aspects of the plans (Carrasco 1999a: 2-7).

The 1990s marked the end of the Cold War between the two blocks. Geo-political interests did not need to be followed through development aid as harshly as during the previous decades. The competition between communism and capitalism appeared to have found an end. Hence, bilateral agreements decreased and multilateral organizations gained dominance within the global net of development aid.

In the 1990s, the focus was on social development as initiated in the 1970s. Through the integration of good governance, the focus becomes clearer. Diverse theories broaden the scope of development aid and are developed to underpin the programmatic switch. The human capital theory and the good governance theory are the two most popular theories of the decade. Several scholars argue for the human capital theory which confirms that human capital and income are prerequisites for reaching institutional development (Svensson 2005: 25; Adelman 1999: 12-13). Especially World Bank researchers are in favor of the good governance theory; "corruption, bad policies, and weak governance will make aid ineffective" (Wolfensohn in Easterly 2003: 25).

In 1992, the UN held the first international *Earth Summit* in Rio de Janeiro, Brazil to find adequate solutions for environmental protection and socio-economic development. Among others, the Rio Declaration on Environment and Development and the Agenda 21 were adopted (A/CONF.151/26). The Agenda 21 was seen as a milestone in the history of development. Its guiding principle was to conduct development in a way that meets the needs of the present as well as future generations. It focused on sustainable development and set its main emphases on poverty, education, health, sanitation, and rural development through a criteria catalogue. The *World Summit on Sustainable Development* held in Johannesburg, South Africa in 2002 (A/CONF.199/20) reaffirmed the importance of the implementation and respect of the wide ranged commitment stated in the Agenda 21.

Three years after the Earth Summit, the UN held the *World Summit for Social Development* in Copenhagen, Denmark. The purpose was to find a new, post-Cold War concept for development assistance. Based on the summit, assistance seemed to create a distance to equalizing development aid and economic growth.

> Under a people-centered framework of social development, the governments urged a political, economic, ethical and spiritual vision for social development that is based on human dignity, human rights, equality, respect, peace, democracy, mutual responsibility and cooperation, and full respect for the various religious and ethical values and cultural backgrounds of people (Carrasco 1999b: 4-5).

Programs increasingly focused on governance aspects by promoting good governance. "Good governance was a euphemism for strong and credible institutions, transparent rule of law and economies free of rampant corruption" (Moyo 2009: 22). It became the key word of the decade along with transparency, accountability, and sustainable development. Another keyword was human capital. Special assistance was provided to promote reforms in the sectors of education and health. Education was seen as a core factor in reaching self-sufficient economic growth (Adelman 1999: 12-13). In addition, market-friendly policies were considered. They comprised development strategies through

> non-inflationary growth, fiscal discipline (i.e., wise government spending), high savings and investment rates, trade and foreign investment liberalization, privatization, and domestic market deregulation (Carrasco 1999b: 1).

Despite the variety of strategies and concepts, the focus on poverty reduction and meeting basic needs remained during the 1990s. Through governance and social service reforms, development projects were to be planned, implemented and evaluated in an open and fair manner. By means of newly established measurements such as the Human Development Index (HDI) by the World Bank, the Human Poverty Index (HPI) and the Gender-related Development Index (GDI) by UNDP, the international community revealed the integration of economic and social development within policies (Fischer et al. 2007: 31-33).

3.1.3. The new Millennium until 2009

With the new millennium, changes took place in international development assistance initiated through a series of various international summits and high-level forums. The starting point of this series was in September 2000. The UN held a summit and presented the Millennium Declaration (A/Res/55/2) including the Millennium Development Goals (MDGs). The declaration commits the UN member states to a global partnership on achieving the goals by 2015. The MDGs comprise a list of eight goals:

> 1. Eradicate Extreme Hunger and Poverty; 2. Achieve Universal Primary Education; 3. Promote Gender Equality and Empower Women; 4. Reduce Child Mortality; 5. Improve Maternal Health; 6. Combat HIV/AIDS, Malaria and other diseases; 7. Ensure Environmental Sustainability; 8. Develop a Global Partnership for Development.

The MDGs reflect the new vision pursued through development assistance now focusing on social development, security, and well-being. The former distinct focus on economics through the equalization of development and economic growth moved to the background. Although economic development remains to be realized, further sectors have become more dominant.

The question of how to finance development was raised in the International Conference on Financing for Development in Monterrey, Mexico in 2002. The *Monterrey Consensus of the International Conference on Financing for Development* (A/CONF.198/11) comprises all outcomes of the conference; a paper that underlines the importance of

> Mobilizing and increasing the effective use of financial resources and achieving the national and international economic conditions needed to fulfil internationally agreed development goals, including those contained in the Millennium Declaration, to eliminate poverty, improve social conditions and raise living standards, and protect our environment, will be our first step to ensuring that the twenty-first century becomes the century of development for all (A/CONF.198/11: 5).

Five years later, in 2008, a follow-up conference took place in Doha, Qatar. The Doha Declaration on *Financing for Development: outcome document of the Follow-up International Conference on Financing for Development to Review the Implementation of the Monterrey Consensus* (A/CONF.212/L.1/Rev.1) re-ensures the importance of mobilizing financial resources for development assistance. It reaffirms the *Monterrey Consensus* and therefore highlights the value of the different aid flows on the national, bilateral and multilateral levels.

In 2003, the first High Level Forum on *Harmonization* was held in Rome, Italy. It called for improved coordination and streamlining of development activities at the national level. It was followed by the second High Level Forum on *Joint Progress Toward Enhanced Aid Effectiveness* in Paris in the beginning of 2005. Its result was the Paris Declaration on Aid Effectiveness, which stressed ownership, harmonization, alignment, results and mutual accountability. It committed countries and organizations to increased and continuous efforts in harmonizing, aligning, and managing aid. The third High Level Forum took place in Accra, Ghana in 2008. The Accra Agenda for Action found its foundation in the Paris Declaration but goes further; it aimed to achieve progress through four factors:

> Predictability – donors will provide 3-5 year forward information on their planned aid to partner countries.
> Country systems – partner country systems will be used to deliver aid as the first option, rather than donor systems.
> Conditionality – donors will switch from reliance on prescriptive conditions about how and when aid money is spent to conditions based on the developing country's own development objectives.
> Untying – donors will relax restrictions that prevent developing countries from buying the goods and services they need from whomever and wherever they can get the best quality at the lowest price (DCD-DAC 2009).

In recent years, new donors entered the network of development assistance. In addition to the private sector, new bilateral relations have developed. China is assuming an increasingly important role in development assistance through bilateral agreements. China assists governments of developing countries, particularly in Africa, "in terms of grants, interest-free loans and concessional loans" which is strongly debated throughout the international community due to rather obvious geo-political interests. It has not occurred with such intensity since the end of the Cold War. China is investing in "resource-rich countries such as Angola, Sudan, Nigeria and Zambia, as well as more politically strategic countries, such as South Africa, Ethiopia and Egypt" (Davies 2008: 3, 1).

3.2. Inclusion of Gender in Development

In the 1970s, gender issues and special needs of the sexes started to be integrated in development assistance. The switch from the focus on economic growth to social development entailed the integration of new factors and aims such as equality, participation, democracy, protection of natural resources, and liberty (Fischer et al. 2007: 24-27).

The first attempts to integrate gender aspects in development assistance were through the approaches of Women in Development (WID), Development Alternatives with Women for a new era (DAWN), and Gender and Development (GAD). The DAWN approach entailed the empowerment concept which has been an integral part of discussions ever since the 1980s. The idea of "women's rights are human rights" manifested during the integration of the GAD approach and remained to be a broadly applied slogan to underline the importance of respecting the needs of both sexes (Maral-Hanak 2007: 180-184).

Gender mainstreaming and diversity management are concepts applied in contemporary development assistance. They pursue the vision of equality between men and women, boys and girls, which is utterly supported by the underlying idea of Human Rights. While diversity management is still less applied in practical development aid, gender mainstreaming is a broadly accepted concept. "It involves the reinvention, restructuring, and rebranding of a key part of feminism in the contemporary era" (Walby 2007). It contains a revised understanding and structure of gendered politics, policy practices and theoretical strategies for development and improvement. Rees defines gender mainstreaming as "the systematic integration of gender equality into all systems and structures, policies, programmes, processes and projects, into ways of seeing and doing, into cultures and their organisations" (Rees 2002: 1).

Returning to a more abstract level of the connection of gender and development assistance, Sen's definition of development as "a process of expanding the real freedoms that people enjoy" is used in my research. His definition requires the necessary step to provide freedom to all persons with no regard to their sex, religion or culture (Sen 1999: 3). His argumentations are thus not only fundamental because they underline the crucial inclusion of political, economic, and social factors in the concept of development. They are furthermore agent-oriented (Sen 1999:19) which brings individual "members of the public and as a participant in economic, social and political actions" to the table. In accordance with the feminist idea of taking both the public and private sphere into account, Sen's understanding of development clearly emphasizes the inseparable relations of the term to the need of integrating gender equality activities. Furthermore, one of his five types of instrumental freedoms is social opportunities (Sen 1999: 10); if social opportunities are to be offered to all persons, the male orientation must be overcome.

Sen raises the issue of inequality several times in his book. He announces that "inequality between women and men afflicts [...] the lives of millions of women, and, in different ways, severely restricts the substantive freedoms that women enjoy" (Sen 1999: 15). Due to the persisting patriarchal societal structures and "boy preference" systems in many developing countries, poverty affects women to a greater degree (Sen 1999: 88-89; McFadden 2000; Tamale 2004: 22; Blanchard 2003: 1298). Avin argues in *Engendering Development* that his "definition of economic development [...] make[s] it obvious that economic development is a multidimensional process that can contribute to the empowerment of women and reduce gender equality" (Avin 2006: 67).

Activities that target to support the process and progress of gender equality are thus crucial in development assistance. A more radical view is the one stated Fréchette: "No development strategy is likely to work unless it involves women as central players" (Fréchette 2001).

Development, growth, and peace consolidation are connected social processes. Development implicates that sustainable growth is advanced through supporting social, ecological, economical, and political stability of a country. This is to be done by operating in a politically consolidating and economically strengthening manner, as well as with commitment to natural resource protection and gender equality advancement. If programs and projects are conducted in a way that excludes women, half of the society becomes excluded. Reaching the targeted freedom of all people would thus be impossible.

Chapter IV Development-oriented Refugee Assistance

In this chapter, the focus is on the historic process towards combining refugee assistance and protection with development initiatives. After examining previous concepts, features for development-oriented refugee assistance are elaborated.

1. Background Information

After the 1967 Protocol was adopted and therewith the refugee definition revised, the geographical scope became broadened to refugee-related issues worldwide. Although UNHCR already operated outside of Europe under the 'good office', its international protection and assistance mandate was manifested and institutionalized.

1.1. Significance of Development-oriented Refugee Assistance

Considering that the majority of refugees remain in the global South, the inclusion of development in refugee assistance may carry the potential to improve conditions. As Bützer puts it, "[i]ronically, most refugees are forced to flee from one developing country to another and seek refuge in countries with similar political economic instabilities" (Bützer 2007: 47). Refugees face long-term encampment with few opportunities. They are captured in protracted situations in their host countries. Refugee hosting regions suffer from refugees' stay with possible tensions caused.

Betts (2009a: 9-12) outlined a list of potential positive benefits for donor nations and refugee hosting countries as well as refugees and local communities when refugee assistance becomes linked to development activities. Northern donor states will profit from limited humanitarian aid, in case additional development aid is integrated in refugee assistance. Due to long-term encampment of refugees, refugee protection and assistance loses its immediate and short-term relief character. Budget lines are extended annually and constitute a 'burden' for donors. "[A] significant proportion of the budget of organizations such as UNHCR now goes towards long-term refugee camp management" (Betts 2009a: 10). Due to the linkage of refugee aid and development, self-sufficiency and self-reliance can be promoted and hence, dependency decreased. Northern states will also benefit from reduced irregular secondary movements towards them. Protracted refugee situations without development integration may cause conflicts within camps and/or with local communities. Regardless, long-term encampment may have negative impacts on refugees due to the lack of opportunities. By means of integrating development initiatives, potential terrorist activities could be eliminated. New or more broadly ranging scopes of activities are developed and offered to refugees who therefore could "reduce the likelihood of radicalisation and recruitment and be part of a preventative approach to terrorism" (Betts 2009a: 10). Moreover, due to adequate protection with livelihood opportunities in the country of asylum, further movements may not be observed as necessary by the refugees.

Southern refugee hosting countries of first asylum will benefit from infrastructural developments. Refugees are predominantly located in rural underdeveloped regions close to borders. By means of integrating development initiatives such as reconstruction or rehabilitation measures, the regions' development will be facilitated. Moreover, at times, neighboring local communities assume that assistance is only received by refugees. When refugee assistance is connected with development, local communities are integrated as beneficiaries. A range of "significant new services in the area of education, health, infrastructure and markets" will be designed and made accessible by refugees and local communities (Betts 2009a: 10). Both, development initiatives in underdeveloped refugee hosting areas of the country of first asylum as well as the new range of services offered to both beneficiary communities, will result in fewer social tensions and insecurity.

Hence, development-oriented refugee assistance can constitute a "win-win" situation for donors, refugee hosts, refugees and local communities (Betts 2009a: 9-13). Before elaborating features to understand what is necessary to achieve this win-win situation, the previous initiatives towards linking refugee aid and development are to be analyzed.

1.2. Changing Political Conditions since the 1970s

According to Macrae, today's view on peace as a vital factor for development has not always existed. Geo-political interests caused by the Cold War shaped the focus and featured the "distinction between relief and development assistance [that] is grounded in politics, rather than in any assessment of the changing needs of particular communities" (Macrae 1999: 5). While the Cold War was still ongoing, the principle of national sovereignty set limitations for intervention or assistance in conflict zones. However, as an aftermath of decolonialization, conflicts occurred almost simultaneously in several countries and caused numerous refugee waves. The number of refugees worldwide arose "from 2.4

million in 1975 to 4.6 million at the end of the decade" and 60 per cent was in Africa (Crisp 2001: 2).

The Cold War superpowers followed their geo-political interests while providing assistance and aid. Receiving access to conflict zones required not only the "consent of governments, including those which were belligerent parties to the war" (Macrae 1999: 6). Moreover, bilateral biases and alliances of Western countries with developing nations formed the nature of politics. The mutual understanding — as an unwritten law — therefore revealed that it was the responsibility of these respective superpowers to prevent expansions of the conflicts. Due to that, "the humanitarian impact of conflict remained [between the coalitions and thus] largely hidden from public view and from public action" (Macrae 1999: 6; cf. Loescher et al. 2008: 35-38).

In the mid-1980s, the intensity of the Cold War slowly alleviated in some developing countries, which "was signaled by a steady political disengagement of the West" (Macrae 1999: 6). The political disengagement of the West referred to an eased comprehension of national sovereignty. Humanitarian situations were discussed more openly and interventions were considered and took place. Relief assistance was therefore also provided in conflict zones. The other side of the coin revealed reduced funding due to violent conditions. War and violence became widely accepted as obstacles to development while peace became the fundamental factor that pushed development forward. When the Cold War ended, the international community recognized this linkage and applied a political formula that supported the transitional process from war to peace.

Macrae portrayed the formula with the below demonstrated illustration. According to her explanation and the figure, development and relief aid are two different, yet interrelated processes. Development reflects on relief and is based on peace (Macrae 1999: 6-9).

Figure 1. The political and aid continua by Macrae.

The political continuum				
War	------------------->	peace accords/ peace-keeping interim administration	----------------------->	peace/election
The aid continuum				
Relief	------------------->	rehabilitation	----------------------->	development

In addition to the changing political structures, the Western world became less open for resettlement initiatives for refugees from the developing world. While resettlement was applied as the main solution during the 1960s, this view altered in the 1970s. By the following decade, asylum policies had been revised and indicated strong restrictions. This complicated resettlement activities for UNHCR and individual asylum applications. The number of asylum-seekers in

Europe nevertheless continued to increase; from the mid-1970s to the end of the 1980s, the number of applications rose more than twentyfold.[21] Since UNHCR could not resettle refugees, yet conflicts subsisted, massive refugee waves developed.[22] Not only Western countries became hesitant towards the refugee influx. Also "many Third World governments that had once welcomed and sheltered refugees, particularly during the era of anti-colonial struggles, were becoming inhospitable and hostile" (Loescher et al. 2008: 35). As a result, refugees were rejected at borders and forcibly repatriated. The decade that characterized the end of the Cold War is thus known as the decade of repatriation; "more than 9 million refugees returned home between 1991 and 1996" (UNHCR 2006b: 130). The manner of these sometimes forcible repatriation activities attracted international attention.[23] In the 1970s and 1980s, "[t]he international community failed to devise comprehensive or long-term political solutions or to provide any alternatives to prolonged camp existence" (Loescher 1994: 363-364). Moreover, appropriate actions and solutions were needed (Loescher et al. 2008: 33-36).

2. *Initiating the Connection of Refugee Assistance and Development Aid*

As shown, factors accumulated that disturbed providing fluent and adequate refugee protection and assistance by the 1980s: conflicts, refugee influx, diminishing funding, restricting asylum policies, involuntary repatriation, and an overall disengagement of the West and the South.

After UNHCR opened its operational scope to the refugee-world outside of Europe and started engage in refugee assistance in Africa, Asia, and South-America. Thus, the assistance and protection scopes had to adjust to new

21 In 1976, 20,000 and by the end of 1980s, 450,000 applications reached Europe annually (Loescher et al. 2008: 34).

22 From about three million refugees in 1997, it increased to more than ten million in 1982 worldwide (Loescher et al. 2008: 35).

23 Chimni states that it was the idea that "all refugees desired to go home" which was guiding (Chimni 1999: 5). Many scholars criticized the involuntary repatriation. Harrell-Bond stated that "what is being promoted as the most desirable solution to refugee crises is a poorly understood social and spatial phenomenon". She later indicated that the "policy to promote repatriation evolved in context of the concerns expressed by the donors over the increasing costs of maintaining refugees, the fear that industrialized countries would be overwhelmed with numbers of asylum seekers, the economic and political pressures which refugees place on host governments, and the interests of the governments of the countries of origin" (Harrell-Bond 1989: 43, 56).

challenges. The former High Commissioner Prince Sadruddin Aga Khan stated in a global meeting in 1966:

> In all these [sub-Saharan refugee-hosting] areas we have been faced with a completely different problem from that which existed in Europe. In Europe, the solution to the refugee problem was essentially through resettlement to countries overseas [...]. In Africa, however, refugees have to be settled locally, this means that, as a result, the relief stage of any operation which my office sets up. It consists of distribution of food, distribution of blankets, medical supplies and the possibility of having the refugees settled on land which is made available by the governments of asylum. This has to be immediately followed with what we call the consolidation of the refugees' integration (Sadruddin Aga Khan 1966a).

The less or least developed countries not only suffered due to internal issues, but also due to incoming refugees. While the Southern states supported local integration initiatives for rural refugees in the 1960s and 1970s, the perspective changed due to "economic adjustment and democratization" (UNHCR 2006b: 130). Since conflicts remained in decolonialized regions, repatriation took place in rather involuntary forms while the Western states were restrictive towards asylum-seekers. "UNHCR and its operational partners found themselves trapped in long-term 'care-and-maintenance' programmes, providing refugees with basic needs such as food, water, shelter, health care and education" (Crisp 2003b). Additionally, the great majority of refugees were imprisoned in "protracted refugee situations (PRSs), being confined to camps, settlements or located in urban areas for over five years and facing severe restrictions on their access to rights because of the absence of opportunities for durable solutions such as repatriation, resettlement, or local integration" (Betts 2009a: 1). Loescher adds, that these situations "have moved beyond the emergency phase [...] but for whom solutions in the foreseeable future do not exist." He notes that the majority of refugees were "left behind [...] to live under terrible conditions warehoused in camps or stuck in shanty towns, exposed to dangers and with restrictions placed upon their rights and freedoms" (Loescher 2009: 3-4).

The search for solutions found its way to the idea of linking refugee assistance with development activities. Yet, it was not only an idea but rather a plan. In the 1967 Report of the United Nations High Commissioner for Refugees, the wish is clearly expressed

> that provision for settlement of refugees be as far as possible included in projects of the United Nations Development Programme (UNDP), invited members of the specialized agencies to take note of the particular needs of refugees in developing countries and invited Governments which contribute to development assistance programmes to take the needs of refugees into account (A/6711: 15).

2.1. Integrated Zonal Development Approach

The idea of linking refugee protection and assistance with development contributions was understood as the way forward. The debate on linking refugee and development aid was initiated in the 1960s. This was the time when numerous changes occurred. UNHCR applied the 'good office' approach to tackle worldwide refugee situations including those beneficiaries, who have not been embraced by the original refugee definition (A/RES/1388). The operational scope of UNHCR had to adapt to the new challenges and receive a global orientation (Loescher et al. 2008: 26). The need for adjustment becomes particularly unambiguous while seeing that "out of 222,558 refugees assisted under UNHCR programmes throughout the world in 1965, 208,000 — 94 per cent — were in Africa" (Loescher 2001: 144). It was a growing number. The international focus of the UN was clearly to shift to development assistance, which was verified by the establishment of UNDP in 1966 (Crisp 2001: 1).

The required global adjustments included overcoming long-term care and maintenance programs in developing countries, and finding actual durable solutions. As said by Crisp, the connection between displacement and development, particularly in developing countries, "became increasingly clear in the late 1960s". It was the time, "when UNHCR and its operational partners began for the first time to launch large-scale refugee relief programmes in Africa and other low-income regions of the world" (Crisp 2001: 1).

The first initiative linking refugee and development aid was named the *integrated zonal development approach*. This approach is at times also referred to as 'integrated rural development' due to its concentration on rural regions. During the 1960s and 1970s, it was implemented by UNHCR, other UN agencies, operational partners and governments. According to the former High Commissioner Prince Sadruddin Aga Khan, it targeted to "strengthen and consolidate the settlement of the refugees and at the same time benefit the local population." While seeking to provide benefits to both groups, the long-term solution remained to be repatriation and "return home one day" (Sadruddin Aga Khan 1969).

The approach integrated the local settlement schemes; this means that settlements were established on, thus far, uncultivated land and refugees received plots for house building activities instead of tents provided by agencies. With this, the operating agencies aimed to "equip the settlement for community centre use" (Sadruddin Aga Khan 1966b). It incorporated infrastructure plans and self-reliance strategies, e.g. education, to facilitate independence. According to the 1969 annual report of UNHCR, "education and remunerated employment would help to prevent refugees from becoming a burden on their country of asylum, while, at the same time benefiting the economic and social development of the country" (A/7211: 81; cf. Loescher 2001: 142-144; Crisp 2001: 1-2; Chambers 1986: 261; Gorman 1986: 283).

The integrated zonal development approach was realized, among others, in Burundi to assist Rwandan refugees in the 1960s. The particular plan was "drawn up by the ILO for Burundi and Kivu Province of the Congo" (A/5511/Rev.1/Add.1: 96). From 1962 to 1965, it was employed in four refugee settlements. According to the 1965 annual report of UNHCR, "the local authorities were very interested in the zonal development plan" (A/5811/Rev.1/Add.1: 85). Hence, not only UNHCR, the League of Red Cross Societies and the ILO but also the Government of Burundi provided assistance to the refugees at different stages. They offered "necessary support for the refugee population, including food distribution, tools and seeds for cultivation". Later, "the drainage of marshland, the reclamation of arable land, the construction of workshops and community centres, road building, improvement of livestock, and other related programmes" were initiated (Goetz 2003: 2; cf. A/6011/Rev.1/ Add.1: 102).

The 1968 Report of the High Commissioner for Refugees draws a rather positive interim conclusion on the implementation and progress of the development approach in Burundi:

> The situation improved considerably in the course of 1966. The refugees became self-supporting and it was possible to discontinue the distribution of food by the World Food Programme. The UNHCR/ILO integration and zonal development project, which has been in operation in the three settlements since 1964, brought about considerable improvements in the infra-structure of the area. By the end of 1966, 500 hectares of marshland had been reclaimed under this project, including 350 hectares actually brought under cultivation during the 1966 dry season; agricultural output had increased considerably; and the buildings planned for the three settlements had been completed. Other items on which work was completed were the water supply conduits, the provision of a ferry service on the river Ruvubu and the installation of workshops (A/6711: 98).

However, despite positive statements of UNHCR and the variety of projects, the program failed to succeed. Schmidt points out that in this particular case, expertise and long-term planning were missing, objectives were insufficiently defined, projects inadequately managed, personnel changed too often due to the different agencies and political insecurity (Schmidt 2003: 9). Goetz also emphasized the lack of planning and added low morale as a reason for failure (Goetz 2003: 2).

In general terms, the 'integrated zonal development approach' remains to be a poorly evaluated and researched approach that is often criticized. Critique of, among others, Jacobsen (2001), Harrell-Bond (1985), Gorman (1987), Loescher (2001), and Crisp (2001) stress that it was an ill-faced or obscure approach that simply failed. Loescher draws attention to a rather pragmatic factor to explain the failure of the integrated zonal development approach:

> this policy never received the full support of the development agencies because of the high capital outlay of some of these schemes, and languished as a result of a lack of adequate funding. Instead of becoming self-sufficient, many refugee camps and their inhabitants continued to rely on international assistance (Loescher 2001: 143).

Nevertheless, what must be kept in mind is that the number of refugees in Africa continued to grow and that UNHCR was forced to come up with adjustment plans. It was the first time that UNHCR, an emergency aid agency, cooperated with development organizations. While the approach was not successfully realized, it was the initial idea of connecting refugee assistance with development initiatives which produced the forthcoming of the linkage.

2.2. Developments in Africa in the 1970s

During the 1970s, programs on the integrated zonal development approach were terminated. Despite the failures, the debate on linking refugee and development assistance was carried on. While the budget of UNHCR decreased by "more than 50 per cent [per refugee] in constant US dollars" during the 1980s (Loescher 2001: 227), UNHCR faced heavily increasing refugee numbers "from 10 million in 1980 to 17 million by the end of the decade" (Loescher et al. 2008: 37). Since both factors influenced each other, the rising asylum restrictions set by Western countries towards Southern refugees added to the difficulties. Through such restrictions, Western countries reacted to the growing number of asylum seekers during the 1970s. Then, resettlement was the most frequently applied durable solution (Loescher et al. 2008: 30).

Since the growing refugee number was foreseeable and the resulting issues obvious, the search for adequate solutions was ongoing and the integration of developmental approaches subsisted. Already in 1986, Chambers highlighted

> that a development approach to refugees is much more acutely needed now. In implementing development programs in refugee-affected areas, the lessons of past failures and successes [of the zonal approach] should improve performance. In addition, the deprivations, needs and capabilities of the weaker hosts as well as those of the refugees deserve to be taken into account. In the next decade, especially in Sub-Saharan Africa, hosts will be more vulnerable. Unless deliberately included in relief programs, services and development, many poorer hosts will be hurt while refugees are helped (Chambers 1986: 261).

Against that backdrop as presented by Chambers, linking refugee relief aid and development assistance was recognized as being of great importance. Gorman furthermore notes hat

> [s]everal factors generated new interest in exploring the connection between refugees and development in Africa. First, the African refugee population exploded in the late 1970s. Second, many of the refugee situations seemed unlikely to be resolved in the immediate future. Consequently, African countries hosting the refugees continue to face a long-term

> refugee-related development burden. Their ability to cope with these burdens is often limited by their already extreme poverty and in many cases by the exacerbating effects of drought (Gorman 1986: 284).

In 1970, the number of refugees in Africa was about one million and growing. The great majority was located in rural regions of host countries (A/8012: 70). According to the 1972 annual report of UNHCR, the local settlement schemes have been used for more than 95 per cent of the beneficiaries in Africa since 1970. UNHCR continued to aid various self-supporting projects. Medical assistance and primary education were integral parts and "vital elements of the rural settlement of refugees". Both was supported if the host country's "facilities were insufficient". The report states several examples of development-oriented assistance particularly in the agricultural and infrastructural sectors. Also, "in some cases the local population also benefited from these facilities [which] has had a beneficial effect on refugee integration" (A/8712: 61, 45, 46). This reveals that not all projects targeted the refugee and national populaces as beneficiaries; it was rather a positive side effect if nationals also took advantages of projects.

In the following years, UNHCR in cooperation with various partners continued to focus on the local settlement scheme in its assistance programs in Africa to support refugees "to become self-sufficient [...], either in organized settlements or in the villages where they have mingled with the local population." Programs remained to be dependent on "available resources, including land, communal services and expertise" (A/9012). In connection to the schemes, UNHCR supported infrastructural activities (A/10012).

In the mid-1970s, broad repatriation activities were carried out more intensively while new refugee influxes were observed. The local settlement schemes in rural regions continued to be the main focus of assistance programs in Africa. Some projects had local integration activities (A/31/12).

In 1978, refugee influxes reached a number of 1.5 million refugees with an additional 1.8 million IDPs in Africa. The majority of displaced persons were located in rural local settlements due to their "agricultural background" (A/33/12: 84, 81). However, by the end of the decade, "the local settlement approach became unsustainable as the number of refugees in Africa continued to climb and refugee populations became increasingly dependent on international assistance to meet their basic needs" (Loescher et al. 2008: 39).

The importance of linking refugee and development assistance nonetheless remained to be stressed. In the 1979 annual report of UNHCR, the establishment of a fund for durable solutions was reasoned as below:

> The Deputy High Commissioner emphasized that the proposed fund would be intended for the resolution of refugee problems all over the world, would be used to pursue all possible durable solutions and would provide assistance to developing countries in their efforts to aid refugees. It would serve a catalytic purpose, linking projects for refugees with national economic and social development programmes, and would enhance the High

> Commissioner's and the international community's capacity to react more effectively and more speedily (A/34/12/Add.1: 137).

At the Pan-African Conference on the Situation of Refugees in Africa held in Arusha, Tanzania in 1979 (Eriksson et al. 1981; A/35/12: 12; A/36/12: 70; A/36/12/Add.1: 26; A/34/12/Add.1: 10), "African states acknowledged their responsibilities as host countries of first asylum and local settlement, reasserting their commitment to the 1969 OAU Refugee Convention" (Betts 2004: 6). Yet, issues were also raised. Besides addressing general asylum questions (Goodwin-Gil 1986: 193), the problem of self-settled refugees was addressed. They were widespread on the African continent and "estimated to be 40 per cent of the total" (Schmidt 2003: 2; cf. Freund/Kalumba 1986: 299; A/34/12: 63). Funds were insufficient to handle the refugee influx and to offer adequate assistance. The creation of a fund for finding durable solutions was thus "supported" by the participants. In this context, the issue of burden-sharing was addressed because "the refugee burden borne by poor countries [...] could ill afford" to provide assistance (A/34/12: 24). The "disproportionate burden" (Betts 2004: 6) needed to be tackled due to poor conditions in most refugee hosting countries and increasing asylum restrictions in Western nations. One of the recommendations therefore revealed "getting refugees out of charity situations into a position of integrated development and self-reliance" (Betts 2004: 6). It was also recommended that assistance to self-settled refugees would be integrated in "the context of national, subregional and regional development plans, that the approach should be one of integrated development and that the aim should be refugee self-reliance and that the aim should be refugee self-reliance" (Freund/Kalumba 1986: 299).

Based on these recommendations, a new approach was required to be developed to assist the constant refugee influxes, share burdens, and incorporate development aspects. On the 25th of November 1980, the General Assembly — strongly influenced by the new, decolonized African member states — reacted with Resolution 35/42 calling for an International Conference on Assistance to Refugees in Africa in the following year (A/35/42; Loescher et al. 2008: 39-40).

2.3. Refugee Aid and Development

2.3.1. ICARA I and II

The first International Conference on Assistance to Refugees in Africa (hereafter: ICARA I) took place in Geneva on the 9th and 10th of April in 1981 and was prepared by UNHCR and the OAU (A/36/12: 81, 368). The second

International Conference on Assistance to Refugees in Africa[24] (hereafter: ICARA II) was held in Geneva from July 9 to July 11, 1984.

ICARA I intended "(1) to focus world attention on Africa's refugee problem; (2) to mobilize additional resources for the problem; and, (3) to assist host countries through the application of these addition resources" (Loescher et al. 2008: 40). Hence, during ICARA I, burden-sharing and responsibility-taking was strongly emphasized. The impacts of hosting refugees should not only be handled by the countries of first asylum; the international community was requested to take responsibility and share the burden with the African nations.

The General Assembly adopted Resolution 37/197 after ICARA I. The resolution underlines that refugee assistance provided in African countries is required "to strengthen their social and economic infrastructure so as to enable them to cope with the burden of dealing with large numbers of refugees and returnees" (A/RES/37/197). It also highlights unambiguously that

> the economic and social burden imposed on African countries of asylum by the growing influx of refugees and its consequences for their development and of the heavy sacrifices made by them, despite their limited recourses, to alleviate the plight of those refugees (A/RES/37/197).

The idea behind burden-sharing was first and foremost rooted in financial support between Northern and Southern nations. Out of 128 projects discussed during ICARA I (A/39/12: 6), UNHCR handed selected ones "to the donor community in order to solicit burden sharing" (Betts 2009a: 7). All projects applied development aid in the context of their refugee protection and assistance agenda. The participating governments of ICARA I targeted to involve development activities to refugee aid "in order to support refugee protection and refugees' access to durable solutions" (Betts 2009a: 7). Hence, self-sufficiency and local integration were assumed to reach specific outcomes. Through ICARA

24 While ICARA concentrates on Africa, two further international conferences focusing on revised refugee protection and assistance concerning Central America and Asia took place during the 1980s: the International Conference on Indo-Chinese Refugees Indo in Geneva in June 1989, and the International Conference on Central American Refugees (CIREFCA) in Guatemala City in May 1989. While the conference on Indo-Chinese refugees has been broadly neglected by the research community, it is often its outcome that is treated; as an outcome of this conference the Indo-Chinese Comprehensive Plan of Action (CPA) was adopted in Geneva in 1989 (A/44/523). According to Betts, "CIREFCA and the CPA focused on resolving very specific mass influx or protracted refugee situations, partly on the basis of northern state interests, rather than on developing general principles of sustainable responsibility-sharing" (Betts 2005a: 4). See also: Betts 2006b, Betts 2006a: 15-16, Loescher /Betts/Milner 2008: 41-46, Betts 2009a: 7, Martin et al. 2005: 237-239; Fielden 2008: 13-14, A/44/12, A/44/12/Add.1, A/45/12, A/46/12, A/47/12, A/50/12.

I, the need for finding solutions was converted into a framework, the so-called *Refugee Aid and Development* framework.

Debates on long-lasting refugee presences in certain African regions and adequate assistance were continued in the succeeding conference ICARA II in 1984. It targeted to establish adequate solutions to solve issues of refugees in Africa, as the title of the event reveals: *A Time for Solutions*. In spite of the acknowledged necessity to continue emergency aid where needed, "the vital importance of the complementarity between refugee aid and development aid" was stressed in the concluding statement by the president of the conference. He accentuated that the integration of refugee assistance into development aid is essential "to ensure lasting solutions" (A/39/402: 59). Based on specifically developed country reports, assessments were conducted on assistance needs of refugees and hosts "to better cope with the refugee burden" (Loescher et al. 2008: 41). International burden-sharing — in addition to co-operations with potential development agencies — hence remained to be a great concern.

The Declaration and Plan of Action adopted at the end of ICARA II declares that the participating governments and thus

> [t]he Conference recognizes that the condition of refugees is a global responsibility of the international community and emphasizes the need for equitable burden-sharing by all its members, taking into consideration particularly the case of the least developed countries (A/39/402/Annex I: A1).

Both documents revealed that both dimensions of adequate assistance and durable solutions were respected and discussed. The approach to solutions showed that voluntary repatriation "has been [and still is] recognized as the best means of promoting permanent and durable solutions" (A/39/402/Annex I: G8). Since the principle of non-refoulement shall be respected, involuntary return was not supposed to be promoted. In impossible repatriation cases, host countries were considered to create adequate conditions for temporary settlement or local integration. The second dimension — protection and assistance in host countries — was targeted to be promoted especially through self-sufficiency, capacity-building, participation and infrastructural activities. These activities were expected to "take into account the needs of the local people as well" (A/39/402/Annex I: G8, Annex II). Projects and programs were assumed to be planned and implemented in partnerships between UNHCR and development agencies such as the UNDP, the World Bank, and further development-oriented agencies and organizations. The need for cooperation was also expressed by the General Assembly in its Resolution 40/118 (A/RES/40/118: 8).

In brief, ICARA I and II focused on involving development initiatives to refugee contexts to provide assistance and share burdens. As Betts states, "the ICARA process focused on using development assistance as a means to enhance refugee protection in Africa, particularly through promoting self-sufficiency and local integration" (Betts 2005a: 10).

While some scholars note that ICARA I was less recognized internationally (Betts 2009a: 7), others stress that ICARA II received less attention by the international community (Loescher et al. 2008: 41). Despite opposing perspectives on international interests, ICARA I and II and hence the refugee aid and development framework were internationally considered as failures. Scholars agree that the core reason[25] for their failures was the polarization between the North and the South about burden-sharing. Views on how burdens were supposed to be shared differed tremendously. African countries aimed to receive additional resources to assist refugees in connection with developmental progress. Donors targeted to find durable solutions to overcome refugee issues. They became increasingly reluctant due to the "very limited commitment to durable solutions", while the "very limited 'additionality' […] disappointed African states" (Betts 2009a: 7; cf. Loescher et al. 2008: 41; Crisp 2003).

Regardless of opposing views or failing conferences, the succeeding strategy to the integrated zonal development approach was established. While the integrated zonal development approach was last mentioned in the 1970 annual report of UNHCR (A/8012/Add.1: 34), it was not until the early 1980s that the succeeding strategy was developed. *Refugee Aid and Development* was the new and widely applied approach.

2.3.2. Key Attributes of the Refugee Aid and Development

By analyzing and explaining the contents and targets of ICARA I and II, some features of the refugee aid and development approach have already been stated. What the approach is about in detail is shown hereafter.

First and foremost, refugee aid and development do not constitute one particular strategy but rather a framework, which encompasses aspects that should be taken into account while elaborating strategies (Chamber 1986: 144). As revealed above, refugee aid and development aims to integrate development activities in refugee assistance to prevent and overcome long-term care and maintenance programs in refugee camps, to share the burden among the international community, and to involve the national populace as an additional

25 In addition to the dispersing perspectives on burden-sharing, the extensive famine in the Horn of Africa in the mid-1980s required immediate emergency response rather than development inclusion which was counterproductive to initial plans (Crisp 2003).

group of beneficiaries next to the refugee population. The framework is furthermore exercised "in order to avoid the dependency syndrome [of refugees], to reduce the resentment of local citizens towards refugees and, whenever possible, to remedy environmental damage and to compensate for some of the burden imposed by the presence of refugees" (A/42/12: 3).

According to a UNHCR Evaluation Report, refugee aid and development is a type of refugee assistance that

- is development-oriented from the outset;
- enables refugees to self-sufficiency; move towards self-reliance and helps least developed host countries to cope with the burden that refugees place on their social and economic structures;
- provides benefits to both refugees and to the local population in the areas where they have settled; and,
- is consistent with the national development plan of the host country (UNHCR 1994: 5)

The applied central durable solutions — in the context of refugee aid and development — are voluntary repatriation and local integration.[26] (A/39/402/Annex I: G8) Under the methodological umbrellas of local integration, UNHCR in cooperation with developmental agencies integrates a wide range of activities to promote the interaction of refugees with national communities. Local integration is based on "interrelated dimensions". According to Crisp, it is a legal, economic, and social process. Rights need to be granted to refugees by host states. Economically, "refugees [...] improve their potential to establish sustainable livelihoods". Through the "growing degree of self-reliance" the beneficiaries are successively "less reliant on state aid or humanitarian assistance". As a social — or rather socio-cultural — process, refugees are supported to coexist with and are integrated in communities of the host countries. The socio-cultural process, however, does not require an assimilation of refugees to the host culture (Crisp 2004: 1-2).

Local integration programs therefore support self-reliance of refugees. Self-reliance strategies constitute an integral part of local integration. They aim to create a foundation on which refugees establish sustainable livelihoods, are less

26 Particularly in the initial period, resettlement was less exercised as a solution in the context of refugee aid and development, due to political developments towards heavy asylum restrictions. While the durable solutions of the 1951 Convention are not proposed in a hierarchical order, voluntary return receives a "growing precedence over resettlement and local integration" by the international community (Crisp 2004: 4). An Executive Committee conclusion from 1983 states that despite the non-hierarchical intention of all durable solutions that "in creating conditions favourable to and promoting voluntary repatriation, which whenever appropriate and feasible is the most desirable solution for refugee problems" (quoted in Crisp 2004: 5).

dependent on aid and learn to self-support and to sustain themselves (Crisp 2004: 1-2). Self-reliance activities are predominantly addressed and applied in connection with local rural settlements schemes (A/40/12: 6-7). In practice, local integration and self-reliance activities in rural areas are often applied together in local settlement schemes. Hence, they are understood to be an integral part of local integration. Yet, Crisp raises a crucial aspect.

> The relationship between the concept of local integration and that of local settlement is a somewhat ambiguous one, complicated by the tendency of some commentators to use them interchangeably" (Crisp 2004: 3).

The local settlement arrangements are "best defined as a strategy for dealing with mass refugee movements" (Crisp 2004: 2). Refugees receive land for housing and agriculture. They are encouraged to "participate on an equal footing in its social and economic life and contribute to [...] development" in the hosting region" (A/39/402/Annex II: B3). Although settlement schemes vary and face numerous obstacles (E/1998/7: 44), in principle they hold the opportunity for self-sufficiency for refugees (Fielden 2008: 5). Whereas definite and distinct advantages exist for refugees, local settlement arrangements also contain benefits for the hosting country. Settlements are predominantly located in remote regions; aid agencies support infrastructural activities to rehabilitate the region that creates a great gain for the host society. To sustain undertakings, the Programme of Action of ICARA II stresses that "settlement programmes should be development-oriented and, wherever possible, be linked to existing or planned economic and social development schemes for the area or region" (A/39/402/Annex II: B3).

Local integration incorporates various activities of diverse sectors to enhance the livelihood of refugees and local communities. In addition to environmental and infrastructural reconstruction and rehabilitation endeavors, among others, rural income-generating activities, primary education provision, and social counseling regarding training and employment are performed (A/44/12; A/41/12; E/1998/7). According to Harrell-Bond, refugees are integrated when they

- are not in physical danger (and do not live under the threat of refoulement);
- are not confined to camps or settlements, and have the right of return to their home country;
- are able to sustain livelihoods, through access to land or employment, and can support themselves and their families;
- have access to education or vocational training, health facilities, and housing;
- are socially networked into the host community, so that intermarriage is common, ceremonies like weddings and funerals are attended by everyone, and there is little distinction between refugees' and hosts' standard of living (Harrell-Bond 2002: 18).

Integrating development components in refugee assistance by means of refugee aid and development is hence understood while considering environmental, economic, and social elements and taking the '3Rs' into account that refer to relief, rehabilitation, and resettlement (Betts 2005a: 23; Betts 2004: 2). This is because refugee aid and development seeks "to strengthen the absorptive capacities of host countries and to enhance the refugees' contribution to their host States", as stated by the former UN High Commissioner for Refugees Jean-Pierre Hocké (A/43/12/Add.1/Annex I: 32).

The debate on refugee aid and development eventually subsided. At times inadequate planning and implementation are raised as the main obstacle to success; though, the primary difficulty is found to be "the fact that UNHCR is not a development agency" (UNHCR 1994). While referring to Loescher, Betts notes that the framework already died in the mid-1980s due to "the [ICARA II] conference failure" (Betts 2004: 12).[27] This failure, more distinctively explained above, is based on the North-South-Polarization. Despite these perspectives, in a resolution of December 1987, the General Assembly was "[r]eiterating once again the vital importance of the complementarity between refugee aid and development assistance." Immediately before underlining the complementarity, the General Assembly was

> [e]mphasizing the collective responsibility of sharing the urgent and overwhelming burden of the problem of African refugees through effective mobilization of additional resources to meet the urgent and long-term needs of the refugees and to strengthen the capacity of countries of asylum to provide adequately for the refugees while they remain in those countries, as well as to assist the countries of origin in rehabilitating voluntary returnees (A/RES/42/107).

27 While Betts and Loescher are most certainly able to prove their perspective, the timeline might be too sharp. Since both the International Conference on Indo-Chinese Refugees Indo of June 1989 and the International Conference on Central American Refugees (CIREFCA) of May 1989 took refugees and returnees into account, the end of the period may be needed to be extended until the 1980s. Betts notes that CIREFCA understands "refugees and returnees […] [as] the principal beneficiaries" (Betts 2006: 12). Moreover, through the annual reports of UNHCR the change can be traced. The 1992 report strictly refers to 'refugee aid and development' as one of the durable solutions and only mentions 'returnee aid and development' within the body of the text (A/47/12: 61 ff, 62). The following report, however, calls 'refugee/returnee aid and development' one of the durable solutions (A/48/12: 63-66). Hence, while the end of the refugee focus and the beginning of the returnee concentration was introduced, programs continued until completion. The view of the end of the framework at the end of the 1980s is in line with the analysis of Macrae (Macrae 1999: 15).

2.4. Returnee Aid and Development and Quick Impact Projects

The succeeding model to refugee aid and development was returnee aid and development.[28] During the 1990s, UNHCR pursued repatriation as "most desirable durable solution"[29] which is why it was declared the "decade of repatriation" (UNHCR 2006b: 130). Owing to the shifting focus from refugees to returnees and from host countries to countries of origin, the new developmental objective in the country of origin becomes obvious. Livelihood matters after return became a greater concern of UNHCR's "interest and involvement [that] was very much focused on the reintegration of returnees in countries of origin – rather than self-reliance amongst refugees in countries of asylum" (Crisp 2003). The idea behind the change was "the underlying assumption that refugees cannot be successfully repatriated if the receiving society does not sustain a certain level of development" (Chimni 1999:1).

According to a UNHCR evaluation report, returnee aid and development "appears to satisfactorily resolve these issues" of the preceding refugee aid and development approach. While repatriation — as the most desired durable solution — is applied, donors are satisfied and "aid [...] brings direct benefits to their citizens and society" (UNHCR 1994: 21).

Returnee aid and development has the following assumptions and principles:

- Returning refugees can only be properly reintegrated if longer-term programmes for political, economic and social reconstruction and reconciliation are established;
- Post-repatriation assistance should be development-oriented from the outset, and bridge the traditional gap between immediate relief and the longer term rehabilitation, reconstruction and development process;
- Reintegration assistance should be provided to entire communities, benefiting not only returnees, but also other needy groups such as demobilized soldiers and internally displace persons, as well as the resident population;

28 The overall agreement in refugee research tends to collate refugee aid and development and returnee aid and development (Loescher/Milner/Betts 2008: 40, 48-50, 116; Betts 2004: 12). However, a clear distinction between the end of one model and the beginning of the other one is hardly viable. As stated by UNHCR, both models were applied simultaneously for certain duration. The concentration on returnees simply strengthened in the 1990s (UNHCR 1994).

29 According to UNHCR's State of the World's Refugee Report 2006, voluntary repatriation may not be the "most desirable durable solution" especially due to "pressure from host countries." International examples of pressure "raised fresh questions about the degree of voluntariness and the role of compulsion in 'imposed return'. Moreover, arguably premature repatriations [...] have renewed debate on sustainable reintegration and its relationship to post-conflict reconstruction" (UNHCR 2006b: 130).

- Assistance programmes established for returnee-affected communities should be consistent with and incorporated into national reconstruction and development efforts;
- Many agencies work at different stages along the relief to development continuum, and their contribution to reintegration programmes must be properly clarified, integrated and coordinated (UNHCR 1994: 26).

Returnee aid and development was realized through small-scale and short-term projects. They may appear to be an old model because short-term projects were also applied before the returnee aid and development model received serious consideration.

> The post-repatriation assistance provided by UNHCR until the early 1990s normally took the form of short-term relief such as food assistance for a period of up to one year, as well as shelter materials, seeds, tools, cash grants and other agricultural inputs, directed primarily towards individual refugees. In addition, a number of UNHCR repatriation programmes provided some community-based assistance for returnee populated areas, usually in the form of infrastructural repairs (UNHCR 1994: 23).

In the context of returnee aid and development, projects were especially developed and adapted to meet immediate regional needs in the home country. The majority of the projects were connected to the repatriation programs. They were led by the idea that they "would be followed up with long-term development assistance supplied by international development agencies" (Loescher et al. 2008: 49). UNHCR called these particular types of small endeavors Quick Impact Projects (QIPs) (Betts 2004: 12).

UNHCR defines QIPs as "small, rapidly implemented projects intended to help create conditions for durable solutions through rapid interventions. They can, for example, provide for small-scale initial rehabilitation and enable communities to take advantage of development opportunities" (UNHCR 2005c: Glossary 9).

The QIPs were originally developed to support first aid programs of natural disasters. Macrae explains that the "continuum concept"[30] designed was anchored in

30 The continuum concept aims to support transitional progress. It was initially mentioned in the beginning of this chapter. A figure developed by Macrae was displayed (see Macrae 1999: 6-9). Mehreteab explains that "[t]he difficulties of achieving a transition from relief to rehabilitation, and from rehabilitation to sustainable development, and of planning and implementing the appropriate support measures have resulted in what is called "the gap", meaning more or less long interruptions between the two categories of support programs. In order to prevent the gap, emergency relief has to give way to rehabilitation support without delay, by a smooth and timely hand over from one agency to the following, establishing what is called a "continuum" of measures" (Mehreteab 2000: 78).

> the idea that well-planned relief could be used to reduce the vulnerability of communities to future hazards, for example, by using emergency food-for-work schemes to invest in key infrastructure. Similarly, well planned development assistance needed to take account of the hazards faced by populations, particularly the poor. In addition to strengthening infrastructure, reducing the financial vulnerability of communities and developing networks for the collection of early warning information could all help to prepare and protect communities better against known hazards, so helping to prevent them from becoming disastrous (Macrae 1999: 11).

In the context of UNHCR's work, QIPs targeted "to support the immediate developmental needs of returnee integration" and "to facilitate sustainable returns" and thus obtained the character of "emergency development projects" (Betts 2009a: 85, 129; Chimni 1999: 15). UNHCR pursued to achieve peace-building elements of reconstruction and reconciliation through QIPs (Macrae 1999:12). While holding on to the continuum concept, UNHCR aimed to address "humanitarian needs and concerns in a community context" (A/50/12: 78).

The operational sectors of returnee aid and development and the QIPs were regional, area-based and wide-ranged. The approach was based on the 3Rs. Access to education, social services and livelihood opportunities as well as (re-) construction of infrastructure constituted some of the sectors that were included in QIPs (Betts 2009a: 88, 129). For instance, the 120 QIPs in Somalia focused on "water, health, agriculture, livestock and infrastructural development" (A/48/12: 98). The overall aim of the efforts was to "promote self-sufficiency of returnees and their communities" (A/50/413: 8).

In planning and implementation processes, UNHCR operated in partnership with UN agencies such as UNDP, development-oriented NGOs, and other development organizations (Betts 2009a: 129; Chimni 1999: 15; Macrae 1999: 13; A/42/12; UNHCR 1994). Betts highlights that "it was only because of UNDP's involvement with the 'refugee issue' that the states in the region were able to effectively link development and refugee protection" (Betts 2006a: 13). In spite of Betts' observation, the partnership between UNHCR and UNDP continued to be difficult which was already traceable during earlier co-operations in the context of refugee aid and development (UNHCR 1994: 38). While UNHCR expected development agencies and in particular UNDP to engage in follow-up and long-term programs in returnee-affected areas, the transitional process was too slow (Loescher et al. 2008: 49). The handover-culture did not present the anticipated success, which is why UNHCR increasingly cooperated with other development agencies besides UNDP (Macrae 1999:13).

Despite complicated partnerships, the continuum concept and the QIPs revealed further difficulties. The continuum concept may envisage the logically identifiable linear transitional process 'conflict - relief - rehabilitation - sustainable development'. In reality, however, sequences take place simultaneously; "repatriation and reintegration may start before the war is over, but rehabilitation may continue for some time" (Mehreteab 2000: 80) Mehreteab furthermore emphasizes that a comprehensive strategy is needed in order to avoid failures. "The continuum argument of a linear transition from relief to development has proven ineffective as a model for dealing with complex crises and may actually have exacerbated those crises" (Mehreteab 2000: 80; cf. 78-80). The concept not only failed due to its idea of linearity, the distinct distribution of responsibilities among involved agencies was also missing.

The QIPs facilitated to reach certain intended outcomes, yet they remained to be small-scale and short-term projects. As Chimni notes, issues of "recurrent costs and sustainability" continued to exist and caused greater problems (Chimni 1999: 15). In addition to researchers, program staff also believed that "[q]uick impact projects are not sustainable and not development" (Helton 2002: 83). Regarding the criticism on lacking sustainability, Weiss Fagen explains that "[a]ll development processes demand continual balancing and bridge building between achieving short-term results and preparing for long-term goals" (Weiss Fagen 2003: 203). While both arguments seem viable, the sustainability question can only be answered after specific projects terminated.

3. Recent Progress under the Umbrella of TDA

Even at the beginning of the new millennium, the majority of refugees were hosted in least developed or developing countries (between 1997 and 2001, about 66 per cent). Refugees lived predominantly in camp or settlement arrangements in remote rural regions of the hosting country of first asylum. These regions were often underdeveloped, unstable, and insecure border regions close to the refugees' countries of origin. Development aid rarely reached these regions. In long-term cases, protracted refugee situations emerged which not only resulted in lengthy care and maintenance programs, but also had negative impacts on refugees and hosting countries. While camp structures kept beneficiaries dependent on aid, settlement structures often promoted self-reliance and capacity building programs to refugees. When local society did not benefit from those programs, it could provoke jealousy (Betts 2009a: 10).

The main issue remained the gap between emergency relief and development aid. As discussed earlier, the new millennium brought several improvements of UNHCR. UNHCR and the World Bank started to cooperate and link development and refugee aid (Macrae 1999: 4). In 2001, the EC initiated its program on Linking Relief, Rehabilitation and Development to "fill the gap between relief and development aid [...] arguing that better relief aid contributes to development and that better development reduces the need for relief aid"

(Bundegaard 2004: 14; EU 2007). The EC also introduced and incorporated a budget line for targeted development assistance in 2003.

> In the follow-up to the budget line B7-667, the Commission intends to propose setting up and implementing from 2004 onwards a multi-annual programme designed both to provide a specific, additional response to the needs encountered by third countries of origin and transit in their efforts to manage more effectively all aspects of migration flows, including those related to international protection (EC 2000).

Due to criticism on UNHCR's refugee protection, the *Global Consultation on International Protection* was launched in late 2000 (EC/GC/01/7). The *Agenda of Protection* of 2002 was the outcome and presented a Plan of Action with the following six goals:

> 1. Strengthening implementation of the 1951 Convention and 1967 Protocol; 2. Protecting refugees within broader migration movements; 3. Sharing burdens and responsibilities more equitably and building capacities to receive and protect refugees; 4. Addressing security-related concerns more effectively; 5. Redoubling the search for durable solutions; 6. Meeting the protection needs of refugee women and refugee children (UNHCR 2003c: 29).

In particular the third goal incorporated the idea of pursuing the linkage of refugee assistance and development further. In the same year of UNHCR's *Agenda for Protection*, Harrell-Bond concluded a paper by stressing that "[t]he development plans of governments must include refugees if they are going to meet the challenges of these additional populations" (Harrell-Bond 2002: 22). UNHCR embraced a similar yet broader idea in its *Agenda for Protection.* In the fifth objective of the third goal, UNHCR accentuated that "[r]efugee issues [must become] anchored within national, regional and multilateral development agendas". The Office also targeted the "[a]chievement of self-reliance for refugees" and the "[r]ehabilitation of refugee-impacted areas in former host countries" (UNHCR 2003c: 60-61, 80-81). Both objectives were stressed in the fifth goal.

In 2003, the *Convention Plus* was initiated. It is a forum that is directly based on the 1951 Convention and the 1967 Protocol. According to the former High Commissioner Ruud Lubbers, the Convention Plus sought to develop "special agreements or multilateral arrangements to ensure improved burden sharing, with countries in the North and South working together to find durable solutions for refugees." Lubbers furthermore emphasized that these arrangements were to be "aimed at better targeting development assistance" (UNHCR 2003c: 6). Thus, as one aspect of Convention Plus, the Targeted Development Assistance (TDA) was initiated.

"Targeted Development Assistance (TDA) refers to the way in which donor states can provide overseas development aid to host countries of first asylum as a means to enhance refugees' access to protection and durable solutions" (Betts 2009a: 1). The discussions about TDA intended to build revised standards on the linkage between development aid and refugee assistance while continuously concentrating on durable solutions. According to Betts, "TDA has the potential to benefit both Northern and Southern states because of its ability to address the most serious negative consequences of protracted refugee situations" (Betts 2009a: 1; cf. Betts 2009b: 147f).

In 2005, UNHCR joined the United Nations Development Group (UNDG) (Betts 2009a: 16). While UNHCR was a humanitarian agency, its membership with UNDG could be observed as an indicator or catalytic factor for the intensified aim to connect refugee protection with development activities. This argument was strengthened through the *Guidance Note on Durable Solutions for Displaced Person* by UNDG in 2004. It highlights that there is a lack of achieving durable solutions. The Guidance Note also explains that "[t]he integration of displaced persons and preventing forced displacement from occurring are development challenges. When pursuing durable solutions, displaced persons should be treated equal to other nationals, while taking into account the increased vulnerability and specific protection concerns that they may face" (UNDG 2004).

In 2006, the attention of the international community towards this linkage increased. The General Assembly held a *High Level Dialogue on International Migration and Development* (cf. UNHCR 2006g). It acknowledged the scope of persons moving across borders of their countries of origin. The dialogue targeted the "global implications of international migration and the mutually beneficial interaction between migration and development" (GFMD 2007). It also focused on "identify[ing] ways and means to maximize the developmental benefits of international migration and to reduce its negative impacts" (A/61/515: 6). As a result, in the General Assembly Resolution 61/208, member states acknowledge

> the important nexus between international migration and development and the need to deal with the challenges and opportunities that migration presents to countries of origin, transit and destination, and recognizing that migration brings benefits as well as challenges to the global community (A/RES/61/208).

The resolution's highlights are the call for contributions and the inclusion of "[i]nternational migration and development" into the following session (A/RES/61/208).

Based on the High Level Dialogue, numerous UN member states revealed their interest in pursuing dialogues and actions with regards to the nexus of migration and development. The Secretary General proposed the idea of launching a global forum to find a foundation for discussions (A/61/515: 20). Belgium initiated the first *Global Forum on Migration and Development* (GFMD). It took place in Brussels in 2007 (GFMD 2007; UN 2009).

GFMD became the global platform where various actors such as civil society actors, national governments and international organizations discussed related issues. It was "a voluntary, informal and government-led process to advance understanding and cooperation on the mutually reinforcing relationship between migration and development and to foster practical and action-oriented outcomes" (A/C.2/64/2: 4). Representatives from 156 nations attended the first GMFD in 2007 (Ban 2008: 1). It resulted in six key conclusions. They embrace, among others, the establishment of a new approach to migration in connection with development, the need to share responsibilities between developed and developing countries, and the establishment of national-based focal points (A/C.2/62/2: 4).

The follow-up GFMD had the title of *Protecting and empowering migrants for development.* It was held in Manila, Philippines in 2008. "More than 1,100 delegates representing 163 Member States of and Observers to the United Nations and 33 international organizations [...] [and] [s]ome 220 participants, representing a broad range of civil society organizations from the different regions of the world, attended [...]" (A/C.2/64/2: 1). The forum focused on "rights and security" to shed light on additional issues and on the "economic implications of migration for development" (A/C.2/64/2: 7). Proposed outcomes were multifaceted and wide-ranging. Among others, it was proposed to develop best practices, to perform capacity-building, to establish a standard lexicon or dictionary on terms relating to migration processes, to conduct monitoring and evaluation activities, and to assess pilot schemes, and to set up methods of data collection and analysis of trafficking.

The third GFMD took place in Athens, Greece in 2009. The title of the third forum — *Integrating Migration policies into development strategies for the benefit of all* — reveals its aim for strategies that comprise positive implications for all involved beneficiaries (GFMD 2009).

In addition to the GFMD, the European Union and the United Nations launched a joint enterprise tackling issues on the connection of migration and development. The so-called *EC-UN Joint Migration & Development Initiative* is organized by UNDP and EC along with UNHCR, UNFPA, ILO, and IOM. During the three-year project, a budget of 15 million Euros was planned to "support civil society organizations and local authorities seeking to contribute to linking migration and development" (UNDP 2010).

The aims of this Joint Initiative were to establish networks of actors engaged in the field, to identify best practices and promote information sharing, and to enhance policy-making. Sixteen countries were identified in which projects are currently implemented. The EC-UN Joint Migration & Development Initiative also opened an online platform (www.migration4development.org/), which "brings individuals and groups from around the world together to exchange information and ideas on migration and development, develop skills and provide each other with mutual support" (UNDP 2010).

All of the abovementioned initiatives and objectives aim to close the gap between humanitarianism and developmentalism, emergency relief and sustainable development, refugee assistance and development (Betts 2009b: 148; EC/GC/01/7).[31] Fundamental preconditions are the political will for commitment and to share responsibilities. During his term as the High Commissioner, Lubbers strove towards building a bridge between relief and development. In his first year, he called "burden sharing [...] the key to finding solutions for refugees. It is about achieving a productive symbiosis between host countries and cash-donor countries" (Lubbers 2001a). Lubbers also urged donors to allocate "development assistance funding for the inter-related issues of refugees, internally displaced people and affected local populations" (Lubbers 2001b).

In May 2003, UNHCR published the *Framework for Durable Solutions for Refugees and Persons of Concern.* While repatriation, resettlement, and local integration remained to be the durable solutions, they were developed further. The document underlines and explains three frameworks which are interrelated and developed under the umbrella of TDA: Development Assistance for Refugees, Development through Local Integration, and the 4Rs (UNHCR 2003d). The overall objective is to better target development assistance.

3.1. Development Assistance for Refugees

Lubbers' call for further development aid goes along with the concept of Development Assistance for Refugees (DAR). The concept seeks to overcome the issue of excluding refugees and neglecting refugee-affected areas from poverty reduction plans and development agendas.

In its *Framework for Durable Solutions*, UNHCR defines DAR as

> additional development assistance for: improved burden-sharing for countries hosting large numbers of refugees; promoting better quality of life and self-reliance for refugees pending different durable solutions; and, a better quality of life for host communities (UNHCR 2003d: 8).

By means of DAR, UNHCR attempts to mobilize donors to provide further funding and hence to close the gap between relief and development, as well as to prevent and overcome protracted refugee situations that keep refugees in dependent on aid. For reasons of the availability of additional funding, UNHCR

31 The aim to close the gap was pursued at earlier stages (Betts 2004, 2005; Crisp 2003, 2001; Fielden 2008).

pursues to share burdens and responsibilities between the funding North and the refugee-hosting South (UNHCR 2005c: vii; UNHCR 2003d: 8).

DAR constitutes a concept that prepares refugees for any of the three durable solutions, repatriation, local integration and resettlement. While observing refugee situations in a strongly simplified timeline of 'refuge — arrival in country of asylum — residence — solution', DAR was and is applied after the arrival and during the stay in the host country. It thus represents an integral part of the framework (UNHCR 2005c: One-4).

DAR is directly dependent on multi-level co-operations. These "broad-based partnerships between governments, humanitarian and multi-and bilateral development agencies [...] may vary from country to country". The "commitment of the relevant host government and the related central and local authorities", however, remains essential due to the aim of the development of regions of the host country (UNHCR 2003d: 10).

Based on co-operations and commitment, DAR pursues the following objectives:

> Simultaneous improvement of lives and livelihoods (refugees and hosts); Focus on medium and long-term development of refugee hosting areas benefiting both host communities and refugees; Focus on gender/age equality, dignity and improving the quality of life; Enhancement of productive capacities resulting in self-reliance of refugees; Empowers refugees to make their own choices for durable solutions; Broad-based partnership/cooperation with all stakeholders; Burden-sharing with host community and country; Promotion of peaceful co-existence (UNHCR 2005c: One – 4).

UNHCR expects refugees to benefit, among others, from educational facilities, income generating opportunities, and strengthened community arrangements and capacities. Host countries are presumed to benefit from poverty reduction in the respective regions, increasing parity of refugees and hosts, and better infrastructure and services (UNHCR 2005c: One – 4).

DAR is planned and realized in an area and community-based manner. That means methods and strategies are precisely adjusted to needs and interests. As a process, DAR is launched to prepare refugees for the durable solution (predominantly repatriation), however can be initiated at different phases (UNHCR 2005c: One – 5).

The implementation of the concept is led by the refugee-hosting country. While UNHCR continues to provide protection, it merely obtains a supporting role. It facilitates finding partners, providing protection, and offers capacity and expertise (UNHCR 2003d: 12-14). Thereby, the host country ensures to pursue its intentions and interests; hence, national ownership and sustainability become promoted (UNHCR 2005c: One – 5). The critique that funds are only used for refugees and locals are left out is less common.

Thus, DAR is a concept integrated in a wider framework. It is the means to reach the solution. Through empowerment of both refugees and members of the society of the host country, the concept intends to build capacity and promote self-sufficiency (A/58/12: 4). Then, they may not be perceived as such burdens to the host country anymore.

As highlighted in the Framework for Durable Solutions, UNHCR finds

> The tendency to think of refugees as a burden […] understandable. […] [However, they] bring human and material assets and resources […]. When given the opportunity refugees become progressively less reliant on State aid or humanitarian assistance, attaining a growing degree of self-reliance and becoming able to pursue sustainable livelihoods, equally contributing to the economic development of the host country (UNHCR 2003b: 9).

In addition to the focus on self-reliance, beneficiaries may also benefit from newly-acquired skills after their repatriation to their country of origin. As examples proved, "refugees have contributed to the local economy, retained the rights to free movement and to earn a livelihood on land provided by the state, and yet have returned home once conditions have allowed" (Betts 2005a: 9).

While the idea of DAR might appear to be the way forward and examples[32] show its feasibility, the political will of the involved parties is the core prerequisite (UNHCR 2003d: 10). It is a particular prerequisite to mobilize additional funds.

> Southern states have generally been unwilling to consider either local integration or self-reliance unless it is accompanied by significant additional development assistance. Meanwhile, Northern states have been unwilling to provide the levels of additional development funding that might entice Southern states to reconsider this position (Loescher et al. 2008: 116).

3.2. Development through Local Integration

As a second framework captured under TDA,[33] *Development through Local Integration* (DLI) is to name. Local integration has been a fundamental element of the refugee assistance and development in the past. Due to success indications, it was further developed to DLI. The strategy focuses on those

32 The implementation of DAR in Uganda is internationally referred to as a best practice example (Loescher et al. 2008: 116; Betts 2009a: 8; Betts 2009b: 168; De Vriese 2006; EC/54/SC/CRP.5). However, the concepts applied in Uganda benefited from a development orientation in the past. SRS is to be noted (Betts 2005a: 13).

33 While the *Framework for Durable Solutions for Refugees and Persons of Concern* captures the three concepts, the 2002 report of UNHCR integrates DLI in the DAR model: "DAR incorporates two concepts. Firstly, the "4Rs" […] [a]nd secondly, the "DLI" strategy" (A/58/12: 4). Since this may be misleading, I follow the explanations of the framework.

refugees "who are unable to repatriate and are willing to integrate locally" (UNHCR 2003d: 24).

UNHCR defines DLI in its *Framework for Durable Solutions* as

> a programming approach applied in protracted refugee situations where the state opts to provide opportunities for the gradual integration of refugees. It is based on the understanding that those refugees who are unable to repatriate and are willing to integrate locally will find a solution to their plight in their country of asylum. DLI is achieved through additional development assistance (UNHCR 2003d: 24).

DAR is understood to be used as an assistance method while refugees are in the country of asylum and DLI is considered a durable solution (UNHCR 2005c: Figure 1.1). However, DLI constitutes more than a durable solution due to its implementation framework. It is temporary assistance, as well as a durable solution. While means of self-sufficiency can be applied to support refugees during their stay, DLI eventually strives for identifying a permanent solution for the refugees in the hosting country. "Over time the process should [hence] lead to permanent residence rights and perhaps ultimately the acquisition of citizenship in the country of asylum" (UNHCR 2003d: 25; cf. Dryden-Peterson/Hovil 2003: 3).

The process of local integration is based on legal, economic, social and cultural components. Refugees must be granted rights by the country of asylum to "become less d pendent on humanitarian aid and increasingly become self-reliant contributors to the local economy" (EC/55/SC/CRP.15: 21). The social and cultural component is rooted in the relations of the refugee and the host population. When living side-by-side UNHCR expects discrimination and exploitation to be prevented (UNHCR 2003d: 24).

Several features are similar to the DAR concept. DLI is also based on broad-based partnerships and the political will of the relevant parties. The host governments take the lead in programming and UNHCR receives a supporting or substantial role. DLI is also a community and area-based approach that needs to be adjusted to respective situations and conditions (UNHCR 2003d: 24-25). The prerequisite of success is anchored in the integration of refugee issues in national development plans and poverty reduction agendas (cf. EC/54/SC/CRP.5: 26). Its realization is strongly connected to the political will of a host country.

Along with DAR, DLI targets social and economic improvements. According to UNHCR, it

> aimed at creating an improved and conducive situation for refugees to become productive members of their host communities as well as improvements in the quality of life of host communities and refugees, realising poverty reduction, promoting peace, security and stability in the region (UNHCR 2003d: 25).

DLI integrates self-sufficiency and reliance strategies to prevent and overcome enduring dependencies on humanitarian aid and to reach the integration in the local host society. The host societies' "own potential for development can thus be significantly enhanced" (A/58/12: 4). Hence, not only refugees but also the host population can benefit from the additional developmental support. However, applying self-reliance strategies does not present durable solutions. As stated by the Executive Committee of UNHCR, "its gradual achievement provides an indication of the extent to which economic and social integration has been attained and forms part of a continuum progressively opening up opportunities for a sustainable solution, whether within the host country or elsewhere" (EC/55/SC/CRP.15: 14).

Local integration and the revised DLI concept in particular, appear to have proven its feasibility.[34] As DAR, DLI comprises a complex process that primarily depends on the willingness of involved parties. While the host countries must provide legal and institutional foundations, donors are required to financially support capacities. In addition, DLI shall help to perceive refugees as "agents for development" instead of a "burden" (EC/57/SC/CRP.19: 11).

Nevertheless, local integration also reveals obstacles. In their article on Local integration as a durable solution, Dryden-Peterson and Hovil point out that integration and assimilation are often inadequately perceived.

> According to the 1951 [...] Convention, restoring refugees to dignity and ensuring the provision of human rights includes an approach that would lead to their integration in the host society. Indeed the Convention uses the word, 'assimilation,' which implies the disappearance of differences between refugees and their hosts as well as permanence within the host society (Dryden-Peterson/Hovil 2003: 2-3).

Crisp furthermore notes that "local integration is not a solution that is available or feasible for a large proportion of Africa's refugees - either because their country of asylum does not want them to settle permanently, or because the refugees themselves would prefer to return to their homeland" (Crisp 2003: 25).

3.3. The 4Rs

The third concept captured under TDA is the *4Rs*. The 4Rs are repatriation, reintegration, rehabilitation and reconstruction. While former frameworks such as refugee aid and development or returnee aid and development concentrated on the 3Rs (relief, rehabilitation and resettlement), TDA was extended to include

34 DLI was applied in Zambia which is often referred to as good practice. "The Zambia Initiative, launched in 2001, is one example of a successful effort to enhance the self-reliance of refugees and provide support to the communities that host them" (UNHCR 2006c: 24).

repatriation and reintegration. The 4Rs now constitute a logical development-oriented concept that targets the improvement of "the sustainability of repatriation by fostering the capacity and institutional partnerships necessary to ensure the smooth transition from emergency relief to long-term development planning within countries of origin" (Betts 2009b: 148).

In its *Framework for Durable Solutions*, UNHCR defines the 4Rs as

> a programme concept referring to the related repatriation, reintegration, rehabilitation and reconstruction processes of a given operation and which aims to ensure linkages between all four processes so as to promote durable solutions for refugees, ensure poverty reduction and help create good local governance. The concept provides an overarching framework for institutional collaboration in the implementation of reintegration operations allowing maximum flexibility for field operations to pursue country specific approaches (UNHCR 2003d: 18).

The 4Rs approach is particularly important because of the unsystematic reintegration assistance. Needs and interests of returnees have often not or only insufficiently been integrated in national development agendas. Capacities and needs were hence rather excluded in development programs, "transition and recovery plans by governments concerned, the donor community and even the UN system" (UNHCR 2003d: 20). Moreover, "[b]y engaging in post-conflict reconstruction, UNHCR's approach potentially facilitates repatriation by tackling 'root causes'" (Betts 2004: 15).

The greatest distinction between DAR and DLI to the 4Rs is the region of concern. While DAR and DLI focus on refugees and development assistance in the country of asylum, the 4Rs embrace returnees and the country of origin (Betts 2004: 3). Hence, while the first two concepts are based on the refugee aid and development models, the 4Rs is rooted in returnee aid and development.

Similarities to DAR and DLI embrace the usage of self-reliance strategies. In case they were applied, returnees have been "capacitated" and are assumed to be able to facilitate the "reintegration process" (UNHCR 2005c: Figure 1.1). It is an integrated approach that is incorporated in national development agendas and poverty reduction plans. The approach is also led by the government "showing strong commitment and assuming ownership of the entire process" while UNHCR and further partners are supportively involved (UNHCR 2003d: 19-20).

Additional funds and strong partnerships are required to reach success. Partnerships are depending on the political will, which has been underlined as an essential prerequisite for success and a potential obstacle in the context of DAR and DLI. As Betts stresses with reference to Duffield, the idea of the 4Rs is "uncontroversial". He furthermore explains that "[s]tates of origin rarely pose objections to return, asylum states are keen to emphasize it as the 'ideal durable solution', and donor states often have specific economic and political interests in reconstruction" (Betts 2004: 3).

Hence, the 4Rs can be a durable solution that takes place after voluntary repatriation (UNHCR 2005c: Figure 1.1). It targets to "facilitate sustainable return and reintegration" (UNHCR 2005c: One – 3).

The concept of the 4Rs also aims to close the gap between relief and development. However, in comparison to DAR and DLI, the context is broader. The 4Rs concept intends to connect "humanitarian, transition and development approaches throughout the different stages of a reintegration process in a structured manner similar to the institutionalised DDR (Disarmament, Demobilisation and Reintegration) process" (UNHCR 2003d: 19).

According to the *Framework for Durable Solutions*, the "guiding principles and critical success factors" for the 4Rs are:

> a) ownership by host governments of the processes which the 4Rs concept embodies; b) integrated planning process at the country level by the UN Country Team; c) strong institutional cooperation and commitment to support punctually and at decisive moments, the needs and efforts of country teams to bridge essential gaps in transition strategies; and, d) participation of the plethora of actors who form part of the development community - UN agencies bilateral and multilateral institutions (UNHCR 2003d: 18).

Pilot projects have been launched in the beginning of the new millennium.[35] The 4Rs concept is seen to be promising. Through the applied bottom-up approach, respective governments lead the programs and ensure the respect and integration of interests and needs (UNHCR 2003d: 19, 22). Moreover, by focusing on returnees and assistance in the country of origin, all involved parties appear to be satisfied: states of origin, former refugee hosting countries, and donor states (Betts 2004: 3). However, post-conflict regions in transition often face instable structures with "limited capacities". Hence, involved agencies need to consider whether they need to support the governments in "building of national capacities through a decentralized approach" as UNHCR did in Afghanistan (A/AC.96/1024: 60).

3.4. Operational Comments

Since the activities running under the umbrella of TDA are ongoing, evaluations are not yet completed. Interim comments on successful progress of implementations can be made nonetheless. The majority of the progress information available is based on the two pilot programs. "The Zambia Initiative

35 According to UNHCR's 2002 report, pilot projects were initiated in Sierra Leone and in Eritrea (A/58/12: 44). The 4Rs approach was applied in five countries (A/AC.96/1024: 60).

and the Uganda Self-Reliance Strategy are two pilot projects aimed at gearing development assistance towards attaining durable solutions for refugees while addressing state interests" (UNHCR 2006b: 6).

Betts notes that TDA can produce 'win-win' situations for both sides the Northern donor side and the Southern refugee-affected side (Betts 2009a). UNHCR's Forum 2005 report reveals that successful results are already visible. The report underlines that the Zambia Initiative shows "firm progress towards achieving economic and social empowerment of refugees, and poverty reduction and enhanced food security among the local host communities. After only one year of implementation, the refugee hosting areas reached the target for food self-reliance for the first time in 36 years" (De Vriese 2006: 14).

Despite, Southern states remain to be reluctant to applying TDA methods, "suspicious that it may be a form of burden-shifting". Moreover, "inter-agency collaboration has proved equally elusive" (Betts 2005a: 21, 22). Hence, achievements in countries of origin were of more success than those in host countries. It is stressed, that "a framework for institutional collaboration [must be built] to ensure the smooth implementation of such approaches [of DAR, DLI, and the 4Rs]" (EC/57/SC/CRP.19: 5). UNHCR indicates another crucial aspect while going beyond potential failure areas. In spite of the value of development initiatives for durable solutions, "[i]n the case of protracted refugee situations, the focus […] should not overlook the importance of addressing and resolving political problems" (UNHCR 2006b: 179).

4. *Guiding Principles for Development-oriented Refugee Assistance*

The different frameworks encompassing the linkage of refugee assistance and development applied in the past four decades, revealed great international interest. The majority of refugees was and still is located in the global South, in regions which suffer from poverty and underdevelopment. The industrialized and wealthier North was required to assist. Not only scholars and policy-makers recognized and accepted this fact but also UNHCR, operational agencies, and donors. Hence, the linkage has mainly been pursued for burden and responsibility-sharing reasons. In addition to supporting the less developed South with refugee issues, handling and overcoming protracted refugee situations was and is the objective. As Betts said clearly,

> [i]f the impasse in north-south cooperation could be overcome in such a way as to channel resources into improving protection standards, it may be possible to resolve the underlying causes of encampment and the corresponding rights violations that commonly result from mass influx and protracted refugee situations in the south (Betts 2005a: 6).

The above analyzed frameworks embrace assistance to refugees and returnees, asylum countries and countries of origin, bridging the gap between relief and development through the application of a variety of methods. They have been realized globally, yet, widely acknowledged success is still missing. While main rationales for framework failures have been analyzed in academic and operational spheres, studies fail to present a catalogue of very fundamental features necessary for success. In other and rather simplified words, we know which frameworks failed and why but we do not know what the very basic prerequisites for success are. What is needed?

Hereafter, the reasons for failure of previous frameworks and a recapitulation of goals are summarized. These contents form the foundation to then elaborate a catalogue of fundamental features.

4.1. In Retrospect: Review of Failures of Past Initiatives

The idea of linking refugee protection and assistance with development aid was born in the 1960s. The *'integrated zonal development approach'* was the first initiative developed from the 'good office' and implemented in the 1960s and 1970s. The approach remains poorly evaluated and researched, and it is often criticized. Critical voices accentuate that it failed due to lacking support of respective development agencies, excessive costs, and deficient funding among other reasons. As a result, beneficiaries remained dependent on aid.

The *Refugee Aid and Development* framework forms the second initiative developed in ICARA I and was implemented during the 1980s and 1990s. While external factors impeded the successful implementation, positions between Northern donor nations and Southern nations polarized regarding the burden-sharing. In connection to that, the framework failed due to the missing will and commitment on both sides, hardening of attitudes and a lack of funds.

Returnee Aid and Development is the pendant to refugee aid and development predominantly implemented during the 1990s. Reasons for failure are attached to unsatisfying cooperation of involved agencies and unexpected long transitional processes. In addition, the QIP concept was criticized to be ineffective due to its small-scale and short-term nature, which opposes the development ascribed feature of sustainability.

Targeted Development Assistance (TDA) is the revised framework and now focuses on three areas of commitment. It takes refugees and returnees into account. Since pilot project are ongoing, final criticism cannot yet be accentuated. Yet, current findings expose that the reluctance of Southern states and lacking collaborations of agencies could lead to failures.

In addition to that, the previous frameworks to TDA lacked an adequate integration of the gender perspective. As earlier explained, my research assumes that the transitional sphere refugee women undergo can be used to further promote gender equality. In connection with development, it is even believed that gender equality strengthens the developmental progress. However, I believe it is only feasible and achievable, if projects are gender-sensitive. In brief, it is assumed that gender-sensitive operations are crucial to benefitting from the opportunities for transformation in the refugee context and to achieve progress in the development assistance context.

The previous frameworks seem to have insufficiently integrated the gender perspective. Also, gender roles — which produce images and ideas and therewith oppress women — appear to have been unsatisfactorily tackled. One needs to keep in mind that the gender aspect only reached international agendas in the 1970s, which explains why it has been insufficiently integrated.[36] The first regional *Forum on* a *Gender Approach in the work with Refugee, Returnee and Displaced Women in Central America* (FOREFEM) was held in 1992 in the context of CIREFCA returnee aid and development implementation. It targeted "to generate awareness of the legal impediments faced by uprooted women and to promote initiatives for self-help" (Betts 2006b: 11, 14; cf. A/47/12: 79; EC/47/SC/CRP.45; A/AC.96/814). However, there is evidence to suggest a clear link between failures of the frameworks and the inadequately or missing integration of the gender perspective. A recent TDA approach "integrates a gender perspective in all programmes" (De Vriese 2006: 2). Since TDA activities are on-going, success can only be evaluated after project completion.

36 Gender issues were only incorporated in development and relief agendas during the 1970s. For example, the UN's Declaration on the Elimination of Discrimination against Women (A/RES/2263) was adopted in 1967, and UNIFEM, the women's fund of the UN, was not established until 1976, nine years after the adoption of the Declaration. Ever since, the importance and scope of the integration of gender continuously changed and increased up to today. UNHCR's commitment to women's and gender issues started in the 1980s. Its Executive Committee adopted the first conclusion on Refugee Women and International Protection in 1985. In 1987, the Executive Committee stressed that there is a distinct need for "taking into account all relevant factors such as age, sex, personality, family, religion, social and cultural background" which infers to Age, Gender, and Diversity Management (UNHCR 1987). UNHCR elaborated a Policy on Refugee Women in 1990, a strategy on Refugee Women and Mainstreaming a Gender Equality Perspective and a paper on UNHCR's Commitments to Refugee Women both in 2001.

4.2. Regarding the Pillars

In the refugee context, several factors come together. Refugee waves cannot be foreseen, and occur spontaneously for multiple reasons. Refugees often flee from violent conflicts or natural disasters to seek security and to ensure their survival. Refugees have often suffered from conflict and experienced forms of violence; they were tortured, trafficked, and lost relatives. Once they reached a hosting country that allowed them to stay until durable solutions are found, they finished a long journey. Immediate assistance through emergency humanitarian aid is necessary. With aid support, they are in a new country, surrounded by unknown natural and social conditions. Many refugee women live without their husbands or greater family circles that used to head households and make decisions; now, they head households, make their own decisions, and take care of their subsistence. Thus, with their arrival, transitional conditions are caused. These conditions could be used to release the strict hierarchical social structures, the structures that define gender role allocations. Refugee assistance could initiate adequate activities to support a psychological transformation towards women's empowerment and gender equality. The transitional process they undergo while being in a hosting country of first asylum and after their repatriation can consequently be utilized to further gender equality through gender-sensitive operations. According to Ferris, "[g]ender roles often change in refugee camps" (Ferris 2007: 586). UNHCR also noted that

> forced displacement and return can be an empowering experience for women. Their experience and the changes in gender roles brought about by displacement may enable them actively to challenge traditional gender roles [...]. Where they have organized, they may be able to claim their right to participate in different aspects of camp or urban life and in return communities (UNHCR 2008a: 40).

While refugee protection and assistance are often only understood as emergency aid, the international community accepted the importance of connecting it with development initiative and hence bridging relief and development for long-term achievements. In the development context, an inextricable linkage between peace, developmental progress and full female inclusion has been detected. Development of a country can successfully progress if it has a stable political system. Caprioli proved that "gender inequality increases the likelihood that a state will experience internal conflict" (Caprioli 2003: 14). Hence, if gender equality is pursued or already exists, than this indicates the stability and the developmental readiness of a country. Development also means to reach independence, enjoying economic opportunities and social security. In view of that, a prior aspect that is this strongly connected with development is freedom. Sen explains development as "a process of expanding the real freedoms that people enjoy" (Sen 1999: 3). Understanding development through freedom furthermore indicates that an entire society shall benefit from development and freedom; an entire society consists of both men and women. If refugee assistance attempts to link protection activities with development initiatives, sustainability is immediately pursued. Sustainable development is understood as a type of development assistance that strives for identifying durable solutions which improves the lives of current and future generations by intentionally respecting and protecting the limited natural resources available, supporting economic growth, recognizing cultural factors, and promoting balanced social relations between the genders to reach freedom. In order to achieve that, efforts must be efficient in terms of performing activities in a resource-friendly mode to reach maximum results. If refugee assistance intends to be development-oriented, actions are required to respect all resources, including natural and human resources. This is only possible if — again — the entire society is involved, which reveals the importance of integrating women.

Consequently, gender equality and sensitivity obtains a dual imperative in the context of development-oriented refugee assistance: adequate refugee assistance would support the psychological transitional process in promoting equality aims for reaching gender parity, and development aid can only be performed sustainably and efficiently if both men and women are involved in the process.

4.3. Brief Recapitulation of Goals

In order to create a catalogue of fundamental features, which are indispensable for the successful linkage of refugee assistance and development aid, the goals pursued through the linkage must be kept in mind. While some aspects are pursued in all frameworks and programs, others may depend on specific frameworks and their applied methodologies. Hence, it is of importance to recapitulate and emphasize the goals.

Finding durable solutions is the superior objective of refugee assistance regardless of the possible integration of development aid. Resettlement, repatriation and local integration have officially been accepted as durable solutions. Development initiatives linked to adequate refugee protection and assistance can lead to interim and durable solutions. While local integration entails a link to development, repatriation can be brought together with development activities such as reconstruction and rehabilitation in the countries of origin. The returnee aid and development as well as parts of TDA reveal the linkage. Development as an interim solution can be applied through self-reliance activities among others.

Burden and responsibility-sharing between the North and South has been an overall objective when refugee assistance is linked with development aid initiatives. While in cooperation, the Northern governments provide additional funding to the Southern regions, which are asylum countries hosting refugees. The idea of the refugee as a 'development agent' stems from increased funding Southern countries may receive.

Protracted refugee situations are long-term conditions in which refugees remain to be dependent on humanitarian assistance. Protracted refugee situations are to be prevented, assisted, and/or overcome. While seeking durable solutions such as repatriation, development offers interim or even final solutions. By using initiatives like local integration as a potentially long-term solution or self-reliance strategies as interim solutions, refugees are enabled to escape lives in which their needs are unfilled.

Finally, the linkage of refugee assistance and development aid pursues the aim of assisting *countries of asylum and of origin*, and hence, *refugees and local communities* mutually. Thereby, potential conflicts or disputes between the two groups of beneficiaries may be prevented because refugees may be less seen as the only ones receiving aid and assistance. While *reconstruction and rehabilitation* takes place in countries of asylum and of origin, they can promote *peace consolidation.* A long-lasting development is launched which is, however, only detectable in a peaceful arrangement.

4.4. Features

Based on the above stated information, one needs to ask now what is needed for the successful linkage of refugee assistance and development aid. What fundamental features are to be addressed to perform development-oriented refugee assistance?

4.4.1. Betts' 'Ingredients' for Success

In his recent writing on *Development assistance and refugees towards a North-South grand bargain?,* Betts produced lists on "ingredients for political agreement" and "ingredients for practical viability" (Betts 2009a: 13-18), which are necessary for successful realizations of TDA. The "ingredients for political agreement" target engagements of both Northern and Southern countries (Betts 2009a: 2). Northern states are required to provide

- significant additional development assistance that does not substitute for existing budget lines that would otherwise benefit country nationals and
- an integrated approach that targets both refugees and citizens (Betts 2009a: 2).

He emphasizes that Southern states are required to offer

- self-sufficiency and possibly local integration;
- a commitment to enhance refugee protection capacity. In order to facilitate political agreement, a neutral arbiter and a credible negotiation process will be required (Betts 2009a: 2).

"[I]ngredients for practical viability" for a successful implementation of TDAs comprise:

- institutional collaboration between UNHCR and development actors;
- joined-up government and new budget lines that can transcend government department divides; and, most crucially;
- the right kinds of interventions, which are based on an integrated approach, focus on livelihoods, use pre-existing community structures, and use evaluations to monitor and follow-up on project implementations (Betts 2009a: 2).

Betts explains how TDAs can reach the status of win-win situations (Betts 2009a: 9-13) for both sides and which ingredients for political agreement and practical viability are needed (Betts 2009a: 13-19). Loescher refers to Betts' findings in a lecture on *Human Rights and Refugees: The Global Crisis of Protracted Displacement*. He summarized that

> successful past approaches were based on a number of practical principles. They were comprehensive in the sense that they drew on all possible solutions: repatriation, resettlement and local integration as well as expanding migratory opportunities. They were cooperative in that they were based on burden sharing between countries of refugee origin, host countries and resettlement countries. And finally they were collaborative meaning they involved a broad range of UN agencies, NGOs and other actors and recognized that humanitarian actors alone could not find solutions (Loescher 2009:12).

In this research, Betts "ingredients" are seen as "pre-conditions" (Betts 2009a: 2, 6). They are indispensable for success, traceable and realistic, which is why I agree with him. Yet, he rather focuses on the 'high' levels of Northern and Southern states. Those decision-making or elite levels are certainly determining successful planning and implementation processes. A simple example reveals their importance: In case Northern states do not provide Southern nations with additional funds, projects cannot be initiated in the first place.

4.4.2. Features for Development-oriented Refugee Assistance

Betts focuses on the relations of 'decision-making actors', or in other words, Northern donor countries and Southern refugee hosting nations. While these levels are significant, I go beyond it. I extend the scope by integrating the 'low' level, or in other words, the grass-roots level of beneficiaries. Beneficiaries are refugees and local community members. The features are based on Betts' "ingredients"; yet, they aim to capture a broader scope.

The proposed features are based on the previous frameworks and their reasons for failure. They are understood to be fundamental, as they are required in order to execute development-oriented refugee assistance successfully and to achieve durable solutions. Since development-oriented refugee assistance is understood to incorporate the three pillars of sustainability, efficiency, and gender sensitivity, specific hints are stated in the explanation of the features. They encompass situational, timely, and actors' dimensions. Thus, they are multi-dimensional and practice-oriented.

4.4.2.1. Involved Actors

- *Political will* is necessary to have for both Northern and Southern spheres at the government and decision-making level. The political will incorporates the acceptance of a changing or revised perspective, authority to launch reforming strategies, and the ability to perform the alteration. The issue of donors' earmarking of funds already causes shortages and leaves UNHCR with inappropriate amounts to react to sudden mass influxes of refugees. On the one hand, donors therefore consider providing funding not earmarked to UNHCR in order for it to take the chance of using the funds according to their own assessment of its necessity. In relation to the development integration, Northern donor nations accept the need for further additional financial resources needed by the Southern refugee hosting countries to share burdens as well as responsibilities.[37] However, if donors are unable to provide for the financial additionality to facilitate the integration of development into refugee assistance, one factor of the political will of the Northern country is not fulfilled. On the other hand, Southern refugee hosting countries of first asylum accept the implications of the integration of the developmental aspects and provide additional arable land to establish refugee settlements instead of camps. Yet, if, for example, they do not have the capacity to provide arable land, the ability factor is not fulfilled either. The political will of funding institutions, refugee hosts and refugee assistance providing institutions is the foundation to create a type of assistance that is sustainable, efficient and gender-sensitive.

37 Thielemann (2006) adds interest- and norm-based factors to burden-sharing.

- *Political willingness*[38] refers to the dedication of Northern and Southern countries to link refugee protection and assistance with development initiatives and hence share burdens.[39] Political willingness is therefore crucial at the government and decision-making level. Donors are committed to develop an approach that links refugee assistance with development and lobby for it. Refugee hosting nations integrate refugee issues in their national development papers such as the Poverty Reduction Strategy Papers (PRSPs) in order to use the significant additionality as needed. They allow strategies such as local integration or self-reliance to be included in policies and frameworks of refugee protection and assistance. Hence, the authorities or political actors develop and maintain a common understanding of the development orientation and strive towards mutually shared results. According to Betts, unwillingness "led to disillusionment and disengagement. It is important that in reviving such an approach, states endeavour to build trust and confidence. There must be a clear expression of willingness [and credibility] to make concessions – for the North in relation to burden sharing and for the South in relation to self-sufficiency" (Betts 2009a: 15). Political willingness of funding institutions, refugee hosts and institutions providing refugee assistance to engage in development-oriented refugee assistance is also the foundation to create a type of assistance that is designed and implemented efficiently and gender-sensitively. Political willingness is also fundamental for reaching sustainable impacts.
- *Initial global consultations*[40] are trend-setting to establish agreements and co-operations between the global North and the global South. While agreements on development-oriented refugee protection and assistance can be

38 The political willingness refers to political dedication, commitment and engagement to launch and implement a revised strategy. Betts refers to the willingness and honest strive towards development-oriented refugee assistance as "credibility" (Betts 2009a: 15).

39 Thielemann adds two norm-based motivations. According to him, there is a great solidarity among the political communities. He says that this type of "[s]olidarity can be understood as a concern for other members of a group which may be expressed by an unwillingness to receive a benefit unless the others do, or an unwillingness to receive a benefit when this will harm them." In addition to his norm-based motivations among the actors, he explains solidarity towards refugees. The evidence shows that mass influxes of refugees did not receive adequate protection and assistance activities in the past. Hence, "[s]tates might therefore accept an agreement on the basis of their commitment to human rights, despite the fact that the redistributive effects of a particular burden-sharing regime are not stacked in their favour" (Thielemann 2006: 12, 14).

40 This feature is based on Betts' "political ingredient" of the "neutral arbiter" as a factor for institutional process (Betts 2009a: 14). For this study, "initial global consultations" is used as a heading because it covers a broader extent and refers to the need for multi-lateral communications.

based on bi-lateral, regional, and multi-lateral agreements, a global discussion to reach a mutual understanding of goals and principles "would certainly contribute to the overall process" (Betts 2009a: 14). Hesitating actors might become aware of the potentials of development-oriented refugee assistance and see benefits for themselves. Previous approaches to a framework on the nexus of refugee and development aid proved the importance of initial debates to find common grounds. The Global Forum on Migration and Development (GFMD), which first took place in Brussels in 2007, may offer such room to initiate debates on general principles and goals. Even if those principles cannot be established at GFMD, participating states of GFMD may agree on launching an additional round table aiming to find shared principles and goals. Finally, "[a]n inclusive North-South dialogue with UNHCR facilitation [to mediate between the interests of states] is required at the multilateral level in order to establish a common understanding of general principles" (Betts 2009a: 14). Additionally, global consultation may have the power to lobby for a type of development-oriented refugee assistance that is sustainable, efficient and gender-sensitive.

- *Collaboration* of involved actors[41] is essential to successfully implement development-oriented refugee assistance. It is especially necessary at the level of individual countries in which refugees are hosted, or in relation to specific programs of refugee assistance. Actors are donors, hosting countries, UNHCR, operational and implementation partners, development organizations, such as UNDP and the World Bank, and respective government authorities, which are responsible for refugee matters. These actors are able to influence planning and implementation processes to certain extents. Their collaborations must reach an open level of information sharing and transparency in order to reach best results. Only that way can coherence and appropriate usage of capacity be ensured. Hence, donor-only meetings are counterproductive to information sharing. Refugee hosting countries as well as UNHCR and development representatives should be present at meetings in order to capture scopes, grasp activity intensities, and launch adequate initiatives. By means of

41 Betts refers to this content while speaking about the need for institutional collaboration between agencies. Despite the phrasing, the content reveals the need for inter-agency cooperation (Betts 2009a: 16). Collaboration is important while taking past failures into account. But what contributed to the failure? Collaborations and partnerships between UNHCR and development agencies, particularly UNDP, were not built on fertile grounds. "UNHCR has found it difficult to achieve concrete partnerships with development agencies" (Betts 2005a: 20). These difficulties reflect on the levels of interaction and cooperation as well as the one of and after handovers (Betts 2006b: 18-19). To realize development-oriented refugee assistance, collaboration and partnership are crucial.

collaboration of involved actors, it may be possible to design respective assistance programs that are sustainable, efficient and gender-sensitive.

- *Regular correspondences* of actors, which are involved in specific programs on refugee assistance, are important to promote information sharing and transparency. By means of that, they are able to react immediately in urgent cases. In the context of the previous approaches to link refugee und development assistance, one reason for failure was the lack of cooperation between the actors. It was continuously raised as an issue that contributed to the little success of the approaches. Regular correspondences may improve that. Cooperating is indeed more than corresponding; cooperation is based on officially agreed project goals and jointly conducted operations. It entails mutual efforts towards outlined objectives. The imperative of regular correspondences may be a starting point on which actors meet periodically and find a common ground for exchange. Although it may not guarantee a productive and constructive cooperation, it is at least a start. Particularly UNHCR, development organizations and implementing partners need to find a way to maintain ongoing communications. The different actors observe different processes, which may be indicators for progress or obstacles. Internal means of sharing information are assumed to have to potential to avoid or prevent failures, and to initiate immediate and appropriate responses to complications, and thus to ensure to achieve planned results. Regular correspondence furthermore promotes the involvement and continuous willingness of political actors and therefore ideally supports in efficient assistance programs.

- *Monitoring, reporting, evaluating, and accounting processes* are understood to be vital to implement in a timely manner and to be able to react to changes instantly. Details of procedures may be content of agreements and regularities. While political willingness and credibility were stressed above, accountability is significant in order to maintain both the credibility and willingness. Misusage and misappropriation of funds, inadequate recognition of capacities, ineffective program implementation, and any discrepancies in documents will not only produce further costs but also provoke anger and irritation among all involved actors and stakeholders.[42] To avoid resentment, monitoring, reporting, evaluation, and especially accounting processes need to be

42 UNHCR's field staff, operating partners and development agencies should pursue the implementation according to agreements with respective governments, and communicate findings to country and branch offices. In addition to the field staff and in case donors obtain the capacity, undertaking regular follow-up missions to research the correctness of stated information in reports of implementing partners may be recommendable.

performed regularly and according to existing rules and regulations. Information is understood to be shared to promote transparency and to ensure coherence. Good and 'bad' practice examples should be examined and taken into account to carry out lessons-learned activities and to possibly revise applied strategies appropriately. Appropriate monitoring, reporting, evaluating, and accounting processes form the foundation to design and maintain development-oriented refugee assistance programs that are sustainable, efficient and gender-sensitive. Through collaborative program planning, all necessary parameters can be integrated. Respective monitoring and evaluation ensures that potential gaps and failures are detected and activities revised. Moreover, gender is to be mainstreamed in planning and implementation processes through program cycles to ensure gender sensitivity and support a process towards gender equality.

- *Ownership of development initiatives* are understood to be necessary to ensure sustainability. Research and international operations have shown that ownership of national actors play a significant role in achieving sustainable development. Already in the context of CIREFCA, the importance of ownership was highlighted. "Rather than being passive recipients of external support, the countries in the region were active participants throughout the two processes. The active involvement of not only the countries of origin but also the countries of asylum ensured that there was 'buy-in' by all of the relevant actors" (Betts 2006b: 58). The UNDG also incorporated the important aspect of ownership as a factor of TDA. "Ownership and active engagement by the national/local Government is critical. As the timing of the CCA/UNDAF process is being aligned with the formulation of national development plans and the PRSP, concerted efforts should be made to incorporate durable solutions for displaced persons into these instruments" (UNDG 2004). Hence, refugee hosting countries of first asylum are understood to hold ownerships and responsibilities. Hence, they include developmental questions of refugee hosting areas into their PRSPs in order to address issues appropriately. Based on that, they ensure that the development initiatives benefit the host country. They go beyond the so-called basic needs of refugees and encompass national developmental needs and benefits. Thereby, refugee hosting countries and their respective authorities are especially responsible that care and maintenance programs include activities that aim to be sustainable. Through that, livelihood and social justice of the national population may be improved, natural resources protected and economic development supported.

In addition to ownership on the level of stakeholders, ownership of beneficiaries is understood to be important as well. "Early participation and ownership by refugees will also contribute to the promotion of socio-economic empowerment, thus leading to maximum self-reliance in preparation for durable solutions" (UNHCR 2003b:51). Since refugee assistance is supposed to gain the development orientation, members of the host country are included in addition to refugees. In the context of the community-based approach, UNHCR states the following:

> Ownership is achieved when persons of concern assume full responsibility for the continuation of the work and manage the activities and services that they consider priorities. It is the natural outcome of a process that has respected the principles of meaningful participation and empowerment. Support and assistance from external actors might still be required, however, because of an absence of resources or opportunities (UNHCR 2008b: 21).

Hence, besides refugee hosting countries also the beneficiaries are supposed to have ownership. Through that, participation, commitment and empowerment are part of the process which may eventually lead to self-sufficiency.

- *Integrity and solidarity* of staff (particularly field staff) are assumed to be important and necessary to exist according to certain maxims. Even if decision-making actors agree on principles and standards, it is the staff that implements programs and is in daily contact with the beneficiaries. They not only need to pursue regularities and strive towards results. Moreover, they are to be informed about long-term objectives. Most staff operating in the field is from the refugee hosting country. Their operational commitment is therefore directly contributing to the development of *their* country. Jacobson quoted an observer who said that "[i]n a refugee context questions of development and human capabilities are put on hold – the situation is supposed to be merely temporary after all" (Jacobsen 2001: 3). Although operations may be temporarily limited, objectives are about sustainable progress. Hence, information and value sharing is required to take place in order to involve staff from all levels in activities and pursued results. It must be clarified, that development-oriented refugee assistance is not supposed to be of short-term usage but rather of sustainability, for refugees but also for the local refugee-hosting communities. Integrity and solidarity of staff towards development-oriented refugee assistance is important to implement a type of assistance that is sustainable, efficient and gender-sensitive. Due to their engagement and commitment, durable results can be pursued by means of suitable and innovative program activities and both men and women can be integrated in such programs.

4.4.2.2. Consideration of Time and Situational Dimensions

- *Contextual recognitions* are understood to be important because despite similarities of refugee context, the exact specifics need to be known and incorporated in programs. Before program design and operation plan processes are even initiated, the context of the anticipated program needs to be clarified. Which donors and what country of first asylum are involved? Where are beneficiaries from and where shall they be settled? What is the timeframe of the funding and of the refugees' anticipated stay? What results are to be achieved? What development organization cooperates? While some of these factors are content of agreements, the entire scope of the context must be understood to launch program planning procedures that prevent potentially harmful activities but rather implement sustainable, efficient and gender-sensitive programs. The method of Do-No-Harm in addition to other assessment methods is widely accepted and used. Through its application, so-called dividers and connectors are identified to avoid negative impact from the outset. The contextual recognition would therefore create the foundation of programs.

- *Situational considerations* are seen to be necessary to tailor programs suiting the exact situation. Specific situational criteria and measures need to be taken into account to develop most appropriate programs. Criteria encompass precise information on circumstances of refugees and local communities respectively in the country of first asylum or of origin.[43] Based on detailed information, an in-depth situation assessment is necessary for the respective case. The specific situational and regional factors are to be considered to compile a catalog of needs, operational focal areas, and potential obstacles. According to the findings of the situation analysis, a program design can be commenced, which considers sustainability, efficiency and gender sensitivity. Based on the situational considerations, appropriate program constellations can be developed. They include an innovative mix of suitable activities, the pursuit of durable results and improved livelihoods, and the promotion of the process towards just social relations between men and women and help to integrate both in programs.
- *Time factors* are to be kept in mind and on paper at all times. Ultimately, the overall objective of development-oriented refugee protection and

43 Possible questions that need to be raised to receive in-depth background information are: Where are the refugees from? Why did they flee? What is their gender constellation? How many refugees are located in which areas and settlements? Which host country of first asylum did they settle in? What geographical and regional features does the country have? Is there a history of violent conflicts within the host country and the specific refugee hosting area? Does the country of origin and asylum have a violent history? Is there a current potential for conflict re-escalation? What is the development status of the country of first asylum and refugee hosting area? What are the social structures of the local communities close to the refugee settlements? Which development organizations have been actively operating in the country? Is voluntary repatriation feasible, and if so, when could it possibly be carried out? These questions should be raised vice versa in the context of development-oriented returnee assistance towards the needs of returnees, reintegration into communities of the country of origin, and development of the country of origin, particularly the returnee affected areas.

assistance is to share burdens and bridge the gap between relief and development. Enduring encampment and connected long-term care and maintenance programs of UNHCR are targeted to be overcome. In order to achieve that, reasonable timeframes need to be determined. The awareness of the need for long-term planning is not new.

Already in 1953, the former High Commissioner of UNHCR van Heuven Goedhart said "[i]f any solutions are to be found for the refugee problem, an element of long-term planning is required" (van Heuven Goedhart 1953). Further High Commissioners announced similar needs (Hartling 1983a; Aga Khan 1966a). Regarding optimized services in the field, Hunt-Matthes and Shishkova reemphasize the need for "[e]ngaging in more foresight, long-term planning and priority setting" (De Vriese 2006: 89). Macrae refers to the gap between relief and development by noting that "all the relevant actors – national and international – [fail] in long-term planning for reintegration and development" (Macrae 1999: 13).

When 'scaling up' towards the integration of development in refugee aid takes place, methods and timeframes must be adjusted. UNHCR's annual program cycles are ineffective for medium or long-term planning procedures in relation to development aid. That short-term project do not support the development idea proved the failure of the QIPs. When returnee aid and development was implemented, QIPs were used to push for progress in the countries of origin. Research has shown that the reason for failure is directly connected to the need for long-term planning and programming when pursuing sustainability (Chimni 1999: 15; Helton 2002: 83; Weiss Fagen 2003: 203). However, until now, UNHCR depends on the annual cycles. Nevertheless, long-term objectives should be categorized and pursued through the annual planning modes. As noted by Macrae, short-term programs related to emergency relief run "three to six months" while medium and long-term programs rather target development lasting from "three to 10 years" (Macrae 1999: 18). Hence, programs concerning development-oriented refugee protection and assistance should run over a period of at least three years to involve refugee and local communities, to build awareness, and to reach durable results. Time factors are important to be known by authorities that design programs. By doing so, they can design programs that suit specific timeframes and reach respective results. Program design and implementation can then ensure that a type of assistance that is sustainable, efficient and gender-sensitive is designed.

4.4.2.3. Target Groups of Beneficiaries

- *Integration of refugees and nationals* of the hosting country of first asylum is required when refugee protection and assistance is targeted to be development-oriented. While refugee assistance originally only targets the refugee community and related groups of beneficiaries, the development orientation entails to include members of local communities as a group of beneficiary. UNHCR understands local integration as one of the durable solutions. According to UNHCR, "[i]t is based on the understanding that those refugees, who are unable to repatriate and are willing to integrate locally, will find a solution to their plight in their country of asylum" (UNHCR 2003d: 24). Local integration is, however, only one method to integrate both groups of beneficiaries. It is also possible to have both groups benefit from activities and services though access. Planning and implementation processes as well as a wide range of activities thus need to ensure a broader scope. This broader scope discovers a multi-linearity of beneficiaries. Programs and activities are important to be designed and implemented in a way that sustainably increases livelihoods and integrates both men and women of both groups in a gender-sensitive manner.
- *Manners of integration* depend on the refugee hosting country of first asylum. While it is clear that refugees and citizens are supposed to benefit, it is to decide whether refugees shall become locally integrated or rather only become self-reliant and sufficient, and hence live side by side with local communities. While local integration comprises self-sufficiency, the latter can also be adopted on its own. These two options of local integration and self-sufficiency have numerous positive impacts. Refugees benefit from prevented or overcoming protracted refugee situations and lasting encampment. Both refugee and local communities gain from new, revised, or newly-created service structures, which improve lives and livelihoods. Local communities can benefit from sustainable results and potentially improved economic growth through infrastructural development. Natural resources may also be sustainably and efficiently protected. The innovative mix of activities within a program is important not only to reach durable results, but also to assist beneficiaries towards the process of social justice. In operations, men and women of both groups should be integrated and participate in activities, which may revise traditional gender roles and support the process towards gender equality. If both work side by side and prove to be able to achieve equal results, acceptance may be increased. Northern donor nations profit because long-term humanitarian funds are limited and potential irregular secondary movements are prevented.
- *Inter-active levels* are understood to have to potential to create awareness between beneficiaries and therefore reduce the likelihood of violence. In addition to avoid conflict, inter-action may also prevent the feeling of neglect

and to be left out on the side of local communities. These inter-active levels include peaceful meeting points as platforms for exchange for refugees and locals so they can generally meet, get to know one another, decrease potential prejudices and perhaps learn from each other. These platforms may also be used for trading and local markets to further improve economic empowerment. It is important for local communities and their members to get used to their "new neighbors" and to overcome potential tensions or clashes. It is indispensable to share information of processes through local authorities so that the understanding of the refugee's stay is raised and maintained among both respective communities. Inter-active levels may support the idea behind development-oriented refugee assistance not only being of benefit to refugees, but also to local communities. Thereby, especially the integration of women and men from both communities as well as their participation is promoted. It thus can be of use to support gender sensitivity.

4.4.2.4. Comprehensive Methods towards Beneficiaries

- *Inclusive and comprehensive frameworks* are required to be developed on a situation-specific foundation to reach syntheses of refugee and development activities and inclusivity of refugees and local communities. In itself, it therefore refers to a dual imperative towards activities and beneficiaries. In order to achieve this, a comprehensive scope of integrated and interwoven approaches and methods need to be applied. UNHCR understands the integrated approach as "a planning approach that brings together issues from across sectors, institutions and national and local levels, as well as different population groups" (UNHCR 2005c: Glossary 7). With the feature of inclusive and comprehensive frameworks, I am at going on set further. These frameworks not only include operational sectors and groups of beneficiaries but also methods. The success of a program depends on the interrelatedness and simultaneity of the three components. Hence, based on the findings of the situational analyses and needs assessments, programs apply several approaches and methods at the same time that are suit the exact situation which makes them innovative. Gender mainstreaming should be included in all operational sectors in order to pursue the progress towards gender equality. They furthermore target to reach the most sustainable results for refugees and local communities. Inclusive and comprehensive frameworks are important to support sustainable, efficient and gender-sensitive programs.
- *The rights-based approach* is needed to ensure the respect of human rights. UNHCR explains: "In a rights-based approach, human rights determine the relationship between individuals and groups with valid claims (rights-

holders) and State and non-state actors with correlative obligations (duty-bearers)" (UNHCR 2006d: 17). Planning and operations procedures are to create the foundation for refugee protection and assistance to ensure that their rights are fulfilled. In the context of linking refugee aid and development initiatives, UNHCR understands the rights-based approach as "a conceptual framework for the process of human development that is normatively based on international human rights standards and operationally directed to promoting and protecting human rights" (UNHCR 2005c: Glossary 11). Hence, all activities of development-oriented refugee assistance should be based on the protection and realization of human rights, regardless of the integration of development.

> Applying a rights-based approach entails: i. understanding the structural causes of the non-realization of rights and analysing who bears the obligation to uphold the specific rights; ii. assessing the capacity of rights-holders to claim their rights, and of duty-bearers to uphold their obligations, and then develop strategies to build these capacities; iii. monitoring and evaluating programmes according to human rights standards and principles; and iv. informing programming on the basis of recommendations of international human rights bodies and mechanisms (UNHCR 2006d: 17).

Incorporating the rights-based approach furthermore includes an in-depth awareness building sequence because enjoying human rights also means to allow others to enjoy the same human rights. This is because human rights are egalitarian[44] (Fritzsche 2004: 17).

Applying the rights-based approach additionally highlights to include to mainstream gender, and to ensure that rights of men and women are met. Since neither the 1951 Convention relating to the Status of Refugees nor the 1967 Protocol obtain a gender dimension, the rights based approach (besides additional mechanisms) ensures that discriminative inequality between men and women or between social groups is prevented. Optimally, through the awareness building and empowering sequence, the process towards equality and sustainable social justice is promoted.

- *A gender-sensitive approach* is essential in order to use the transitional period to further the process towards gender equality. Due to their refuge into a country of first asylum, refugees experience changing or transitional conditions, which can be used to further women's empowerment and gender equality. Especially in early phases of a program of refugee assistance, psychological support should be provided to beneficiaries. Operating gender-sensitively and

44 Fritzsche created a list of ten features of human rights: inalienable, supra-state, individual, egalitarian, moral, legal, universal, fundamental, interdependent, critical (translated: Fritzsche 2004: 16-19).

mainstreaming gender in programs means to integrate the resource, capacity, and special needs of both refugee women and men in all spheres and at all levels of program planning and implementation what UNHCR intends to do (UNHCR 1990: 5). When refugee assistance is linked with development, activities should strive for gender equality to an even greater extend. Developmental progress depends on a relatively stable political system. Hence, peaceful circumstances are required. It is proven that gender equality decreases the likelihood of conflicts and consequently strengthens political stability (Caprioli 2003: 14). Due to the development integration in refugee assistance, not only refugees but also local communities are targeted. All activities should be created in a way that targets refugees and locals, as well as women and men equally. Thereby, livelihoods are improved and social justice is supported. Planning, implementation, and evaluation processes must be conducted in a gender-equitable manner to pursue, promote, and ensure a positive and sustainable impact of the activities towards gender equality.

- *Results-based management* (RBM) targets to focus on reaching sustainable results. RBM helps taking relevant steps to achieve goals. In action-based management, the focus is directly on activities. Since they (but not the results) count, it is less sustainable. In RBM, activities are seen as the way to attain a result but are not explicitly included in this type of management because several ways may lead to acceptable outcomes. By narrowing goals, the project per se becomes narrowed. UNHCR defines RBM as

> [a] methodology within the Operation Management System (OMS) which emphasises results that have a positive impact on target populations, instead of controlling project inputs. There are four components to RBM: 1. Participatory analysis among stakeholders; 2. Core problem analysis; 3. A hierarchy of objectives and objective setting; and 4. Performance monitoring (UNHCR 2005c: Three – 31).

In the context of development-oriented refugee assistance, RBM assists planning and implementation processes to remain focused on sustainable long-term results, rather than short-term interim achievements. This is particularly important considering the intended sustainable effects of development initiatives.

- *Impact-considering operations* seek to consider possible impacts of actions. Impact-considering operations are based on in-depth analyses to grasp the complexity of the targeted area with its economic, environmental, political, and social conditions. Impact-considering operations also integrate Do-No-Harm approaches. According to UNHCR, Do-No-Harm means "never should the work or interests of providers or their proxies cause further suffering to those dependent on their aid" (UNHCR 2002: 423). In the context of development-oriented refugee assistance, the range of programs must be designed and performed while considering the impact on local and refugee communities. For example education: Are schools built? Where are they built? Can they be reached by beneficiaries? Is the access to education for girls and boys ensured? Are female and male teachers available and/or present to provide equal access and show that both are capable of equal duties? Impact-considering also captures to respect national environment resources and treating them accordingly. Impact-considering operations are therefore of a broad scale and target to first assess and then ensure sustainable, efficient and gender-sensitive program implementation.

- *Rural local refugee settlement structures*[45] instead of refugee camps are to be used when refugee assistance is development-oriented. UNHCR defines local settlement schemes "where voluntary repatriation is not yet possible, covers assistance to help refugees become self-supporting in the country of first asylum and to integrate into the economic and social life of the local community" (UNHCR 2005c Glossary: 7). While a pre-condition for the establishment of refugee settlement is sufficient land provided by the hosting country, refugee settlements are preconditions for promoting self-reliance and self-sufficiency of refugee communities. Due to the arrangement of settlements, refugees are more likely to become less depended on aid and agencies. While refugee settlements still constitute a type of encampment, their structures are less limited and can lead to durable self-contained social and economic units when beneficiaries receive land for housing, arable land for agriculture, trainings on farming methods, and seeds. Their independence can then be used for local integration. Through rural local settlements, livelihoods can be increased sustainably and gender-sensitively by integrating women and men. Moreover, through a suitable use of seeds, agriculture may be conducted. Since refugees may not be aware of the appropriate type of seeds, it would be innovative and new to them. Capacities would be built. If they reached a surplus from farming, they could sell it on markets. Hence, economic growth would be supported. Rural local settlements therefore contain the potential to be sustainable, efficient and gender-sensitive.
- *Community-based methods* are to be applied in order to reach beneficiaries and their specific needs. Political context, social and cultural dynamics, gender-roles and their allocations, and possible fields of tension must be understood and taken into account when designing and implementing a community-based approach. Approaches based on communities and their needs

45 The idea of refugee settlements is controversially debated in the academic world; e.g., Clark and Stein called it an "operational myth" (Clark/Stein 1985: 47). Owen indicates the negative possibility that refugees may only think and act short-term in settlements due to lacking ownership and hence do "not consider the longer-term implications of their practices for the well-being of the land" (Owen 2001:15). Cf. Harrell-Bond 2002; Crisp 2003, 2004; Schmidt 2003; Dryden-Peterson/Hovil 2003; UNHCR 2006d.

incorporate comprehension of conditions of refugees, citizens and social structures. A refugee community often consists of different nationalities, ethnic groups or tribes, religions, and languages or dialects. That is why they often do not observe or consider themselves as one community. The local community of the refugee hosting country possesses social structures, which need to be known in order to introduce them to the refugee population. Activities of such approaches must consider the above aspects. Hence, community-based approaches must be planned and implemented in a way that meets the needs of both beneficiary groups. It then "recognizes the resilience, capacities, skills and resources of persons of concern, builds on these to deliver protection and solutions, and supports the community's own goals" (UNHCR 2008b: 14). As stated by Lippman and Malik in the context of the 4Rs, "community participation [and] communities should be at the heart of the process" (Lippman/Malik 2004:10). Community-based methods thus have the potential to create sustainable results through efficient methods and integrated gender sensitivity. This can promote revised traditional gender roles and the process towards gender equality through the visibility of equal capabilities.

- *A livelihood-based approach*[46] is necessary to be applied because the connection of refugee aid and development eventually aims to improve livelihood conditions. UNHCR defines livelihood according to DFID as "a combination of the resources used and the activities undertaken in order to live. Resources include individual skills (human capital), land (natural capital), savings (financial capital), equipment (physical capital), as well as formal support groups and informal networks (social capital)" (UNHCR 2005c Glossary: 7). According to this understanding, integrating the livelihood approach into development-oriented refugee assistance aims to design a type of operation that is sustainable, efficient and gender-sensitive. When refugee protection and assistance is linked with development initiatives, improved and sustainable livelihoods of the refugee and local communities are targeted. This is done through cross and multi-sectoral operations incorporating social, socio-economic, and further human and public services.
- *Pre-existing social structures* and chains of command shall be respected and used in the case of local integration. These social structures of local communities — as noted above — must be introduced to the refugee population that is to be integrated locally. If social systems are not respected and used, dual systems develop in which refugees will most likely remain. Adjusting structures

46 Betts also referred to the livelihood-based approach as a necessary factor for the "right intervention" (Betts 2009a: 17f).

within refugee settlements to pre-existing structures is particularly of durable use. For example, when the health and education sectors should be adopted to national structures in order to later integrate the structures into local schemes. This reveals a great level of sustainability through durable use. If gender is mainstreamed and both sexes are integrated, the process towards gender equality may be promoted.

- *Cross and multi-sectoral strategies* are to be elaborated and included in development-oriented refugee assistance. While the multi-linearity was explained above as the inclusion of refugee and national communities, the multi-sectoral approach is somewhat based on a broadened scope. The strategies comprise several sectors. Activities in these sectors have to take place simultaneously to enhance services and livelihood conditions. The most notable sectors are education, health, infrastructure and markets. To plan in coherence with national development aims, the refugee issues should be added to the national poverty reduction plan. By doing so, national needs and those of the refugees can be best targeted. In best practice, educational and health facilities are provided and accessible for both refugees and national communities. Thereby, possible tensions are prevented because nationals benefit from the 'refugee funded services' as well. Infrastructural development takes place by means of reconstruction and rehabilitation. Roads are built, houses improved, and water supplied through, e.g. boreholes, and electrification promoted. In the long run, local communities take great advantage of these initiatives, especially because refugee settlements are mainly located in rural and underdeveloped regions of the host country. In addition to that, refugees should be able to access and contribute to markets. While they may receive skills or vocational trainings, they are not only empowered but can also use their capacities to become self-reliant. This is of advantage for the host nation because these then constitute an additional labor force for markets.[47] Cross and multi-sectoral operations thus entail that activities of the different sectors are simultaneously and coherently implemented with the aim to design a type of development-oriented refugee assistance that is sustainable, efficient and gender-sensitive.
- *Environment-friendly or ecological methodologies* are assumed to be necessary to protect and revitalize natural resources. UNHCR comprehends environmental consideration as "an integral part of refugee assistance operations,

47 The argumentation presented above shows an ideal-typical process. In reality, especially the integration of refugees into local markets has proven to be complicated. Due to restrictive rights of movements, obstacles to accessing market are created. Even if refugees gain access to local markets, they may be seen as competition which could lead to tensions.

and thus should not be considered in isolation" (UNHCR 2003b: 54). The Office aims to operate in consideration of the environment in the three phases of "emergency, care-and-maintenance and durable-solutions" (UNHCR 1996: 5). When refugee settlement structures are set up and refugees receive land for farming, they subsequently need to be taught how to cultivate the land in a sustainable manner. The farming methods in the host country may be new to the refugees which means that their capacities in farming would have to be built first. It should be innovative and suitable to the soil conditions. In addition to that, the considerate use of natural resources such as firewood is to be taken care of. Sustainability is eventually the aim of development. UNHCR sees environmental actions in the bigger picture because "impacts on natural resources and the environment are always accompanied by social impacts of some kind, and commonly by associated health, cultural and economic impacts. Unless due attention is given to the breadth and scale of possible environmental impacts, local populations can easily suffer as much as refugee populations" (UNHCR 2009: 2). Development organizations cooperating with UNHCR send experts to train local staff in environment-friendly and appropriate ecological farming methods. Trained local staff can then inform beneficiaries and build their capacity. They will spread their knowledge among further beneficiaries. Through follow-up visits of the trained staff, awareness of gained knowledge and skills will be maintained. Through trainings, refugees may be prevented from acting with short-term perspectives. They may start to consider long-term implications that their actions potentially have on the land. This would falsify the statement of Owen about ownership issue in refugee settlements (Owen 2001:15). The sequence of trainings will result in a knowledge catalyst with an amplifying and multiplying effect, because in best case scenarios they transfer knowledge and thus act as multipliers. According to this understanding, integrating the environment-friendly or ecological methodologies into development-oriented refugee assistance aims to protect the natural resources efficiently and sustainably. Again, if programs mainstream gender and involve women and men as participants, equal capabilities may be highlighted and traditional gender roles eventually revised.

4.4.3. Additional Remarks on the Fundamental Features

The need for additional funds to implement development-oriented refugee assistance is undisputable. Donor states, however, can hardly be pressured to provide the additional funds. The majority of funds is earmarked and cannot be used according to UNHCR's will or rather where needed. As said above and underlined by Betts (2009a: 3-20), there is a need for global discussions and agreements on basic principles. It must be clarified why development-oriented refugee assistance is important for all sides, donors, hosts, refugees and local communities. Also, standards on implementation durations are to be elucidated.

'Common but differentiated responsibility-sharing' (Hathaway/Neve 1997a; Betts/Milner 2006; Betts 2005a and 2005b) is a scheme developed by Hathaway and Neve used by several international researchers. The scheme "would allow more good to be done for more refugees than is possible under the present regime." It basically "would provide a principled yet flexible framework within which to reconcile the needs of refugees to the legitimate concerns of states" (Hathaway 1997: xxvi, xxiv). Betts explains that it is based on bi-lateral cooperation to reach an interest-convergence between the different groups.

> Hathaway and Neve's idea is that states should be able to contribute to the global refugee regime in different ways that are in their mutual interest. This is a particularly important idea when we recognize that most states contribute to refugee protection selectively and in areas in which they derive some kind of supplementary state-specific benefit (Betts 2009b: 155).

Hence, national contributions to refugee protection and assistance do not need to be linear or "identical". States should rather contribute according to their capacities. While some offer financial support others provide physical contributions. In the context of a common but differentiated responsibility-sharing and not earmarking all funds, Harrell-Bond announces that

> [e]ven if 'burden sharing' has been construed by the rich northern donors as simply the obligation to provide money to poor southern asylum countries, governments should insist that these monies are granted in a flexible manner that allows them to initiate development programmes as well as provide relief (Harrell-Bond 2002: 22).

In order to implement a type of aid that allows actors to contribute according to their capacities, a "consensus" must be agreed upon by all involved actors. This consensus will lead to the ability to "offer [assistance in] the most efficient way to maximise the protection space available to refugees"[48] (Betts 2009a: 11).

Local communities of the refugee hosting countries become an additional group of beneficiaries. This criterion is accepted throughout by policy-makers, researchers, and operating staff. In spite of the acceptance, refugee protection and assistance remains to be the center of operations. Does that convey to an asymmetric assistance? Betts writes that "UNHCR has operationalized a rights-based framework for one particular group of people on the move: refugees"

48 Betts also notes that the "common but differentiated responsibility-sharing" constitutes the status quo which has been implicit and needs to become explicit (Betts 2009a: 11-12).

(Betts 2008a: 16).[49] Are local communities secondary or inferior to the primary or superior refugee communities in terms of receiving aid? Is it not, that activities in underdeveloped refugee hosting areas are provided merely because refugees are located in the respective area? No, UNHCR and its operating partners are not supposed to implement asymmetric assistance in favor of refugees. Planning and implementation modes are to be according to integrated, inclusive and comprehensive approaches. UNHCR's *DAR Handbook* explains, what that means: agreements and operations are "based on partnerships between host governments, humanitarian and development partners [...], refugees, host communities, local authorities [...] and other actors [...]" (UNHCR 2005c: vi).

49 To avoid misunderstandings, the context of Betts' statement must be clarified. He explains the collaborative approach and the particular role of UNHCR. He notes the mandate and experience of UNHCR on vulnerable irregular migrants, yet emphasizes its expertise in "one particular group of people on the move: refugees" (Betts 2008a: 16).

Chapter V Development-oriented Refugee Assistance on the Case Study of Rhino Camp

In this chapter, the focus is on the case study of Rhino Camp in Uganda. After providing background information about Uganda, the refugee situation and operations at Rhino Camp are analyzed.

Figure 2. Map of Uganda

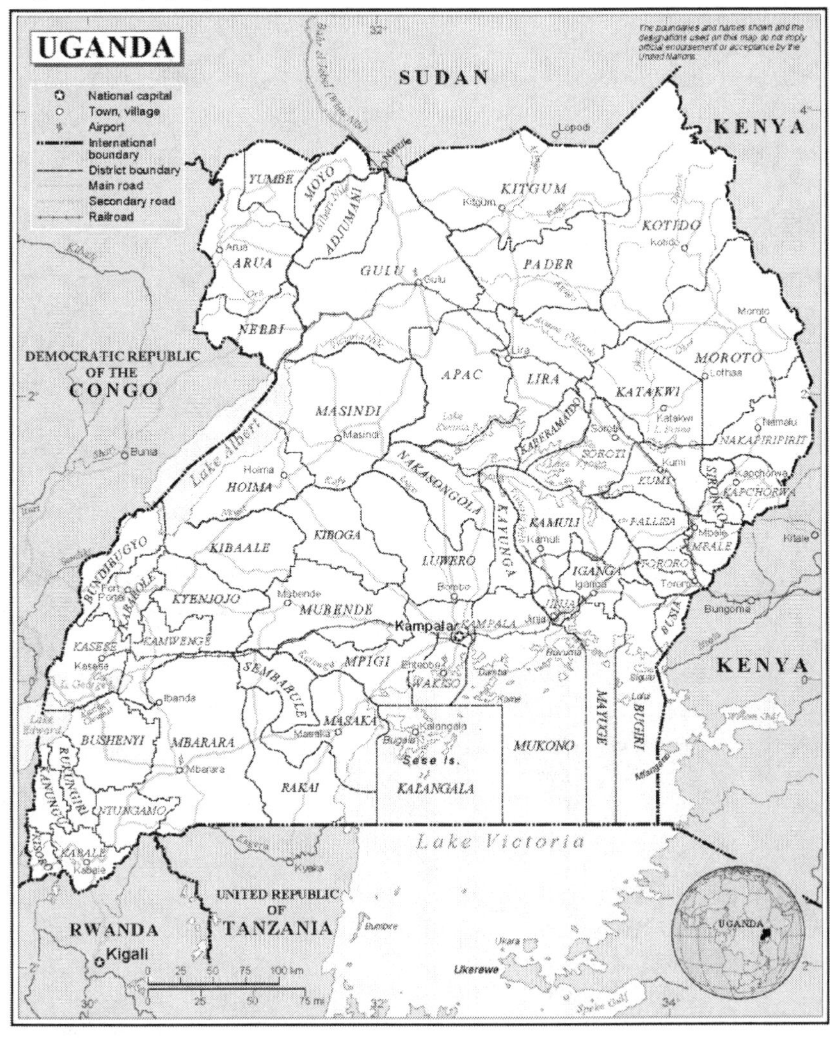

1. *Background Information about Uganda*

When the former British Prime Minister Winston Churchill visited Uganda in the beginning of the 20th century, he named the country 'the Pearl of Africa' (UNDP 2005: vi). Despite the soft name, Uganda experienced a great degree of violence since its independence in 1962.

1.1. Brief historical Overview

In 1962, Uganda gained its independents from the British colonial power and became a republic. However, the country lacked a "political party that was national both in its composition and behavior" (Otunnu 1992: 27). Leaders — whether at district or national level — followed tribal biases and acted in favor of such. The leading kingdoms continued to possess power, although the establishment of a monarchy failed.

Milton Obote created the first independent government through an alliance of the Uganda Peoples Congress (UPC) and the Kabaka Yekka in the same year of independence. Obote became the prime minister and a Kabaka[50] of Buganda became the first president, which gave the Kingdom of Buganda greater power. Discrimination against ethnic groups and tribes remained, but deadly violence broke out when Obote dismissed officials from Buganda (Ottunu 1992: 27). "[A] lot of Baganda were butchered by Obote" (Tejani 1974: 64). Northern troops attacked the Kabaka led by Idi Amin and the North-South axis within Uganda dispersed increasingly by the end of the 1960s. Obote's first administrative period lasted from 1962 until 1971 (Lomo/Hovil 2004: 2).

In 1971, Idi Amin, a general of a military group, "upstaged Obote, while the latter was away attending the Commonwealth Conference in Singapore" (Otunnu 1992: 28). Amin started its ruling rather cooperatively by, e.g., offering that Obote rules "by emergency" (Otunnu 1992: 28) but continued to strengthen the military, which was predominantly recruited in the West Nile region (Eckert 2008: 13-14). It targeted to ensure his political power. Its result reveals a great degree of cruelty. Amin's anarchic administration caused "total destruction of the infrastructure and the gross violation of human rights such as imprisonment without trial, murder, abductions and state sponsored violence" (Mulumba 2005: 89). Amin was dispossessed in 1979 by the Uganda National Liberation

50 Kabaka means King in Luganda.

Front/Army (UNLF/A) supported by the Tanzania People's Defense Forces (TPDF) (Lomo/Hovil 2004: 4). This, however, caused conflicts among Amin's soldiers who were mainly located in the West Nile region and recommended to move towards the border areas of South Sudan and DRC (Eckert 2008: 13-14). Until the elections in 1980, interim governments were in place.

In 1981, the UPC won the elections and Obote became the new president. His second administration lasted from 1981 until 1985. The neutrality and openness of the election was officially questioned. Among others, Yoweri Museveni raised his voice and launched the National Resistance Movement and Army (NRM/A). The NRM/A constituted of several tribes, namely "the Baganda, Banyankole, Banyarwanda, Bakiga and Rwandese refugees" (Otunnu 1992: 31). Museveni "wage[d] a guerrilla war against the UPC government led by Obote until it was defeated in 1985" (Mulumba 2005: 89). Obote performed massacres to overcome the NRM/A. However, Obote was dispossessed and General Tito Okello assumed power for a brief period. The NRM occupied Kampala and Museveni took over (Mulumba 2005: 91).

In 1986, the NRM took over the lead and Museveni became the new president of Uganda. He "initiated a positive policy toward southern Sudan" and the Sudan People's Liberation Army (SPLA), which was an opposing regime to the Sudanese government (Otunnu 1994: 7). Museveni was officially elected in 1996 and has been leading the country ever since.

Internal disputes subsisted. The West Nile region suffered especially from issues caused by "the Former Uganda National Army (FUNA), the first Uganda National Rescue Front (UNRF), the UNRF II, and the West Nile Bank Front (WNBF)". The rebel groups were mainly based in the bordering countries of Sudan and DRC. They affected the stability of the West Nile region significantly (Lomo/Hovil 2004: 3; cf. Hovil/Lomo 2005; Lomo/Naggaga/Hovil 2001). In Northern Uganda, the conflict between the Lord's Resistance Army (LRA) and the current political regime led by the NRM/A were a source of serious instability since 1987. The LRA operated primarily in the districts of Acholi Land and the Langi District, all located in Northern Uganda. The LRA's activities "have inflicted harm, injury and death not only to the Acholi but also to the Sudanese refugees settled in Acholi Pii refugee settlement in Pader district" (Mulumba 2005: 75). While solutions to the conflict have been approached mainly in recent years, most notable the 2006 ceasefire agreement, "the consequent impact on the civilian population has still been profound" (Lomo/Hovil 2004: 3; cf.: Lenhart 2008; IDMC 2008a; IDMC 2008b).

1.2. Country Profile

Uganda is located in sub-Saharan Africa. It borders Tanzania, Rwanda, and Lake Victoria in the South, the Democratic Republic of Congo (DRC) in the East, South Sudan in the North, and Kenya in the West. Uganda has a national population of an estimated 30.9 million, and an average annual growth rate of 3.2 per cent. About 13 per cent reside in urban areas (World Bank 2008).

Economic statistics of the World Bank (state of 2007) reveal that Uganda had a gross domestic product (GDP) of 11.3 billion US$ with an estimated GDP annual growth of 4.7 per cent in 2007. Agriculture takes up 29 per cent, industry 18.2 per cent and further services 52.8 per cent of the GDP. In the trade market, coffee is the most important export good. It is traded with 227 million US$ per annum. Its gross national income (GNI) is more than 340 million US$ per capita. The poverty line is about 38 per cent (World Bank 2008, 2010a, 2010b).

Social statistics of the World Bank (state 2007 and 2008) show that life expectancy is about 52 years, which is similar to that of other sub-Saharan countries. The mortality rate of under-five-year old children is 130 per 1,000 live births. The gross school enrollment to primary schools is about 97.1 per cent in 2008, which is generally high in comparison to further sub-Saharan countries. However, the primary completion rate is only 56.1 per cent of the enrolled children. In comparison to primary school enrollments, only 19.2 per cent enrolled in secondary schools in 2007 and only 3.7 per cent in tertiary education in 2008. The official prevalence of HIV among a populace aged between 15 and 49 is 5.4 per cent (World Bank 2010a; World Bank 2010b).

The World Bank notes, that "[s]ince 1986, Uganda has evolved from a nearly "failed state" battered by violent dictatorships to a country with a track record of growth and institutional reform" (World Bank 2009: 1). National development took place through a "strong economic growth [...] accompanied by a reduction in the population of Ugandans living in absolute poverty from 56% in 1992 to 38% in 2004" (UNDP 2005: ix). With a population of 30 million, Uganda ranks 157 out of out of 182 countries in Human Development Index (HDI). The HDI for Uganda was 0.514 in 2007 (UNDP 2009a; UNDP 2009b).

Despite the strong economic performance at the national level, positive and sustainable impacts are not translating into better livelihoods for all Ugandans countrywide. Although the incidence of income poverty declined significantly from 56 per cent in 2002/03 to 31 per cent in 2005/06, a large proportion of the population remains trapped in chronic poverty (IFAD 2001: 1). The population growth rate was 3.4 per cent in 2005. This is significantly higher than the sub-Saharan Africa average (UNDP 2005: vi). It poses challenges to job creation, agricultural production, income distribution, and the delivery of social services.

The latest developments include the *Poverty Eradication Action Plan* (PEAP). It was signed in 1997 and aims to eradicate mass poverty by enabling households to earn decent incomes and facilitate the improvement of the quality of their lives. In 2010, the PEAP was partly replaced by the National Development Plan. The *Peace, Recovery and Development Plan* for Northern Uganda was introduced by the Government of Uganda in October 2007. This Plan theoretically aimed to provide an overarching structure for the recovery and development approach – and inject much needed resources into newly established and/or fragile district government councils, enabling them to meet their statutory obligations (UN OCHA 2010). In April 2008, the *Karamoja Integrated Disarmament and Development Plan* was officially launched by the government in partnership with UN agencies. The plan reveals a coordinated long-term development program to address the roots of violence and instability of which voluntary disarmament is just one component (OPM 2007).

While the Northern (Lango and Acholi) region has been covered with development activities, the West Nile region has largely been neglected. This is particularly unfortunate because the region has been hosting refugees and remains at risk for violence due to the close location to Sudan and DRC.

The below table states socio-economic indicators from 1992 and 2006. Based on the data, significant changes are traceable.

Table 2. Socio-economic indicators of Uganda in comparison: 1992 and 2006.

Country Indicators	1992	2006
GDP growth	3,4	10,8
GDP per capita (US$)	177	320
Inflation (consumer prices, %)	42	7.2
Gross domestic savings (% of GDP)	0.6	13.2
Exports of goods and services (% of GDP)	7.2	15.5
External debt (% of GDP)	106	53.9
Private sector investment (% of GDP)	6.5	16.6
Poverty incidence (%)	56	31
Net primary school enrollment (%)	68 (1995)	91,7
Under-five child mortality (per 1,000 live births)	160 (1990)	137
Population (millions)	22 (1996)	29.9

2. *Refugees in Uganda*

2.1. Displacement in Uganda: A Brief Introduction

The Great Lakes region and neighboring countries of Uganda, such as South Sudan and Kenya, constituted a broad and fragile conflict zone. The region suffered from various violent outbreaks during the second half of the 20th century. Most conflicts took place internally and occurred between rebel groups and national governments, or among ethnicities and tribes. The impact on neighboring countries is particularly feasible through refugee waves. Uganda faced several waves, originating from the DRC, South Sudan, Rwanda, Ethiopia, and Somalia, and smaller numbers of refugees from, among others, Burundi, Eritrea, and Kenya (UNHCR 2003c: 214; UNHCR 2007d: 143-144).

Refugees entering Uganda primarily crossed the border in the west and northwest of Uganda from the DRC and Sudan. While the majority of Rwandan refugees entered Uganda in 1994, those from the DRC mainly arrived in 2002 and again in 2009 (UNHCR 2007d: 142-143). South Sudanese refugees experienced protracted situations in Uganda.

> The Sudanese refugees, mainly comprising farmers displaced by the conflict in the south of Sudan, dating back to 1989 (Adjumani and Moyo) and 1993 (Arua). This is a young population (more than half are below the age of 18) representing several ethnic groups (UNHCR 2005e: 144).

Uganda has not only received but also caused displaced persons. The political instability, including massacres triggered by former political leaders, as well as fights between government and rebel groups, such as the LRA, provoked Ugandans to flee from their country of origin to seek safety and asylum in other nations. Besides Ugandan refugees leaving, internal displacement had an impact on the country. The most affected region is Northern Uganda, where widespread IDP camps have been maintained since the 1990s (UNHCR 2007d: 143). The conflict between the Government of Uganda and the LRA lasted for more than twenty years and hampered developments in the North. Improved conditions can only be traced back to developments accomplished in recent years. In 2006, the Cessation of Hostilities Agreement was signed and the Juba Peace Process was initiated. It resulted in the signing of all but the final part of a multi-component peace agreement. Ever since, the Northern (Acholi and Lango) regions have faced relative security. A crucial opportunity for recovery in the North has come, and with it, an opportunity to address the development gap between that region and the rest of the country.

Against this backdrop, the regions have experienced large-scale movements of IDPs out of the camps and returning toward their original homesteads. The 1.6 million IDPs encamped in 218 IDP camps in 2006 were encouraged to return to their villages after security had stabilized. In 2009, only 853,000 IDPs remained in camps. While the homecoming evoked other issues, such as land conflicts, the returning IDPs still emphasized the relative stability and security in Uganda (UNHCR 2006f: 164; UNHCR 2007e: 233-237; UNHCR 2007d: 141-145).

While it needs to be acknowledged that Uganda has caused refugees and IDPs, as well as hosted a great number of foreign refugees, the focus of this analysis is on refugees. Hence, the IDPs perspective, although of great significance, is excluded from here on.

2.2. Statistics and Geographical Location of Refugees

According to UNHCR's Statistical Online Population Database, the refugee concentration in Uganda increased from 1997 until 2000, decreased in 2001, and grew again until 2005. The table below reveals the Refugee Population Statistics from 1997 until 2006 nationwide.

Table 3. Annual refugee population statistics from 1997 until 2006 in Uganda.

1997	1998	1999	2000	2001
189,883	205,685	218,611	239,533	200,518

2002	2003	2004	2005	2006
218,109	236,041	252,382	259,089	223,970

The population figures provided above are holistic and include all refugees located throughout the country. Most refugees have been settled in camps and local settlement arrangements in the north-western and western regions of Uganda by UNHCR in cooperation with the Office of the Prime Minister (OPM). Figure 3 reveals the locations of refugees.

Refugees were located in the north-western and western regions because on the one hand, most refugees crossed the borders in the west and north-west. On the other hand, these regions are less developed in comparison to central and central-western Uganda (Merkx 2000: 10). Extended stretches of land were economically idle and sparsely populated or completely uninhabited. By establishing the refugee settlement systems, infrastructure was developed. Neighboring local communities were to potentially benefit from that as well.

Figure 3. Map of refugees and IDPs in Uganda, December 2005.

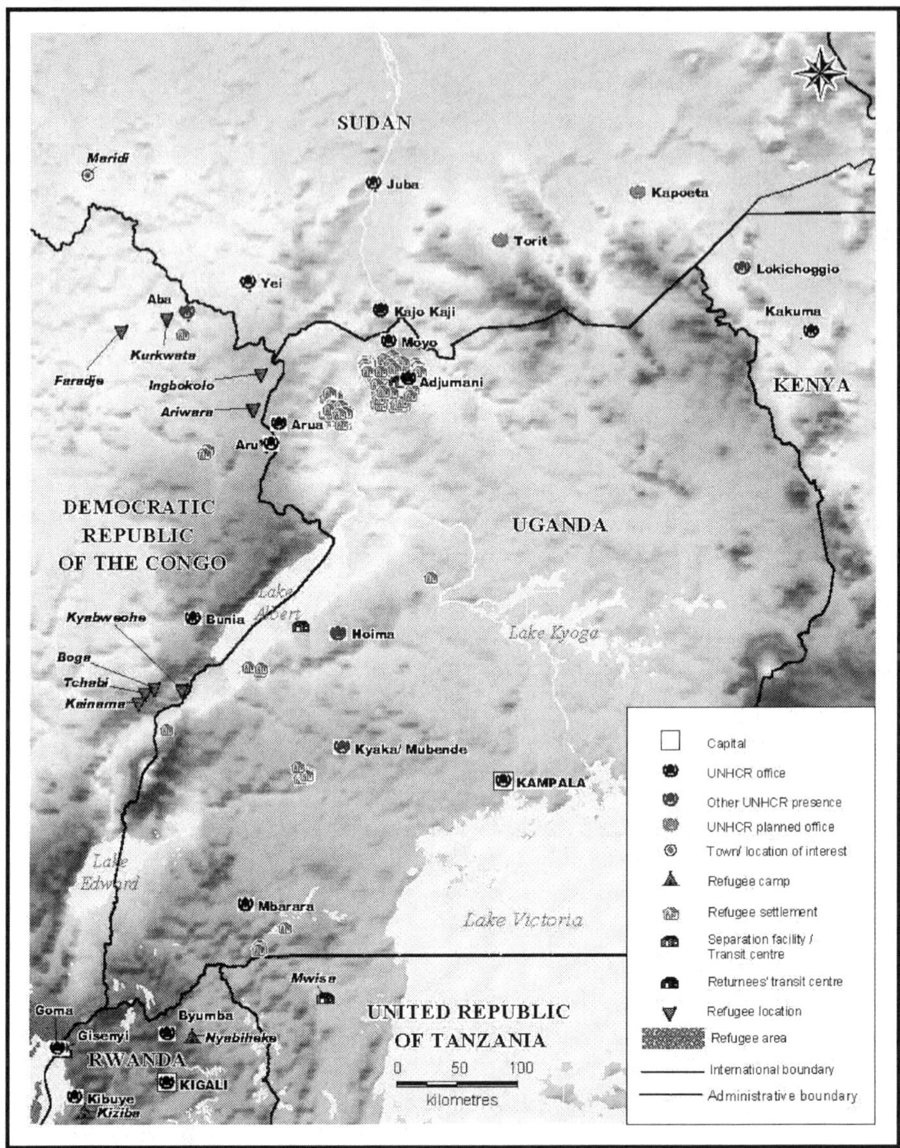

2.3. West Nile Region

The region is in the North-West of Uganda bordering South Sudan and DRC.

Figure 4. Map of West Nile region, Uganda.

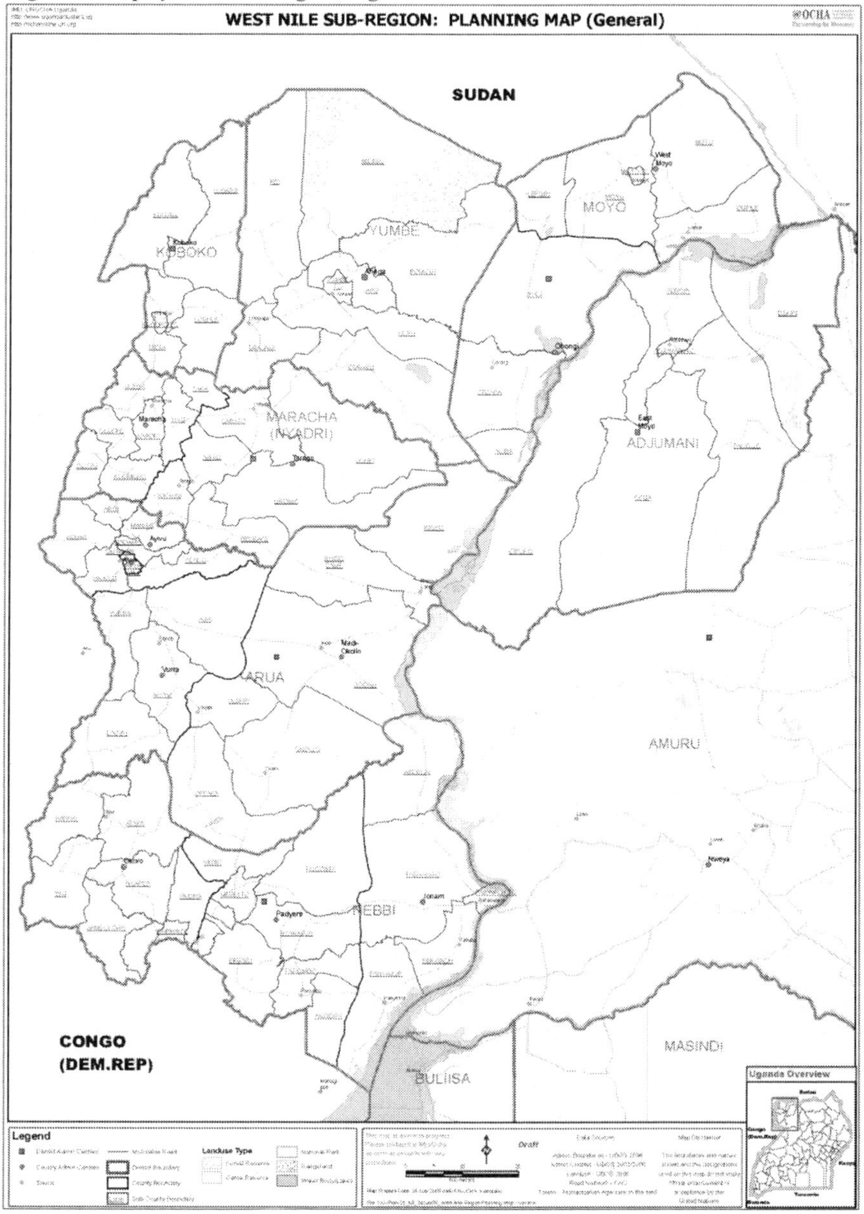

West Nile region has mainly been hosting South Sudanese refugees. Movements of displaced persons have been taking placing since the 1960s (Merkx 2000: 13-16). The first rather small group of South Sudanese refugees arrived in the West Nile region in 1986 along with returning Ugandan refugees. Ugandan refugees fled Uganda after Idi Amin was defeated and conditions became increasingly unsafe. The conflict in South Sudan ignited in 1993 between the Government of Sudan and South Sudanese rebels. It was coupled with ethnic conflicts, forced recruitment of youths into the army and wrangles between factions of the Sudanese People's Liberation Army (SPLA) leadership. When the SPLA attacked Ugandan refugees, they returned. Some Sudanese fled from violence along with the Ugandans (Rowley/Burnham/Drabe 2006: 167).

Increased intensity of violence resulted in the displacement of the South Sudanese to Uganda, particularly to the Arua District. The first major refugee wave arrived at the border town of Koboko from South Sudan in August 1993. Large transit camps were established in Arua and Adjumani Districts where refugees were initially located (DED LS/403 2006: 2). Ogujebe and Koboko were occupied by the majorities of refugees. Koboko is still utilized (Merkx 2000: 17). Transit centers were used because the incoming refugees were expected to return to South Sudan soon. Care and maintenance programs with basic service provision were set up. Since the refugee population in transit centers went beyond 100,000 beneficiaries in the first year, the need for alternative solutions became more urgent (Payne 1998: 7). Merkx estimates that up to 210,000 Sudanese fled to Uganda between 1986 and 1994 (Merkx 2000: 16). While several thousand returned in 1997, "the vast majority stayed, and many Sudanese have lived in West Nile for ten years or more" (Rowley/Burnham/Drabe 2006: 167).

The need for alternatives to transit centers due to the lasting conflict in Sudan was grasped by Uganda's Government and UNHCR in the early 1990s, because camps grew and the security was at risk. The transit centers were located in the Uganda-Sudan borderland and the conflicts affected the wellbeing of the refugees (Payne 1998: 7). Under pressure to keep them safe, refugees were transferred to local settlement arrangements, which aimed at pursuing self-reliance of beneficiaries. The pressure triggered errors.

> There were many misunderstandings between refugees, implementing non-governmental organizations (NGOs), the Ugandan government and UNHCR. All of them had different ideas as to how best to assist the refugees to achieve self-sufficiency. One of the issues frequently mentioned as problematic was the relationship between hosts and refugees. The settlement programme did not manage to involve the hosts from the start, and refugee settlements became "islands," where parallel services were provided to the refugees (Merkx 2000: 17).

Despite initial errors, local settlements were established and refugees located. Rhino Camp was set up in 1992, Ikafe in 1994, and Imvepi in 1995. In 2003, Madi Okollo was set up as an additional settlement.

In addition to the focus on meeting basic needs, the Government of Uganda intended to provide refugees with a medium-term solution through local settlements that was more than simply assistance and protection:

> Refugees were transferred from the transit centres to agricultural settlements with the aim of becoming self-sufficient, concentrating on food production. After the large influxes of 1993–94, the settlement scheme had to be expanded and new areas were made available (Merkx 2000: 17).

All settlements are in Arua District of West Nile region (DED LS/403 2006). Refugees were transferred to Ikafe, Imvepi, and Rhino Camp between December 1994 and July 1997. Spreading insecurity caused by the West Nile Bank Front rebels from early 1996 to March 1997 severely affected refugee allocation and settlement. By the end of 1996, nearly all of the 40,000 refugees settled in Ikafe were displaced. Most of them moved in a mass exodus back to Sudan in March 1997, emptying the whole Ikafe settlement and the remaining transit centers in Koboko. Imvepi and Rhino Camps were maintained (DED LS/403 2006: 2).

It is important to emphasize that the establishment of settlements instead of camp structures under the approval of the government is progressive, especially when one considers that this was a time of internal conflict and displacement as well. Moreover, establishing local settlements for refugees went beyond the National Refugee Policy that was in force at the time.

2.4. National Refugee Policy in Brief

The original refugee policy in Uganda was the Control of Alien Refugees Act, Cap. 64. It was adopted in 1960 (Uganda 1960). According to article 3.1, an alien is defined as

> a person who is not a citizen of Uganda or a Commonwealth citizen within the meaning of section 13 of the Constitution, or a protected person within the meaning of section 2 of the Uganda Citizenship Act, or a citizen of the Republic of Ireland (Uganda 1960: article 3.1)

A refugee is understood to be

> any person being one of a class of aliens declared by the Minister by statutory instruments to be refugees for the purpose of this Act but shall not include – (a) any person ordinarily resident in Uganda; (b) any person with diplomatic immunity; (c) any agent or employee of any Government who enters Uganda in the course of his duty; or (d) any person or class of person declared by the Minister by statutory instrument not to be a refugee (Uganda 1960: article 3.1)

Arrival and departure of refugees in Uganda is handled by authorized officers. Refugees entering Uganda have to be provided with a permit to stay, which includes their registration. Article 71 c of the Uganda Citizenship and Immigration Control Act, Cap. 66 stresses that "an alien recognised as a refugee by the Government and the United Nations High Commissioner for Refugees" is entitled to receive an identity card (Uganda 1999b: article 71 c). The Government of Uganda reserves the right to refuse the permit "without signifying any reason" and to "order any refugee or class of refugee to return by such means or route as he shall direct, to the territory from which he or they, as the case may be, entered Uganda, or to return to the country of which he or they is a national or are nationals" (Uganda 1960: articles 6, 20). However, a permit is not to be refused or a refugee deported to the country of origin if the refugee may face punishment for "an offence of a political character [...] or be subject to a physical attack" (Uganda 1960: articles 6, 20 3).

Refugees in Uganda live under restrictive laws with regards to movement and settlement. The Government of Uganda, through authorized officers, reserves the right to decide where refugees are to be located and settled. This entails that the government or respective ministers are able to order a relocation of refugees within the country (Uganda 1960: articles 6, 7, 8). In case of criminal activities, unauthorized and unregistered stays in the country, or possession of arms, refugees can be detained in prison and/or legally charged (Uganda 1960: articles 9, 11, 12). Moreover, if refugees intend to leave the settlement or even the country, they are required to inform respective officers and seek their approval. Refugees are charged with imprisonment if they fail to comply with the order of return to their country of origin by the Government of Uganda, or if they have committed an offence and crime (Uganda 1960: articles 20 4, 19). Refugees who neither informed authorities nor received the permit to move within the country "shall be guilty of an offence and shall be liable on conviction to imprisonment for a period not exceeding three months" (Uganda 1960: article 17). This is contrary to the 1951 Convention relating to the Status of Refugees. Its article 26 on the Freedom of Movement clearly states the following:

> Each Contracting State shall accord to refugees lawfully in its territory the right to choose their place of residence and to move freely within its territory subject to any regulations applicable to aliens generally in the same circumstances (A/RES/429 (V): article 26).

The restrictions have also been criticized in research. Kaiser highlights precisely that "[i]n practice, refugees do not enjoy their right to freedom of movement, and this has consequences for their enjoyment of socioeconomic and political rights too" (Kaiser 2005b: 354).

Time spent in the country shall not refer to an automatic reception of the Ugandan citizenship (Uganda 1960: article 18 2). However, according to article 16 of the Uganda Citizenship and Immigration Control Act, Cap. 66 any alien can ask for citizenship by naturalization, if the person applies for the citizenship and meets all set requirements (Uganda 1999b: article 16).

Organization, structure, safety, and efficient management of refugee settlements are the responsibility of the director and settlement commandant. This includes, among others, ensuring adequate reception, treatment, health, and well-being of refugees (Uganda 1960: articles 13 1, 2). Safety is targeted to be maintained by restricting access to refugee settlements (Uganda 1960: article 14). To ensure a level of livelihood, employment of refugees is permitted and "shall be paid [...] at the appropriate rate of wages" (Uganda 1960: article 15).

Deportation and involuntary forced return of refugees in Uganda is prohibited according to the Control of Alien Refugees Act (Uganda 1960: articles 6, 20 3). In theory, it proves the verification of the non-refoulement norm of international refugee law. Yet, heavily restricted rights of movement, rights for arbitrary acts and decisions of authorized officers to charge refugees are critical. Article 6 states that an officer "in his discretion without signifying any reason refuse to issue a permit" (Uganda 1960: articles 6). However, article 19 states that

> the Minister or the Director may in his discretion, by writing under his hand, direct that such refugee shall be detained in custody and any such direction shall be authority for any police or prison officer to arrest and detain such refugee in custody as an unconvicted prisoner (Uganda 1960: articles 19).

Moreover, Article 22 enables authorized persons to "arrest without warrant any person whom he has reasonable grounds for suspecting has committed an offence or a disciplinary offence [...]." Article 23 supports the above and even allows authorized persons to "use such force, including the use of firearms, as may be necessary to compel any refugee to comply with any order or direction, whether oral or in writing, given pursuant to the provisions of this Act" (Uganda 1960: articles 22, 23).

The 1960 refugee policy is the guiding policy for refugee protection and assistance in Uganda until the 2006 revised Refugee Act was agreed upon. The bill constitutes a revised policy for refugee protection and assistance and clearly manifests Uganda's goal to connect refugee assistance with development by "implement[ing] national and regional development plans relating to refugees, in line with current international refugee practices" (Article 8, 2 g). Due to the focus on the time scope from 1997 until 2006, the revised Refugee Act is not analyzed.

3. *Rhino Camp and Operations between 1997 and 2006*

3.1. Location and Context Information

The Government of Uganda allocated a large area for hosting refugee in the West Nile region. Rhino Camp is one of these settlements. It is situated in the Terego County of the Arua District, about 66 kilometers east of Arua town. It covers an area of approximately 225 square kilometers (DED LS/403 2001: 2). The location is indicated on the map below:

Figure 5. Location of Rhino Camp with Wanyange I and II as cluster examples.

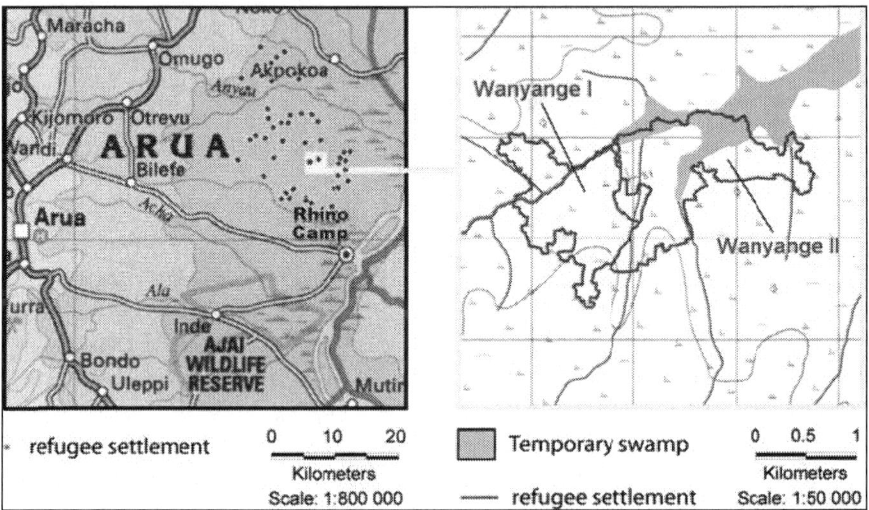

Topographically, Rhino Camp is located in a graben. The environmental study of IRD explains that "[t]he elevation varies in that area between 600 and 800 metres. On either side of the rift, the elevation rises sharply to over 900 metres on the East and to 1,100 metres on the West" (Beaudou et al. 2003: 30). The map below presents the topography of the settlement.

Figure 6. Topography of Rhino Camp.

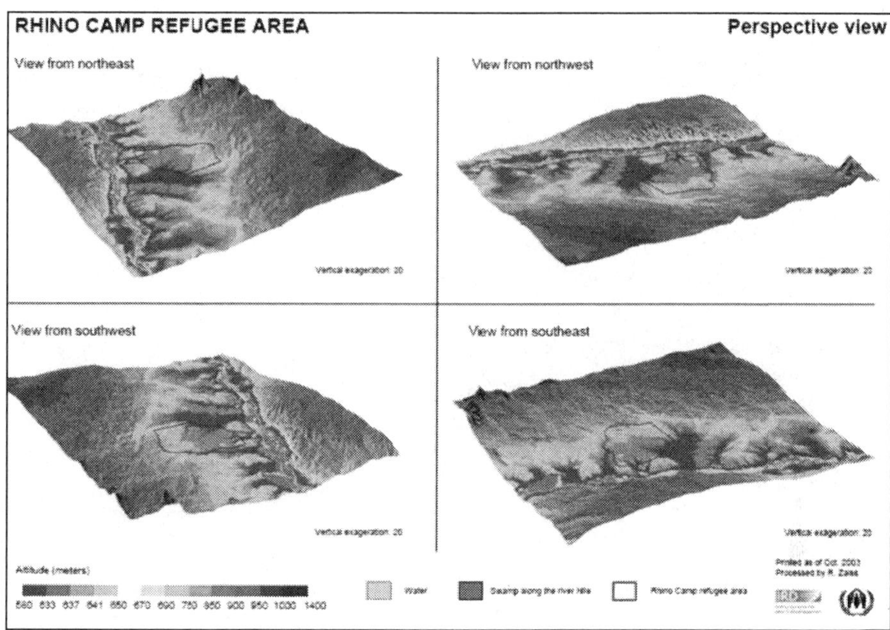

In regards to the regional context, it is to be noted that the West Nile region was neglected in comparison to other parts of Uganda. At time of allocation, this border region between Uganda, Sudan and DRC lacked socio-economic infrastructure and trade (Merkx 2000: 10). It was sparsely populated by nationals, underdeveloped, and "relatively impoverished and marginalized" (Kaiser 2005a: 8). A large size of land was allocated for refugee settlements. Merkx explains that

> [i]t is remarkable that the Government of Uganda was willing to allow refugees to occupy large areas in the north. The land itself was made available to the refugees by local communities, represented by elders and local councils. Land available for settlement was still abundant; the local population was not interested in settling in many areas because of their isolation and because of security problems. It should also be noted that settlement land is of rather poor quality with a lot of sandy soil (Merkx 2000: 18).

By allowing it to be used for refugee settlement, the region would benefit from activities through development. Infrastructure was going to be built and maintained. UNHCR with implementing partners would be able to set up local settlements in which refugees could become self-sufficient through agriculture. Hence, refugees and nationals alike were to benefit.

3.2. Structure and Capacity

Rhino Camp was established in 1992 as the first refugee settlement in the region. It has an estimated carrying capacity of 32,000 refugees, provided the national population within the settlement area would not increase. Despite this estimation, the number was reduced to 17,000 refugees in 1995 due to severe water shortages. Insecurity and spontaneous repatriation further caused a rapidly changing refugee population and destabilized the settlement and involved agencies (DED LS/403 1997: 2).

Rhino Camp has 10 zones and 42 clusters, which are set up as villages with local markets (DED LS/403 2001: 2). The zones and clusters are spread out in the area of the settlement. The map below presented in Figure 7 shows how Rhino Camp is set up.

Figure 7. Set-up of Rhino Camp and population density, 2001.

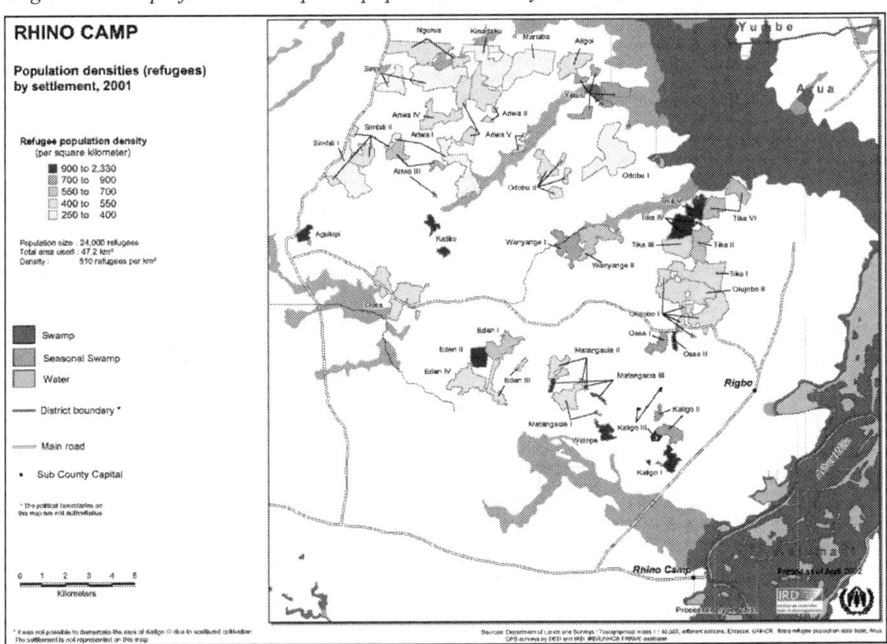

Clusters contain several compounds with huts in which people live. The huts are built with locally produced mud bricks and have grass-thatched roofs. UNHCR's camp structures typically use plastic tents for beneficiaries to live in. Since Rhino Camp is a local settlement, these plastic tents are very rare (Hoenig 2004: 6-7; personal observation).

Between 1997 and 2006 service delivery facilities were built and maintained. During these years, medical services were provided in four health centers in the settlement (namely, Siripi grade 3, Olujobo grade 3, Odobu grade 2 and Ocea grade 2). In addition, Arua town had the Arua District Hospital and the Koluba Mission Hospital. Access to education was provided through thirteen primary schools (namely Ocea, Kaligo, Olujobo, Siripi, Tika, Walope, Matangacia, Odobu, Eden, Yelulu, Ariwa, Wanyange, and Kiliadaku) and one secondary school (named Quiver Self Secondary School), as well as one skills training center called Ocea. Sixty-nine boreholes were drilled throughout the settlement and in walking distance of all refugees and nationals. Refugees and nationals were allowed to access medical and education services in the settlement. Their living standards were equal. One mosque and several churches under trees were spread all over the settlement (Interview Mwesigwa; 01.10.2010).

3.3. Beneficiaries: Number and Origin

The below table shows the refugee population statistics in Rhino Camp.

Table 4. Annual refugee population statistics from 1997 until 2006 in Rhino Camp.

1997	1998	1999	2000	2001
28,571	27,677	30,817	35,333	24,727

2002	2003	2004	2005	2006
25,453	**25,836**	**26,418**	**25,157**	**20,231**

The Government of Uganda recognized all refugees at Rhino Camp and granted them blanket *prima facie* status. Most refugees at Rhino Camp originated from rural areas and towns in South Sudan, mainly from Equatoria Province. The majority of Sudanese refugees were of Kakwa ethnicity from Yei County. Other ethnicities were Pojulu, Moru, Madi, Bari, Kuku, Kaliko and Zande. The Nilotic Dinka, Dinka-Nuer cattle keepers from Upper Nile and Bahr el-Ghazal and the Acholis from Eastern Equatoria, were minor groups. A few other South Sudanese tribes such as Lotuko and Didinga were present. Other beneficiaries were Congolese, Kenyans and Nigerians. The Congolese refugees were of Lendu and Hema origin. Most of the refugees had an agricultural background with some skilled artisans in masonry, carpentry, tailoring as well as mechanics and civil servants as teachers and health workers (DED LS/403 2001, 2003, 2006).

In Rhino Camp, refugees were not settled according to ethnicity or tribal origin. Villages were rather mixed. The map below shows where tribes settled and how dense settlements were.

Figure 8. Number of refugees by ethnic group and settlement, April 2002.

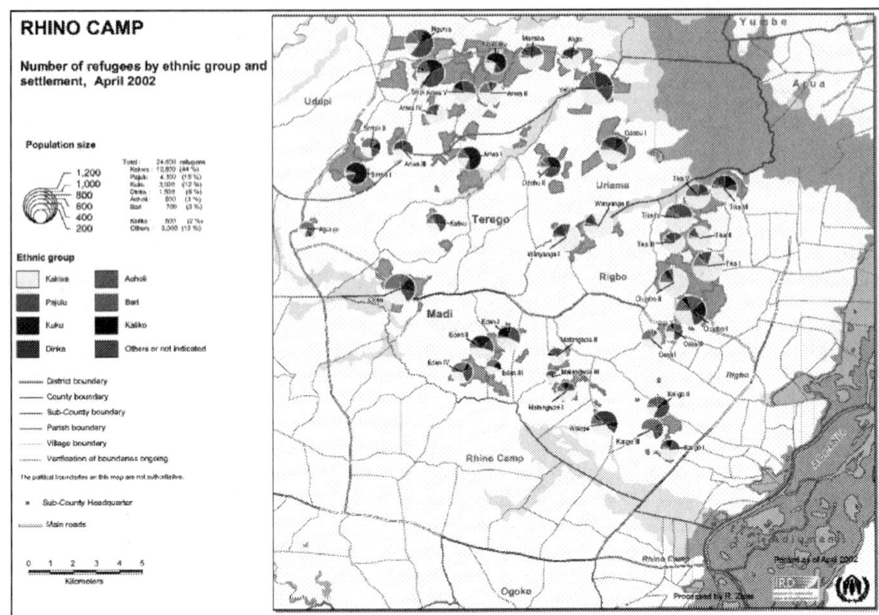

The national population living in or close to Rhino Camp was relatively small. An estimated 18,000 persons lived there (DED LS/403 2006: 6). The map below reveals that sparse population. Most villages were outside of Rhino Camp.

Figure 9. Number of refugees by ethnic group and settlement, 2002.

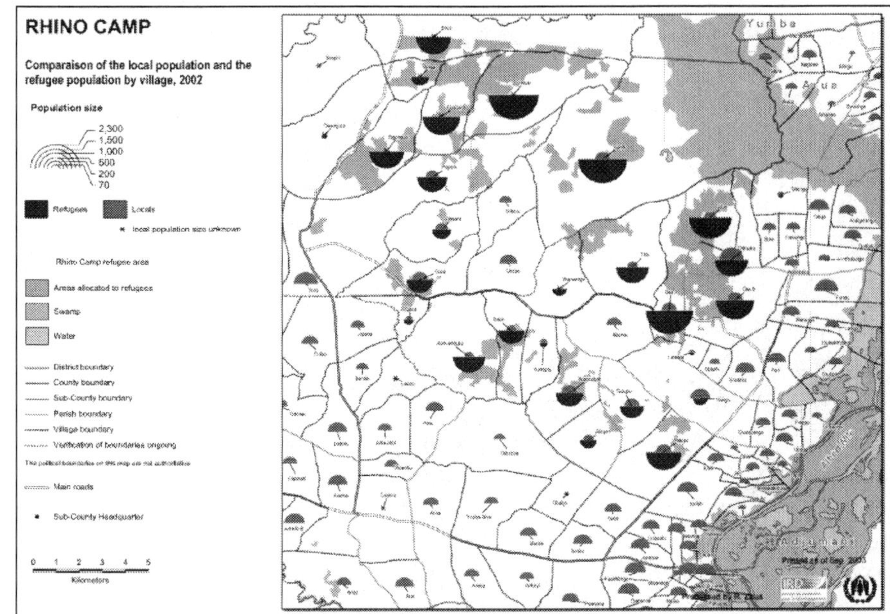

3.4. Beneficiaries: Gender Structures and Relations

Female and male refugees were settled and lived throughout Rhino Camp. The demographic age structure of female and male refugees is shown in Figure 10. According to the figure, it is traceable that the demographic age structure of female and male refugees was not even. Especially in the groups of 15 to 19 year olds, great differences are visible. Almost twice as many male as female refugees lived in Rhino Camp. Although less significant, the group of 20 to 24 year olds shows similar trends.

Figure 10. Age structure of the refugee population at Rhino Camp, end of year 2001.

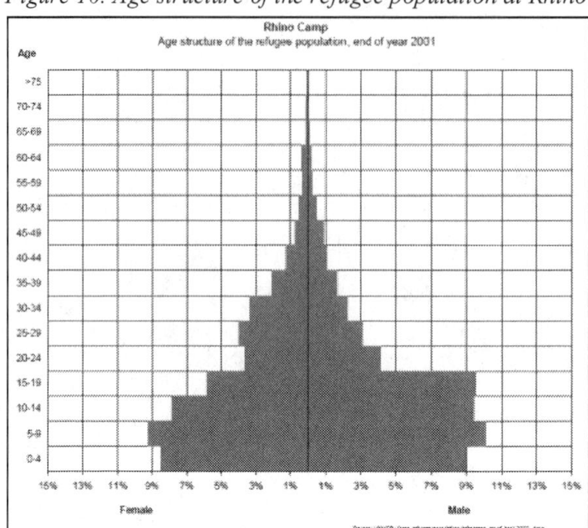

The size of households varied throughout the settlement of Rhino Camp. The map below reveals the broad extent of them in Rhino Camp.

Figure 11. Number of households by settlement, April 2002.

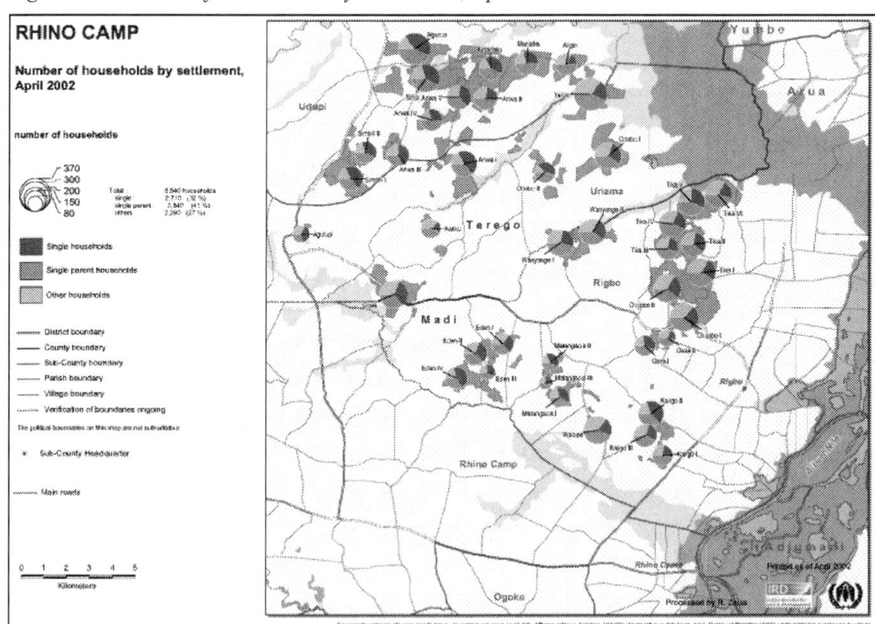

As shown, single households and single-parent households constituted the majority of all households. The map is lacking detailed information with regard to whether these single and single parent households were headed by women or men. This is of importance in order to distinguish if traditional gender structures in terms of family set-ups remain for refugees, or if they changed in a way that women possessed additional responsibilities. The table below identifies the lacking information and reveals the percentage of female and male single-parent households with respect to the age structures.

Table 5. Age of the head of family in one-parent families in Rhino Camp in 2001.

Age	Female	Male	Female	Male
0-4	0	1	0.00%	0.00%
5-9	4	2	0.10%	0.10%
10-14	2	3	0.10%	0.10%
15-19	59	38	1.70%	1.10%
20-24	396	81	11.20%	2.30%
25-29	615	144	17.40%	4.10%
30-34	644	202	18.20%	5.70%
35-39	371	157	10.50%	4.40%
40-44	248	118	7.00%	3.30%
45-49	**106**	**97**	**3.00%**	**2.70%**

Hence, it is to note that the great majority of single-parent households were headed by females. As noted above, single female-headed households with several children and single women are classified as especially vulnerable (DED LS/403 1998: 23).

However, how does the information about age structures and single-parent households affect the so-called gender roles? "[G]ender relations are an aspect of broader social relations and, like all social relations, are constituted through the rules, norms and practices by which resources are allocated, tasks and responsibilities are assigned, value is given and power mobilized" (Mulumba 2005: 176). In very general terms, gender relations comprise gender identities; "they invariably start from basic premises about masculine and feminine roles in a specific class and culture […]" (Mulumba 2005: 26). According to post-modern feminism, the sex-specific roles are to be clarified in order to deconstruct gender stereotyping and hence to promote the process towards equality. In order to do that, the very basic gender relations are to be understood.

Traditional gender role paradigms are based on ascribed role allocations. In very basic terms, the local Ugandan communities, as well as the refugee communities, are patriarchal and thus male-dominated. Men are superior to women. In her book *Gender and Development. The Role of Religion and Culture*, the Ugandan researcher Tuyizere explains gender roles as "job behavior in a given social context." She generally speaks about Africa and notes that

> [g]ender roles are socially defined and prescribed and they shape and condition tasks and responsibility into masculine or feminine. Gender roles are affected by factors such as age, class, religion, ethnicity, race, regional origins and history. It can also be affected by changes brought about through development interventions or efforts. Throughout the African continent, roles are divided according to sex. African society is patriarchal in nature, where men are seen at the centre. It is a culture that oppresses women. Gender has been defined as a set of roles which, like costumes or masks in the theatre, communicate to other people traits which are masculine or feminine. These include appearances, dress, attitudes, personalities, work (both in and outside the household), sexuality and family commitments. Most religious teachings have encouraged maintenance of traditional male and female roles. [...] Female roles in most African societies include cooking, doing housework, looking after children, fetching water, collecting firewood, digging, making pots and mats and grinding grain. Male roles include hunting, fishing, going to market, making weapons, building boars and minding. In Uganda most of the agricultural work is done by women (Tuyizere 2007: 125).

The Ugandan gender researcher Mulumba distinguished in her research the micro and macro level in the context of negotiating gender relations. At the micro level, women and men appear to "work out their own gender boundaries and norms in the privacy of their homes or in their workplaces or in social gatherings." However, at the macro level, "men have greater influence and through institutionalized frameworks such as religion and politics they have historically made decisions about women's well being" (Mulumba 2005: 26).

Exemplified in the Madi ethnic group of South Sudanese refugees[51], Mulumba extracted information that explains the type of their traditional gender relations. This incorporates the gender roles. In summary, Madi "are organized on a patrilineal clan structure and practice patrilocal marriage [which] means that the children belong to the husband's clan and family." Clan membership transmission proceeds through male members and their offspring. Women receive their membership through patrilineage. Marriages in one clan are not permitted. Reproduction is therefore patrilineal. This is perpetuated in ownership aspects. The residential lives of the Madi generally comprise "people from two to three generations living together in huts, either in a compound, or spread out within a clan area. Family clusters form the basic household. Men are figures of authority and all junior members, regardless of gender, are expected to respect their elders." The male offspring obtains special value and responsibilities due to the future authority role for maintaining and leading family and clan (Mulumba

51 Mulumba notes "I consider this information to be largely illustrative of the gender relations of the Southern Sudanese refugees in general. This is because the Madi have quite a number of similar characteristics as the other Sudanese including the Kuku, Kakwa and Bari. Moreover they comprise (35%) (out of the 8 ethnic groupings) of the total refugee population in Rhino Camp" (Mulumba 2005: 175-176).

2005: 176). Resources are transmitted patrilineally. While men receive land through their fathers, women obtain the right to use the land of their husbands and his family after marriage and giving birth to his children. "In case of land disputes, these were solved by clan elders" (Mulumba 2005: 178). Gender roles are traditionally patrilineal.

> Madi men are the head of households and make most important non-routine decisions. The behaviour of men is sanctioned by the clan elders to whom women and younger men may resort in case of family conflicts [...]. The men's role of protecting their wives and children ensured they have access to land. And when sick, he is supposed to make sure they receive the required treatment. [...] The women are expected to be submissive to their husbands and their in-laws irrespective of gender. They are expected to cultivate and provide food to their households and to help the husband with cash crops. In addition women are expected to undertake all the duties in the home that concern the wellbeing of the households. Thus, it is with the foregoing gender expectations that the socialization of girls and boys is undertaken. The socialization process is enforced further by participation in rituals such as child naming, marriage, death, burials and last funeral rites. Women's position in subordination changes with time. The elder wife assumes authority over her co-wives. It also changes when she acquires a daughter-in-law, whom she has power over (Mulumba 2005: 179).

Hence, the traditional role allocations between men and women are based on cultural and social factors and are historically formed. Among other things, polygamy is permitted (Mulumba 2005: 223).

The refugee situation changed the above explained gender relations and role allocations. Due to their flight, families and clans were separated, which disorganized the traditional settings. While at Rhino Camp, refugee men and women received land for residential and agricultural use. Hence, women were not dependent on men (Mulumba 2005: 179). By cultivating land, women took over men's traditional work. Mulumba found that women perceived this change "as a form of liberation, since [...] they have 'gone beyond culture'" (Mulumba 2005: 181). Refugee women perceived this process as becoming equal to the status of men. Despite the female perception, Mulumba indicates that these changes were provoked primarily "by the absence of men in the refugee settlements and their (men's) failure even when present to live up to the expected behavior" (Mulumba 2005: 181). Moreover, food was traditionally provided by men. In the refugee setting, however, food was merely provided as a part of assistance. In addition, women headed households and thus obtained additional responsibilities for decision making in household settings (Mulumba 2005: 179).

Traditional conflict resolution mechanisms through the elders of clans were also dysfunctional due to separation and refuge. Mulumba notes that the integration of different clans and tribes in communities at Rhino Camp affected these mechanisms: "the social support and conflict resolution mechanisms to a great extent also disintegrated." She also highlights that men felt cheated regarding their diminished authority. They consequently tended to solve disputes violently and women felt disempowered (Mulumba 2005: 179).[52]

Mulumba concludes by highlighting that women took over numerous additional responsibilities while in the refugee settlement. She explains "that the refugee experience increases the tasks and activities for the women and lessens men's" (Mulumba 2005: 182).[53]

3.5. Operating Actors

Since the establishment of Rhino Camp, the Office of the Prime Minister (OPM) and UNHCR have been involved as guiding institutions. Both have offices in Arua town (Bützer 2007: 65). OPM is in charge of refugee issues respectively for the Government of Uganda. While initially managed by UNHCR, the German Development Service (DED) took over the camp management in 1996 (DED LS/403 1997; 1998). DED constitutes the main implementing partner of UNHCR in Rhino Camp, which acts according to regularities and guidance of the agency. The general hierarchical structure involved UNHCR, OPM and DED as the main agencies since DED took over the camp management. UNHCR provides its implementing partner with programmatic concepts and guidclines, as well as required funds to realize adequate refugee assistance. OPM holds a supervisory function ensuring that operations proceed in accordance with agreements between UNHCR and the Government of Uganda. The actual implementation of projects is done by the DED Refugee/IDP Programme which is part of DED.

3.5.1. Government of Uganda and Office of the Prime Minister

The Government of Uganda and respectively the Office of the Prime Minister (OPM) provided land for the establishment of the settlements and covered the salaries and benefits of staff of OPM. This included staff assigned to the field in the settlement. Civil servants such as teachers, medical personnel and community workers were assigned to work in the settlements at the government's expense (DED LS/403 2001). The Directorate of Refugees of

52 In my research, no information was collected or found to falsify these statements.

53 Mulumba developed a list of responsibilities for men and women while at Rhino Camp. It reveals that women have quantitatively more responsibilities. (Mulumba 2005: 195)

OPM assumed responsibility in providing security and regulating public information, facilitating provision of land, moving relief items and providing work permits for relief workers. OPM also educated local authorities on the obligations of the government towards the refugees (DED LS/403 2001). The District of Arua, as part of the local Government of Uganda, provided supervisory visits and overall technical advice on refugee services in the key sectors of water and sanitation, education, forestry, community development and agriculture. District authorities furthermore assisted through seminars and workshops (DED LS/403 1997: 2).

3.5.2. United Nations High Commissioner for Refugees

UNHCR in cooperation with the Government of Uganda and especially OPM, has been in charge of ensuring adequate refugee assistance. As the lead actor in the refugee field globally, UNHCR identified the rather progressive approach that connects development with refugee protection and assistance. In 1993, UNHCR and the Government of Uganda committed themselves to a new strategy, which would improve ad-hoc and short-term refugee aid. The development aspect was integrated and became a central feature. Development refers to the belief that sustainable growth can be advanced through supporting the social, ecological, economic, and political stability of a country. This is to be done by operating in a politically consolidating and economically strengthening manner, as well as a commitment to natural resource protection and gender equality advancement.

3.5.3. German Development Service

The German Development Service (Deutscher Entwicklungsdienst, DED), and especially the DED Refugee/IDP Programme, has been the main implementing partner of UNHCR for activities in Rhino Camp. From 1994 to 1995, DED was only in charge of the health sector and related services. Engagement and responsibility of the organization expanded instantly; in 1996, DED became the lead agency for health, agriculture and forestry, construction, settlement, and community services. In 1997, DED took over the primary education sector as well (DED LS/403 1997: 2). While DED implemented activities financed by and under the overall guidance of UNHCR, DED also funded various additional activities. Besides short-term assistance measures, DED has facilitated the program through personnel in form of a Programme Coordinator and by providing funds to run the program office in Arua (DED LS/403 2007: 8-9).

3.5.4. World Food Programme

WFP has been involved in basic food assistance to refugees. Food rations consisted of cereals, pulses, CSB, salt, sugar and oil. WFP also provided funds to DED for the management of Extended Delivery Point and food monitors, as well as the overall responsibility of food distribution activities to refugees in settlements. The agency also implemented Food for Education (FFE) programs (DED LS/403 2007: 9). DED maintained a contract with WFP to ensure food security and assistance (DED LS/403 2001; 2006). Despite the necessity of food distribution, refugee assistance was aimed at supporting refugees to attain the level of self-sufficiency. This was targeted to be done through, i.e., agriculture.

3.5.5. Additional temporarily involved Actors

Between 1997 and 2007, several additional actors were operating or providing assistance in Rhino Camp on a short-term basis. The following actors are, among others, to be named (DED LS/403 1997 – 2007; cf. Bützer 2007: 65-66):

- UNFPA funded reproductive health activities and provided family planning support;
- Transcultural Psychosocial Organisation offered psychosocial counseling for traumatized people;
- Community Empowerment for Rural Development and Netherlands Development Organisation implemented projects on education in Arua District;
- German Technical Cooperation provided assistance through its Food and Nutrition Security project;
- Jesuit Refugee Service conducted peace education activities;
- UNICEF supported the improvement of water and sanitation in primary schools in Arua District;
- Right to Play supported sports activities in Rhino Camp;
- African Development Initiative implemented vocational and skills training and worked with loan schemes for refugees.

3.5.6. Steering and Leadership Structures

When looking at Rhino Camp, two different leadership structures need to be distinguished. On the one hand, organizational and operational program structures, which steer project execution. These structures define who makes decisions and who implements them. On the other hand, there were leadership structures among refugees. These structures identified which committees are in charge of specific issues.

The steering structure at Rhino Camp contained predominantly three actors:[54] OPM, UNHCR and DED. The decision-making level was led by the Government of Uganda and respectively OPM along with UNHCR. Both parties possessed primary roles.

OPM was responsible for providing security and regulating public information, in addition to facilitating the provision of land, movement of relief items and work permits for relief workers. OPM also educated local authorities on the obligations of the government to refugees.

As noted earlier, UNHCR is mandated to support refugees, IDPs, and other groups of disadvantaged people by means of emergency assistance, aid, and relief. UNHCR's mission is to build, manage, and maintain refugee camps and settlements, provide legal protection and advice as well as to supply beneficiaries with shelter, food, water, sanitation, and medical care in order to meet their basic needs (UNHCR 2007: 21). In the example of Rhino Camp, UNHCR registered refugees and ensured their legal protection and tracing through its partner, the Red Cross Society. It operated through an implementing partner by providing financial assistance to the implementing partner, DED, which in turn realized activities. Hence, OPM and UNHCR guide processes and make decisions, which are implemented by DED.

DED and in particular the DED Refugee/IDP Programme was the implementing partner in charge of general settlement management of Rhino Camp, including management of infrastructure, such as road maintenance, the water sector and community services, including skills training. Sectoral committees on food, water, health etc. were formed by the community with the advice of OPM and support of DED.

Official leadership structures existed among refugees in Rhino Camp as well. The overall management of the settlement fell under the Refugee Welfare Council (RWC), which was equivalent to Local Council (LC) III in the national local council system. Each RWC is composed of ten refugee members, which was headed by a Chairperson and a Vice Chairperson and a Secretary General. The post of the Vice Chairperson was reserved for women only. The rest of the members were referred to as Secretaries for law and order, education, finance,

54 Other short-term actors might be involved in operational processes. However, in the context of the research, only three parties are involved over the long term and have key roles. The steering structure presented is based on the interview with Astrid Peter, former Programme Coordinator (Interview Peter; 01.12.2010).

women affairs, youth and adolescence, production/environment and people with disabilities. It was mutually agreed that at least thirty per cent of the representatives have to be women. Under the RWC, there are Point/Zonal Executives made up of ten members from each point/zone. This was equivalent to the LC II system in the national setting. The level below the point/zone set-up was the Village executive. The lowest level in the settlement setting was the block with one leader per block (DED LS/403 2005: 4; DED LS/403 2006: 5). Hence, existing local leadership structures were replicate and applied.

3.6. Operational Sectors

The main operational areas in Rhino Camp were as follows:

Settlement management and General Project Management Services: These management activities ensure an effective and efficient execution of activities to provide basic services to meet the needs of beneficiaries. Organizational processes are being designed and realized.

Health and nutrition: Activities under health and nutrition target to ensure access to primary care in terms of preventive, as well as curative actions of refugees. Reproductive and maternal health is to be provided and aims to reduce mortality rates of mothers and children. Sufficient food ratios according to international standards are to be handed to refugees and therewith prevent malnutrition. HIV and Aids control and prevention measures are in place and offered to beneficiaries, with the aim to reduce additional infections (DED LS/403 2006: 26-27).

Education: Primary education for refugee children is a basic need that is to be met. Therefore, refugee children and adolescents are offered to attend school to acquire basic knowledge, skills and complete recognized levels of qualification. In this context, required furniture and equipment along with scholastic and sports materials and qualified staff are procured to provide these services (DED LS/403 2006: 44-49). In addition, vocational trainings were also offered at Ocea Skills Training Center. Among others, trainings was given in bricklaying and concrete practice, carpentry, tailoring, tin and blacksmithing, woodcarving, agriculture and domestic science (DED LS/403 2006: 7).

Food: Food ratios according to the international standard are to be provided to refugees in order to meet their basic needs. WFP was responsible for providing basic and supplementary food assistance; despite support, self-sufficiency of refugees was targeted. In addition, extended delivery points (EDPs) were set up for the management of food storage and delivery (DED LS/403 2001: 5).

Water: Access to adequate quantities of clean drinking water and hygiene purposes are also a basic need of refugees, which needs to be met. Water supply plans of operation are to be developed and implemented according to updated refugee population data. At Rhino Camp, water was not only provided in tanks, but also through boreholes, which were maintained and rehabilitated regularly in order to remain sustainable. Boreholes were not to be too far away from beneficiaries. DED targeted a distance to the water points of not more than 500 meters. To promote involvement and self-reliance, refugees formed and participated in community-based water management committees with emphasis on female representation. These water management committees were knowledgeable of safe water chains and participatory hygiene and sanitation transformation (DED LS/403 2006: 16-21).

Sanitation: Whether in protracted refugee situations or in short-term camp conditions, sanitation has a great impact on health. Well-organized sanitation through hygiene and latrines will support healthy conditions. Hence, risks of diseases and their transmission and outbreaks among the beneficiaries are reduced. Along with that, awareness building measures are to be promoted. Sanitation and hygiene promotion committee members are knowledgeable in vector control and personal hygiene, and raise awareness among the population. Peer trainings or child-to-child trainings shall be conducted to inform each other about hygiene standards (DED LS/403 2006: 22-25).

Infrastructure and shelter: This sector primary focuses on refugees living in adequate conditions and having access to relevant service deliveries. In particular, access to farming land, residential plots and markets is to be ensured. Physical security plays an important role. Road maintenance and improvement of school and health facilities also fall under this sector (DED LS/403 2006: 35-37).

Community Service: Community services projects seek to improve the capacity of refugees and nationals to meet their social human and emotional needs and support vulnerable community members. Prevention and treatment of SGBV, as well as awareness building is an integral part of community service to strengthen structures. Gender mainstreaming aims to promote women's participation in projects. Also, among others, nursery schools and kindergartens and adult literacy classes are supported (DED LS/403 2006: 38-43).

Community-based environmental management: Environmental operations and sensitization activities have been conducted at Rhino Camp since refugees were settled. One of the major and most durable activities was to re-forest land taken for refugees. The more refugees came, the more wood they needed for fire, building houses etc. Sensitization activities are multifaceted and captured among others environmental-friendly behavior, energy-saving stoves and agricultural methods. To up-scale operations, DED started to implement a sub-project precisely focusing on community-based environmental management; it was funded by UNHCR and ran under LS 453. It addressed the negative impact of the settlement activities related to residing refugees on the environment.

Depletion of vegetation is one of the immediate effects refugees caused on the environment due to a sudden increase in demand for firewood, house materials, land clearance for settlement and agriculture (DED LS/453 2006).

Voluntary Repatriation: Due to overall peaceful conditions, voluntary repatriation of refugees back to South Sudan was offered from 2006 onwards. The signing of the Comprehensive Peace Agreement between the SPLM/A and the Government of Sudan laid the foundation for the return to their country of origin. Prior to that, a photographic refugee registration exercise was conducted in 2006 to grasp the actual scope of the population. In March 2006, a tripartite agreement was signed between the Government of Uganda, the Government of National Unity of the Sudan and UNHCR. Based on that, DED received an additional sub-project on "Voluntary Repatriation of Sudanese Refugees from Uganda" (RP 331). This agreement enabled the legal and voluntary return of Sudanese refugees to their country of origin (DED RP/331 2009: 2-7).

Cross-cutting issues and policy priorities: According to the annual reports of DED, refugee women/gender equality, specific needs of children and adolescents, disabled persons and elderly, HIV/AIDS and environment were treated as cross-cutting issues and policy priorities. Hence, specific needs of these most vulnerable groups and themes are considered.

4. *Analysis of Operations*

As shown above, refugee protection and assistance at Rhino Camp was complex. In cooperation with partners, needs of beneficiaries were pursued to be met. The main operational sectors were settlement management and general project management services, health and nutrition, education, food, water and sanitation, infrastructure and shelter, community service, environment and forestry.

While the first years up until 1999 rather demonstrated an emergency aid character in terms of reacting to a challenge, conditions successively stabilized. From 1999 onwards, the development orientation became clearly visible. How is the development orientation visible? Which strategies contribute to the development orientation of refugee assistance? Is the implemented development-oriented refugee assistance at Rhino Camp sustainable, effective and gender-sensitive? These are the guiding questions when analyzing the operations.

4.1. Main Strategies and Policies

In accordance with the definition by Sen, development is understood as "a process of expanding the real freedoms that people enjoy" (Sen 1999: 10, xii).

Development-oriented refugee assistance aims to prevent protracted refugee situations. Finding durable solutions is the superior objective of refugee assistance, regardless of the possible integration of development. Resettlement, repatriation and local integration have been accepted as the durable solutions. While looking for joint durable solutions, development offers interim, if not even the final solution. By using initiatives such as self-reliance strategies as interim solutions, refugees may build capacity and are enabled to escape lives in encampment in which needs are unsatisfied. Has this been achieved at Rhino Camp? Which strategies may have contributed to the development orientation of refugee assistance?

4.1.1. Local Settlement Schemes

Several strategies contributed to development orientation in refugee assistance at Rhino Camp. First and foremost, local settlement schemes instead of tent arrangements in camps have been set up in the early 1990s (Payne 1998: 7). Rhino Camp's local settlement was established in 1992 (DED LS/403 2006).

After refugees were relocated from transit camps to settlements, they received two plots of land for residential and agricultural usage. Local settlement schemes were arranged as villages. Refugees were able to move within the surrounding area and cultivate their land (Government of Uganda 1999).

Although research often stated that the local settlement scheme has been existing since the 1990s in Uganda (Merkx 2000: 17), "[t]he policy of local settlement has been in place since the arrival of the early refugees in Uganda (1940s/50s). It is estimated that Government of Uganda (GOU) has allocated well-over 3300 km^2 of land to refugees in consultation with communities and Districts" (RLSS Mission Report 2004/03: 2).

As a part of the local settlement scheme, Rhino Camp was set up in form of villages. It has 10 zones and 42 clusters with local markets (DED LS/403 2001: 2). Clusters have several residential compounds with huts. The huts were constructed with locally-produced mud bricks and had grass-thatched roofs (Hoenig 2004: 6-7). Refugees also received plots of land for agricultural use. The agricultural plots had a size of 0.3 ha (Beaudou et al. 2003: 71).

Access to services was provided to refugees and local communities. Medical services were made available in four health centers in the settlement and one hospital in Arua town, education in thirteen primary schools and one secondary school (Interview Mwesigwa; 01.10.2010).

4.1.2. Self-Reliance Strategy

The overall goal of Uganda's Self-Reliance Strategy (SRS)[55] policy is "to improve the standard of living of the people in Moyo, Arua and Adjumani districts, including the refugees", while the ultimate goal is

> to integrate the services to refugees in the eight key sectors of assistance (health; education; community services; agricultural production; income generation; environmental protection; water and sanitation, and infrastructure) currently provided for the refugees into regular government structures and policies. This means also enhancing the government's (and district) capacity to take over this responsibility and monitor and coordinate the implementation of its refugee policy (RLSS Mission Report 2004/03: 3).

The specific objectives are:

- to empower refugees and nationals in the area to the extent that they will be able to support themselves; and
- to establish mechanisms that will ensure integration of services for the refugees with those of the nationals (RLSS Mission Report 2004/03: 3).

The key elements of Uganda's SRS are as follows:

> (i) allocation of land to refugees in designated "settlements" (for both homestead and agricultural purposes), to enable refugees to become self-sufficient in food production; (ii) relatively free access of refugees (registered or self-settled) to education, health and other facilities built by the government; (iii) the openness and generosity of local communities – related to the fact that many Ugandans had been refugees once and the cultural and ethnic affinities between Ugandans and many of the refugees – which has been a major factor in facilitating refugee integration into Ugandan society (RLSS Mission Report 2004/03: V).

According to Kaiser, "[a]t the time this was written in 1999 it was envisaged that, by 2003, refugees would be able to grow or buy their own food, access and pay for basic services, and maintain self-sustaining community structures" (Kaiser 2005b: 355). By inheriting SRS activities in district development plans, dual structures and "'special treatment' of refugees by UNHCR and NGO implementing partners" were to be avoided (Kaiser 2005b: 355).

In line with that, Uganda's SRS was pursued based on the local settlement schemes and was done in that manner at Rhino Camp. Agriculture was promoted and aimed for. By means of agriculture, involved agencies encouraged beneficiaries to become engaged in individual food production and therefore less

55 Self-reliance is defined by UNHCR as "the ability of an individual, household or community to depend (rely) on their own resources (physical, social and natural capital or assets), judgment and capabilities with minimal external assistance in meeting basic needs, and without resorting to activities that irreversibly deplete the household or community resource base" (UNHCR 2005c: Glossary 12).

depended on food distribution. The 'normal' life was intended to be stabilized by means of a rather self-sufficient life style instead of being reliant on aid. Agencies facilitated that process through providing seeds and seedlings along with technical support (DED LS/403 2001: 44). Through that, self-reliance of refugees was promoted and SRS became the main objective in refugee policies.

However, Uganda's SRS only aimed to integrate services and service structures. This is clearly outlined as an objective of the policy, namely "to establish mechanisms that will ensure integration of services for the refugees with those of the nationals" (RLSS Mission Report 2004/03: 3). Hence, and as noted in research, SRS rather seeks to reduce expenses and to avoid dual service structures. It also intends to integrate "refugee assistance, rather than the refugees themselves [...]. A programme of social integration is far from being the objective of the strategy" (Kaiser 2005b: 355). It subsequently does not intend to promote local integration processes of refugees within neighboring local communities in the West Nile region.

Service integration is nevertheless traceable. Infrastructural development initiatives and activities further promoted the functionality of the local settlements and the SRS. The DED-managed database on infrastructure reveals that 350 infrastructural facilities were constructed at Rhino Camp. These fall under the categories of education, health facility, sanitation facility, residential, office, security facility, energy, store, communication, maintenance, environment, production, physical education/exercise, roads, bridges, water, health centers, and culverts. Developments not only targeted to meet basic needs through such facilities as health and educational centers. Also, sanitation facilities such as pit latrines, boreholes for improved water access, security, roads and bridges were set up. Energy was mostly provided by generators, which ran with fuel. Offices and residential buildings were predominantly established for personnel of the implementing agency.

The infrastructure developments were mainly built with local materials. All facilities were used by refugee and locals. In an interview, the former coordinator of the DED Refugee/IDP Programme, Astrid Peter, confirmed the infrastructure's mutual benefit for refugees and locals. She said, "[t]he refugees and the local population in a lot of cases shared the same facilities, i.e. health centres, schools and boreholes" (Interview Peter; 01.12.2010).

Despite the variety of activities, DED's database revealed that infrastructure developments lacked usability and functionality. The state of some infrastructure was insufficient.[56] Over time, especially frequently used facilities such as pit latrines and boreholes did not function anymore. It was not noted in the database whether or not regular and adequate maintenance activities were undertaken. Hence, it was not clear at that point (DED 2008).

Another factor of SRS is agriculture. The goal of agricultural production is to promote empowerment of "refugees and nationals in the area to the extent that they will be able to support themselves" according to the SRS policy (RLSS Mission Report 2004/03: 3). The agricultural plots are provided to beneficiaries for them to cultivate and receive crops. This may be seen as a step towards self-sufficiency. While researchers continue to indicate the assumption of insufficiently fertile soil in Rhino Camp (Kaiser 2006: 611f; Merkx 2000: 18; Hoenig 2004: 17, 19; Orach/Brouwere 2005: 54), a geographical study finally provides evidence and proof for the above criticism. The study is about the "Geographical information system, environment and camp planning in refugee hosting areas". Findings reveal that neither size of agricultural plots nor soil quality nor applied farming methods are satisfactory.

Sizes of plots are insufficient according to the study.

> We can say then that the larger the family (with, by consequence, a larger number of young children and old people) the smaller becomes the proportion of its members who are active and available for working in the fields. That boils down to saying that the larger the family, the less are the conditions adequate to be able to rely on agriculture for survival (Beaudou et al. 2003: 68-69).

Later, the study concludes that the "agricultural site surface areas are insufficient for ensuring respect of the allocation rule of 0.3 ha per refugee, […] the cultivated land surface per refugee is around 0.15 ha". The size of agricultural plots were therefore too small and "should distinguish – for each family -, the allocated land surface from that which is in cultivation". Hence, the study proposes to determine the size of agricultural plots on the number of family members (Beaudou et al. 2003: 71).

The soil quality is not only an issue refugees complain about. The sandy and poor soil prevents them from conducting fruitful farming (Kaiser 2005a: 22). The environmental study verifies the unsuitable soil conditions for farming in connection with the existent vegetation. It reveals that Rhino Camp had little rainfall due to its location "on the floor of the rift [, as shown in the map of *Figure 6. Topography of Rhino Camp*]. Moreover, the temperature is higher during the whole year. Evapotranspiration by the vegetation is higher and sandy soils have a low water-retention capacity" (Beaudou et al. 2003: 38). The study

56 An analysis of the state of all infrastructures would go beyond the scope of research.

later concludes that "those [areas] located in flood zones in Rhino Camp offer distinctly less favourable conditions for agriculture" (Beaudou et al. 2003: 40). Moreover, the study distinctively announces that "some land proves to be unsuitable for agriculture" (Beaudou et al. 2003: 70).

Fallow seasons are crucial for agricultural cycles. Continuous use of soil and practicing agriculture without a crop-free period will decrease the productivity and fertility of the land.

> By taking account of the existence of land impossible to cultivate, the low values of these figures appears to confirm that fallowing is only practised when the soils have lost the essential part of their fertility. Owing to this, the indications are that the non-respect of the rule of 0.3 ha per refugee leads farmers to bring down the extent of land surface cultivated without any real possibility of practising the necessary fallow cycle. In the end, the excessive population load per agricultural site (or the insufficient surface area of sites in relation to the number of refugees) is threatening both the prospect of any true food self-sufficiency and the conservation of the environmental resources (Beaudou et al. 2003: 70).

The density of the refugee population created additional agricultural problems. The population was unequally spread across the area of Rhino Camp, which the map of *Figure 8. Number of refugees by ethnic group and settlement, April 2002* shows. The extent of agricultural land is insufficient for the capacity of refugees Rhino Camp can hold and "[t]his deficit poses an extremely serious problem" (Beaudou et al. 2003: 67). The study calculates "whereas with 24,665 refugees, the total surface area of all agricultural land put together should not be less than 7400 ha, at the very minimum 3490 ha is lacking" (Beaudou et al. 2003: 67).

It is to conclude that SRS was implemented, and services were integrated in all eight sectors of "health; education; community services; agricultural production; income generation; environmental protection; water and sanitation, and infrastructure" (RLSS Mission Report 2004/03: 3). While SRS was officially initiated in 1999, some activities and projects implemented at Rhino Camp aimed at the overall goal of improving living standards, as well as at the specific objective to empower refugees and nationals. While agricultural constrains existed, other activities were of benefit. Among others, schools, skills and vocational trainings were offered at Ocea Skills Trainings Centre to refugees and nationals already in 1997. Skills trainings in "leather, carpentry, tailoring and blacksmith" were offered as income-generating activities, which in turn empower participants (DED LS/403 1997: 17).

4.1.3. Local Integration

Local integration is understood to be one of the durable solutions promoted by UNHCR. According to UNHCR, "[i]t is based on the understanding that those refugees, who are unable to repatriate and are willing to integrate locally, will find a solution to their plight in their country of asylum" (UNHCR 2003d: 24).

Based on Uganda's SRS, local integration was not targeted in the manner defined above. Integration focused on the integration of services. It did not mean to integrate refugees into local communities.[57] Yet, according to the annual reports of the DED Refugee/IDP Programme, several efforts appear to have been undertaken in Rhino Camp to pursue local integration, which was not limited to service structures (DED LS/403 2001: 2; DED LS/403 2006: 3).

At Rhino Camp, local integration was partly realized through a twofold approach. On the one hand, refugees and nationals were provided with access to services through SRS, such as health care and education, and organized recreational sports and joint social events. Services and service structures were aligned with national systems in accordance with SRS (RLSS Mission Report 2004/03). Thereby, equal treatment was promoted and refugees were not perceived by nationals as being in an aid-receiving position. Potential disputes about resource distribution were therefore prevented. On the other hand, leadership structures of and within refugee communities were adjusted to local government structures. Among others, the RWC, which assumed the overall management of the settlement, was set up in the same way as the LC III in the national local council system. Point/Zonal Executives were below the RWC and equivalent to the LC II system in the national setting (DED LS/403 1999: 30; DED LS/403 2005: 5).

Participation of refugees and nationals was promoted throughout program activities. For example, already in 1999, water committees for boreholes were created. Boreholes were used by refugees and nationals. The committees were to ensure maintenance and functionality of the facilities as well as awareness regarding the usage of the boreholes. The committees consisted of nationals and refugees (DED LS/403 1999: 12). By means of such integration efforts, participation as well as local integration was promoted to some extent.

In spite of that, the focus remained on service integration and coherence. Interviews revealed the same. The former Assistant Programme Coordinator for Rhino Camp stated in an interview that integration was conducted rather automatically due to the long-lasting stay of refugees in Uganda's settlements. She said "[r]efugees have been integrated, it is a gradual process that has no clear planning but given the long period refugees have stayed, integration has come automatically as they continue to coexist" (Interview Namyalo; 12.01.2011).

57 The SRS pursues the object "to establish mechanisms that will ensure the integration of services for the refugees with those of the nationals" (RLSS Mission Report 2004/03: 3).

The former Programme Coordinator of the DED Refugee/IDP Programme revealed in an interview, that although refugee and national communities were enabled to use facilities, this "did not necessary lead to integration." Lives rather proceeded side by side. "Friction between the two communities remained. It is my impression that integration remained the exception rather than the rule" (Interview Peter; 01.12.2010).

In line with her information, the former Head of Section Agriculture of the DED Refugee/IDP Programme, Moses Obbo gave the following explanation.

> The very fact that refugee settlement were distinctly curved out and demarcated from the hosting communities means that there was little or no integration of the two communities. The refugee settlements were located in areas that were perceived to be non-occupied or least populated by local nationals [...] (Interview Obbo; 08.01.2011).

Despite different perspectives, local integration was not targeted according to SRS. Only structures were to be aligned with and integrated in national systems.

4.1.4. Development Assistance for Refugees-Hosting Areas

The program on Development Assistance for Refugees-Hosting Areas (DAR) is based on SRS. The overall goal of DAR

> is to improve the overall standard of living of Refugees and the hosting communities, with special emphasis on increasing household and communal resources that serve to reduce poverty and foster durable solutions given their specific social-economic needs (Wafula, OPM 2010).

Refugee hosting regions are predominantly under-developed, which was already targeted to be improved through SRS. With DAR, the Government of Uganda and UNHCR aim to "address some of the problems of poverty and under-development in refugee hosting districts which could promote further peace, security and stability in the region." The objectives are

- Burden sharing with the host country
- Development of the host community
- Gender equality, dignity and improved quality of life of both refugees and host communities
- Empowerment and enhancement of productive capacities and self reliance of refugees, particularly of women, pending durable solutions (RLSS/ DOS Mission Report 2003: 6).

DAR aims to assist the broader refugee-hosting communities and is therefore not necessarily implemented in the direct context of refugee settlements. Astrid Peter and Safinah Namyalo indicated during interviews that DAR was not realized in Rhino Camp (Interview Peter; 01.12.2010; Interview Namyalo; 12.01.2010).

Nevertheless, activities that run under DAR add to the development orientation of refugee assistance in the West Nile region. It can be observed as conflict-preventing initiatives since refugees are not merely the recipients of aid. Aid, assistance and benefits are shared. Local communities benefitting from DAR are assumed to be aware of it and also receive assistance. Refugees may therefore not be perceived as the recipients of international goods only.

4.2. Features for Development-oriented Refugee Assistance met?

In order to 'measure' if refugee assistance at Rhino Camp was development-oriented, the elaborated features are to be applied. These would then also provide information on sustainability, effectiveness and gender sensitivity. Hereafter, operations at Rhino Camp are analyzed against the features.

4.2.1. Involved Actors

- *Political will* refers to the ability of donors and host countries to engage in development-oriented refugee assistance. Based on the abovementioned analysis, it is to conclude that political will was given. The North and South were generally able to share burdens. The Government of Uganda had the ability to provide land for local settlement schemes for refugees to engage in agriculture and become self-sufficient and self-reliant. This indicates the aim for sustainability and improved livelihood conditions. Uganda's restrictive refugee law based on the Control of Alien Refugees Act, Cap. 64 of 1960 (Uganda 1960) is to be observed critically because it reduces refugees' livelihoods. Moreover, SRS involves environmental protection and hence the protection of natural resources as one key element (RLSS Mission Report 2004/03: 3). This leads to the aim to implement development-oriented refugee assistance in a sustainable and efficient way for the nature in the refugee hosting region in Uganda. However, SRS predominantly concentrates on the integration of service structures in national systems. It is not intended to integrate refugees. Moreover, SRS neither incorporates a gender perspective nor does it promote gender-sensitive programming. Its midterm review nevertheless refers to the need to engage in gender mainstreaming in the context of the follow-up policy of DAR. Gender mainstreaming, however, remains vague and undefined; specific activities or an action plan are not noted (RLSS Mission Report 2004/03). In DAR, the Government of Uganda agreed to promote "[g]ender equality, dignity and improved quality of life of both refugees and host communities" (RLSS/ DOS 03/11: 6). This appears to generally state the commitment to promote gender-sensitive programs. However, DAR programs are not implemented in the area of Rhino Camp. It is thus to infer, that these gender-sensitive programs do not reach refugees and have little, if any, effect and impact on program measures for refugees.

Northern donors appear to have provided UNHCR with sufficient funds for long-term assistance at Rhino Camp.[58] To what extend additional funds were needed to provide more elaborated assistance, is not possible to distinguish due to the lack of access to specific budget-related information. Nevertheless, based on the allocation of land from the side of the hosting country of Uganda and the long-term assistance of refugees from the side of donors through UNHCR, it is to conclude that political will was present in principle.

- *Political willingness* refers to the dedication of the Government of Uganda, UNHCR and donors to link refugee protection and assistance with development initiatives and hence to share burdens. The willingness to provide land to implement refugee assistance was given by the Government of Uganda. Moreover, the government agreed to establish the local settlements, developed SRS and intended to apply local integration of services and infrastructures. The positive effect for Uganda was the promotion and support of the development of the West Nile region. The focus was therefore not only on refugee assistance, but also on developing the rather neglected region. Refugee communities and implementing agencies used natural resources while they were on the allocated land. Regional profit was extracted through infrastructural development and service provision to local communities. Moreover, DAR targeted directly national host communities as primary beneficiaries who benefited through initiatives. As explained above, the willingness to promote gender sensitivity in programs remains questionable due to the reasons stated above. It is therefore to conclude that the Government of Uganda indeed shows willingness to host refugees; nevertheless, gender aspects appear to be of little importance. Sustainable development and natural protection seem to be positioned higher on the agenda, which is proven through the environmental-friendly local settlement schemes and infrastructural initiatives.

UNHCR along with the funding donors invested funds in order to engage in strategies and programs. UNHCR in Uganda receives its operational guidelines from the respective headquarters. Thereby, there is room to individually plan

58 Neither budgets and funding amounts, nor planning meetings were accessible or could be attended. UNHCR publishes budget amounts for entire countries. However, this information does not help to discern how much of a financial contribution is allocated for each refugee settlement or program. Hence, the political will cannot be analyzed in terms of financial contributions or earmarked contributions by donors and donor states. This constitutes a limit to draw a rather holistic conclusion on the political will of Northern and Southern states.

program activities. DED's reports provide insight to the programming focus, which now helps to conclude whether and to what extend UNHCR had the willingness to implement sustainable, efficient and gender-sensitive programs. The conclusion is possible to be drawn since the reports are based on submitted proposals by DED, which UNHCR agrees with. Hence, although the proposals were not accessed, an objective conclusion is possible. Based on the information collected through DED's annual reports, the main operational focus was on care and maintenance assistance to refugees. This includes providing aid in the various sectors of settlement management and general project management services, health and nutrition, education, food, water and sanitation, infrastructure and shelter, community services, environment and forestry. In the context of gender-sensitive programming, the main focus was on meeting the needs of women and providing political participation. In addition, some campaigns were realized. It is therefore to conclude, that based on the collected information the willingness to promote and reach progress towards gender equality in the refugee and local communities appears to be little. While sustainable development and efficiency is discernible through the various infrastructural and natural resource activities, comparatively little was done to achieve gender sensitivity.

- *Initial global consultations* are understood to be trend-setting to establish agreements and cooperation between Northern donors and Southern refugee hosts. These global consultations take place at a high international level of decision-makers including governments, international organizations and other relevant institutions. In *Chapter V, 3. Recent Progress under the Umbrella of the TDA*, a number of global initiatives to commence and improve relevant global consultation is listed. The importance to link refugee assistance with development was accepted by the international community. Through different fora, authorities discussed ways to come to conclusions and to realize ideas. Since global consultations and initial agreements are not merely guided by single nations such as the Government of Uganda or agencies such as UNHCR, it is not traceable to what extent the subject of the case study located in Uganda benefitted from it. Additional information can therefore not be provided at this point. Nevertheless, it is traceable that discussions about the significance of integrating development into refugee assistance have been taking place. Since Uganda engages in the development orientation since the 1960s (Merkx 2000: 13-16), it can be assumed that global debates may have had an effect.
- *Collaboration* of involved actors is understood to be essential to plan, to implement and to evaluate programs targeting development-oriented refugee assistance coherently and to act in concert. It is also significant in order to plan and implement programs that incorporate sustainable, efficient and gender-sensitive results.

According to the annual reports of DED, involved actors complement each other well. A clear steering structure was in place and implementation was done in accordance to it. The former Programme Coordinator confirmed the sufficiency of collaboration of UNHCR, OPM and DED at Rhino Camp. Quarterly coordination meetings took place for all stakeholders involved. However, she indicated the need for consistent and regular coordination meetings at the settlement level (Interview Peter; 01.12.2010).

At this point of time, it is impossible to objectively verify or falsify if collaboration of actors involved in programming at Rhino Camp collaborated in a way that ensured sustainable, efficient and gender-sensitive operations. To identify how the collaboration contributed to programming operations that are sustainable, efficient and gender-sensitive, the participation of planning meetings over the research period may have been helpful. If it would have been possible to access minutes and protocols of meetings, the chosen focus and set of activities including the respective argumentation may have led to a conclusion. This was, however, not possible. Based on the annual reports, it is to conclude that the overall collaboration between the involved actors existed.

- *Regular correspondence* of involved actors is understood to be important. The regular monitoring reports on monthly basis, as well as bi-annual and annual reports reveal official correspondence with regard to progress. In addition to that, personal meetings with all stakeholders including UNHCR, OPM and DED took place on a quarterly basis at district level in Arua. In addition, as the Programme Coordinator explained during an interview, "[t]here also are impromptu meetings, usually on a bilateral basis, of the agencies whenever the need arises" (Interview Peter; 01.12.2010). At the settlement level, the former Assistance Programme Coordinator for Rhino Camp noted that meetings were scheduled "daily/whenever need arises since all agencies are present in the settlement" (Interview Namyalo; 12.01.2010).

Hence, regular correspondence took place. Although it is not discernible to what extent correspondences of actors involved in programming at Rhino Camp ensured that operations were sustainable, efficient and gender-sensitive. Since the interviewees mentioned that meetings were held whenever need arose, it is assumable that programmatic gaps may have been discussed to find alternative methods. This would in turn refer to the support of sustainable, efficient and gender-sensitive operations; though, it does not prove it. In spite of unknown intensity, regular correspondence of actors involved in programming existed.

- *Monitoring, reporting, evaluating, and accounting processes* are essential for quality assurance of program execution, and for ensuring that intended impacts are achieved. As the implementing party, DED monitored progress and presented outputs against proposals in monthly, bi-annual and annual reports to the donor agencies.[59] The reports consisted of narrative reports and accountability documents. During regular meetings of all stakeholders or on a bi-lateral basis, progress and potential obstacles were also discussed in person.[60] Evaluation of progress was conducted by DED in bi-annual and annual reports. Lessons-learnt and constrains are clearly stated in the respective reports. They furthermore include suggestions of what may be needed to improve conditions in the following program cycle. Evaluations of accountabilities are conducted through a neutral agency and submitted to DED and the respective donor.[61] Peter explained the process in detail:

> The programme team is in charge of compiling the narrative parts of the monthly, bi-annual and annual reports, including the required evaluations of programme activities, which are then checked and amended by the Deputy Programme Coordinator and Programme Coordinator. The accounts departments is in charge of compiling the financial parts of the monthly, bi-annual and annual reports which are checked by the Deputy Programme Coordinator and Programme Coordinator. There are external donor audits on an annual basis verifying programme outputs, assets as well as accounts. DED has also conducted internal financial audits on a few occasions (Interview Peter; 01.12.2010).

Hence, it is possible for donors and implementing partners to trace progress. Moreover, due to regular monitoring, programmatic gaps can be detected instantly. These gaps could lead to stagnation in assistance provision or progress. Based on early detection, necessary adjustments can be proposed to donors and partners and alternative activities can be initiated. The annual reports provided by DED reveal that activities were broadened or changed over a period of time. Since neither needs assessments, nor program proposals were accessible in the context of this research, it is not feasible to identify to what extent gaps existed and revised alternatives program components were integrated.

All annual reports show that women's needs and empowerment were part of the overall cross-cutting issues and policy priorities. However, it is to ask

59 Parts of these bi-annual and annual reports were provided to author by DED. Hence, content and structure were personally observed. Further information about processes was provided in interviews by the Programme Coordinator and Assistant Programme Coordinator for Rhino Camp (Interview Peter; 01/12/2010 and Interview Namyalo; 12/01/2010).

60 Minutes of meetings were not provided to by DED and could therefore not be accessed.

61 These reports were, however, not accessible for this research.

whether this is sufficient for operating in a gender-sensitive manner. UNHCR's handbook on *Partnership: An Operations Management Handbook for UNHCR's Partners* lists aspects to ensure that women's needs are regarded and assistance integrates gender sensitivity (UNHCR 2003b: 15). Under protection and assistance to refugee women, the handbook notes the need to provide protection, ensure active participation in planning and implementation, as well as the overall integration of these measures in operations so they are not treated separately.

According to DED's annual reports, gender-related activities were integrated in all operational sectors. Protection appears to have been provided through the overall security measures, which were under OPM. Though, details on security measures were not accessible. The active participation in planning and implementation cannot be discerned from DED's annual reports. In an interview, Obbo noted that

> [...] the beneficiaries (refugees) participated in decision making in the form of one semi-illiterate refugee leader representing thousands of other refugees in a committee populated by powerful and articulate managers and heads of programs, I don't think this representation gave the beneficiaries an actual means of voicing their concerns because the representative had neither the audacity nor power to speak and challenge any decisions already made (Interview Obbo; 08.01.2011).

Based on that, it is to conclude that active participation may not have been fulfilled to the extent necessary. UNHCR's aforementioned handbook furthermore notes a list of "practical measures [that] concern procedures to be applied within the context of programme and project management". Summarized, these measures include assessments of needs and resources, application of the POP, and the mentioning of the impact of protection and assistance programs in monitoring reports (UNHCR 2003b: 15-16). According to an interview with Peter, assessments were conducted (Interview Peter; 01.12.2010). POP was neither traceable in any of DED's reports, nor mentioned in any interview. Hence, it is to conclude that the framework was not applied. Since POP was developed in 1992, it should have been part of monitoring, reporting and evaluation. Finally, mentioning the impact of protection and assistance programs in monitoring reports was done in DED's reports. The reports included bullet points of impacts, which contain few explanations.

In conclusion, monitoring, reporting, evaluating, and accounting processes included assessments and references to gender aspects, natural resources and progress towards sustainable infrastructure development. However, based on the collected information through DED's annual reports and the interviews, gaps remain. The beneficiaries' voices appear to be vaguely heard and considered. No reference to the application of POP was found.

- *Ownership of development initiatives* is assumed to be vital to ensure a sustainable use and impact of measures. Refugee-hosting countries of first asylum should take the ownership, responsibility and have a voice in priority setting. The Government of Uganda with OPM work along with UNHCR on refugee issues to develop and finalize policy, strategy and programs. For example, SRS "was jointly developed by OPM, Directorate of Refugees and UNHCR Uganda" (RLSS Mission Report 2004/03:2). In the context of DAR, OPM clearly highlights its engagement and leadership.

> Government-led development initiative, which is linked to a number of national development programmes especially the Universal Primary Education (UPE), Uganda's Poverty Eradication Action Plan (PEAP) and the Millennium Development Goals (MDGs). The programme is also in line with UNHCR's global framework for Durable Solutions for Refugees – as part of the High Commissioners "Convention - Plus Initiative" (Wafula, OPM 2010).

In addition, interviewees confirmed that stakeholders and especially OPM attended regular meetings (Interview Namyalo; 12.01.2010). It is therefore assumable that national interests of Uganda were represented and provided by the respective OPM representatives.

The strategies of SRS and DAR show ownership and engagement in national development and that refugee assistance targets to promote sustainability. The integration of service structures is an element of SRS and eventually aims for improved livelihood conditions, because services are accessible to refugee and local communities. The development-oriented strategy of DAR is a good example for ownership. While refugees are allowed to stay in Uganda, DAR is implemented in refugee hosting areas yet to reach nationals. This is in favor of the refugee-hosting country of Uganda and shows ownership.

At the operational level, the staff structure of the DED Refugee/IDP Programme may reveal further information. The Programme Coordinator is the only fixed international position. All other posts are held by Ugandans. By doing so, the Ugandan staff can actively engage in program design and implementation and hence take ownership in what is done. In addition to their basic engagement, one furthermore needs to take note of women in leadership positions. Although Human Resource documents were not accessible due to confidentiality, I noted in interviews and field visits that women were in leadership positions as well as other hierarchical levels.

On the level of the beneficiaries, ownership is distinguished through their participation, having their voices heard, and engagement in implementation. While political participation of women and men was promoted through various committees, it was revealed in an interview that voices were hardly heard (Interview Obbo; 08.01.2011). In operations, female and male refugees and nationals, among others, were involved through small-scale employment. Infrastructure development and maintenance constitute one example. The 2001 annual report notes that "road maintenance contracts [were] awarded to refugees and nationals within the catchment area as a source of income". Later, it is stated that only one refugee woman was among the contractors. According to the report, the reason for low female engagement was that "[w]omen are encouraged to participate in manual road maintenance but the traditional society makes it difficult for them to take contracts and mobilise labour force" (DED LS/403 2001: 28). Since no further details were accessible about the contractors' work, it is impossible to conclude whether or not women were indeed treated equally in the context of operational engagement and taking ownership.

At the government level, it is to conclude that ownership seem to be pursued before and during operations. This was done especially through specific policies, as noted above. At the operational and beneficiaries' level, attempts to promote ownership are feasible. Two main aspects were found to be counterproductive: voices were insufficiently heard and societal disparity between men and women due to tradition was detected.

- *Integrity and solidarity of staff* (particularly field staff) should exist towards maxims. I.e., information and value sharing is required to take place in order to involve staff of all levels in activities and pursued results. It is to be clarified, that development-oriented refugee assistance is not supposed to be of short-term usage but rather sustainable, especially for the local refugee-hosting area. The level of integrity and solidarity of staff is very difficult to assess from a research point of view.

Indicators to find out to what extent staff showed integrity and solidarity towards the organization and the work are challenging to create. One may ask how often criminal offences were committed or for how many years staff remained on their posts or in the organization. While I did not have access to confidential information from the Human Resource Department of the DED Refugee/IDP Programme, both responses would also only yield superficial assumptions regarding integrity and solidarity. Criminal offences may have been committed by other per-sons but staff and jobs are rare in the West Nile region, which is why individuals could have remained in the organization although they may have disliked their work. To obtain a comprehensive view, an option would have been to try to conduct an all-staff survey. However, this would have gone beyond the scope of this research project. Hence, it was decided to raise the question during interviews to receive personal impression. In order to weigh up, critical opinions of a former local staff member and a former international staff member were used.

Obbo said that "[t]o a large extent I think that the staff in DED Rhino Camp acted in the best interest of the program. This was shown in their commitment to meeting and achieving their respective sector goals, targets and objectives, which collectively fed into the program objectives and goals." However, he also indicated that lacking initiatives concerning staff development and great remuneration gaps caused obstacles. "This tended to create some form of antipathy among staff that felt they were left out of the big picture. [...] That is why cases of fuel, motorcycle and other equipment theft were common." Obbo also referred to this as a "major cause of the high staff turnover at Rhino Camp" (Interview Obbo; 08.01.2011). Peter explained:

> On the whole, I believe staff did follow the rules and endeavoured to provide good services although there are of course always exceptions. Instances of theft, mismanagement and gross negligence have occurred. It is hard to prevent them completely. However, the individuals in question were brought to account for their improper actions and a clear message was sent to the rest of the staff that such behavior does have severe consequences. The activities on the ground were monitored not only by DED management (Assistant Programme Coordinator) but also by the RWC and OPM who always kept a close eye on the actions of our staff (Interview Peter; 01.12.2010).

Based on the interviews, it is to conclude in very general terms that the staff members of the DED Refugee/IDP Programme at Rhino Camp appeared to have shown integrity and solidarity towards the organization and work. It is, however, not traceable if the staff believed in and represented the long-term idea of development-oriented refugee assistance.

4.2.2. Consideration of Time and Situational Dimensions

- *Contextual recognitions* are required in order to prevent potentially harmful activities, but rather implement sustainable, efficient and gender-sensitive programs. Although context considerations are important, when refugees reach the border of another country, immediate response is necessary. Long-term planning is unlikely to take place within days. Right then, it is necessary to provide assistance and meet basic needs.

However, before protracted situations appear, contexts need to be taken into consideration. In Uganda, the government and UNHCR has done this by allocating land for long-term refugee assistance and the application of strategies such as the local settlements, SRS and DAR.

Contexts are to be respected not only in the beginning of assistance phases but also during ongoing assistance. According to interviews, needs assessments were conducted towards refugee and local communities (Interview Namyalo; 12.01.2010). Peter added specific details on how contexts were regarded:

> Needs were considered by taking into consideration the findings of the annual Joint Assessment Mission (JAM) and the Age, Gender, Diversity and Mainstreaming (AGDM) exercise carried out jointly by all partners. In addition, DED took into consideration the results of (formal and informal) surveys and evaluations, especially with regard to what type of skills training should be offered to the refugees (Interview Peter; 01.12.2010).

How thorough and complex these assessments and surveys were, and to what extent findings were integrated in program designs and proposals, is not traceable due to a lack of access to respective documents. However, since these activities of assessments and surveys were conducted, the importance of knowing contexts and programming according to needs seem to have been understood and done. It is thus assumable that they built a foundation to programs. Since programs contained different program components from all sectors simultaneously, it can be assumed that it was innovative. The focus on improved livelihood, engagement in infrastructural development, and the protection of natural resources furthermore indicates the tendency towards sustainability. Women and men were also integrated and promoted to participate in activities within Rhino Camp. This furthermore refers to some extent of gender sensitivity. However, as revealed above, the POP was not found to having been applied and voices of beneficiaries were apparently little heard, although committees existed and beneficiaries were promoted to actively engage in them. In addition, Mulumba found that land allocation was based on little cultural sensitive manners. According to her, tribes were separated and land was allocated randomly which "resulted in different ethnic groupings finding themselves with 'strangers' for neighbours and this reduced the network system" (Mulumba 2005: 180).

- *Situational considerations* to operations were targeted to be done at Rhino Camp through proposals for and execution of annual program cycles. Along with distinct needs of beneficiaries, it was criticized that situational considerations were insufficient, because "whatever planning DED was involved in was biased and aimed at meeting/fulfilling the donors targets, goals and objectives" (Interview Obbo, 08.01.2011). According to Peter, work plans were, however, developed according to needs and gaps identified and based on lessons learnt exercises. Situation analyses were therefore carried out at the operational level (Interview Peter; 01.12.2010).

Situational consideration furthermore refers to the question how sustainable, efficient, and gender-sensitive program cycles were. With regard to sustainability, efforts towards reforestation and infrastructural development are particularly to be emphasized. Investments were made to maintain natural resources and to develop the region. The DED-managed databases on infrastructure developments, as well as my field visits revealed that many sites had been neglected over the years (DED 2008). Some infrastructures were insufficiently maintained and hence, some was not of sustainable use for the national population after refugees repatriated. How efficiently were funds spend in retrospective? Maintaining infrastructure that is damaged may produce high costs at that moment, which indicates a certain degree of inefficiency. Nevertheless, the infrastructure may then be of rather sustainable use. On a positive note, it is necessary to highlight that local contractors of national and refugee background were involved in infrastructure maintenance. Women were attempted to be engaged with little success due to traditional societal structures, according to DED (DED LS/403 2001: 28).

Situational considerations towards gender-sensitive operations are particularly important by taking into account the numerous households headed by single women and their vulnerability. DED's annual reports contain information — yet with little explanation — on specific activities that aim to meet the special needs of women, and to promote empowerment, and to create awareness between women and men. Moreover, the skills and vocational trainings offered appeared to include a balanced number of participants from both sexes. However, DED's reports predominantly refer to activities for women and not both sexes. Gender integrates both, men and women. Gender-sensitive operations should therefore include both. It is to be asked to what extend men were integrated in activities, which integrate gender considerations. DED's reports provide little information about attempts to include refugee men and refugee men's activeness in gender-related measures. The potential lack of male participation and failure of acceptance of such measures could lead to the implementation of a single-edged approach in which women are promoted and empowered without men simultaneously learning about the social process. In addition to that, the extent of gender sensitivity in the context of violence is little traceable. Due to a lack of information it remains unclear how exactly sexual offences are treated and whether victims of SGBV receive psychological support.

- *Time factors* are important to take into account in order to achieve the overall objective for development-oriented refugee protection and assistance, which is to share burdens and to bridge the gap between relief and development. The likelihood of refugees' long-term stay in Uganda was kept in mind when operations were planned and executed at Rhino Camp. Long-term consideration was conducted through local settlements, SRS and DAR. By applying these strategies, the long-term character of refugees at Rhino Camp was considered. With the establishment of local settlements for refugees and the integration of nationals into service structures, a higher living standard and self-sufficiency was targeted. Nationals benefit in particular from infrastructural development of, for example, education and health structures. SRS and DAR further strengthen operations. Through operational periods of four years for each concept, medium to long-term planning ensures the development orientation of refugee protection and assistance. It bridges the gap between emergency aid and development and is also sustainable. Women and men were intended to be integrated and their participation promoted in program components during the annual program cycles. This generally supports the intent for gender-sensitive programming. UNHCR was nevertheless restricted though annual program cycles.

Regarding *contextual recognitions, situational considerations* and *time factors* potential financial constraints are to be kept in mind. Funding is limited to donors, UNHCR and implementing agencies such as DED. Funds made available need to be spent wisely. For example, although some activities may have been needed to increase the livelihoods of refugees and local communities, funds may not have been available to the amount requested. Peter explained that "[b]udget cuts result in the need to concentrate on life-saving activities only (and to scrap the more development-oriented activities)" (Interview Peter; 01.12.2010). The DED-managed database on infrastructure furthermore confirms the broad extent of assistance, not only towards meeting basic needs of refugees, but also integration of a clear development orientation. Based on information from the database, situational considerations in regard to what is needed at the settlement level were taken into account (DED 2008).

4.2.3. Targeted Groups of Beneficiaries

- *Integration of refugees and nationals* of the hosting country of first asylum is observed as important, especially in protracted and long-term situations. According to SRS, refugees were not intended to be integrated in local communities. SRS pursues the objective "to ensure integration of services for the refugees with those of the nationals" (RLSS Mission Report 2004/03: 3). Although DED undertook efforts to integrate refugees locally, interviews also revealed that success remained scarce (Interview Peter; 01.12.2010; Interview Obbo, 08.01.2011). In addition to efforts, it is to note that few local communities resided in or close to Rhino Camp. Integration and interaction was therefore limited. As explained above, interaction may have been limited because the land allocated for Rhino Camp was sparsely populated by national communities (DED LS/403 2001: 2). In 2000, almost twice as many refugees as nationals lived in the area of Rhino Camp. During the years of 1997 until 2006, the number of refugees continued to be significantly higher than that of nationals.

Nevertheless, integration took place on the basis of services. Local communities, as well as refugees were enabled to use services. This led to interaction rather than integration. Peter noted that the interaction of locals and refugees was nevertheless promoted.

> The skills training courses, for example, were always mixed, i.e. attended by both refugees and nationals. School days were attended by the parents of all pupils, i.e. from the refugee as well as the local community. Celebrations, i.e. World Aids Day or Women's Day, also brought the two communities together (Interview Peter; 01.12.2010).

In addition to the clear focus on service integration, a potential integration of refugees in local communities would have been complicated due to restrictive rights to movement stated in Uganda's Control of Alien Refugees Act, Cap. 64

of 1960 (Uganda 1960). According to article 17, refugees were to inform authorities and receive a permit to be allowed to move within the country.

To conclude, local integration took place on the basis of the integration of services in the national system. This infers a durable use of service structures and increased livelihoods for refugee and local communities. Hence, efforts strive for sustainability. Due to the access to both groups of beneficiaries, it can also be assumed that it is efficient because dual structures are avoided and infrastructure is aimed to be used over long-term, even after the repatriation of refugees. Men and women benefited from the provision of services. Special attention was paid to women to further their participation. Among other things, girl child education and the sanitation needs of women were regarded. It can thus also be concluded, that programs aimed at being gender-sensitive. However, the integration of refugees in local communities was not targeted.

- *Manners of integration* at Rhino Camp were focused on the integration of services as explained above. A clear strategy to integrate persons did not exist. It is known from DED's annual reports that the setup of services was conducted in correspondence with respective local authorities. I.e., DED's 2001 report states that "refugee health services [were integrated] into the District Health according to the government Health Strategic Policy and finally to enhance smooth effective hand over according to SRS policy" (DED LS/403 2001: 20).

Integration was conducted at the level of service delivery. Both refugee and local communities had access to services. Service structures were developed during that period of refugee assistance. Through the provision of services, livelihoods were improved. Aside from the durable use of services and service structures, natural resources were protected through reforestation activities. All sectors were implemented simultaneously. This reveals the cross-cutting nature of operations. Through an innovative mix of activities within the operations at Rhino Camp both groups of beneficiaries — nationals and refugees — received benefits and had advantages. For example, instead of providing water tanks only, boreholes were drilled. To ensure their maintenance, committees with local and refugee members were created. Moreover, both men and women were targeted to be integrated in programs especially through participatory measures. In the educational sector including schools and vocational trainings, men and women, as well as locals and refugees, were targeted to be integrated. They had access and support to attend educational programs. Female participation was not only promoted, but required in committees which support their representation and visibility of equal capabilities. That, in the long run, may support the process towards gender equality. Hence, sustainability, efficiency and gender sensitivity aspects were regarded in the manner of integration.

- *Interactive levels* were promoted by DED at Rhino Camp. Despite limited efforts for local integration, certain patterns of life of both communities were shared; religious facilities, schools, and further trainings were attended by nationals and refugees. Refugees and nationals had access to community services and interacted there. For example, to overcome language barriers, national and refugee teachers were recruited in 1997 to teach at primary schools (DED LS/403 1997:17). The DED Refugee/IDP Programme supported the interaction of refugees and nationals by setting up and offering vocational trainings as a part of UNHCR's income-generating activities. Trainings were offered to refugees and nationals. These activities build capacities and human capital; hence, they contributed to sustainable development.

The most distinct example for a precise interactive level is recreational activities; refugees and nationals organized sports and social events jointly from 1997 onwards. Peter explained the following:

> Interaction was limited but promoted in some ways. The skills training courses, for example, were always mixed, i.e. attended by both refugees and nationals. School days were attended by the parents of all pupils, i.e. from the refugee as well as the local community. Celebrations, i.e. World Aids Day or Women's Day, also brought the two communities together (Interview Peter; 01.12.2010).

In another interview, Obbo is of similar understanding as Peter.

> The only visible sort of interaction between refugees and national was in schools, health centers and agriculture field-days where the two groups had to inevitably meet in their quest for health services and education. But even here the level of interaction was quite subtle. I can't imagine that any beneficial level of interaction could be realized between two sick people or between kids whose only opportunity of mixing in during break time at school (Interview Obbo, 08.01.2011).

According to him, the restrictive right to movement limits interaction. Moreover, he notes that the "preferential treatment for refugees in the provision of humanitarian aid and other development assistance in the region created a kind of barrier between the two communities" (Interview Obbo, 08.01.2011).

It is to conclude, that interaction between refugees and nationals took place but at an insufficient level, which may be related to lacking local integration. Despite some points of meeting each other, the two groups rather lived side by side than with each other. Nevertheless, clashes were not mentioned in reports or during interviews. If these meeting points promoted any type of gender-related activities and the process towards equality, it is not traceable. Since very few meeting points existed, a distinct effect is not to be assumed.

4.2.4. Comprehensive Methods towards Beneficiaries

- *Inclusive and comprehensive frameworks* are required to be developed on a situation-specific foundation to reach syntheses of refugee assistance and development activities and inclusivity of refugees and local communities.

At Rhino Camp, refugees and nationals had access to community services, organized recreational events and took part in decision-making through sectoral committees, such as for boreholes and food. Although the local integration of refugees in Ugandan communities was not targeted, both groups of beneficiaries had access to services and were therefore included in operational frameworks.

A multi-sectoral approach was applied that included work in the fields of health and nutrition, education, food, water and sanitation, infrastructure and shelter, community service and environmental work with agriculture and reforestation. UNHCR defines the multi-sectoral approach as an integrated approach as "a planning approach that brings together issues from across sectors, institutions and national and local levels, as well as different population groups" (UNHCR 2005c: Glossary 7). The intended impact on cross-cutting issues and policy priorities of activities - including gender mainstreaming - was applied. In practice, i.e., sanitation facilities were built to advance health aspects. By means of drilling boreholes, access to water is ensured. Moreover, traditionally women maintain households. By drilling boreholes close to communities, walking distances for women are being significantly minimized.

Both women's participation and representation were continuously noted in the annual reports of DED. Gender equality was moreover understood as a cross-cutting issue. Although, according to DED's reports, it is traceable that women's participation and integration in program activities were promoted, it is questionable whether gender equality itself was indeed promoted. DED's reports reveal that most gender-related activities strove towards the active integration of women with little reference to men and their roles. In the context of political and educational participation as well as meeting medical needs, men and women were included. Women and men were furthermore promoted to participate in vocational trainings. However, during awareness building measures, the focus was demonstrably on female issues and participation. Neither the details on campaign implementation, nor the empirical reference allow me to determine female and male attendance rates during awareness campaigns.

Hence, it is to be reasoned that inclusive and comprehensive frameworks were partly gender-sensitive. In the broad context of participation, both sexes were promoted to be included. The softer measures of awareness building show little evidence for a sufficient inclusion of refugee men and women.

Overall, it is nevertheless to conclude that this dual imperative of inclusive and comprehensive frameworks towards beneficiaries and activities appeared to have been applied at Rhino Camp. Both refugees and nationals were included in operational frameworks. Also, the frameworks were comprehensive due to the nature of the multi-sectoral approach. The usage of infrastructure and access to services by refugees and nationals can be understood as innovative since dual structures were avoided. That indicates efficiency. It can be assumed that final costs were minimized since refugee related services were integrated in local schemes. Hence, the application was efficient. Due to the integration of services and service deliveries into the national system, it can be assumed they, or at least those services needed after the repatriation of refugees, will continuously be used. This reveals sustainability. In regard to the sustainable use of infrastructure, it noted that DED's database on infrastructure revealed that numerous sites showed a lack of usability and functionality.

- *The rights-based approach* in operations fundamentally targets to ensure that human rights are met. DED's annual reports reveal inconsistent information on the application of the rights-based approach.

From 1997 until 2002, the reports primarily provided operational information about service delivery, but no details on applied approaches or strategies. They also did not state any information whether or how the human rights of beneficiaries were protected. However, operations contained some activities that promoted specific human rights. For example, the 2001 report states that the "[s]ensitization of the communities on children's rights [...] covering 906 participants in R/Camp" were conducted and that "[t]he establishment of the schools, recruitment of the teachers and provision of all the teaching/learning inputs ensured the right of the child to education" (DED LS/403 2001: 29, 43). Nevertheless, the implemented activities targeted the well-being of beneficiaries and promotion of human rights.

It was not until 2003, that the rights-based approach was traceable. In the context of the assessment of sub-project results, one of the overall impacts achieved was: "Protection for the refugee population, guarantee of basic human rights and physical security" (DED LS/403 2003: 64). Exactly this sentence was included in all reports from 2003 until 2006 (DED LS/403 2004: 69; DED LS/403 2005: 36; DED LS/403 2005: 54).

The 2005 and 2006 reports also noted that their superior commitment is to keep beneficiaries alive, to offer protection and to meet their basic needs. It was stated to be a policy priority:

> The Protection of the Beneficiary Population: The legal rights of the beneficiaries were accorded and protection was ensured through special programmes under the various sectors. These programmes catered for the physical, psychological, social, economic and security needs of the special groups.
>
> These programmes improved the economic life of these groups of beneficiaries while at the same time offering them social and psychological acceptability within the communities (DED LS 403 2006: 6; DED LS 403 2005: 5).

Hence, up until 2003, a clear reference to the rights-based approach is missing in DED's reports. Reports of the following years demonstrated an increasing positioning towards the application of a rights-based approach. In spite of that, it is not discernible whether activities were created on the foundation of the rights-based approach. One could argue that the activities implemented targeted the well-being of beneficiaries. However, it would be questionable if this was sufficient to fulfill UNHCR's understanding of a rights-based approach as

> a conceptual framework for the process of human development that is normatively based on international human rights standards and operationally directed to promoting and protecting human rights (UNHCR 2005c: Glossary 11).

Based on the state of information collected through research, it is not possible to provide a distinct inference whether or not the holistic rights-based approach was applied throughout the research period from 1997 until 2006. During the entire timeframe, basic needs of refugees were targeted to be met. From 2003 onwards, clear references to human rights were stated in the annual reports.[62] Hence, some degree of awareness about the need to indicate and promote human rights coherent operations was reflected, especially in comparison to previous reports. It is not possible, however, to verify the application of the rights-based.

- *Gender-sensitive approach* is essential in order to use the transitional period to support the process towards gender equality. It is understood that due to the refuge into a foreign country of first asylum, refugees experience changing or transitional conditions. These conditions can be used to further women's empowerment and gender equality. Both men and women need to be included in this process because gender equality is a social process.

In the context of gender-sensitive operations, gender relations and roles are vital to be taken into account. In Chapter V, *3.4. Beneficiaries: Gender Structures and Relations*, the set-up within Rhino Camp was illustrated. Also, traditional gender roles and changed roles while at Rhino Camp were explained based on the example of the South Sudanese Madi tribe. In brief, there was a clear patrilineal clan structure which traditionally existed. The male dominated culture in terms of decision making and heading the household, left women with inferior and rather supportive roles. While settled in Rhino Camp, gender

62 It is to add, that the state of reports from DED to UNHCR have changed and improved over the years. While from 1997 until 2002, reports merely explain implemented activities, reports of the following years state further information about result orientation. Reports are to be submitted from DED as the implementing partner to UNHCR in specific formats, as explained in 5.2 "Monitoring, Reporting and Evaluation, Sub-Project Monitoring Reports (SPMRs)" of UNHCR's Operations Management Handbook of 2003 (UNHCR 2003b: 104-108). Only one previous guideline for operations management of UNHCR from 2001 was found referred to, the entire document was, however, not accessible. Moreover, reporting guidelines from UNHCR were increasingly created from 2002 onwards (UNHCR 2001a) but no guidelines accessible previous to that. Hence, reporting standards have changed but the exact standards are not traceable. It can be assumed that reporting guidelines previous to 2003 may have simply not required data about the application of a rights-based approach and were therefore not integrated in DED's annual reports.

relations and roles altered. Women obtained additional responsibilities and fields of action. Households headed by single females included that women were in charge of maintaining the household, cultivating land, ensuring food provision. While women perceived the process as liberating, men felt cheated because they lost part of their traditional authority. In spite of that, polygamy was still practiced by men (Mulumba 2005: 175-183).

DED's activities at Rhino Camp show that the inclusion of women, their concerns and needs in operations and programs were pursued. All annual reports reveal that it was part of the overall cross-cutting issues and policy priorities. While in 1997, special female needs were primarily taken care of, community sensitization was increasingly implemented in the years from 1998 until 2006. Examples show how this was realized. Sanitary and medical support was a continuous aspect of work throughout the research period. In 1998, a workshop on women and food distribution was held to support "more women leaders in Camp Committees" (DED LS/403 1998: 8-9). From 1998 until 2000, communities were sensitized towards the vulnerable and in 2000, the initiative "Sports for Girls" was launched to "[s]ensitise girls, parents of girls on the importance of sports/games for women" (DED LS 403 1998: 23; DED LS 403 1999: 31; DED LS 403 2000: 33). From 2000 onwards, one specific objective was to ensure that the role of women was integrated in project implementation (DED LS/403 2000: 2). From 2001 onwards, sensitization about SGBV became an integral part of operations. The 2001 report states that the target was to "[s]ensitise the community and women in particular on gender issues so as to create gender equity in decision-making at all levels and helping to reduce Sexual and Gender Based Violence (SGBV)" (DED LS 403 2001: 31). "Gender responsive planning" was integrated in 2002. Thereby, it was aimed to "[s]trengthen women's participation in sports and decision making" (DED LS 403 2002: 30-37). From 2003 onwards, gender aspects were included in all sectors of health and nutrition, education, food, water and sanitation, infrastructure and shelter, community service and environmental work. Special attention was then aimed to be provided wherever possible (DED LS 403 2003; DED LS 403 2004; DED LS 403 2005; DED LS 403 2006). From 2004 until 2006, gender mainstreaming was applied. Women and men were targeted to be involved in committees in order to ensure that their voices and specific concerns are heard (DED LS/403 2004: 33).

In 2005 and 2006, "Refugee Women/Gender Equality" was listed as policy priorities. This reveals that the focus was not only on women's empowerment but also on both men and women into programs. The following was noted:

> Refugee Women/Gender Equality: The programme ensured that clean and safe water was accessible within walkable distances to all the beneficiaries in adequate quantities, which improved the living conditions especially of women and children. [...] To promote gender equality, girl child education has been promoted through sensitisation workshops and

> provision of sanitary materials for both girls in secondary and primary schools. [...] To empower refugee women, the programme through its revolving loan scheme ensures that women have access to funds by giving 70% of its loans to women. Women and girls had access to skills training within the settlement and to sponsorship for special courses outside the settlement. Through OPM, women participation in leadership was ensured at 30% representation in the RWC therefore ensuring women views and concerns were taken into consideration in policy and decision making (DED LS 403 2006: 7).

In an interview, Namyalo confirmed the promotion of women's empowerment. "Women leadership is maintained at 50% and above. Female headed households are given priority" (Interview Namyalo; 12.01.2010). Peter also confirmed the engagement.

> The participation of women in community life/activities was always actively promoted although the numbers aimed for were often not achieved. This was in part due to the fact that a large percentage of women still lack the required formal education for leadership positions on the various committees. Participation of women in skills training was very encouraging though (Interview Peter; 01.12.2010).

Besides the operational level, it is of interest to look at DED's staff involved in operations and implementations and which is therefore visible to beneficiaries. Since staff details are not provided by the Human Resource department due to confidentiality, the following information is based on observations. The Programme Coordinator and Assistant Programme Coordinator were women. Other staff positions and holders of the posts were observed during field visits at Rhino Camp. The number of men and women appeared to be rather equal. Exact figures were not accessible. Based on observations, women and men realizing similar assignments may reflect equal abilities to the outside. At the DED Refugee/IDP Programme and in particular the Rhino Camp, women held management positions. They work hand in hand with other stakeholders and leading agencies of UNHCR and OPM.

DED's reports and the interviews reveal a positive trend in regard to gender sensitivity in operations. During the research period, several critical factors were, however, discovered. At a very fundamental level and based on the available reports, it is not traceable if DED applied UNHCR's POP. The aspect has already been criticized above. Through the module, gender-related aspects could have been integrated in program planning and implementation in a more in-depth manner. Analytical and empirical assessments before planning may have helped to incorporate specific activities more strategically. According to UNHCR, POP supports the process towards gender equality by means of specific measures and actions integrated in the broader program (UNHCR 2003b: 15-16).

Little information about SGBV was accessible. While DED's reports from 2001 onwards announce that awareness building measures were implemented in order to sensitize the communities (DED LS/403 2001: 24, 30-31, 34; DED LS/403 bi-annual 2005: 6, 26), it was not until the 2006 report that the documentation contained additional background information in terms of types of violence with empirical data (DED LS/403 2006: 7, 28-29, 32, 38). The 2001 report merely notes that "[o]nly 8 cases were reported to health units." Considering the number of refugees living in Rhino Camp in 2001, 8 cases appear unrealistically low. Later, the report notes different case data: "A total of 21 SGBV cases [were] reported for action to office of Settlement Commandant in R/Camp." However, "[f]ield staff intervened in 56 minor cases of SGBV [...] reported to OPM" (DED LS/403 2001: 22, 30, 34). The report also notes that sensitization campaigns were carried out (DED LS/403 2001: 34). Since the report provided inconsistent data, it is not verifiable how many SGBV cases took place and how victims were supported.

In 2005, 24 SGBV cased were reported. In 2006, the number rose to 182 cases. DED's reports reason that the increased numbers of reported SGBV cases were due to the establishment of community-based SGBV centers (DED LS/403 2006: 38). Based on such a significant increase of reported cases, it can be assumed that case registration and reporting as well as support and treatment was insufficient before 2006.

For the first time, the 2006 report contains a categorized table with types of violence and number of incidences. The table furthermore includes a gender breakdown, which clearly shows that men and women were similarly affected by SGBV. In spite of that, women are demonstrably much more frequently affected by SGBV. The 2006 report reveals that almost three times as many women as men suffer from SGBV incidences. 47 men and 135 women reported the incidences (DED LS/403 2006: 38).

Table 6. SGBV incidences with gender breakdown in Rhino Camp in 2006.

Incident type	Male	Female	Total	# Assisted
Domestic violence	19	51	70	8
Psycho-social violence	6	20	26	--
Early marriage	4	14	18	--
Child abuse	5	12	17	3
Social economic violence	7	7	14	--
Early pregnancy	0	13	13	13
School drop outs	4	8	12	6
Sexual harassment	0	4	4	4
Defilement	0	3	3	3
Physical violence	2	0	3	--
Social tendency	0	1	1	1
Assault	0	1	1	--
Marital rape	0	1	1	--
Total	**47**	**135**	**182**	**38**

Although the report does not provide definitions of the types of SGBV case reports, it nevertheless reveals a more realistic picture of the broad scope of

SGBV. Through the establishment of community-based SGBV centers, SGBV cases were reported. Victims appeared to use the opportunity to receive support and bring incidences to court. According to the report, victims "benefited from routine guidance and counseling services" (DED LS/403 2006: 39). Moreover, all reported cases were filed and brought to "legal justice in Arua", the town nearby Rhino Camp. It remains uncertain, which sentences were appealed. In addition to legal support, community sensitization meetings and campaigns were continuously realized to raise awareness of SGBV (DED LS/403 2006: 39). While awareness building measures were included, none of the reports indicate awareness measures for boys and men that sensitize the community towards violence experienced by them. Since it was not mentioned, it can be assumed that anti-violence trainings were not offered or implemented.

Despite the more detailed presentation of SGBV cases and following support, in 2006, the trend of previous reports towards equating 'gender' with 'women' continues to be traceable. From the very outset, the trend of equating 'gender' with 'women' can be exemplified through the following information stated in the reports. For example, in the earliest DED report from 1997, gender-related activities were, among others, the distribution and provision of sanitary cotton clothes to refugee women as a part of meeting female needs (DED LS/403 1997: 11). In 2001, a targeted result is to "[s]ensitize the community and women in particular on gender issues so as to create gender equity in decision-making at all levels and help to reduce Sexual and Gender Based Violence (SGBV)". DED reports that the following outputs were achieved:

- Women hold 30% of leadership position in R/Camp […].
- A total of 21 SGBV cases reported for action to office of Settlement Commandant in R/Camp.
- 4 teachers in R/Camp disciplined (dismissed) on reports of defilement originating from the section in a bid to pass the information on SGBV.
- A total of 441 members of food committees trained of which 173 are women in Rhino camp […] (DED LS/403 2001: 30-31).

Aside from the SGBV cases, it appears that the focus is on women by highlighting what percentage of women participated in leadership positions and how many women were trained. While the data on women's involvement respond to the set target "to create gender equity", the actual number is to be highlighted. Only about one third of the above mentioned beneficiaries were female. The majority still constituted males. However, only data on females is especially underlined. In addition to that, the manner and scope of male integration and awareness building is neither mentioned, nor apparently intended. The 2006 report pursued this trend with some visible improvements.

While the gender-aggregated data now included male and female data, and workshops for leaders on gender mainstreaming and gender-sensitive planning were held, 'gender' was still equated with 'women' through an emphasis on women. For instance, the report reads that the "[p]articipation of women is encouraged in management of school programmes by ensuring that at least 40% of the school committees are women" (DED LS/403 2006: 38, 28, 42). Yet again, the report does not indicate if, how and to what extent men were involved. Awareness building measures appear to be realized for women. This may eventually be counterproductive in the process towards gender equality because it reverses authority structures for women without men understanding why.

In addition, the 2005 and 2006 DED reports highlight "Refugee Women/Gender Equality" as policy priorities. (DED LS/403 bi-annual 2005:6; DED LS/403 2006: 7). However, men are not mentioned which could be understood as positive discrimination.

There is a great information gap concerning psychological and psycho-social support and counseling. Despite brief indications in the DED's reports, no specific information about procedures and contact points were mentioned. Even during interviews, no information was provided. Therefore, it remains to be unknown to what extent and how psychological and psycho-social support and counseling was provided to SGBV victims.

It was found that gender-sensitive activities were integrated in operations. First and foremost, it is to note that men and women of local and refugee communities enjoyed benefits through active implementation. In the context of special gender-related activities, it is to note that they were cross-cutting. Due to the cross-cutting nature of these activities, they were implemented in all sectors as exemplified above. However, gender-related activities predominantly targeted women and their empowerment and participation. Considering that the refugee and national beneficiaries are mainly from patriarchal societies, the emphasis on women's protection and participation was important and will lead to awareness and, if further pursued, to the empowerment of women. In spite of that, it was found that men's inclusion was insufficient in the context of specific gender activities. The inclusion of men was, nevertheless existent in community sensitization measures because they targeted entire communities. How great the impact on revising traditional gender roles in fact is, cannot be concluded. Nevertheless, it can be assumed that the variety of activities conducted had effects on gender images. Women proved to be capable to participate successfully in committees next to men.[63]

63 To eventually find out how great the impact was on women, additional analyses especially after repatriation to the country of origin are required. In that case it would be interesting to examine if women continue to engage in participative assignments or whether they return to more traditional role allocations.

Finally, a clear focus of gender sensitivity is hardly feasible. There is no clear mission statement of DED or the cooperation of OPM, UNHCR and DED that clarifies the way gender sensitivity is understood and intended to be promoted. Neither DED's reports, nor the interviews clarified how the 'gender-sensitive operations' are to be implemented, and by means of which underlying method. Political participation is a method highlighted throughout all DED reports; women and men are being promoted to participate in committees. Although continuously used, it is, however, not strong or often insufficiently applied to identify it as the operational focus for gender sensitivity. Another focus on women's needs is also frequently mentioned throughout all reports; it is, however, only focused on women. It is therefore little gender-sensitive because particular needs of men were not mentioned once. The lack of a clear focus is thus traceable and to be noted critically.

- *Results-based management (RBM)* targets to manage operations in a way that aims for reaching sustainable outcomes, rather than to focus on activities. At Rhino Camp, assistance was not based on ad hoc activities to keep refugees alive and safe. The local settlement scheme and SRS was applied. Both aim to provide medium and long-term assistance. Activities were selected in a way to achieve specific results. In both cases, the targeted result was the refugees' self-reliance. The SRS policy states that one of the specific objectives was to "to empower refugees and nationals in the area to the extent that they will be able to support themselves"; hence self-reliance was targeted to be achieved (RLSS Mission Report 2004/03: 3). The policy furthermore sets out key elements to achieve the result. Among others:

> (i) allocation of land to refugees in designated "settlements" (for both homestead and agricultural purposes), to enable refugees to become self-sufficient in food production; (ii) relatively free access of refugees (registered or self-settled) to education, health and other facilities built by the government (RLSS Mission Report 2004/03: V)

Since DED provided regular reports, operations are traceable. Reports prior to 2001 merely contained information about progress and therefore only stated what was done and where gaps existed. In 2001, monitoring templates were altered. DED started to report on previously developed impact and performance indicators and explained the actual progress of operations. In the following years from 2002 up until 2005, a more advanced monitoring, evaluation and reporting system was applied. Sections about current situations and expected outputs were added and thus provided a more thorough context. In 2006, one further adjustment was made by means of adding the particular objective to activities. Hence, expected or planned outputs along with objectives were compared to actual progress, which was indeed reached.

It is to conclude that from the policy side, results-based management was principally pursued through the local settlement scheme and SRS. Operations were not done based on a catalog of activities, but rather aimed at achieving greater results. The activities identified and put together in a way to pursue and eventually achieve specific results. Hence, results-based management was implemented at Rhino Camp.

Through results-based management reporting, it is now possible to screen that certain activities were implemented to achieve sustainability. For example, trees were planted to substitute for the use of natural resources by refugees and the "[c]onservation of natural resources" (DED LS/403 2003: 50).

- *Impact-considering operations* take potential negative effects of programs into account. All monitoring reports from DED from 1998 onwards reveal explanations under each sector lists' intended impacts to be reached, achievements reached, constraints faced, and solutions applied. All reports from 2003 onwards contain lessons-learnt sections. While that information is useful for improving the following year's program cycle, they do not provide any background details about impacts regarding initiatives such as needs assessments or do-no-harm analyses. These types of analyses or assessments should be conducted prior to an annual program cycle. Information collected should be used in proposals for a new annual cycle and therefore shape the nature of activities planned to be conducted. Proposals were not made accessible to do this research project.

However, interviewees stated that needs assessment were conducted before planning programs. Namyalo said that "[a]ssessments, surveys, interviews of the beneficiaries are conducted". She also referred to frequent meetings with stakeholders (Interview Namyalo; 12.01.2010). Peter provided a broader view and listed examples for assessments done:

> Needs were considered by taking into consideration the findings of the annual Joint Assessment Mission (JAM) and the Age, Gender, Diversity and Mainstreaming (AGDM) exercise carried out jointly by all partners. In addition, DED took into consideration the results of (formal and informal) surveys and evaluations, especially with regard to what type of skills training should be offered to the refugees (Interview Peter; 01.12.2010).

By doing so, impacts to fulfill these distinct needs and to prevent possible negative effects were analyzed.

Conflict-sensitive planning modes are especially important to prevent further clashes in a region that is characterized by conflict. Since the Government of Uganda allocated sparsely populated land of local communities, possible land ownership conflicts were avoided. By providing assistance to refugees and local communities, potential conflicts due to jealousy were prevented. On the program level, services were accessible for refugees and nationals alike. Although this is done in theory, Obbo noted that

> [...] preferential treatment for refugees in the provision of humanitarian aid and other development assistance in the region created a kind of barrier between the two

> communities. Imagine two groups with similar levels of deprivation but receiving different types of assistance from the same helper? (Interview Obbo, 08.01.2011).

To provide an objective response to whether impact was sufficiently considered in program planning and implementation, too little information was available. The access to possible assessments per se, information about the use of assessments to consider impacts and proposals including this information are lacking. Although two interviewees said that impacts were considered through assessments, another interviewee spoke about a barrier between communities without reference to conflict preventing measures. Furthermore, no evidence about possible clashes or preventive activities for conflicts between local and refugee communities was found in annual reports. Data only referred to the interaction of both communities.

Besides considering potential impacts of programs and operations, impact-considering operations also mean to contemplate existing groups of beneficiaries and national environment resources. Knowing what happens on the ground and who to deal with is important to design programs accordingly. At Rhino Camp, agriculture was targeted to be done by refugees to reach self-sufficiency. According to a geographical study, soil was not sufficient to do so and agricultural plots were too small (Beaudou et al. 2003). Hence, in this respect, impacts were inadequately considered and were treated accordingly.

On a positive note, however, DED provided information about beneficiaries and their origin and ethnicity in all annual reports. Based on that data, staff was aware of constellations. Also, the impact of refugees on the natural environment was considered. Since, refugees would use a large quantity of firewood, respective activities were implemented.

No detailed information on psychological and psycho-socio counseling to beneficiaries was accessible, which may have also supported gender equality and women's empowerment. It remains to be unknown if the settlement structures and assistance caused psychological issues for beneficiaries, and if/ how counseling support was offered. As explained earlier, traditional gender relations and roles altered while refugees lived in Rhino Camp. However, it is not traceable if and to what extent the changes were known by the staff.

As argued above, obvious impacts on special needs were nevertheless considered. Women's needs in relation to medical and sanitation were taken care of. This is part of ordinary refugee assistance and meeting refugee's basic needs. Consequently, based on the research findings, potential impacts were little considered. Effect on sustainability, efficiency and gender sensitivity can therefore not be summarized positively in brief. The only precise factor that is to be highlighted is the protection of natural resources through reforestation. This illustrates sustainability and efficiency. Insufficient evidence that would infer to respecting gender sensitivity in the context of impact consideration was found.

- *Rural local refugee settlement structures* were applied at Rhino Camp from the very beginning as stated. The local settlement provided the foundation to refugees to have increased living standards and livelihoods, to engage in agriculture despite unsuitable soil conditions, and to access services. SRS along with vocational trainings supported capacity-building. It is to note that the rural local settlement at Rhino Camp targeted to create durable use of structures and protection of natural resources through cross and multi-sectoral operations, which indicate sustainability and efficiency.

Although the rural local refugee settlement scheme is generally widely accepted as a positive means to work against protracted refugee situations and towards self-reliance of refugees, research reveals a notable critical aspect about gender sensitivity. As noted under impact consideration, Mulumba found that land allocations to refugees were conducted without consideration of tribal connections. Clans and family structures were detached and communities within Rhino Camp somewhat randomly developed.

Based on the "first come first serve" mentality, diverse ethnic and tribal groups were mingled in the clusters (Mulumba 2005: 180). While this may positively impact on empowerment through revised roles and responsibilities of men and women, it simultaneously annuls authority and support structures, which could then cause disempowerment. A clear response towards to the two options cannot be provided. Research reveals advantaging and disadvantaging factors for refugee women and men (Mulumba 2005: 179-180).

- *Community-based methods* were to be applied in order to reach beneficiaries and their specific needs. According to interviews, they were applied. Obbo, for example, noted that "activities were community based because they were implemented in the communities for the communities and in some cases by the communities" (Interview Obbo, 08.01.2011). The political, social and ethnic context was analyzed in needs assessments and gender-aggregated data was developed in demographic profiles; that information was provided in a description of the beneficiary population in the monitoring and evaluation reports of DED. Hence, OPM, UNHCR, and DED were aware of whom it dealt with and what needs may arise.

Needs, but also interests of refugee and national communities were considered through numerous community-based sectoral committees. These sectoral committees consisted of female and male members which can be attributed to the promotion of female representation. Moreover, sensitization campaigns on SGBV, children's rights, sanitation, or HIV/AIDS were carried out and targeted communities directly. Capacities and knowledge was aimed to be built. In addition, various committees as well as the RWC represented beneficiaries and their concerns. In spite of that, during interviews it was questioned if their voices were heard and sufficiently expressed. Obbo doubted that the representation was adequate. Although representatives were voted by refugees, these leaders were "semi-illiterate" and they "had neither the audacity, nor power to speak and challenge any decisions" (Interview Obbo, 08.01.2011).

It was already explained above that there is a lack in the application of UNHCR's POP. This application may have supported a more precise focus on communities and their needs, especially because POP seeks to collect data about communities which help to design adjusted and fully suitable programs.

It is to conclude that activities aimed to reach communities and were partly implemented by beneficiaries. This builds capacity. They targeted to satisfy basic needs, and to improve livelihoods. Nevertheless, the representation of beneficiaries may not be strong enough to sufficiently voice concerns.

- *The Livelihood-based approach* targets to improve the livelihoods of the beneficiaries. UNHCR defines livelihood according to DFID as "a combination of the resources used and the activities undertaken in order to live. Resources include individual skills (human capital), land (natural capital), savings (financial capital), equipment (physical capital), as well as formal support groups and informal networks (social capital)" (UNHCR 2005c Glossary: 7).

At Rhino Camp, several methods and tools used to target livelihoods. For example, through local settlement schemes agriculture promoted a greater degree of independence and self-reliance of the refugees and therefore improved livelihood. Skills and vocational trainings built the capacities of female and male students and enabled them to receive employment opportunities after the completion of trainings, which promotes their economic empowerment. No documents that revealed employment rates of graduates of the vocational trainings were accessible. Sustainability of trainings is therefore not traceable.

The development of infrastructure, including roads and facilities for refugees and nationals will be sustained for the local communities if they continue to use what was built. As aforementioned, the DED-managed database on infrastructure revealed a certain lack in usability of infrastructure developments (DED 2008).

Contrary to the abovementioned activities, which support increased livelihood, it is important to refer to the refugee law of Uganda. Refugees do not enjoy the right to freedom of movement according to article 26 of Convention relating to the Status of Refugees. The national refugee policy in Uganda limits this right. According to Article 17, refugees were to inform authorities and to receive a permit to be allowed to move within the country (Uganda 1960: article 17). This greatly impacts on livelihood conditions of refugees. They are limited in access to markets and enjoying economic freedom. Self-reliance observed under the restrictive Freedom of Movement is complicated to implement because refugees cannot sell agricultural goods and gain independence from services. Moreover, they cannot offer their human capital acquired through completed vocational trainings to possible employers.

It is to conclude that constraints exist, especially due to the limited freedom of movement for refugees. However, the improved livelihood for beneficiaries was pursued by the programmatic work of DED in Rhino Camp. Due to the composition of activities in the different sectors, self-reliance is targeted to be achieved. This indicates sustainability. Skills and vocational trainings built the capacities of female and male participants. Due to the integration of both, gender sensitivity was regarded. Despite the lacking documentation of graduates' employment, it will impact the economic conditions. Revitalizing and protecting the natural environment illustrates the optimum usage and hence also efficiency.

- *Pre-existing social structures* and chains of command shall be respected and used for local integration in order to avoid dual structures. The local integration of refugees into national communities was not pursued, but only the integration of services based on the SRS policy. In spite of that, social structures within Rhino Camp were tailored to local structures. Leadership structures for refugees were adjusted to the existing ones in Uganda. For example, the structure of the RWC was adapted to the LC III of the national local council system. Under the RWC, there are Point/Zonal Executives composed of ten members from each point/zone which is equivalent to the LC II system in the national setting. The level below the point/zone set-up is the village executive followed by the lowest level of the block which has one leader each (DED LS/403 2005: 4; DED LS/403 2006: 5). In addition to the RWC, water committees were built in a way to consist of female and male refugee and national members in order to ensure that the voices of both were heard. Female participation was particularly promoted (DED LS/403 2000:13; DED LS/403 2001:17).

Service structures were also integrated in national schemes. By doing so, local communities and refugees accessed services. Even after refugees repatriate, these structures will remain if needed. Therefore, the local communities will benefit from the developed infrastructure on a long-term basis, and have durable use for such. Hence, adjustments took place and dual systems were prevented.

In the context of refugee communities, it is also important to ask if pre-existing social structures were considered. When refugees were settled at Rhino Camp, they received plots of land for residential and agricultural usage. It was conducted randomly without taking into account the ethnic origin of the refugees (Mulumba 2005: 180). This may be rated positively because respective staff has little room to give some beneficiaries preferential treatment over others. Although the relative improbability of preferred treatment (which could potentially be based on ethnic reasons), pre-existing social structures of refugee communities were not considered. This manner of land allocation "resulted in different ethnic groupings finding themselves with 'strangers' for neighbours and this reduced the network system" (Mulumba 2005: 180) The network systems were in other words the pre-existing social structures. They not only included support structures, but also conflict resolution systems, often through the elders of communities. The ethnic split-up and ethnic diverse grouping furthermore transformed the rather traditional household system including gender roles. Although it can be criticized that these refugee structures were not taken into account, it is to be kept in mind that at the time of settlement and land allocation, several thousand refugees were relocated from transit camps close to the border to South Sudan in 1992 until 1994. The relocation procedure was to take place relatively rapidly and instantly, which left little time for systematically allocating residential and agricultural plots to ethnic groupings.

- *Cross and multi-sectoral strategies* are important to be assessed in the context of development-oriented refugee assistance in order to simultaneously enhance services and livelihood conditions. First, it is to note that the national Poverty Eradication Action Plan (PEAP) of Uganda from 1997 includes refugees and their assistance. Refugees fall under pillar 3 of "Security, conflict-resolution and disaster management". In PEAP, refugees constitute a central factor to "poverty reduction initiatives over the PEAP period." It is furthermore noted that "[t]he management of the issue will be mainstreamed into district planning. Government will continue to implement the policy on self-reliance of refugees" (MFPED 2004: 29, xxi). In that regard, the effect of refugees in Uganda is considered, and needs of locals and refugee can be targeted.

Under the guidance of UNHCR, DED was responsible at Rhino Camp, for the planning and the implementation of operations for eight sectors. DED linked sectors and complemented activities to enhance results for refugees and nationals. For example, from 1998 onwards, DED promoted energy-saving stoves and sensitized communities with regard to their usage and impact. The agencies built capacities about how to use a device that requires less wood and which is therefore environmental-friendly. Since it produces less smoke, it is also healthier. Energy-saving stoves were more sustainable and efficient because less fuel and wood needed to be used. Natural resources were needed and therefore fewer trees had been planted to maintain the natural environment. It was stated in an ero-epic dialogue during a field visit in January 2011 that since these stoves were used, men also entered the kitchen because there was less smoke. It can therefore be assumed that the purpose of the exercise, which was supposed to primarily save energy, also has had a positive impact on gender constellations (Ero-epic dialogue 07.01.2011).

It is to conclude that at Rhino Camp in particular, cross and multi-sectoral strategies were applied. Since the DED Refugee/IDP Programme managed all sectors, complementing activities were possible. Due to the complexity of programs implemented and by means of the already given examples about sustainable, efficient and gender-sensitive efforts, one can conclude that the cross- and multi-sectoral operations supported all three pillars.

- *An environment-friendly and ecological methodology* is important to be applied in order to ensure the protection of natural resources during the refugees' stay. Moreover, the bigger picture of a negative impact of the environment on economic and social contexts needs to be considered (UNHCR 2009: 2). According to a governmental report on environment-related issues in Arua district, refugees are one of the "[m]ajor causes of deforestation" (Adrabo 2004: 27). Moreover, the PEAP notes that refugees may entail "environmental challenges" (MFPED 2004: 105).

DED's annual reports throughout the research period contain activities to protect natural resources and the environment. Already in 1997, cultural methods for pest control instead of inorganic options were promoted, and trees were planted to re-forest land that suffered from settling refugees (DED LS/403 1997: 13, 7). Seedlings were distributed, forest plantation activities carried out, and environmental awareness campaigns were held in schools and homesteads (DED LS/403 2001: 49-50). Sensitization campaigns and the installation of energy-saving stoves "led to the increased use of energy saving devices and willingness of the beneficiaries to plant multipurpose trees" (DED LS/403 2006: 9). Environmental education was even part of the curriculum at primary schools (DED LS/403 2006: 7). Moreover, instead of continuously providing great water tanks, which are cost-intensive and need to be transported to the remote location of Rhino Camp, boreholes were drilled as early as 1997. Nationals and beneficiaries therewith received access to clean drinking water. This is not only sustainable, but also efficient. Water committees were responsible for the maintenance of the boreholes (DED LS/403 1997: 5).

Agriculture was conducted to the possible extent. What needs to be critically observed are the lacking fallow seasons. Continuously practicing agriculture without fallow seasons not only reduce the productivity of the soil, it furthermore decreases the fertility of the land (Beaudou et al. 2003: 70). Although too little land was made available to refugees for them to take a break from farming, this may have long-term negative effects on the soil. During the interview with Peter, she noted that "[a]fforestation and camp clean-up (after the voluntary repatriation of the refugees to South Sudan) have been integral parts of the programme" (Interview Peter; 01.12.2010). This took place after the research period. It nevertheless shows the commitment to environmental protection.

Based on the information and variety of activities, one can conclude that operations at Rhino Camp were environmental-friendly and targeted to protect and maintain natural resources.

Chapter VI Summary and Conclusion

1. Linking Refugee Aid with Development

Linking refugee assistance with development to close the gap between ad hoc relief and long-term development is not a new idea. In Chapter IV, I analyzed what different concepts about the linkage of refugee assistance and protection with development initiatives existed, and how they changed over time. By means of that, the first sub-question of the overall research question of "how has the approach of development-oriented refugee assistance been developed over the past years?" was analyzed.

Four concepts were found: Integrated Zonal Development Approach, Refugee Aid and Development, Returnee Aid and Development and Targeted Development Assistance.

1.1. Integrated Zonal Development Approach

This approach was a first initiative to link refugee assistance with development. It was developed from the 'good office' and implemented in the 1960s and 1970s. Therefore, the idea of combining refugee and development aid was born then. The approach is sometimes also captured as 'Integrated Rural Development' due to its concentration on larger rural regions. It targeted to "strengthen and consolidate the settlement of the refugees and at the same time benefit the local population." While seeking to provide benefits to both groups, the long-term solution remains to be repatriation and "return home one day" (Sadruddin Aga Khan 1969). The approach integrated the local settlement schemes as a major feature to improve long-term encampment. Little information is available about the implementation of the approach. It remains poorly evaluated and researched, and it is often criticized. Critical voices accentuate that it failed due to a lack of support of respective development agencies, excessive costs, and insufficient funding, among other reasons.

1.2. Refugee Aid and Development

This framework forms the second initiative. It was developed in ICARA I. During the conference, the burden-sharing and responsibility-taking of authorities was strongly emphasized. The impacts of hosting refugees should not only be handled by the countries of first asylum; the international community was asked to take responsibility and to share the burden with the African nations.

The idea behind burden-sharing was primarily founded in financial support from Northern to Southern nations. Participating governments of ICARA I targeted to involve developmental activities to refugee aid "in order to support refugee protection and refugees' access to durable solutions" (Betts 2009a: 7).

Refugee Aid and Development was implemented during the 1980s and 1990s. It aims to integrate development activities in refugee assistance to prevent and to overcome long-term care and maintenance programs in refugee camps, to share the burden among the international community, and to involve the national populace as the additional group of beneficiaries next to the refugee population. The method of local rural settlement continued to be applied. The framework was exercised "in order to avoid the dependency syndrome [of refugees], to reduce the resentment of local citizens towards refugees and, whenever possible, to remedy environmental damage and to compensate for some of the burden imposed by the presence of refugees" (A/42/12: 3).

Voluntary repatriation and local integration were the preferred durable solutions. The '3Rs' of relief, rehabilitation, and resettlement were considered (Betts 2005a: 23; Betts 2004: 2). The framework targeted "to strengthen the absorptive capacities of host countries and to enhance the refugees' contribution to their host States" (A/43/12/Add.1/Annex I: 32). It was found that Refugee Aid and Development lacked a precise strategy. They do not consist of one particular strategy. It is rather a framework, which encompasses aspects that should be taken into account when elaborating strategies (Chamber 1986: 144). While external factors impeded the successful implementation, positions about burden-sharing between Northern donor nations and Southern nations polarized. In connection with that, the framework failed due to the missing will and commitment on both sides, a hardening of attitudes and a lack of funding.

1.3. Returnee Aid and Development

Returnee Aid and Development is the third concept. During the 1990s, UNHCR pursued repatriation as the durable solution. Owing to the shifting focus from refugees to returnees, and from asylum countries to countries of origin, the new developmental objective on the country of origin was identified. Livelihood matters after return became a greater concern of UNHCR to successfully reintegrate returnees. The idea behind the change was "the underlying assumption that refugees cannot be successfully repatriated if the receiving society does not sustain a certain level of development" (Chimni 1999:1).

Returnee Aid and Development was realized through small-scale and short-term projects especially created and adapted to immediate regional needs. They were called Quick Impact Projects (QIPs). UNHCR pursued to achieve peace-building elements of reconstruction and reconciliation through the QIPs. The operational sectors of returnee aid and development and its QIPs were regional, area-based and wide-ranging. The approach is still based on the 3Rs. Access to education, social services and livelihood opportunities, as well as the (re-)construction of infrastructure constitute some of the sectors that were included in QIPs. In planning and implementation processes, UNHCR operated in partnership with UN agencies such as UNDP, development-oriented NGOs, and further development agencies. It was found that reasons for failure are attached to the unsatisfying cooperation of involved agencies and unexpected long durations of transitional processes. In addition, the QIP concept was criticized to be ineffective due to their small-scale and short-term nature, which opposes the development feature of sustainability.

1.4. Targeted Development Assistance

Targeted Development Assistance (TDA) is the fourth and revised framework, which was initiated in the new millennium. It brought about several changes in the international refugee regime. The international community conducted global consultations and dialogues and added budget lines to push for a closing of the gap between emergency aid and development. In 2003, UNHCR published the *Framework for Durable Solutions for Refugees and Persons of Concern.* While repatriation, resettlement, and local integration continued to be the durable solution, they were further developed. The document underlines three frameworks that are interrelated and captured under the umbrella of TDA: Development Assistance for Refugees, Development through Local Integration, and the 4Rs. By doing so, it was aimed to better target development assistance to refugees and returnees, as well as the regions of their residence. Development Assistance for Refugees (DAR) pursues the following objectives:

> Simultaneous improvement of lives and livelihoods (refugees and hosts); Focus on medium and long-term development of refugee hosting areas benefiting both host communities and refugees; Focus on gender/age equality, dignity and improving the quality of life; Enhancement of productive capacities resulting in self-reliance of refugees; Empowers refugees to make their own choices for durable solutions; Broad-based partnership/cooperation with all stakeholders; Burden-sharing with host community and country; Promotion of peaceful co-existence (UNHCR 2005c: One – 4)

UNHCR expects for the refugees to benefit from, among other things, educational facilities, income-generating opportunities, and strengthened community arrangements and capacities. Development through Local Integration (DLI) is defined in UNHCR's Framework for Durable Solutions as

> a programming approach applied in protracted refugee situations where the state opts to provide opportunities for the gradual integration of refugees. It is based on the understanding that those refugees who are unable to repatriate and are willing to integrate locally will find a solution to their plight in their country of asylum. DLI is achieved through additional development assistance (UNHCR 2003d: 24).

DLI is understood as temporary assistance and durable solution. While means of self-sufficiency can be applied to support refugees during their stay, DLI eventually strives for a permanent solution for the refugees in the hosting country of asylum. The 4Rs stand for repatriation, reintegration, rehabilitation and reconstruction and enhance the 3Rs by repatriation and reintegration. UNHCR defines it as

> a programme concept referring to the related repatriation, reintegration, rehabilitation and reconstruction processes of a given operation and which aims to ensure linkages between all four processes so as to promote durable solutions for refugees, ensure poverty reduction and help create good local governance. The concept provides an overarching framework for institutional collaboration in the implementation of reintegration operations allowing maximum flexibility for field operations to pursue country specific approaches (UNHCR 2003d: 18).

The 4Rs approach is particularly important because of the unsystematic reintegration assistance. Needs and interests of refugees and returnees are regarded.

TDA cannot yet be criticized under the above frameworks since pilot programs are ongoing. Nevertheless, current findings expose that the reluctance of Southern states and lacking collaborations of agencies could lead to failures.

2. Features for Development-oriented Refugee Assistance

One of the aims of this research project was to develop features of development-oriented refugee assistance that ensure successful realization. The features were elaborated based on findings about the previous concepts, UNHCR's revised and current working standards, and academic debates — in particular Betts' lists on "ingredients for political agreement" and "ingredients for practical viability" (Betts 2009a: 13-18). Betts focuses on the relations of 'decision-making actors'. While these levels are certainly significant, I extended the scope and integrated the grass-roots level of the beneficiaries' sides and specific methods into the catalog of features. Beneficiaries are refugees as well as local communities. They also capture the operational level. They are understood to be practice-oriented and most fundamental, they are required in order to execute development-oriented refugee assistance successfully and to achieve durable solutions. They encompass situational, time, and actors' dimensions, and are thus multi-dimensional. The developed features are categorized in four sections.

Section 1: Involved Actors

- Political will of Northern and Southern spheres on government and decision-making levels means to accept changing perspectives and launching reform strategies.
- Political willingness of Northern and Southern countries means to be dedicated to linking refugee protection and assistance with development initiatives and hence share burdens.
- Initial global consultations are trend-setting to establish agreements and co-operations between Northern donors and Southern refugee hosts.
- Collaboration of involved actors ensures successful implementation of development-oriented refugee assistance through commitment.
- Regular correspondence of actors involved in programs ensures and promotes information- sharing and transparency, and enables prompt responses to obstacles if necessary.
- Monitoring, reporting, evaluating, and accounting processes support accountability to maintain the credibility and willingness.
- Ownership of development initiatives ensures that refugee hosting countries take ownership and responsibility.
- Integrity and solidarity of staff (particularly field staff) should exist towards maxims to implement a type of assistance that is sustainable, efficient and gender-sensitive.

Section 2: Consideration of time and situational dimensions

- Contextual recognition ensures program planning and implementation that takes specific background data into account.
- Situational considerations ensure program planning and implementation that takes situational and regional factors into account.
- Time factors are to be considered by authorities that design programs to find suitable measures that can reach specific results within a specific timeframe.

Section 3: Targeted groups of beneficiaries

- Integration of refugees and nationals of the hosting country of first asylum is required to be targeted because both groups are supposed to benefit.
- Manners of integration depend on the refugee hosting country of first asylum and should be taken into consideration.
- Interactive levels are to be created for refugees and local communities in long-term refugee assistance programs to avoid conflict and the feeling of exclusion on the side of local communities.

Section 4: Comprehensive methods towards beneficiaries

- Inclusive and comprehensive frameworks are required to be developed on a situation-specific foundation to reach syntheses of refugee and development activities and inclusion of refugees and local communities.
- The rights-based approach is needed to ensure the respect for human rights.
- A gender-sensitive approach is essential in order to use the transitional period to further the process towards gender equality.
- Results-based management targets to reach sustainable results.
- Impact-considering operations target to take into account possible impacts of actions.
- Rural local refugee settlement structures instead of refugee camps are to be used to help refugees to become self-sufficient and to ensure enhanced livelihood.
- Community-based methods are to be applied in order to reach beneficiaries and their specific needs.
- A livelihood-based approach is necessary to strategically improve livelihood conditions of refugee and local communities.
- Pre-existing social structures and chains of command shall be respected and used in local integration in order to avoid dual structures and to harmonize it with existing ones.
- Cross and multi-sectoral strategies are to be developed in order to enhance services and livelihood conditions within all operational sectors.
- Environment-friendly or ecological methodology needs to be applied to protect and sustain the natural resources of the hosting country.

By means of these developed features, the overall research question of "How can the development-oriented approach to refugee assistance be delivered in a way that is sustainable, efficient and gender-sensitive?" is responded to. It is understood that the features are to be fulfilled to successfully implement development-oriented refugee assistance in sustainable, efficient, and gender-sensitive manners.

3. *Assistance at Rhino Camp*

The research project contained a case study conducted at Rhino Camp in Uganda. It was targeted to find out how operations were planned and implemented, what scope operations had, and if and how development was integrated as part of refugee assistance. By doing so, the second sub-question of the overall research question of "How is the approach of development-oriented refugee assistance implemented in practice?" was analyzed.

The case study was based on information drawn from annual reports with the DED Refugee/IDP Programme as the main implementing partner of UNHCR as well as field research. Field research within Rhino Camp as well as the local office of the DED Refugee/IDP Programme in Arua included expert interviews, participative observations, and ero-epic dialogues.

Uganda is a developing country located in sub-Saharan Africa and part of the Great Lakes region. It not only suffered from numerous internal conflicts and instable political conditions since its independence in 1962, but also a slow development and impacts of regional instability. The region has suffered from various violent outbreaks during the second half of the 20th century. Most conflicts took place internally and occurred between rebel groups and national governments, or among ethnicities and tribes. The impact on neighboring countries is particularly feasible through refugee waves.

Refugees in Uganda are predominantly from neighboring countries such as DRC, South Sudan and Rwanda but also from Ethiopia, Somalia, Burundi, Eritrea, and Kenya. Within the research period from 1997 until 2006, about 200,000 refugees were hosted in Uganda according to UNHCR's Statistical Online Population Database. The Government of Uganda agreed on allocating land for local settlement schemes for a medium-term solution to refugees.

The refugee policy of Uganda effective during the research period was the Control of Alien Refugees Act, Cap. 64. It was found that the act contained several strong restrictions. The rights of movement and rights for arbitrary acts were restricted. Authorized officers may press strict charges including imprisonment. Even the use of force was permitted by the act.

Rhino Camp is located in the West Nile region. The West Nile region was rather neglected in development agendas, lacked socio-economic infrastructure and trade, and suffered from internal conflicts and violence in neighboring countries. It has been hosting refugees since the 1960s. Rhino Camp was set up in 1992 and covers an area of approximately 225 square kilometers.

Since Rhino Camp was established, OPM of the Government of Uganda and UNHCR have been the guiding institutions. OPM is in charge of refugee issues for the Government of Uganda. While the settlement was initially managed by UNHCR, DED took over camp management in 1996. DED constitutes the main implementing partner of UNHCR in Rhino Camp. Additional actors were involved in specific service provision or short-term assistance.

According to the annual reports, Rhino Camp obtained an estimated carrying capacity of 32,000 refugees in the case that the national population within the settlement area would not increase about 18,000. During the research period, the refugee populations alternated from 28,571 in 1997 to 35,333 in 2000 — which constituted the absolute maximum reached — to 26,418 in 2004 and 20,231 in 2006. It had 10 zones and 42 clusters. They were set up as villages. Clusters contained several compounds with huts in which people live. The huts were built with locally produced mud bricks and had grass-thatched roofs. The main operational sectors were settlement management and general project management services, health and nutrition, education, food, water and sanitation, infrastructure and shelter, community service, environment and forestry. Refugees and nationals had access to medical services and education through four health centers within the settlement and thirteen primary schools and one secondary school, as well as one skills training center.

3.1. Main Strategies applied

It was found that at Rhino Camp, refugee assistance had a development orientation. The main strategies were the Rural Local Settlement Scheme (LS), Self-Reliance Strategy (SRS), Local Integration (LI) and Development Assistance for Refugees-Hosting Areas (DAR).

The rural local settlement scheme at Rhino Camp prevented long-term encampment and protracted refugee situations with residence in tent structures. Refugees received two plots of land for residential means and agricultural use. The agricultural plots had a size of 0.3 ha.

SRS intended to enhance the livelihoods of nationals and refugees. Services and infrastructure were targeted to be developed and integrated in local systems. Improvement of service structures were part of the development orientation and were considered to be of durable use. Agriculture was promoted and aimed for to reach self-reliance and decrease food distribution. However, it was proven that neither the size of agricultural plots, nor the soil quality or applied farming methods were satisfactory and would thus not lead to self-reliance.

Local integration or rather integration initiatives were part of the SRS. Local integration of refugees in local communities was not intended. The SRS only aimed at an alignment and integration of services and service structures into national systems. According to SRS, it was aimed "to integrate the services to refugees in the eight key sectors of assistance (health; education; community services; agricultural production; income generation; environmental protection; water and sanitation, and infrastructure) currently provided for the refugees into regular government structures and policies" (RLSS Mission Report 2004/03: 3). At Rhino Camp, services of these eight sectors were developed, delivered and integrated in national systems. Refugees and nationals had access to them. Thereby, equal treatment was promoted and refugees were not perceived by nationals as being in an exclusive aid-receiving position. Potential disputes over resource distribution were therefore prevented. Besides distinct services, leadership structures of and within refugee communities were also adjusted to local government structures. Among others, the RWC was set up in the same way as the LC III in the national local council system. Point/Zonal Executives are below the RWC and equivalent to the LC II system in the national setting.

Although local integration of refugees in national communities was not targeted, the annual reports and interviews reveal that the interaction between refugees and nationals was promoted. In addition to enabling both groups of beneficiaries to access services and therewith decreasing the likelihood of disputes over aid, recreational events were organized at Rhino Camp.

DAR aimed at assisting the broader refugee hosting communities. It was not implemented in the direct context of refugee settlements and in line with that, neither at Rhino Camp. DAR was nevertheless part of the development orientation of refugee assistance.

3.2. Final Inferences about the Pillars and Recommendations

In Chapter V, *4.2. Features for Development-oriented Refugee Assistance met?*, assistance provided at Rhino Camp was analyzed against the elaborated features. Based on the collected data about the main strategies, operations and applied features, it is now to conclude whether or not the assistance provided at Rhino Camp satisfied the claims of the three pillars of sustainability, efficiency and gender sensitivity. Recommendations will be made

3.2.1. Sustainability

Operations at Rhino Camp were conducted in local settlement arrangements while taking into consideration Uganda's SRS. Livelihoods were increased by considering the long-term stay of refugees at Rhino Camp by setting up local rural settlement schemes similar to villages, which created a more residential environment. Refugees received two plots of land for residential and agricultural use. They were therefore encouraged to engage in agriculture instead of depending on food aid. This is in line with and part of SRS, which promoted refugees to become self-sufficient. However, it was found that agricultural plots were often not only insufficient in size, but also had in soil quality to successfully practice agriculture. Therefore, refugees were unable to sustain themselves. Refugees fetched their own water from boreholes and ensured the sources' maintenance through their elected committees, while also receiving water from enormous tanks. Tanks exist besides to boreholes in case boreholes cannot be drilled or did not function. Boreholes nevertheless constitute the primary source of water. They will be handed over to district authorities along with other infrastructure, so that nationals can continue to use them after refugees repatriate, which illustrates a sustainable use in properly maintained.

Services delivered in the context of operations were open to refugees and nationals alike. In accordance with the SRS, service structures and infrastructure were aligned with national structures. Human capacities were built by means of offering primary education to children, literacy courses to adults, and vocational trainings. Trainings contributed their empowerment and promoted their economic participation. However, Rhino Camp was very remote. Moreover, refugees faced restricted rights of movement, which had a negative effect on the possibility to find employment, and to further their economic lives.

Natural resources were used and protected while setting up the local settlements instead of tent constructed camps. Engaging in agriculture and attempting to scale down food provision simultaneously decreased waste as well as resulting necessary efforts to clean up and to dispose of the waste. Moreover, DED put an emphasis on engaging in reforestation at Rhino Camp. It aimed at ensuring that natural resources were used, but also protected. To assist the refugee hosting areas directly, environmental programs and the DAR project were initiated. Environmental efforts captured operations and sensitization activities. They targeted to secure natural resources, which may have been affected by the long-term stay of refugees in the region. Among others, activities included the reforestation of the land taken for refugee aid and the promotion of environmental-friendly behavior, the usage of energy-saving stoves and trainings in agricultural methods. The DAR project rather distinctively targeted national communities and the improvement of development in the regions.

Economic growth was promoted by means of facilitating infrastructural development in the refugee hosting region. Infrastructure was developed through refugee aid budgets and was used by refugees and locals. Within the settlement, facilities were not established for the short-term, but rather to be of durable use. Roads, bridges, and buildings were constructed and boreholes drilled. This facilitated the sustainable improvement of livelihoods for nationals because the infrastructures are handed over to the local government after refugees repatriate. The construction of infrastructure therefore is to ensure and to enhance lives of current and future generations. Also, the DAR project contributed to infrastructural development in the refugee-hosting region. According to government information, activities were coherent with the national PEAP (Wafula, OPM 2010). DED's database on infrastructure revealed the broad scope of infrastructure developed. After the repatriation of refugees, infrastructures are to be handed over to the respective district authorities. This would verify the durable benefit and development orientation for local communities. However, the database also revealed a lack of functionality, usability, and access to some of the infrastructure, which limited the durable use. Maintenance is necessary to sustainably benefit from developed infrastructure.

Gender relations and their process towards equality between women and men of refugee and national communities were integrated in planning and implementation processes. Just social relations between women and men were generally targeted and strengthened through gender mainstreaming. Special needs of women were respected and taken care of. Girl child education was promoted and sensitization campaigns carried out to reduce drop-out rates particularly those of girls. Balanced attendance of boys and girls in schools (although unintended) emphasizes equal abilities to learn. Based on these programmatic initiatives, the focus on women in gender-related activities is identifiable at this point. It was already noted above that gender appeared to be equated with women. While women's empowerment — as important as it is — enjoyed diverse operational approaches, men and their roles appeared to be neglected. For a sustainable positive impact on the process towards gender equality, both men and women are to be introduced to the idea of and be involved in activities for empowerment as are women. In addition to lacking gender-related operations, it is to note that neither POP nor the rights-based approach seemed to have been conducted.

In spite of the criticism, men and women were engaged in vocational training. By gaining skills, they became empowered and were able to compete economically by obtaining employment. Political participation was promoted through the encouragement of being part of various committees. In addition, by having women and men working at the management level at DED, the idea of equal capacities and capabilities was reflected to beneficiaries.

Hence, a complex selection of strategies was applied, intend sustainable impact on the development of the country in addition to providing assistance to the primary beneficiaries, the refugees. Development-oriented refugee assistance at Rhino Camp was implemented through diverse multi-linear, cross- and multi-sectoral programs for both groups of beneficiaries at the same time. Thus, activities were comprehensive and interlinked, which created synergies. This promoted sustainable development in Rhino Camp.

Gaps and obstacles in the context of sustainability appeared in particular in three fields as research has shown: the use of infrastructure, gender equality-related assistance, and soil conditions. The durable use of infrastructure even after refugees repatriated is dependent on the district government's decisions. They should make decisions as early as possible for maintenance or demolition reasons. The inadequate soil conditions kept beneficiaries from engaging in agriculture and becoming self-reliant. Gender-related activities revealed a lack of sustainability, especially due to the missing focus and the trend of equating gender-related work with women's empowerment which disregards men.

It is also to note that UNHCR's budget cycles were annual due to funding arrangements from its donors. In line with that, program planning also took place on an annual basis. This conflicts with long-term planning for sustainability.

A recommendation for ensuring the durable use of infrastructure, which according to the DED's database lacked in functionality, would be at the level of policy and local government decision-making. To ensure a sustainable functioning and use of infrastructure, first of all, the local district government needs to decide what is to maintain and rehabilitate. The decision is to be based on an evaluation of population figures in order to discern the need. In case of infrastructure developments are not to be kept, they are to be demolished and plots rehabilitated, e.g. by planting trees to protect the environment. Based on that, financial sources are to be ensured. Since DAR was already initiated, it may be recommendable for the Ugandan government to consider raising the question if UNHCR or development partners can contribute to the rehabilitation. In case of negative responses, internal budgets may be used to maintain and use the already developed infrastructure to ensure sustainable development. In spite of the origin of financial sources, decisions about maintaining or demolishing existing infrastructure should be made as early as possible so that actions can be initiated accordingly and adequately. The recommendation is in line with information provided in an interview with Peter. If district authorities announced, which infrastructure developments are to be kept in advance of the hand-over, respective maintenance may be funded by donors to ensure their durable use and increased livelihoods through continued service delivery.

A second recommendation may be abstract but supports the idea of sustainable use of developed infrastructure. Uganda did not only suffer from refugees but also internal civil conflicts. The conflict between the Lord's Resistance Army and the Government of Uganda in Northern Ugandan region led to large-scale internal displacement. IDPs were kept in protracted situations and encampment. Due to their long-term encampment, the home land of IDPs was occupied by others by the time they returned to their villages of origin. This caused extensive land conflicts. Taking these circumstances into account, it could potentially be considered by the Government of Uganda to offer affected persons to voluntarily settle in the area of Rhino Camp. Therewith, the sustainable running of infrastructures would be ensured and invested funds would be efficiently used.

In the context of the inadequate soil conditions, it may be recommendable to conduct research to find out if there are alternative kinds of seeds that work with the soil conditions. The gender-related gaps will be discussed in the context of gender sensitivity later.

Finally, it is to conclude that the wide range of activities in different sectors were implement while taking into account durable use and improved livelihood conditions. Natural resources were protected. Economic growth was aimed for. Refugees nevertheless suffered from restrictive rights of movement. The process towards just social relations between women and men was attempted to be supported through participatory activities, however, it was not found to be fully satisfactory. Despite the gaps, it can be concluded that the parameters were mainly proven and operations appear to be sustainable.[64] How durable the use of infrastructure indeed is, needs to be analyzed at a later point in time.[65]

3.2.2. Efficiency

Operations at Rhino Camp were found to be implemented in multi- and cross-sectoral manners. Project activities of the different sectors were implemented at the same time. Service delivery was carried out throughout the implementation process. An innovative composition of approaches and activities implemented appears when looking at the type of assistance from the meta-level. Several examples can be listed: boreholes were drilled to access water, a vocational training center was established and trainings offered to build human capacities, energy-saving stoves were installed, loans were provided to promote economic development[66], and farming trainings were offered to refugees. Moreover, innovative stay-in-school campaigns, awareness building campaigns, and recreational events with sport competitions were carried out by and for beneficiaries. These increased awareness and reduced drop-out rates, especially those of girls. Education will eventually contribute to empowerment and economic competitiveness. Despite stay-in-school campaigns and recreational events to reduce drop-out rates, annual reports indicate constant dropouts.

The involvement of political actors seems to have been ensured. The existence of SRS and DAR shows the involvement of political actors of Uganda. The Government of Uganda also attended meetings whenever needed, according to interviews (Interview Peter; 01.12.2010; Interview Namyalo; 12.01.2010).

Natural resources have particularly been taken into account through reforestation, consistent usage of boreholes, and the energy-saving stoves. Through reforestation activities, the natural resources were protected and re-

64 It needs to be emphasized once more that budgets of the DED Refugee/IDP Programme were not provided which is why financial aspects were not considered.

65 Due to the time focus of 1997 until 2006, this was not part of this research. Certain gaps were, however, already attributable through DED's infrastructure database (DED 2008).

66 Information on the loan scheme was not accessible.

vitalized. Drilling boreholes, wherever the water sources allowed for it, throughout Rhino Camp and using natural sources decreased long-term costs. Vast water tanks may not be needed to be provided. Once boreholes were drilled, they merely needed to be maintained. The energy-saving stoves required less firewood for cooking and, produced less smoke which was healthier. Thus, the use of natural resources was decreased; i.e., less new trees need to be planted. This reduced long-term costs. Also, the energy-saving stoves had an unintended and unknown effect on gender-relations. It was found that men started to enter cooking rooms because there was less smoke (Ero-epic dialogue 07.01.2011).

Hence, the programmatic constellation of assistance proves a certain degree of dynamic efficiency. Applied methods - especially local settlements, SRS and DAR - were innovative in their implementation and degree as basic principles. The Government of Uganda and political actors were involved and agreed on providing land for refugee assistance to avoid protracted refugee situations. A diverse constellation of activities was implemented to satisfy needs and establish a sustainable usage. How donor countries reacted and whether they provided comparatively more funds to share the burden is not identifiable. Locals and refugees benefited and long-term facilities were built, which can be used after the repatriation of refugees, if they are maintained. These activities represent dynamic efficiency due to innovative inputs that produced greater outputs.

In addition to that, one needs to ask how efficiently gender-related activities were integrated in the programs, as well as if integration took place in a resource-saving manner and targeted to reach maximum results. When looking at the elaborated parameters of efficiency, the gender context reveals the following: Although the composition of activities to promote women's empowerment was broad, there is little evidence that the activities and their variety were innovative. For example, meeting special (medical) needs of women, providing access to school to boys and girls, promoting the political participation of women and men is rather fundamental refugee assistance. Political actors were somewhat involved. While DAR refers to the need to promote gender equality, SRS does not. Moreover, DAR was not even implemented at Rhino Camp. Since DAR was elaborated based on SRS, it can be assumed that the lack of gender-related aspects was noted and therewith included in DAR. Furthermore is not possible to determine to what extend political actors attempted to promote the process towards gender equality and the inclusion of gender sensitivity in operations. The optimum use of resources is vague because the resources to be used to support gender sensitivity were not defined beforehand. At the beneficiaries' level, one example can be noted. According to the different DED reports, gender-related campaigns to raise awareness on diverse issues were held in different sectors. For that purpose, little resources were used to reach out to several communities and their members. However, as argued above, it was also found that several gender-related activities predominantly targeted to reach refugee women and to support their empowerment with little regard to men and their roles. Subsequently, an overarching conclusion on the efficient inclusion of gender-related activities in programs cannot be drawn.

Gaps existed. In spite of free primary education, stay-in-school campaigns and recreational events to reduce drop-out rates, annual reports proved continuity in the numbers of school drop-outs. Agricultural efforts and related farming trainings were promoted from 1997 onwards. Food supplies nevertheless remained to be provided to beneficiaries up until 2006 due to unsuitable soil conditions. Thus, the target of self-sufficiency was not accomplished. Numerous infrastructural development initiatives were built, which were supposed to be of sustainable use. After refugees repatriate, infrastructures are intended to be handed over to district authorities and it is on them to decide whether to maintain them. Based on the rather small national community residing in or close to Rhino Camp, it is to be questioned whether the construction of constant buildings and facilities were indeed efficient. In addition to that, vocational trainings and loan schemes were provided. It is however not verifiable through literature or interviews how useful or efficient they were to beneficiaries towards economic empowerment. In the context of activities to promote gender equality, gaps remained as well. There was a lack in the degree of innovation; neither activities per se nor the composition of gender-related activities were found to be innovative. In spite of that, gender-related activities were implemented in all sectors. Through community campaigns, little resources were used, but as a result the maximum amount of beneficiaries was reached.

Recommendations are limited. Due to the nature of the above identified gaps in the sectors of education, soil conditions, and infrastructure, it is necessary that experts work on recommendations and develop potential solutions. The gaps therefore create avenues for further research. In the context of gender-related activities, it was noted that measures were little innovative. Considering the current international developments towards technology use, it may be interesting to take into account activities with computers or mobile phones. The use of mobile phones shows great positive impact on the collection and flow of information. This could be applied for SGBV measures and localization.[67]

67 An innovative and currently worldwide new approach in the context of including technology in development assistance is shown by UNICEF Uganda. The office developed a so-called Digital Drum. The rain-proof drums integrate a computer with internet access. By means of that, local communities gain internet access and learn about computers.

Finally, it is to conclude that innovative activities as well as a great composition of projects were applied. Political actors were involved. Natural resources were also found to be protected and well used in several measures. Despite the gaps in agriculture and the lack of functionality of infrastructure, it can be concluded that operations appear to be efficient.[68]

3.2.3. Gender Sensitivity

On a more basic level, the post-modern feminist factor of language was operationalized particularly through references in the DED annual reports. Psychological support and counseling were found to be necessary to be provided due to the transitional period to refugees. However, did gender roles and relations alter as a consequence of their refuge? Based on empirical data, it was found that the demographic age structure of female and male refugees was not even. In the groups of 15 to 19 year olds as well as 20 to 24 year olds, great differences are visible. Almost twice as many male than female refugees lived in Rhino Camp. It was also found that the great majority of single-parent households spread all over the area of Rhino Camp were headed by females. Single female-headed households with several children and single women are classified as especially vulnerable persons (Beaudou et al. 2003: 59, 61a, 61; DED LS/403 1998: 23).

Gender relations were discovered to show distinct differences between men and women at Rhino Camp. Refugee and local communities were found to be based on clear social and authoritarian structures. In brief, gender relations were based on patriarchal and patrilineal clan structures which developed over time and thus can be rated as traditional. Under the umbrella of these traditional role allocations, men possessed a precisely dominating status over the respective family. The male dominated culture was especially shown in terms of decision making and heading the household. Women were in an inferior and rather supportive role. Women maintained households, watched and raised children (Mulumba 2005: 175-183).

Due to refuge and while living at Rhino Camp, these traditionally grown and ascribed gender roles and relations changed, especially because pre-existing

Further information is provided under "UNICEF-developed computer kiosk aims to provide information access to isolated communities in Uganda" via UNICEF 2011.

68 It needs to be emphasized on more that budgets of the DED Refugee/IDP Programme were not provided and accessed which is why financial aspects were not taken into account.

social structures among the refugees were not maintained in the refugee settlement. The clans were separated and therefore could not pursue the working modes from the pre-refuge time. Women obtained additional responsibilities and fields of action. The nature of single female-headed households included that women were in charge of maintaining the household, cultivating land, and ensuring food supply. While women perceived the process as liberating, men felt cheated because they lost part of their traditional authority. Despite the progress, traditional conflict resolution mechanisms through the elders of a clan were dysfunctional, and polygamy on the male side remained to be practiced and accepted (Mulumba 2005: 175-183).

DED's annual reports reveal that some operational measures target the above changes. Among others, it was known that the majority of single (-parent) households were headed by females. Since protective clan structures did not persist at Rhino Camp, they were understood to be especially vulnerable and in need of protection which was provided. Moreover, food provision was also prioritized for female-headed households.

However, these activities put female refugees, despite their vulnerability, on a higher level than male refugees. This is a drastic change and if not perspicuously explained to male refugees, the feeling of being cheated on may be traceable. From their point of view, it may appear that they have not only lost their homes and existence in South Sudan and were forced to leave. Moreover, they have also lost their traditional authority over women. The DED reports do not reveal any information about project activities that aimed at creating awareness and sensitization regarding the way in which women are perceived as being especially vulnerable and why they receive the kind of assistance that they do.

Psychological support and counseling was found to be necessary to not only support both sexes during the transitional period to handle experiences but also to promote the empowerment of women. Annual reports merely revealed that the Transcultural Psychosocial Organisation offered and provided psycho-social counseling to traumatized people. No information was accessible about how the psychological and psycho-social support was provided to beneficiaries, who was supported and when counseling was offered to whom. Neither annual reports nor interviews could reveal any information. Moreover, inquiries remained unanswered. This suggests a significant gap.

Not only information about psychological and psycho-social support and counseling was insufficient. Information about SGBV at Rhino Camp was also inadequately reported on. Little data about SGBV was accessible. Prior to 2001, DED reports do not mention any reference to SGBV. The DED reports from 2001 until 2005 merely indicate few incidences and the implementation of awareness building measures in order to sensitize the communities. For instance in 2005 24 cases of SGBV were reported. Considering that 25,157 refugees lived in Rhino Camp, 24 cases are an unrealistically small number. This is especially obvious when taking into account that the number of incidences increased by more than seven times with 184 cases compared to the 24 cases reported in the previous year of 2005. It was not until the 2006 report, that additional background information was provided. The types of violent incidences were broken down and supported with empirical data. According to the 2006 report, in addition to continuous implementation of awareness-raising campaigns, a community-based SGBV center was established. Victims "benefited from routine guidance and counseling services" and reported cases were announced to be brought to "legal justice in Arua" (DED LS/403 2006: 38-39). This provokes the assumption that SGBV incidences may receive sufficient psychological and medical support. Though, procedures are not explained in the report, which reveals a gap and leaves the above as an assumption rather than a conclusion.

Activities for women's empowerment were conducted throughout. In 2005 and 2006, 'refugee women/gender equality' were even listed as policy priorities. While in 1997, special female needs were primarily taken care of, community sensitization was increasingly implemented in the years from 1998 until 2006. As a basic principle, Age, Gender, Diversity and Mainstreaming (AGDM) assessments and further surveys were conducted for program planning (Interview Peter; 01.12.2010). Gender mainstreaming was also implemented by means of the continuous integration of women and men in program implementation. Both sexes were encouraged to participate in committees, engaged in education and vocational training. Sensitization campaigns were also conducted. Gender-sensitive planning and implementations were therefore attempted to be carried out. How thoroughly assessments and surveys were carried out, however, is not possible to determine. However, based on the collected information through DED's annual reports and the conducted interviews, it was found that beneficiaries' voices appear to be vaguely heard and considered. Also, no reference was found about the application of POP.

On DED staff level, it is important to note that women and men alike were employed to implement operations. Their involvement in operations on a general basis may reflect equal abilities to the outside. At the DED Refugee/IDP Programme and the Rhino Camp in particular, women are on management positions. They work hand in hand with other stakeholders and the leading agencies UNHCR and OPM.

It was found that the already mentioned energy-saving stoves not only protected natural resources but also positively impacted on gender relations. These stoves not only produced less smoke and hence were better for women's health who were traditionally the ones cooking. Moreover, during an ero-epic dialogue, it was explained that men started to enter cooking areas while women were cooking. The reduced production of smoke appeared to have had a positive impact on gender relations.

The annual reports reveal that men and women along with children and youths participated in educational programs. While children and youth had access to primary education, literacy classes and vocational trainings were offered to adults. This holistic approach to education-related empowerment was accessible to refugee and national beneficiaries. Health initiatives did not only include ensuring to meet the special needs of women. It was also encouraged to prevent and treat cases of sexual and gender-based violence. Victims were assisted to pursue legal actions. Yet again, whether or not victims received psychological support remains unknown (DED LS/403 2001: 22, 25). Political participation in representing committees was also encouraged. DED reported to have pursued an equally balanced rate of 50 per cent representation of women and men but not less than 30 per cent of women, which was not only stated in annual reports but was also revealed in interviews.

Further activities restricted in time targeted the promotion of the inclusion women and aimed at increasing awareness. For example, a workshop on women and food distribution was conducted to increase the representation of women leaders in committees at Rhino Camp, the "Sports for Girls" initiative was implemented to decrease girl drop-out rates in schools, and SGBV sensitization campaigns were launched.

Gender relations were targeted to be improved towards equality especially through trainings, the integration of men and women in committees and various sensitization campaigns about HIV/AIDS, education and on further theme. Training sessions on gender issues were offer to DED staff and refugee leaders. "The beneficiaries of these trainings included Senior Women Teachers, Women representatives, Girl Child Coordinators, Youth representatives and Church representatives" (DED LS/403 2001: 34-35). They then acted as multipliers and applied the gained knowledge. Women and men were encouraged to engage in political participation of the various committees. However, more men continued to be present in these committees than women (Interview Peter; 01.12.2010). The campaigns aimed building awareness on various issues. Especially campaigns on HIV/AIDS aimed at provoking behavior changes. For that, men and women need to be involved. While DED's annual reports reveal great numbers of participation, data on results are not available. A gender focal person was also not existent in the DED Refugee/IDP Programme structure.

As revealed above, the term 'gender' has been mentioned and referred to in DED's annual reports. DED's works at Rhino Camp show especially that the inclusion of women, their concerns and needs in operations and programs were pursued. While in 1997, special female needs were primarily taken care of, community sensitization was increasingly implemented in the years from 1998 until 2006. From 2000 onwards, one specific objective was to ensure that the role of women was integrated in project implementation (DED LS/403 2000: 2). From 2001 onwards, sensitization about SGBV became a part of operations. The 2001 report states that it was targeted to "[s]ensitize the community and women in particular on gender issues so as to create gender equity in decision-making at all levels and help to reduce Sexual and Gender Based Violence (SGBV)" (DED LS 403 2001: 31). "Gender responsive planning" was integrated in 2002. By means of that, it was aimed to "[s]trengthen women's participation in sports and decision making" (DED LS 403 2002: 30-37). From 2003 onwards, gender aspects were included in all sectors of health and nutrition, education, food, water, sanitation, infrastructure and shelter, community service and environmental work. Special attention was then targeted to be provided wherever possible. From 2004 until 2006, gender mainstreaming was applied. Women and men were targeted to be involved in committees in order to ensure that their voices and specific concerns are heard (DED LS/403 2004: 33).

Despite mentioning men and women participating in operations, a clear tendency in all DED reports were found towards equating the term 'gender' with 'women'. This is also revealed through the above summary of operational activities under the umbrella of gender. 'Gender'-related activities predominantly focused on women's empowerment and women's protection and meeting women's special needs rather than gender equality. Men seem to be neglected, which could be understood as positive discrimination. This trend conforms to the above mentioned feeling of neglect by refugee men. It was previously noted that refugee women perceived their increased scopes of responsibilities as liberating while refugee men had the feeling of being cheated due to the loss of their traditional roles, which leaves them with the decision-making power as head of the household (Mulumba 2005: 179). Only one DED report noted the need to sensitize men (DED LS/403 1998: 9). The other reports did not indicate project activities that targeted to create awareness and sensitization especially to men explaining why women are viewed as vulnerable, why they receive the kind of assistance they do, why women shall participate in decision-making committees, why the process of changing gender roles comes about, and why women perceive the process towards their empowerment as liberating. Also, although SGBV cases were registered from 2001 onwards, no anti-violence trainings were offered for men and women to grasp that violence does not solve conflicts.

A clear focus and strategy of gender sensitivity is not feasible in DED's reports. There is no mission statement of DED or the cooperation of OPM, UNHCR and DED that clarifies the existence and adaptation of a gender sensitivity strategy. It is therefore vague, what the focus and main implementation methods are. Political participation is a method highlighted throughout all DED reports; women and men are being promoted to participate in committees. Although political participation is continuously used, it is, however, not strongly or often insufficiently applied. Hence, it is not enough to identify political participation as an operational focus for gender sensitivity.

The focus on women's needs is also frequently mentioned in DED's reports; it, however, only focuses on women and is therefore little 'gender'-sensitive because particular needs of men were not mentioned once. The lack of a clear focus is thus recognizable and to be noted critically.

Hence, numerous activities were implemented to strive to empower women. The most consistent and obvious examples are promoting girl child education, integrating women on decision-making positions in camp management and operational sectors, providing access to vocational trainings for economic opportunities, enhancing women's participation in committees, conducting awareness campaigns, satisfying special needs of women in the medical context.

Gaps and obstacles existed despite numerous activities which intended to be gender-sensitive at Rhino Camp. Firstly, it is not possible to confirm how psychological support and counseling were provided. Too little information on counseling and handling SGBV cases was accessible. It remains unknown how support was offered, to whom, who provided support and what follow-up activities existed. I am therefore unable to measure and conclude if and to what extent psychological and psycho-social support promoted the process towards revising traditional gender images and roles towards gender equality. Secondly, during the analyses of operations against the features, it was found that operations lacked a clear application of the human rights-based approach. In line with that, POP was also not clearly visible in any of the reports. This is a significant gap. Thirdly, all above stated examples of activities run under the term "gender-sensitive" but refer to the distinct involvement of women in operations. Yet, gender equality and gender sensitivity include both sexes of women and men. The trend appears in all reports that the term 'gender' is being equated with 'women'. This affects men in negative sense through neglect. One may argue that male beneficiaries automatically had increased access to education, decision-making positions, health services, vocational training and economic life. Eventually, it is not only about access to opportunities but rather enlightening both sexes about equal capabilities, which are to be reached by equal access to education, health, economic life, and decision-making positions. Fourthly, although gender sensitivity appears to have been applied, gender equality was found to be little promoted. Refugee women without family support or husbands were perceived to be in weaker positions and more susceptible. Especially single women and single female-headed households with several children were understood to be a vulnerable group of beneficiaries, who requires additional assistance to meet basic needs, according to DED's reports. If other beneficiaries without considering the sex perceived a smaller group of persons to receive significantly more care and assistance, the feeling of jealousy among beneficiaries may come up. This is in line with the above noted feeling of neglect by men. Fifthly, a clear gender sensitivity strategy is missing. It remains unknown how gender equality is targeted to be achieved strategically and what the specifically intended outcomes and operational goals are.

Recommendations are developed to the above noted gaps and based on ideal-typical operations. Based on international standards and local needs and opportunities at Rhino Camp, a strategy of gender sensitivity would have to be developed which would close the fifth gap. This is to be in line with UNHCR standards. Since the UN is working towards operating in a harmonization under the umbrella of "One UN", it may be feasible to consult with UN Women or UNFPA. These agencies have a great expertise in matters of gender equality and may be able to support the elaboration of the strategy. Nevertheless, UNHCR remains to be the UN's agency most experienced in and mandated for matters of displacement. Their regularities therefore have to be taken into account. Based on the strategy, by appointing a gender specialist it may be possible to improve the other gaps. The employment of such a specialist depends, however, on sufficient budget. The specialist could oversee the general integration of gender sensitivity in program implementation and be responsible for adequate planning, monitoring and reporting. Through integrating gender sensitivity it could lead to the assumption that in fact men and women are integrated equally. Hence, doing so would target to overcome the trend of equating 'gender' with 'women' which means to go against the third and fourth gap. On the planning stage, the second gap of the missing application of the human rights-based approach and POP would be improved due to integration. Ideal-typically, planning sessions would be based on in-depth assessments which identify beneficiaries' needs. Female and male beneficiaries would therefore be able to voice their opinions and have it heard. On the monitoring stage, the first gap would be touched besides keeping an eye on the daily implementation and its effectiveness. The visibility, accessibility and transparency of psychological support and counseling as well as SGBV incidence support could be improved. The gender specialist would not be in charge of implementing the above. S/he would rather be overseeing processes.

Finally, it is to conclude that the collected data reveals the political participation of men and women was promoted and gender mainstreaming took place during planning and implementation processes. How psychological support was given is unknown. Nevertheless, it can be assumed that through the variety of activities, an impact on gender images and roles towards gender equality was reached. How great the impact may be, cannot be precisely indicated and requires further analysis.

At last and in addition to the above gaps and recommendations, final remarks are to be noted while wearing the post-modern feminist glasses. While consulting the research findings of Mulumba, information on traditional and modified gender roles and relations were found. The data was based on the Madi tribe from South Sudan. As summarized above, the ascribed traditional gender relations were found to be based on clear social and authoritarian structures through patriarchal and patrilineal clan structures. Men possessed a dominating status over the respective family, maintained decision making, and headed the household. Women were rather captured in inferior and supportive roles by being in charge of maintaining households and raising children (Mulumba 2005: 175-183). Similar patriarchal and patrilineal structures exist for the local communities in West Nile region in Uganda (Tuyizere 2007: 125).

The refuge and the limited stay at Rhino Camp caused these transitional conditions. Mulumba found that women received numerous additional responsibilities which they perceived as liberating. Among others, women received food provision without being depending on their husbands. Men were found to feel cheated due to the loss of power and authority (Mulumba 2005: 181, 179). Despite different perceptions, it is to note that gender roles changed due to the transitional conditions and assistance provided at Rhino Camp.

In retrospective and in consultation with the research findings of Mulumba, it can be concluded that a liberating process for women's empowerment was launched. Due to the numerous activities targeting the inclusion and promotion of women, they gained additional responsibilities. The pre-existing social structures left refugee women in inferior roles with little power. Due to displacement, the traditional patriarchal and patrilineal clan structures became dysfunctional and allowed women to break out of their ascribed role allocations. Through the accumulation and range of different occurrences, they experienced a movement towards equalization to men. However, as already noted above, men were partly left out. They felt neglected and betrayed. Neither awareness building measures nor a consistent inclusion of men in gender-related activities in the context of refugee assistance was possible to be determined. This leads to the assumption that men were insufficiently integrated in the transitional process and opportunities for transformation.

While wearing the post-modern feminist glasses, the very fundamental idea that gender roles are not inflexible role allocations between men and women is viewed. Thus, post-modern feminism believes that sex-specific roles and identities are flexible and not static. The roles shall be clarified in order to deconstruct gender stereotyping. Thereby, androcentric or, in this case, patriarchal and patrilineal structures can be revised. Stereotypes are seen as counterproductive to improvements and promoting the process towards gender equality. As shown above, women received and handled additional responsibilities while at Rhino Camp. Their role changed significantly and they themselves perceived these changes as liberating. Men also perceived the changes of traditional gender roles although with a negative connotation. This verifies the assumption of post-modern feminism that gender roles are ascribed, can be changed, and are therefore flexible. In the context of DED's annual reports, it becomes clear that the role allocations and the characteristics of gender relations were not taken into account to a satisfactory degree. While women's empowerment was a constant in the reports, the actual interaction between men and women was not reported on and does not appear to have been targeted. From a post-modern feminist perspective, DED would have to take the traditional roles into account in order to create suitable activities to deconstruct them and thereby revise role allocations. Ultimately, this was not done. Nevertheless, according to the annual reports, DED designed and implemented activities to promote women's empowerment. By doing so, they use the psychological transformation opportunities, which may help women to increasingly strive for gender equality.

4. Additional Remarks on Development-oriented Refugee Assistance

Successfully implemented development-oriented refugee assistance depends on numerous factors. While Betts mainly focused on international spheres (Betts 2009a), I included operational levels. This is understood to have great potential for preventing protracted refugee situations, improving the livelihoods of refugee communities in the first country of asylum, and to contribute development in the refugee hosting region of the country of asylum. Whether on the decision-making or operational level, the overall aim of development-oriented refugee assistance remains to be burden-sharing and responsibility-sharing between the global South and the global North.

At a time when refugees predominantly flee from one developing country to another developing country, it becomes obvious that the drive of forced displacement and cross-border migration has changed. When UNHCR was established, it was initially mandated to assist refugees caused by the Second World War. Today's epicenter of forced migrants is, however, in the global South. While this means that refugee issues may be geographically far from the global North, it nevertheless obligates the global North to assist.

One crucial precondition is cooperation, whether through funding, expertise or other means. Cooperation was one of two hypotheses of the research project. The hypothesis was stated in the introduction. It said that development-oriented refugee assistance can only be achieved sustainably, efficiently and gender-sensitively if the direct actors (UNHCR, OPM, DED) cooperate, transparency and information flows exists, and beneficiaries are fully integrated in processes.

Although it is not clearly visible to what extent the global North assisted financially refugee aid in Uganda through UNHCR, the case study conducted at

Rhino Camp proved that cooperation was fundamental to implement development-oriented refugee assistance. On a very basic level, if the Government of Uganda had not allocated the land for refugee settlement, local settlements for long-term assistance could not have been realized. The direct actors appeared to have worked together. Continuous reporting and regular meetings promoted information flows and transparency. This was not only verified in annual reports but also revealed in interviews. Beneficiaries were included in operational processes although local integration was targeted.

The second hypothesis was on the operational level; it was assumed that activities of different sectors are to be combined and implemented simultaneously in an integrated or cross-sectoral manner. In reference to the case study at Rhino Camp, multi and cross-sectoral operations were proven. The main operational sectors were settlement management and general project management services, health and nutrition, education, food, water and sanitation, infrastructure and shelter, community service, environment and forestry. Activities were implemented at the same time. Through the composition of activities and methods applied, livelihoods of refugees and local communities were targeted to be increased.

The hypotheses were focused on the operational level. The contemporary developments of forced migration show that most refugee waves remain in the global South. This needs to be taken into account by the international community and their policies. Adjusting aid to new challenges is particularly important in order to meet human rights and gender equality. Numerous refugee waves are again and again the result of natural disasters such as floods or droughts; environment-induced forced migration and affected persons, however, are still not covered by refugee law and defined as refugees. While refugee waves take place in the global South, Northern donors should provide adequate support although (or maybe especially because) donors are far from the region of the incident. The funding manners and the scope of donors to UNHCR have to be sufficient in order to successfully share burdens and responsibilities between the global North and the global South. This aspect has been highlighted by Betts as well (Betts 2009a).

5. *Avenues for Future Research*

Since sharing burdens and responsibilities between the global North and the global South is a precondition for development-oriented refugee assistance, it is necessary to analyze how cooperation can be improved. Betts already researched the international level and highlighted that strengthened cooperation is necessary (Betts 2009a). Financial contributions and commitments by Northern donors to the global South are fundamental for assistance if resettlement to a third country and immediate repatriation is not a potential durable solution for a refugee influx. Besides funding, burden and responsibility sharing also includes harmonized assistance. In the context of Uganda, it was surprising that UNDP did not appear to have played a role although UNHCR's assistance at Rhino Camp included a development orientation. Several questions came up, which may blaze the trail towards burden and responsibility sharing between agencies: What agency is responsible for which field of operation? How can additional agencies still assist in enhancing knowledge? How can different agencies best cooperate on the policy and operational level? How can funding opportunities best be used to achieve sustainable results? While funding gaps continue to be pointed out in research and operational publications, looking at how to better link operations among the agencies may contribute to more efficient aid. Inter-agency assistance entails intense administrative means; however, the different agencies are specialized and contain expertise. Knowledge-practice gaps may be closed by combining expertise. In recent years, discussions were already initiated between agencies as explained in Chapter VI. Initiatives such as the Global Forum on Migration and Development bring representatives of agencies to one table to discuss options. What needs to be analyzed is how agencies can cooperate and share knowledge at the policy and operational level.

On the basis of previous initiatives to link refugee protection and assistance with development, the features for development-oriented refugee assistance were developed. The features aim to be practice-oriented and fundamental, encompass situational, time, and actors' dimensions, and thus be multi-dimensional. They were applied against the operations at Rhino Camp in Uganda. In order to test their practicability and universality, they need to be applied against additional development-oriented refugee assistance operations. This would be an important avenue for further research for me. An additional field study in a different setting may reveal aspects which were not taken into account in this case.

Gender sensitivity was treated as a guiding pillar in the context of this research. While going back to the dual imperative of gender sensitivity in the context of development-oriented refugee assistance, it was assumed that that the psychological transitional process of refugees could lead to greater gender parity through adequate (hence, gender-sensitive) operations. Moreover, through the involvement and participation of men and women, developmental programs could also lead to revised gender constellations and equality if activities are performed in a gender-sensitive manner. To assess the actual extent of revised gender roles, research would ideal-typically have to be based on refugee identities and how specific roles changed over a scope of time from before refuge, while in the settlement and potentially also after repatriation. Due to this research project's time and regional confinements, the process towards revising gender constellations for a rather equal role set-up between men and women, the focus was on the programmatic sphere. It was included, how men and women were supported and participated in operations. An avenue for further research would be to go into further detail. Based on the findings, it would be interesting to carry out research on returning refugees in South Sudan while integrating refugee identities. It would be important to analyze the gender relations after repatriation to the regions of origin. The focus should be on it was assumed that if women maintained the additional responsibilities gained while being at Rhino Camp. Moreover, do they transfer the gained knowledge to their female and male fellows in the region of origin? Although war-torn, it may be feasible to look at a broader regional area including communities that remained in South Sudan and those that had fled. Comparing both communities and their gender role constellations may bring forward results that could help to judge if gender sensitivity in development-oriented refugee assistance can indeed support the process towards gender equality.

In relation to the case study conducted at Rhino Camp, two particular areas for future research are discernible: research on local communities and services in the former refugee-hosting region in Uganda, and research on agriculture.

Firstly, in the West Nile region of Uganda, it would be interesting to research if the developed infrastructures are sustainably used and maintained. It was found that the area of Rhino Camp was sparsely populated, yet infrastructure developments took place. DED's database on infrastructure already revealed certain lacks in functionality of some of the infrastructure. On a long-term basis, it is to analyze whether infrastructures are maintained and used, and whether service delivery to the national population is provided through governmental organizations. If this was the case, it would reveal that activities of refugee were development-oriented and sustainable.

Secondly, agriculture was supposed to be a part of SRS in Uganda. While efforts were undertaken to promote farming at Rhino Camp, a geographical study provided reasons for little success (Beaudou et al. 2003). Although soil conditions were not suitable, it would be interesting to conduct further research on possible farming methods and produce which could be applied and targeted.

Bibliography

Annual Reports of DED

DED LS/403 1997 - DED Refugee/IDP Programme. Annual Report. PROJECT: 97/AB/UGA/LS/403(a).
DED LS/403 1998 - DED Refugee/IDP Programme. Annual Report. PROJECT: 98/AB/UGA/LS/403(a).
DED LS/403 1999 - DED Refugee/IDP Programme. Annual Report. PROJECT: 99/AB/UGA/LS/403(a).
DED LS/403 2000 - DED Refugee/IDP Programme. Annual Report. PROJECT: 00/AB/UGA/LS/403(a).
DED LS/403 2001 - DED Refugee/IDP Programme. Annual Report. PROJECT: 01/AB/UGA/LS/403(a).
DED LS/403 2002 - DED Refugee/IDP Programme. Annual Report. PROJECT: 02/AB/UGA/LS/403(a).
DED LS/403 2003 - DED Refugee/IDP Programme. Annual Report. PROJECT: 03/AB/UGA/LS/403(a).
DED LS/403 2004 - DED Refugee/IDP Programme. Annual Report. PROJECT: 04/AB/UGA/LS/403(a).
DED LS/403 2005 - DED Refugee/IDP Programme. Bi-Annual Report. PROJECT: 05/AB/UGA/LS/403(a).
DED LS/403 2006 - DED Refugee/IDP Programme. Annual Report. PROJECT: 06/AB/UGA/LS/403(a).
DED LS/403 2007 - DED Refugee/IDP Programme. Annual Report. PROJECT: 07/AB/UGA/LS/403(a).
DED LS/453 2006 - DED Refugee/IDP Programme. Annual Report. PROJECT: 06/AB/UGA/LS/453(a).
DED RP/331 2004 - DED Refugee/IDP Programme. Annual Report. PROJECT: 04/SB/UGA/RP/331(a).
DED RP/331 2006 - DED Refugee/IDP Programme. Annual Report. PROJECT: 07/SB/UGA/RP/331(a).
DED. 2008. Database on infrastructures. Kampala.

Documents of the Government of Uganda or related Institutions

Government of Uganda/Office of the Prime Minister. 2000. Refugee statistics in Arua District, 2000. Kampala: Government of Uganda.
Government of Uganda/Office of the Prime Minister. 2001. Refugee statistics in Arua District, 2001. Kampala: Government of Uganda.
Government of Uganda/Office of the Prime Minister. 2002. Refugee statistics in Arua District, 2002. Kampala: Government of Uganda.
MFPED 2004 - Ministry of Finance, Planning and Economic Development. 2004. Poverty Eradication Action Plan. Kampala 2004.
MFPED 2004/5 - Poverty Eradication Action Plan (2004/5-2007/8). Kampala.

OPM 2007 - Office of the Prime Minister. 2007. Karamoja Integrated Disarmament and Development Programme. Creating Conditions for Promoting Human Security and Recovery in Karamoja, 2007/2008-2009/2010. Kampala Uganda. (http://www.brookings.edu/~/media/Files/Projects/IDP/Laws%20and%20Policies/Uganda/Uganda_Karamoja_2007.pdf).
OPM 2008 - Office of the Prime Minister. 2008. Camp Phase out Guidelines for all Districts that have IDP Camps. Kampala.
Uganda 1960 - Government of Uganda. 1960. Control of Alien Refugees Act, Cap. 64, 13 July 1960 (http://www.unhcr.org/refworld/docid/3ae6b4d2c.html, 02.05.2010).
Uganda 1999 - Government of Uganda. 1999. Self-reliance for refugee hosting areas in Moyo, Arua and Adjumani District, Uganda. Strategy Paper. Kampala.
Uganda 1999b - Government of Uganda. 1999b. Uganda Citizenship and Immigration Control Act 1999, Cap. 66. Act No. 3 of 1999.
Uganda 2003 - Government of Uganda. 2003. Refugees Bill 2003. (http://www.unhcr.org/refworld/docid/3e7700564.html, 02.05.2010).
Uganda 2007 - Government of Uganda. 2007. Peace, Recovery and Development Plan for Northern Uganda. Kampala.
Wafula, OPM 2010 – Wafula, Michael Remy, Office of the Prime Minister. 2010. DAR. (http://opm.go.ug/index.php?curpage=submenus&id=20, 13.07.2010).

UN Documents (legal and advisory)

A/2011 – UNHCR. Refugees and Stateless Persons and Problems of Assistance to Refugees: Report of the United Nations High Commissioner for Refugees, 1951. 1 January 1952.
A/5511/Rev.1 - UNHCR. Report of the United Nations High Commissioner for Refugees. 1 January 1964.
A/5511/Rev.1/Add.1 - UNHCR. Addendum to the Report of the United Nations High Commissioner for Refugees. 1 January 1964.
A/5811/Rev.1/Add.1 - UNHCR. Addendum to the Report of the United Nations High Commissioner for Refugees. 1 January 1965.
A/6011/Rev.1/Add.1 - UNHCR. Addendum to the Report of the United Nations High Commissioner for Refugees. 1 January 1966.
A/6711 - UNHCR. Report of the United Nations High Commissioner for Refugees. 1 January 1968.
A/7211 - UNHCR. Report of the United Nations High Commissioner for Refugees. 1 January 1969.
A/8012 - UNHCR. Report of the United Nations High Commissioner for Refugees. 1 January 1971.
A/8012/Add.1 - UNHCR. Addendum to the Report of the United Nations High Commissioner for Refugees. 1 January 1971.
A/8712 - UNHCR. Report of the United Nations High Commissioner for Refugees. 1 January 1973.
A/9012 - UNHCR. Report of the United Nations High Commissioner for Refugees. 1 January 1974.
A/10012 - UNHCR. Report of the United Nations High Commissioner for Refugees. 1 May 1975.
A/31/12 - UNHCR. Report of the United Nations High Commissioner for Refugees. 1 January 1976.

A/34/12 - UNHCR. Report of the United Nations High Commissioner for Refugees. 11 October 1979.
A/34/12/Add.1 – UNHCR. Addendum to the Report of the United Nations High Commissioner for Refugees. 11 October 1979.
A/35/12 – UNHCR. Report of the United Nations High Commissioner for Refugees. 24 September 1980.
A/35/42 – General Assembly Resolution. International Conference on Assistance to Refugees in Africa. 25 November 1980.
A/36/12 – UNHCR. Report of the United Nations High Commissioner for Refugees. 28 August 1981.
A/36/12/Add.1 – UNHCR. Addendum to the Report of the United Nations High Commissioner for Refugees. 28 August 1981.
A/39/402 - General Assembly, Office of the United Nations High Commissioner for Refugees: Second International Conference on Assistance to Refugees in Africa (ICARA II): Report of the Secretary-General. 22 August 1984.
A/40/12 - UNHCR. Report of the United Nations High Commissioner for Refugees. 13 September 1985.
A/41/12 - UNHCR. Report of the United Nations High Commissioner for Refugees. 1 August 1986.
A/42/12 - UNHCR. Report of the United Nations High Commissioner for Refugees. 27 July 1987.
A/43/12 - UNHCR. Report of the United Nations High Commissioner for Refugees. 4 August 1988.
A/43/12/Add.1/Annex I - UNHCR. Addendum to the Report of the United Nations High Commissioner for Refugees. 26 October 1988.
A/44/523 – General Assembly. Office of the United Nations High Commissioner For Refugees: International Conference on Inco-Chinese Refugees. Report of the Secretary-General. 22 September 1989.
A/44/12 - UNHCR. Report of the United Nations High Commissioner for Refugees. 1 September 1989.
A/44/12/Add.1 - UNHCR. Addendum to the Report of the United Nations High Commissioner for Refugees. 1 September 1989.
A/45/12 - UNHCR. Report of the United Nations High Commissioner for Refugees. 24 September 1990.
A/46/12 - UNHCR. Report of the United Nations High Commissioner for Refugees. 1 January 1992.
A/47/12 - UNHCR. Report of the United Nations High Commissioner for Refugees. 28 August 1992.
A/48/12 - UNHCR. Report of the United Nations High Commissioner for Refugees. 6 October 1993.
A/50/12 - UNHCR. Report of the United Nations High Commissioner for Refugees. 14 September 1995.
A/50/413 - UNHCR. Report of the United Nations High Commissioner for Refugees. 14 September 1995.
A/51/950- General Assembly. Report of the Secretary-General. Reviewing the United Nations: A Programm for Reform. 14 July 1997.
A/52/3 - UN ECOSOC. Agreed Conclusions 1997/2. 18 July 1997.
A/54/227 - General Assembly. Report of the Secretary-General. 1999 World Survey on the Role of Women in Development: Globalization, Gender and Work. 18 August 1999.
A/58/12 - UNHCR. Report of the United Nations High Commissioner for Refugees. 19 August 2003.

A/61/515 – General Assembly. Summary of the High-level Dialogue on International Migration and Development. Note by the President of the General Assembly. 13 October 2006.

A/C.2/64/2 - General Assembly. Globalization and interdependence: role of the United Nations in promoting development in the context of globalization and interdependence. Letter dated 1 October 2009 from the Permanent Representative of the Philippines to the United Nations addressed to the Secretary-General. 12 October 2009.

A/AC.96/814 - UNHCR. Executive Committee of the High Commissioner's Programme. Actions Taken on Decisions of the Forty-Third Session of the Executive Committee. 30 August 1993.

A/AC.96/1024 – UNHCR. Executive Committee of the High Commissioner's Programme. Reports on the Work of the Standing Committee: International Protection. Note on International Protection1. Report by the High Commissioner. 12 July 2006.

A/AC.96/1035 – UNHCR. Conclusion on Women and Girls at Risk, No. 105 (LVII). 6 October 2006.

A/CONF.151/26 Vol. I – General Assembly. Report of the United Nations Conference on Environment and Development. Rio de Janeiro, 3-14 June 1992. Annex I Rio Declaration on Environment and Development. 12 August 1992.

A/CONF.198/11 - Report of the International. Conference on Financing for. Development. Monterrey, Mexico. 18 - 22 March 2002.

A/CONF.199/20 – General Assembly. Report of the World Summit on Sustainable Development Johannesburg, South Africa. 26 August- 4 September 2002.

A/CONF.212/L.1/Rev.1 - Follow-up International Conference on Financing for Development to Review the Implementation of the Monterrey Consensus, Doha, Qatar, 29 November-2 December 2008: Doha Declaration on Financing for Development: outcome document of the Follow-up International Conference on Financing for Development to Review the Implementation of the Monterrey Consensus. 9 December 2008.

A/RES/40/118 - General Assembly. Report of the United Nations High Commissioner for Refugees. 13 December 1985.

A/RES/42/107 – General Assembly. Second International Conference on Assistance to Refugees in Africa. 7 December 1987.

A/RES/42/187 - General Assembly Resolution. World Commission on Environment and Development. Report of the World Commission on Environment and Development. 11 December 1987.

A/RES/48/104 - General Assembly Resolution. Declaration on the Elimination of Violence against Women, General Assembly resolution. 20 December 1993.

A/RES/55/2 - Resolution adopted by the General Assembly. United Nations Millennium Declaration. 13. September 2000.

A/RES/58/153 - General Assembly Resolution. Implementing actions proposed by the United Nations High Commissioner for Refugees to strengthen the capacity of his Office to carry out its mandate. 24 March 2004.

A/RES/61/208 - General Assembly Resolution. International migration and development. 6 March 2007.

A/RES/62/208 - General Assembly Resolution. Triennial comprehensive policy review of operational activities for development of the United Nations system. 14 March 2008.

A/RES/62/277 - General Assembly Resolution. System-wide coherence. 7 October 2008.

A/RES/63/311 - General Assembly Resolution. System-wide coherence. 2 October 2009.

A/RES/428 (V) – General Assembly Resolution. Statute of the Office of the United Nations High Commissioner for Refugees. 14 December 1950.

A/RES/429 (V) – General Assembly. Draft Convention relating to the Status of Refugees. 14 December 1950.

A/RES/430 (V) – General Assembly. Problem of Assistance to Refugees. 14 December 1950.
A/RES/638(VII) – General Assembly Resolution. Integration of refugees. 20 December 1952.
A/RES/639(VII) - General Assembly Resolution. Report of the United Nations High Commissioner for Refugees. 20 December 1952.
A/RES/1165 (XII) - General Assembly Resolution. Prolongation of the Office of the United Nations High Commissioner for Refugees. 26 November 1957.
A/RES/1166 (XII) - General Assembly Resolution. International assistance to refugees within the mandate of the United Nations High Commissioner for Refugees. 26 November 1957.
A/RES/1167 (XII) - General Assembly Resolution. Chinese Refugees in Hong Kong. 26 November 1957.
A/RES/1286 (XIII) - General Assembly Resolution. Refugees in Morocco and Tunisia. 5 December 1958.
A/RES/1388 (XIV) - General Assembly Resolution. Report of the United Nations High Commissioner for Refugees. 20 November 1959.
A/RES/2198 (XXI) - General Assembly Resolution. Protocol relating to the Status of Refugees. 16 December 1966.
A/RES/2263 - General Assembly. Declaration on the Elimination of Discrimination against Women. 7 November 1967.
E/1998/7 – UN ECOSOC. Report of the United Nations High Commissioner for Refugees. 27 April 1998.
EC/47/SC/CRP.45 - UNHCR. Executive Committee of the High Commissioner's Programme. Progress Report on Refugee Women and UNHCR's Framework for Implementation of the Beijing Platform for Action. 15 August 1997.
EC/49/SC/CRP.22 - UNHCR. Executive Committee of the High Commissioner's Programme. Refugee Women and a Gender Perspective Approach. 3 September 1999.
EC/51/SC/SRP.17 - UNHCR. Executive Committee of the High Commissioner's Programme. Refugee Women and Mainstreaming a Gender Equality Perspective. 30 May 2001.
EC/54/SC/CRP.5 - UNHCR. Executive Committee of the High Commissioner's Programme. Economic and Social Impact of Massive Refugee Populations on Host Developing Countries, as well as other Countries. 18 February 2004.
EC/55/SC/CRP.15 – UNHCR. Executive Committee of the High Commissioner's Programme. Local Integration and Self-Reliance. 2 June 2005.
EC/55/SC/CRP.17 - UNHCR. Executive Committee of the High Commissioner's Programme. Report on the High Commissioner's five Commitments to Refugee Women. 13 June 2005.
EC/57/SC/CRP.19 - UNHCR. Executive Committee of the High Commissioner's Programme. Targeting Development Assistance, including International Cooperation for finding Durable Solutions for Protracted Refugee Situations. 9 June 2006.
EC/GC/01/7 – UNHCR. Global Consultations on International Protection/Third Track: Mechanisms of International Cooperation to Share Responsibilities and Burdens in Mass Influx Situations. 19 February 2001.
EC/GC/02/8 - UNHCR. Global Consultations on International Protection. Refugee Women. 25 April 2002.
E/RES/2005/31 – UN ECOSOC. Resolution 2005/31 Adopted by the UN Economic and Social Council: Mainstreaming a Gender Perspective Into All Policies and Programmes in the United Nations System. 26 July 2005.
HCR/GIP/02/01 – UNHCR. Guidelines on International Protection No. 1: Gender-Related Persecution Within the Context of Article 1A(2) of the 1951 Convention and/or its 1967 Protocol Relating to the Status of Refugees. 7 May 2002.
S/RES/1325 - Security Council Resolution 1325 (2000) on women, peace and security. Adopted by the Security Council at its 4213th meeting. 31.10.2000.

S/RES/1820 - Security Council Resolution 1820 (2008) on Women, Peace and Security. Adopted by the Security Council at its 5916th meeting. 19.06.2008.
SC/1998/INF.1 - UNHCR. Progress Report on Refugee Women. 25 May 1998.
ST/SGB/2003/13 - Secretary-General's Bulletin: Special Measures for Protection from Sexual Exploitation and Sexual Abuse. 9 October 2003.
UNHCR. Conclusion on Women and Girls at Risk, No. 105 (LVII). 6 October 2006.
UNHCR. Refugee Women, No. 60 (XL). 13 October 1989.
UN ECOSOC. UN Economic and Social Council Resolution 1997/2: Agreed Conclusions. 18 July 1997.
UN General Assembly. Protocol to Prevent, Suppress and Punish Trafficking in Persons, Especially Women and Children, Supplementing the United Nations Convention against Transnational Organized Crime. 15 November 2000.
UN. Convention on Consent to Marriage, Minimum Age for Marriage and Registration of Marriages. 7 November 1962.
UN. Convention on the Elimination of All Forms of Discrimination against Women, 18 December 1979, and its Optional Protocol to the Convention on the Elimination of All Forms of Discrimination against Women. 6 October 1999.
UN. Convention for the Suppression of the Traffic in Persons and of the Exploitation of the Prostitution of Others. 2 December 1949.

Literature

Abel, Andrew B.; Mankiw, N. Gregory; Summers, Lawrence H.; Zeckhauser, Richard J.. 1989. Assessing Dynamic Efficiency: Theory and Evidence. The Review of Economic Studies. 56, 1.
Adelman, Irma. 1999. Fallacies in Development Theory and their Implications for Policy. Cudare Working Paper Series 887, University of California at Berkeley. Berkley.
Adelman, Irma; Morris, Cynthia Taft. 1997. Development History and its Implications for Development Theory: An Editorial. University of California at Berkeley and at Smith College 1997. (http://are.berkeley.edu/~adelman/, 02.11.2009).
Adelman, Irma. 1999. Fallacies in Development Theory and Their Implications for Policy. Working Paper No. 887. California Agricultural Experiment Station. Giannini Foundation of Agricultural Economics. University of California at Berkeley. Berkley.
Adrabo, Stanley. 2004. The Republic of Uganda. District State of Environment Report. Arua.
Aleman, Ulrich von; Forndran, Erhard. 2002. Methodik der Politikwissenschaft. Eine Einführung in Arbeitstechnik und Forschungspraxis. Stuttgart.
Al-Jurf, Saladin. 1999. Good Governance & Transparency: Their Impact on Development. In: Carrasco, Enrique R.; Berg, Kirsten J. (ed.). The E-Book on International Finance and Development. Revised edition. (http://www.uiowa.edu/ifdebook/ebook2/contents/contents.shtml, 09.11.2009).
Ali-Tani, Nouria. 2006. Zur Transformation internationaler Politik aus feministischer Perspektive. Entspricht die Resolution 1325 des UN-Sicherheitsrats feministischen Konzeptionen von Sicherheit? Magisterarbeit zur Erlangung des akademischen Grades einer Magistra Artium der Universität Hamburg (http://www.gwi-boell.de/downloads/Magisterarbeit_AliTani.pdf, 02.08.2009).
Anderson, Mary B.. 1999. Do No Harm: How Aid Can Support Peace – or War, Boulder, Colorado.
Anderlini, Sanam Naraghi. 2007. Women Building Peace. What They Do, Why It Matters. Boulder, Colorado.

Antle, John M.; Crissmann Charles C.. 1990. Risk, Efficiency, and the Adoption of Modern Crop Varieties. In: Evidence from the Philippines Economic Development and Cultural Change. 38, 3.

Apelt, Maja; Dittmer, Cordula. 2008. About Intervening in Vulnerable Societies: Gender in Military Peacekeeping of the Bundeswehr. In: Carreiras, Helena; Kümmel, Gerhard (ed.). Women in the Military and in Armed Conflict. Schriftreihe des Sozialwissenschaftlichen Institutes der Bundeswehr. Vol. 6. Wiesbaden.

Assmann, Jan. 2002. Das kulturelle Gedächtnis. München.

Avin, Rose-Marie. 2006. Engendering Development. A critique. In: Edith Kuiper,Drucilla K. Barker (ed.). Feminist economics and the World Bank: history, theory and policy. London, New York.

Bakewell, Oliver. 2003. Community services in refugee aid programmes: a critical analysis. New Issues in Refugee Research. Working Paper No. 82. UNHCR. Geneva.

Barnes, Nancy E.. 2004. Why Borrow for Capacity Building? (http://www.iwahq.org/uploads/iwa%20hq/website%20files/task%20forces/sustainability/cost%20considerations/WhyBorrowforCapacityBuilding_Barnes.pdf, 23.02.2010).

Bauhardt, Christine. 2004. Feministische Kritik an einem patriarchalen Mensch-Natur-Verhältnis. In: Becker, Ruth; Kortendiek, Beate (ed.). Handbuch Frauen- und Geschlechterforschung. Theorie, Methoden, Empirie. Geschlecht und Gesellschaft. Vol. 35. Wiesbaden.

Beaudou, Alain; Cambrézy, Luc; Zaiss, Rainer. 2003. Geographical Information System, Environment and Camp Planning in Refugee Hosting Areas. Approach, methods and application in Uganda. Institut de recherche pour le de´veloppement (IRD). (www.bondy.ird.fr/carto/refugies/index.html, 02.06.2010).

Beauvoir, Simone de. 1953/1988. The Second Sex. Translated and edited by H. M. Parshley. London.

Bessis, Sophia. 2003. International Organizations and Gender: New Paradigms and Old Habits. Signs. Issue 29, 2.

Betts, Alexander. 2004. International cooperation and the targeting of development assistance for refugee solutions: lessons from the 1980s. New Issues in Refugee Research. Working Paper No. 107. UNHCR Geneva.

Betts, Alexander. 2005a. International Cooperation Between North and South to Enhance Protection in Regions of Origin. Refugee Studies Centre Working Paper No. 25. University of Oxford.

Betts, Alexander. 2005b. Convention Plus: Continuity or Change in North-South Responsibility-Sharing? Prepared For 'New Asylum Paradigm?' Workshop. Centre on Migration, Policy and Society, Oxford. (http://www.compas.ox.ac.uk/fileadmin/files/pdfs/Non_WP_pdfs/Events_2005/C+%20Paper%20(2).pdf, 10.09.2009).

Betts, Alexander. 2005c. What does 'efficiency' mean in the context of the global refugee regime? Centre on Migration, Policy and Society. Working Paper No. 9. University of Oxford.

Betts, Alexander. 2006a. Conceptualising Interconnections in Global Governance: the case of refugee protection. Refugee Studies Center Working Paper 38. University of Oxford.

Betts, Alexander. 2006b. Comprehensive Plans of Action: Insights from CIREFCA and the Indochinese CPA. New Issues in Refugee Research. Working Paper No. 120. UNHCR. Geneva.

Betts, Alexander. 2008a. Towards a 'soft law' framework for the protection of vulnerable migrants. New Issues in Refugee Research. Working Paper No. 162. UNHCR. Geneva.

Betts, Alexander. 2008b. Cross-Issue Persuasion: Why Northern States Contribute to Refugee Protection in the South. Paper presented at the London Migration Research Group Seminar, SOAS, 14th October 2008.
Betts, Alexander. 2009a. Development assistance and refugees towards a North-South grand bargain?. Forced Migration Policy Briefing No. 2. University of Oxford.
Betts, Alexander. 2009b. Protection by Persuasion: International Cooperation in the Refugee Regime. Ithaka, London.
Betts, Alexander; Kaytaz, Esra. 2009. National and International Responses to the Zimbabwean Exodus: Implications for the Refugee Regime. New Issues in Refugee Research. Working Paper No. 175. UNHCR. Geneva.
Betts, Alexander; Milner, James. 2007. The Externalisation of EU Asylum Policy: The Position of African States. Danish Institute for International Studies. DIIS Brief. Copenhagen.
BMZ/UNHCR-Partnerschaftsprogramm. 2006. Das erste Jahr der strategischen Partnerschaft zwischen dem BMZ und dem Amt des Hohen Flüchtlingskommissars der Vereinten Nationen (UNHCR) über die Zusammenarbeit bei entwicklungsorientierten Flüchtlingsprogrammen. Bonn.
Blanchard, Eric M.. 2003. Gender, International Relations, and the Development of Feminist Security Theory. Signs. Vol. 28, 4.
Carrasco, Enrique; Berg, Kirsten J.. 1999a. E-Book on International Finance and Development. (http://www.uiowa.edu/ifdebook/ebook2/contents/contents.shtml, 09.11.2009).
Blanco, Sandra. 1999. The 1960s and 1970s: The World Bank Attacks Poverty; Developing Countries Attack the IMF. In: Carrasco, Enrique R.; Berg, Kirsten J. (ed.). The E-Book on International Finance and Development. Revised edition. (http://www.uiowa.edu/ifdebook/ebook2/contents/contents.shtml, 09.11.2009).
Blair, Deirdre. 1986. Simone de Beauvoir: Politics, Language, and Feminist Identity. In: Yale French Studies. Simone de Beauvoir: Witness to a Century. Vol. 72.
Blomström, Magnus. 1986. Foreign Investment and Productive Efficiency: The Case of Mexico. The Journal of Industrial Economics. Vol. 35, 1.
Brabandt, Heike; Locher, Birgit; Prügl, Elisabeth. 2002. Normen, Gender und Politikwandel: Internationale Beziehungen aus der Geschlechterperspektive. Welttrends 35.
Bordoff, Jason E.; Deich, Michael; Kahane, Rebecca; Orszag, Peter R.. 2006. Promoting Opportunity and Growth through Science, Technology, and Innovation. The Hamilton project. Strategy Paper. The Brookings Institution.
Boswell, Christina. 2005. The Ethics of Refugee Policy. Aldershot.
Bucci, Alberto. 1998. Market Power and Growth in a Schumpeterian Framework of Innovation. Discussion Papers (IRES - Institut de Recherches Economiques et Sociales). University of Ancona in Ancona, Italy and Catholic University of Louvain in Louvain, Belgium. (http://sites-final.uclouvain.be/econ/DP/IRES/9824.pdf, 03.02.2010).
Bundegaard, Anita Bay. 2004. Convention Plus Issues Paper on Targeting of Development Assistance. Geneva.
Bundesministerium für wirtschaftliche Zusammenarbeit und Entwicklung. 2006. Die Zusammenarbeit des BMZ mit dem Amt des Hohen Flüchtlingskommissars der Vereinten Nationen (UNHCR). Spezial No. 138. Bonn.
Bützer, Christina. 2007. The Long Way Home: Contemplations of Southern Sudanese Refugees in Uganda. In: Spektrum - Berliner Reihe Zu Gesellschaft, Wirtschaft Und Politik in Entwicklungsländern. Vol. 98. Berlin.
Caprioli, Mary. 2003. Gender Equality and Civil Wars. World Bank CPR Working Paper No. 8. Washington, DC.
Carrasco, Enrique R.. 1999a. The 1980s: The Debt Crisis & The Lost Decade. In: Carrasco, Enrique R.; Berg, Kirsten J. (ed.). The E-Book on International Finance and Development.

Revised edition. (http://www.uiowa.edu/ifdebook/ebook2/contents/contents.shtml, 09.11.2009).
Carrasco, Enrique R.. 1999b. Development in the 1990s. In: Carrasco, Enrique R.; Berg, Kirsten J. (ed.). The E-Book on International Finance and Development. Revised edition. (http://www.uiowa.edu/ifdebook/ebook2/contents/contents.shtml, 09.11.2009).
Carreiras, Helena; Kümmel, Gerhard (ed.). 2008. Women in the Military and in Armed Conflict. Schriftreihe des Sozialwissenschaftlichen Institutes der Bundeswehr. Vol. 6. Wiesbaden.
Chambers, Robert. 1986. Hidden Losers? The Impact of Rural Refugees and Refugee Programs on Poorer Hosts. International Migration Review. Vol 20, 2.
Chant, Sylvia; McIlwaine, Cathy. 2009. Geographies of Development in the 21st Century: An Introduction to the Global South. London.
Chimni, B.S.. 1999. From Resettlement to involuntary repatriation: towards a critical history of durable solutions to refugee problems. New Issues in Refugee Research. Working Paper No. 2. UNHCR. Geneva.
Colson, Elizabeth. 1999. Gendering Those Uprooted by 'Development'. In: Engendering Forced Migration. Theory and Practice. Refugee and Forced Migration Studies. Vol. 5. edition. By Doreen Indra. New York.
Conteras, Ricardo. 1999a. How the Concept of Development Got Started. In: Carrasco, Enrique R.; Berg, Kirsten J. (ed.). The E-Book on International Finance and Development. Revised edition. (http://www.uiowa.edu/ifdebook/ebook2/contents/contents.shtml, 09.11.2009).
Conteras, Ricardo. 1999b. Competing Theories of Economic Development. In: Carrasco, Enrique R.; Berg, Kirsten J. (ed.). The E-Book on International Finance and Development. Revised edition. (http://www.uiowa.edu/ifdebook/ebook2/contents/contents.shtml, 09.11.2009).
Crisp, Jeff. 2001. Mind the Gap! UNHCR, Humanitarian Assistance and the Development Process. New Issues in Refugee Research. Working Paper No. 43. UNHCR. Geneva.
Crisp, Jeff. 2003. No Solutions In Sight? The Problem of Protracted Refugee Situations in Africa. New Issues in Refugee Research. Working Paper No. 75. UNHCR. Geneva.
Crisp, Jeff. 2003b. UNHCR, refugee livelihoods and self-reliance: a brief history. (http://www.unhcr.org/3f978a894.html, 11.09.2009)
Crisp, Jeff. 2004. The local integration and local settlement of refugees: a conceptual and historical analysis. New Issues in Refugee Research. Working Paper No. 102. UNHCR. Geneva.
Crisp, Jeff. 2006. Forced displacement in Africa: dimensions, difficulties and policy directions. New Issues in Refugee Research. Working Paper No. 126. UNHCR. Geneva.
DCD-DAC. 2009. Development Co-operation Directorate. The Paris Declaration and Accra Agenda for Action. (http://www.oecd.org/document/18/0,2340,en_2649_3236398_35401554_1_1_1_1,00.html , 09.11.2009).
Danielsen, Dan; Karen Engle. 1995. After Identity. A Reader in Law and Culture. New York.
Davies, Martyn. 2008. How China delivers development assistance to Africa. Centre for Chinese Studies. University of Stellenbosch.
De Vriese, Machtelt. 2006. Refugee livelihoods. A review of the evidence. EPAU/2006/04. Geneva.
DeLong, J. Bradford. 2001. The Last Development Crusade. (http://econ161.berkeley.edu/totw/easterly_neoliberal.html, 02.11.2009).
Diefenbach, Hans; Zieschank, Roland. 2009. Sustainability and growth – towards the description of an area of conflict on the basis of national indicators. (http://www.beyond-gdp.eu/download/BMU_UBA_poloeko_eng.pdf, 12.09.2009).

Dittmer, Cordula. 2007. Gender, Konflikte und Konfliktbearbeitung. Zivile und militärische Ansätze, Forderungen und Probleme. CCS Working Papers No.6. Wagner, Ulrich; Bös, Mathias; Becker M., Johannes (eds). Zentrum für Konfliktforschung der Philipps-Universität Marburg.
Donchin, Anne. 2004. Converging Concerns: Feminist Bioethics, Development Theories, and Human Rights. Signs. Vol. 29, 2.
Dryden-Peterson, Sarah; Hovil, Lucy. 2003. Local Integration as a durable Solution: Refugees, Host Populations and Education in Uganda. New Issues in Refugee Research. Working Paper No. 93. UNHCR. Geneva.
Duffield, Mark. 2005. Getting Savages to Fight Barbarians. Development, Security and the Colonial Present. Conflict, Security and Development. Vol. 5, 2.
Duffield, Mark. 1994. Complex Emergencies and the Crisis of Developmentalism. In: IDS Bulletin: Linking Relief and Development. Vol. 25, 3.
Duffield, Mark. 2001. Global Governance and the New Wars. London.
Easterly, William. 2003. Can Foreign Aid Buy Growth? The Journal of Economic Perspectives. Vol. 17, 3.
Easterly, William. 2006. The White Man's Burden: Why the West's Efforts to Aid the Rest Have Done So Much Ill and So Little Good. London.
Easterly, William; Sachs, Jeffrey. 2006. The Big Push Déjà Vu: A Review of Jeffrey Sachs's "The End of Poverty: Economic Possibilities for Our Time". Journal of Economic Literature. Vol. 44, 1.
EC. 2000. Communication from the Commission to the Council and the European Parliament, 2001. (http://eur-lex.europa.eu/Notice.do?mode=dbl&lang=en&ihmlang=en&lng1=en,de&lng2=da,de,el,en,es,fi,fr,it,nl,pt,sv,&val=278393:cs&page=, 14.01.2010).
Eckert, Florens. 2008. Marginalisation and Identity in West Nile – Colonial Burden, Idi Amin, Rebellion and Islam. In: Dieter Neubert (ed.). Post-Conflict Development in West Nile/Uganda. Bayreuth.
Edwards, Alice. 2003. Age and Gender Dimensions in International Refugee law. In: Feller, E.; Türk, V.; Nicholson, F. (eds.). Refugee protection in international law: UNHCR's global consultations on international protection. Cambridge, New York, Geneva.
Egbert Jahn, Sabine Fischer, Astrid Sahm (ed.). 2005. Die Zukunft des Friedens. Die Friedens- und Konfliktforschung aus der Perspektive der jüngeren Generation. Vol. 2. Wiesbaden.
Enloe, Cynthia. 1989. Bananas, Beaches & Bases. Making feminist sense of international politics. London.
Eriksson, Lars-Gunnar; Melander, Göran; Nobel, Peter (ed.). 1981. An Analyzing Account of the Conference on the African Refugee Problem Arusha May 1979. Scandinavian Institute for African Studies. Uppsala.
Estrin, Saul; Laidler, David. 1995. Introduction To Microeconomics. London.
EU. 2007a. Linking relief, rehabilitation and development (LRRD). (http://europa.eu/legislation_summaries/humanitarian_aid/r10002_en.htm, 14.01.2010).
EU. 2007b. Humanitarian Aid. MEMO/07/238. Brussels.
Farr, Vanessa A.. Notes toward a Gendered Understanding of Mixed Population Movements and Security Sector Reform after Conflict. Signs. Vol. 32, 3.
Farrell, Michael J.. 1957. The Measurement of Productive Efficiency. In: Journal of the Royal Statistical Society, A 120, Part III.
Fielden, Alexandra. 2008. Local integration: an under-reported solution to protracted refugee situations. New Issues in Refugee Research No. 158. UNHCR. Geneva.
Fierke, Karin M.. 2001. Critical Methodology and Constructivism. In: Fierke, K.M.; Jörgensen, K.E. (ed.). Constructing International Relations. The Next Generation. New York.

Finke, Barbara. 2003. Feministische Ansätze. In: Schieder, Siegfried; Spindler, Manuela (ed.). Theorien der Internationalen Beziehungen. Opladen.

Ferris, Elizabeth G.. 2003. The Role of NGOs in the International Refugee Regime. In: Steiner, Niklaus; Gibney, Mark; Loescher, Gil (ed.). Problems of Protection. The UNHCR, Refugees, and Human Rights. New York.

Fischer, Karin; Hödl, Gerald; Maral-Hanak, Irim; Parnreiter, Christof (ed.). 2007. Entwicklung und Unterentwicklung. Eine Einführung in Probleme, Theorien und Strategien. 3. edition. Wien.

Fonow, Mary Margaret; Cook, Judith A. 2005. Feminist Methodology: New Applications in the Academy and Public Policy. Signs. Vol. 30, 4.

Fréchette, Louise. Deputy Secretary-General of the United Nations Secretary-General. Women and Peace. Press Release DSG/SM/123 OBV/196 WOM/1271. 08.03.2001.

Freund, Paul; Kalumba, Katele. 1986. Spontaneously Settled Refugees in Northwestern Province, Zambia. International Migration Review. Vol. 20, 2.

Frey, Regina. 2003. Gender im Mainstreaming – Geschlechtertheorie und -praxis im internationalen Diskurs. Königstein, Taunus.

Friedrich, Wolfgang-Uwe. 1991. Demokratische Realpolitik: Die Deutsche Frage als Problem der deutsch-amerikanischen Beziehungen 1945 – 1990. Eds. von Wolfgang-Uwe, Friedrich. Die USA und die Deutsche Frage 1945 – 1990. Frankfurt, New York.

Fritzsche, Karl-Peter. 2004. Menschenrechte. Eine Einführung mit Dokumenten. Allgemeine Erklärung der Menschenrechte. Paderborn.

Fritzsche, Karl-Peter. 2007a. Human Rights Education – What Is It All About?. (http://www.menschenrechtserziehung.de/publikationen/pdfs/HREtheses.pdf, 14.08.2007).

Fritzsche, Karl-Peter. 2007b. Human Rights Education after September 11 - Empowerment through Human Rights Education. (http://www.menschenrechtserziehung.de/publikationen/pubhereberlin.htm, 13.08.2007).

Frug, Mary Joe. 1995. A Postmodern Feminist Legal Manifesto (An Unfinished Draft). In: Danielsen, Dan; Karen Engle (eds.). After Identity. A Reader in Law and Culture. New York.

Galtung, Johan. 1975. Peace: Research, Education, Action: Essays in Peace Research Volume One. Romania: CIPEXIM, Bucuresti.

GFMD. 2007. Global Forum on Migration and Development. Background. Brussels. (http://www.gfmd-fmmd.org, 20.12.2009).

GFMD. 2009. Global Forum on Migration and Development 2009. Athens. (http://www.gfmdathens2009.org/index.php?id=1&L=0, 20.12.2009).

Ghemawat, Pankaj; Costa, Joan E. Ricart I. 1993. The Organizational Tension between Static and Dynamic Efficiency. Strategic Management Journal. Vol. 14, Special Issue: Organizations, Decision Making and Strategy.

Gibney, Matthew J.. 2002. Security and the ethics of asylum after 11 September. Forced Migration Review. September 11th: Has anything changed?. Vol. 13.

Gilbert, Richard J.; Newbery, David M. 1994. The Dynamic Efficiency of Regulatory Constitutions. The RAND Journal of Economics. Vol. 25, 4.

Girtler, Roland. 2001. Methoden der Feldforschung. 4th revised edition. Wien, Köln, Weimar.

Gode, Dhananjay K.; Sunder, Shyam. 1993. Allocative Efficiency of Markets with Zero-Intelligence Traders: Market as a Partial Substitute for Individual Rationality. In: The Journal of Political Economy. Vol. 101, 1.

Goetz, Nathaniel H.. 2003. Towards self sufficiency and integration: an historical evaluation of assistance programmes for Rwandese refugees in Burundi, 1962 – 1965. New Issues in Refugee Research. Working Paper No. 87. UNHCR. Geneva.

Goodwin-Gill, Guy S.. 1986. International Law and the Detention of Refugees and Asylum-Seekers. International Migration Review. Vol 20, 2.

Goodwin-Gill, Guy S.. 2004. Refugees and their Human Rights. Refugee Studies Centre Working Paper No. 17. Oxford.
Goodwin-Gill, Guy S.. 2006. International Protection and Assistance for Refugees and the Displaced: Institutional Challenges and United Nations Reform. Paper presented at the Refugee Studies Centre Workshop, 'Refugee Protection in International Law: Contemporary Challenges', Oxford, 24 April 2006. (http://www.unhcr.org/47e8d2a82.pdf, 03.01.2010).
Goonesekere, Savitri. 1998. A rights-based approach to realizing gender equality. Colombo, Sri Lanka. (http://www.un.org/womenwatch/daw/news/archive1998.htm; 01.12.2009).
Gorman, Robert F.. 1986. Beyond ICARA II : Implementing Refugee-Related Development Assistance. International Migration Review. Vol. 20, 2.
Gorman, Robert F.; Kibreab, Gaim. 1997. Repatriation Aid and Development Assistance. In James C. Hathaway (ed.). Reconceiving International Refugee Law. The Hague.
Grewal, Inderpal. 1998. On the new global feminism and the family of nations: dilemmas of transnational feminist practice. In: Shohat, Ella (ed.). Talking visions – multicultural feminism in a transnational age. Massachusetts.
Griffiths, Allan; Wall, Stuart (ed.). 2004. Applied Economics. 10th edition. Harlow.
Harding, Sandra. 2001. Comment on Walby's "Against Epistemological Chasms: The Science Question in Feminism Revisited": Can Democratic Values and Interests Ever Play a Rationally Justifiable Role in the Evaluation of Scientific Work? Signs. Vol. 26, 2.
Harding, Sandra. 1986. The Science Question in Feminism. Ithaca.
Harmer, Adele; Macrae, Joanna (eds.). 2004. Beyond the continuum. The changing role of aid policy in protracted crises. Humanitarian Policy Group Research Report. Report No. 18.
Harrell-Bond, Barbara. 1986. Imposing Aid. Emergency Assistance to Refugees. Oxford.
Harrell-Bond, Barbara. 1989. Repatriation: Under What Conditions Is It the Most Desirable Solution for Refugees? An Agenda for Research. African Studies Review. Vol. 32, 1.
Harrell-Bond, Barbara. 1999. The experience of refugees as recipients of aid. In: A. Ager (ed.). Refugees: Perspectives on the Experience of Forced Migration. London.
Harrell-Bond, Barbara. 2000. Are Refugee Camps Good for Children? New Issues in Refugee Research. Working Paper No. 29. UNHCR. Geneva.
Harrell-Bond, Barbara. 2002. Towards the Economic and Social 'Integration' of Refugee Populations in Host Countries in Africa. This document was prepared as a stimulus for discussion at the Stanley Foundation conference "Refugee Protection in Africa: How to Ensure Security and Development for Refugees and Hosts" held in Entebbe, Uganda from November 10-14, 2002. (http://reports.stanleyfoundation.org/hrp/HRP02B.pdf, 08.12.2009).
Harrell-Bond, Barbara, Voutira, E.; Leopold, M.. 1992. Counting the refugees: Gifts, givers, patrons and clients. Journal of Refugee Studies. Vol. 5, 3/4.
Hartling, Poul. 1983a. Opening Statement to the Executive Committee of the High Commissioner's Programme, thirty-fourth session, Geneva, 10 October 1983.
Hathaway, James. 1997. Preface: Can International Refugee Law Be Made Relevant Again?. In: Hathaway, James (ed), Reconceiving Refugee Law. The Hague.
Hathaway, James; Neve, Alexander. 1997. Making International Refugee Law Relevant Again: A Proposal for Collectivized and Solution-Oriented Protection. Harvard Human Rights Journal. Vol. 10.
Hedinger, Sandra. 2002. Krieg und Frieden im Denken von Bertha von Suttner, Rosa Luxemburg, Hannah Arendt und Gegenwartsautorinnen. In: Geschlechterverhältnisse in Krieg und Frieden. Perspektiven der feministischen Analyse internationaler Beziehungen. Opladen.
Helton, Arthur C. 2002. The price of indifference: refugees and humanitarian action in the new century. Oxford, New York.

Herrmann, Christa. 2005. Betriebliches Zeithandeln – Bedingungen für Zeitautonomie am Beispiel von Vertrauensarbeitszeit. Dissertation an der Technischen Universität München. München.

Hoenig, Wiebke. 2004. Self-image and the well-being of refugees in Rhino Camp Settlement, Uganda. New Issues in Refugee Research. Working Paper No. 103. UNHCR. Geneva.

Holland-Cunz, Barbara. Die alte neue Frauenfrage. In: Esser, Josef (ed.). Neue Sozialwissenschaftliche Bibliothek. 2335. Frankfurt a.M..

Holzmann, Nora. 2005. Gender und Konflikte. GTZ Orientation Paper. Eschborn.

Hovil, Lucy. 2002. Free to stay, free to go? Movement, Seclusion and Integration of Refugees in Moyo District. Refugee Law Project. Working Paper No. 4. Kampala.

Hovil, Lucy. 2007. Self-settled Refugees in Uganda: An Alternative Approach to Displacement? Journal of Refugee Studies. Vol. 20.

IDMC. 2008a. Integrated Regional Information Networks. In-Depth: Life in northern Uganda. UGANDA: The Acholi Society. (http://www.irinnews.org/InDepthMain.aspx?InDepthId=23&ReportId=65773, 22.08.2008).

IDMC. 2008b. Uganda: Uncertain future for IDPs while peace remains elusive. 24.04.08. (http://www.internal-displacement.org/8025708F004CE90B/(httpCountrySummaries)/30C1E18695F9FE74C12574330056B5E4?OpenDocument&count=10000, 20.08.2008).

IFAD. 2011. Enabling poor rural people to overcome poverty in Uganda. Rome (http://www.ifad.org/operations/projects/regions/Pf/factsheets/uganda.pdf, 01.03.2011).

IMF. 2000. Poverty Reduction Strategy Paper. Uganda's Poverty Eradication Action Plan. Summary and Main Objectives. (http://www.imf.org/external/NP/prsp/2000/Uga/01/, 07.11.2010).

International Alert; Forum on Early Warning and Early Response; Africa Peace Forum; Centre for Conflict Resolution; Consortium on Humanitarian Agencies. 2004. Conflict-Sensitive Approaches to Development, Humanitarian Assistance and Peace Building. (http://www.conflictsensitivity.org/publications/conflict-sensitive-approaches-development-humanitarian-assistance-and-peacebuilding-res, 09.01.2010).

Jacobsen, Karen. 1996. Factors influencing the Policy Responses of Host Governments to Mass Refugee Influxes. International Migration Review. Vol 30, 3.

Jacobsen, Karen. 2001. The forgotten solution: local integration for refugees in developing countries. New Issues in Refugee Research. Working Paper No. 45. UNHCR. Geneva.

Jacobsen, Karen; Landau, Loren. 2003. Researching refugees: some methodological and ethical considerations in social science and forced migration. New Issues in Refugee Research. Working Paper No. 90. UNHCR. Geneva.

Juma, Monica Kathina; Kagwanja, Peter Mwangi. 2003. Refugee Protection in Europe and the U.S. after 9/11. In: Steiner, Niklause; Gibney, Mark; Loescher, Gil (ed.). Problems of Protection. The UNHCR, Refugees, and Human Rights. New York, London.

Kaiser, Tania. 2002. Participatory and beneficiary-based approaches to the evaluation of humanitarian programmes. New Issues in Refugee Research Working Paper No. 51. UNHCR. Geneva.

Kaiser, Tania. 2005a. "We Are All Stranded Here Together": The local settlement system, freedom of movement, and livelihood opportunities in Arua and Moyo Districts. Refugee Law Project. Working Paper No. 14. Kampala.

Kaiser, Tania. 2005b. Participating in Development? Refugee protection, politics and developmental approaches to refugee management in Uganda. Third World Quarterly. Vol. 26, 2.

Kaiser, Tania. 2006. Between a camp and a hard place: rights, livelihood and experiences of the local settlement system for long-term refugees in Uganda. Journal of Modern African Studies. Vol. 44, 4.

Kibreab, Gaim. 1990. Local settlements in Africa: a misconceived option? Journal of Refugee Studies. Vol. 2, 4.

Kibreab, Gaim. 1993. The Myth of Dependency among Camp Refugees in Somalia 1979-1989. Journal of Refugee Studies. Vol. 6, 4.

Kibreab, Gaim. 1995. Eritrean women refugees in Khartoum, Sudan, 1970-1990. Journal of Refugee Studies. Vol. 8, 1.

Kibreab, Gaim. 1996. People on the Edge in the Horn: Displacement, Land Use and the Environment in the Gedaref region, Sudan. Oxford.

Kibreab, Gaim. 1999. Revisiting the debate on people, place, identity and displacement. Journal of Refugee Studies. Vol. 12, 4.

Klinger, Cornelia. 1994. Zwischen allen Stühlen. Die politische Theoriediskussion der Gegenwart in einer theoretischen Perspektive. In: Appelt, Erna/Neyer, Gerda (ed.): Feministische Politikwissenschaft. Wien: Verlag für Gesellschaftskritik.

Kohlbach, Florian. 2006. The Use of Qualitative Content Analysis in Case Study Research. In: Forum: Qualitative Social Research. January 2006. Vol. 7, 1.

Kolland, Franz. 2007. Zwischen Fortschrittsoptimismus und kritischer Gesellschaftsanalyse. Die klassischen Entwicklungstheorien. In: Karin Fischer, Gerald Hödl, Irim Maral-Hanak, Christof Parnreiter (ed.). Entwicklung und Unterentwicklung. Eine Einführung in Probleme, Theorien und Strategien. 3. edition. Wien.

Koopmans, Tjalling C.. 1961. Convexity Assumptions, Allocative Efficiency, and Competitive Equilibrium. The Journal of Political Economy. Vol. 69, 5.

Kopp, Raymond J.. 1981. The Measurement of Productive Efficiency: A Reconsideration. In: The Quarterly Journal of Economics. Vol. 96, 3.

Krause, Ulrike. 2009. Women in Peace and Conflict. The Need of Female Representation and Participation. A Different View. International Association for Political Science Students. Vol. 33.

Kreisky, Eva. 1995. Der Staat ohne Geschlecht? Ansätze feministischer Staatskritik und feministischer Staatserklärung, In: Kreisky, Eva; Sauer, Birgit (ed.): Feministische Standpunkte in der Politikwissenschaft. Eine Einführung. Frankfurt a.M..

Kreisky, Eva. 2000. Der Stoff aus dem die Staaten sind. Zur männerbündischen Fundierung politischer Ordnung. In: Braun, Kathrin; Fuchs, Gesine; Lemke, Christiane; Thöns, Katrin (ed.). Feministische Perspektiven der Politikwissenschaft. München.

Kreisky, Eva; Sauer, Birgit. 1997. Einführende Bemerkungen zur Begriffsbildung in der Politikwissenschaft. In: Kreisky, Eva; Sauer, Birgit (ed.). Das geheime Glossar der Politikwissenschaft. Frankfurt a.M..

Kreisky, Eva; Sauer, Birgit. 1998. Geschlechterverhältnisse im Kontext politischer Transformation. In: Kreisky, Eva; Sauer, Birgit (ed.). Geschlechterverhältnisse im Kontext politischer Transformation. Opladen.

Krell, Gert. 1996. Feminismus und Internationale Beziehungen. Zwischen Dekonstruktion und Essentialisierung. Zeitschrift für Internationale Beziehungen. Vol. 3.

Krolokke, Charlotte; Sorensen, Anne Scott. 2005. Three Waves of Feminism: From Suffragettes to Grrls. Gender Communication Theories and Analyses: From Silence to Performance. Sage.

Krouse, Clement G. 1975. Measuring Allocative Efficiency with Technological Uncertainty. The Journal of Finance. Vol. 31, 2. (Papers and Proceedings of the Thirty-Fourth Annual Meeting of the American Finance Association Dallas, Texas December 28-30, 1975).

Kumar, Brij Nino; Graf, Ina. 1998. Globalization, Development and Ethics. In: Kumar, Brij Nino; Steinmann, Horst (ed.). Ethics in International Management. Berlin, New York.

Lippman, Betsy; Malik Sajjad. 2004. The 4Rs: the way ahead? Forced Migration Review. Vol. 21.
Locher, Birgit. 2000. Internationale Beziehungen aus der Geschlechterperspektive. In: Braun, Kathrin; Fuchs, Gesine; Lemke, Christiane; Thöns, Katrin (ed.). Feministische Perspektiven der Politikwissenschaft. München.
Locher-Dodge, Birgit. 1998. Internationale Politik – geschlechtsneutrale Paradigmen? In: Geschlechterverhältnisse im Kontext politischer Transformation. Opladen, Wiesbaden.
Loescher, Gil. 1994. The International Refugee Regime: Stretched to the Limit? Journal of International Affairs. Vol. 47, 2.
Loescher, Gil. 2001. The UNHCR and world politics: a perilous path. Oxford.
Loescher, Gil. 2009. Human Rights and Refugees: The Global Crisis of Protracted Displacement Transcript of the Sergio Vieira de Mello Lecture 26 March 2009 at the Supreme Labour Court, Brasilia. (http://www.rsc.ox.ac.uk/PDFs/Sergio%20Vieira%20de%20Mello%20Lecture.pdf, 10.03.2010).
Loescher, Gil; Milner, James. 2003. The Missing Link: The Need For Comprehensive Engagement in Regions of Origin. International Affairs. 79:3.
Loescher, Gil; Milner, James. 2005. Protracted Refugee Situations: Domestic and International Security Implications. Adelphi Paper No. 375. London.
Loescher, Gil; Milner, James. 2009. Understanding the challenge. Forced Migration Review. Protracted displacement. Vol. 33.
Loescher, Gil; Betts, Alexander; Milner, James. 2008. The United Nations High Commissioner for Refugees (UNHCR). The politics and practices of refugee protection into the twenty-first century. In: Weiss, Thomas G.; Wilkinson, Rorden (ed.). Global Institutions. London, New York.
Lenhart, Lioba. 2008. Nord-Uganda. In: Bundeszentrale für politische Bildung. Konfliktportraits. (http://www.bpb.de/themen/SJPWRX.html, 20.08.08).
Lomo, Zachary; Hovil, Lucy. 2004. Negotiating Peace: Resolution of Conflicts in Uganda's West Nile Region. Refugee Law Project. Working Paper No. 12. Kampala.
Lomo Zachary; Naggaga, Angela; Hovil, Lucy. 2001. The Phenomenon of Forced Migration in Uganda: An Overview of Policy and Practice in an Historical Context. Refugee Law Project. Working Paper No. 1. Kampala.
Lubbers, Ruud. 2001a. Opening Statement to the Ministerial Meeting of States Parties to the 1951 Convention and/or the 1967 Protocol relating to the Status of Refugees, Geneva, 12 December 2001a HC Statements, 12 December 2001 (http://www.unhcr.org/cgi-bin/texis/vtx/search?page=search&docid=3c17316c4&query=Ruud%20Lubbers, 05.12.2009).
Lubbers, Ruud. 2001b. Opening Statement at the Fifty-second Session of the Executive Committee of the High Commissioner's Programme (ExCom), Geneva, 1 October 2001 (http://www.unhcr.org/cgi-bin/texis/vtx/search?page=search&docid=3bb851224&query=lubbers%20%22Opening%20Statement%22%202001, 05.12.2009).
Maral-Hanak, Irmi. 2007. Feministische Entwicklungstheorien. In: Karin Fischer, Gerald Hödl, Irim Maral-Hanak, Christof Parnreiter (ed.). Entwicklung und Unterentwicklung. Eine Einführung in Probleme, Theorien und Strategien. 3. edition. Wien.
Macrae, Joanna. 1999. Aiding Peace … and War: UNHCR, Returnee Reintegration and the Relief – Development Debate. New Issues in Refugee Research. Working Paper No. 14. UNHCR. Geneva.
Macrae, Joanna; Zwi, Anthony B.; Gilson, Lucy. 1996. A Triple Burden for Health Sector Reform: ''Post- Conflict'' Rehabilitation in Uganda. Social Science and Medicine. Vol. 42, 7.

Marchand, Marianne H.; Parpart, Jane L.. 1995. Feminism/Postmodernism/Development. London.
Martin, Susan F.; Fagen Weiss, Patricia; Jorgensen, Kari; Mann-Bondat, Lydia; Schoenholtz, Andrew (eds.). 2005. The Uprooted. Improving Humanitarian Responses to Forced Migration. Oxford.
Maybin, Susanna. 1992. A Comparison of Health Provision and Status in Ban Napho Refugee Campand Nakhon Phanom Province, Northeastern Thailand. Disasters. Vol. 16, 1.
McCartney, Matthew. 2004. Dynamic versus Static Efficiency: The Case of Textile Exports from Bangladesh and the Developmental State. Post-autistic Economics Review. Vol. 26, 2. (http://www.paecon.net/PAEReview/development/McCartney26.htm, 09.02.2010)
McFadden, Patricia. 2000. Issues of gender and development from an African feminist perspective. Lecture presented in honor of Dame Nita Barrow, at the Center for Gender and Development Studies, University of the West Indies, Bridgetown, Barbados. (http://www.escueladefeminismo.org/spip.php?article153, 17.11.2009).
Mehreteab, Amanuel. 2000. 'Reintegrating ex-refugees and ex-fighters in the Process of Reconstruction in Post-conflict Eritrea'. Ph.D. Thesis. University of Leeds.
Merkx, Jozef. 2000. Refugee Identities and Relief in an African Borderland: A Study of Northern Uganda and Southern Sudan. New Issues in Refugee Research. Working Paper No. 19. UNHCR. Geneva.
Merkx, Jozef. 2002. Refugee Identities and Relief in an African Borderland: A Study of Northern Uganda and Southern Sudan. Refugee Survey Quarterly. Vol. 21, 1 & 2.
Meuser, Michael; Nagel, Ulrike. 1991. ExpertInneninterviews – vielfach erprobt, wenig bedacht. Ein Beitrag zur qualitativen Methodendiskussion. In: Detlev Garz, Klaus Kraimer (eds.). Qualitativ-empirische Sozialforschung. Konzepte, Methoden, Analysen. Opladen.
Meuser, Michael; Nagel, Ulrike. 1997. Das Experteninterview – Wissenssoziologische Voraussetzungen und methodische Durchführung. In: Friebertshäuser, Barbara; Prengel, Annedore (eds.). Handbuch Qualitative Forschungsmethoden in der Erziehungswissenschaft. Weinheim und München.
Meuser, Michael; Nagel, Ulrike. 2004. ExperInneninterview. Zur Rekonstruktion spezialisierten Sonderwissens. In: Becker, Ruth; Kortendiek, Beate (ed.). Handbuch Frauen- und Geschlechterforschung. Theorie, Methoden, Empirie. Geschlecht und Gesellschaft. Vol. 35. Wiesbaden.
Meuser, Michael; Nagel, Ulrike. 2005. ExpertInneninterviews – vielfach erprobt, wenig bedacht. Ein Beitrag zur qualitativen Methodendiskussion. In: Bogner, Alexander; Littig, Beate; Menz, Wolfgang (eds.). Das Experteninterview. Theorie, Methode, Anwendung. 2. edition.. Opladen.
Meyer, Sarah. 2006. The 'Refugee Aid and Development' Approach in Uganda: Empowerment and Self-Reliance of Refugees in Practice. New Issues in Refugee Research. Working Paper No. 131. UNHCR. Geneva.
Milner, James. 2000. Sharing the Security Burden: Towards the Convergence of Refugee Protection and State Security. Refugee Studies Centre Working Paper No. 4. Oxford.
Milner, James. 2009. Refugees, the State and the Politics of Asylum in Africa. Basingstoke.
Moser, Caroline. 1993. Gender Planning and Development: Theory, Practice, and Training. New York.
Moyo, Dambisa. 2009. Dead Aid. London.
Mulumba, Deborah. 2005. Gender relations, livelihood security and reproductive health among women refugees in Uganda. The case of Sudanese women in Rhino Camp and Kiryandongo Refugee Settlements. Ph.D. Thesis, Rural Development Sociology Group, Disaster Studies, Wageningen University.
Mulumba, Deborah. 2007. The Challenges of Conducting Research among Rural-Based Refugees in Uganda. Refugee Survey Quarterly. Vol. 26, 3.

Nachtigall, Andrea.2006. Frieden - Gewalt - Geschlecht. Friedens- und Konfliktforschung als Geschlechterforschung. H-Soz-u-Kult. 25.05.2006.
Nawratil, Georg; Rabaioli-Fischer, Barbara. 2004. Sozialpsychologie leicht gemacht. Einführung und Examenshilfe. 5. edition. Berlin.
Newland, Kathleen; Patrick, Erin; van Selm, Joanne; Zard, Monette. 2002. Introduction. Forced Migration Review. September 11th: Has anything changed?. Vol. 13.
NRC. 2009. Uganda. (http://www.nrc.no/?aid=9167601, 06.09.2009).
Nuscheler, Franz. 2004. Internationale Migration. Flucht und Asyl. Wiesbaden.
Nuscheler, Franz. 2005. Entwicklungspolitik. Bonn.
Oakley, Ann. 1972. Sex, Gender and Society. New York.
Orach, Christopher Garimoi; Brouwere, Vincent De. 2003. Integrating refugee and host health services in West Nile districts, Uganda. Health Policy and Planning. Vol. 21, 1.
Owen, Matthew. 2001. Evaluation of BMZ-supported environmental activities in refugee-hosting areas of northern Uganda. Engineering and Environmental Services Section. UNHCR. Geneva.
Oxfam International. 2008. Emergency to Recovery. Rescuing northern Uganda's transition. Oxfam Briefing Paper 118. Oxford.
Otunnu, Ogena. 1992. Socio Economic and political crises in Ugandada: Reasons for Human Rights Violations and Refugees. Refugee. Vol. 11, 3.
Panke-Kochinke, Birgit. 2003. Methode der rekonstruktiven hermeneutischen Textanalyse. In: Dies.: Unterwegs und doch daheim. (Über-) Lebensstrategien von Kriegsschwestern im Ersten Weltkrieg in der Etappe. Frankfurt a.M..
Peterson, Spike V.. 1992. Transgressing Boundaries: Theories of Knowledge, Gender and International Relations, Millennium: Journal of International Studies. Vol. 21, 2.
Pies, Ingo; Sass; Peter; Frank, Roland. 2005. Anforderungen an eine Politik der Nachhaltigkeit - eine wirtschaftsethische Studie zur europäischen Abfallpolitik. Wirtschaftsethik-Studie No. 2005-3. Lehrstuhl für Wirtschaftsethik an der Martin-Luther-Universität Halle-Wittenberg und der Sektion Wirtschaftswissenschaften der Stiftung Leucorea in der Lutherstadt Wittenberg (ed.). Halle.
Pateman, Carol. 1989. The Disorder of Women. Democracy, Feminism and Political Theory. Cambridge.
Payne, Lina. 1998. Rebuilding Communities in a Refugee Settlement: A Casebook from Uganda. Oxford.
Peterson, V. Spike; Runyan, Anne S.. 1999. Global Gender Issues. Colorado.
Pettman, Jan J.. 1997. Gender Issues. In: Baylis, John; Smith, Steve (ed.). The Globalization of World Politics. Oxford.
Polk, Merritt. 2001. Gender Equality and Sustainable Development: The need for debate in transportation policy in Sweden. Transportpolitik i Fokus. No. 1.
Reinharz, Shulamit. 1992. Feminist Methods in Social Research. New York.
Reimann, Cordula. 2003. Frauen, gewaltförmige Konflikte und Peacebuilding. In: Feministisches Institut (ed.). Feministische Theorieansätze in der Friedens- und Sicherheitspolitik. Berlin.
Reiman, Cordula. 2002. Gender als analytische Kategorie in der zivilen Konfliktbearbeitung. In: Ruth Stanley. Gender in der zivilen Konfliktbearbeitung. Werkstattbericht. Berlin.
Rees, Teresa. 2002. Gender Mainstreaming: Misappropriated and Misunderstood? Cardiff. (http://www.sociology.su.se/cgs/ReesPaper.doc, 07.08.2007).
RLSS Mission Report / DOS Mission Report. 2003/11. Development Assistance for Refugees (DAR) for Uganda Self Reliance Strategy. Way Forward. 14 to 20 September 2003. Kampala, Uganda.

RLSS Mission Report. 2004/03. Self-Reliance Strategy (1999 – 2003) For Refugee Hosting Areas in Moyo, Arua and Adjumani Districts, Uganda. Report of the Mid-term Review April 2004. Geneva.

Rosenberger, Sieglinde. 1998. Das Geschlecht der Internationalen Beziehungen. Feministische Kritik politikwissenschaftlichen Denkens. In: Kreisky, Eva; Sauer, Birgit (ed.). Geschlecht und Eigensinn. Feministische Recherchen in der Politikwissenschaft. Wien, Köln, Weimar.

Roth, Silke. 2004. Gender Mainstreaming. Eine neue Phase der Frauenbewegung in Deutschland. In: Meuser, Michael; Neusüß, Claudia (ed.). Gender Mainstreaming. Konzepte – Handlungsfelder – Instrumente. Bundeszentrale für politische Bildung. Vol. 418. Bonn.

Rowley, Elizabeth A.; Burnham, Gilbert M.; Drabe, Rabbin M.. 2006. Protracted Refugee Situations: Parallel Health Systems and Planning for the Integration of Services. Journal of Refugee Studies. Vol. 19, 2.

Sadruddin Aga Khan, Prince. 1966a. Statementto the Global Meeting of Resident Representatives at Turin, 1 April 1966. HC Statements, 1 April 1966. (http://www.unhcr.org/cgi-bin/texis/vtx/search?page=search&docid=3ae68fd030&query=Sadruddin%20Aga, 03.12.2009).

Sadruddin Aga Khan, Prince. 1966b. Statement at the Economic and Social Council (39th Session), 1 May 1966. (http://www.unhcr.org/cgi-bin/texis/vtx/search?page=search&docid=3ae68fb71c&query=Sadruddin%20Aga, 03.12.2009).

Sadruddin Aga Khan, Prince. 1969. Statement to the 47th Session of the United Nations Economic and Social Council (ECOSOC), 28 July 1969. (http://www.unhcr.org/3ae68fc920.html, 03.12.2009).

Schmidt, Anna. 2003. FMO Thematic Guide: Camps versus settlements. (http://www.forcedmigration.org/guides/fmo021/fmo021.pdf, 25.11.2009).

Sen, Amartya. 1999. Development as Freedom. New York.

Sengupta, Jati K.. 1988. The Measurement of Productive Efficiency: A Robust Minimax Approach. Managerial and Decision Economics. Vol. 9, 2.

Singer, Hans Wolfgang; Wood, John B.; Jennings, Tony; Jennings, Anthony. 1987. Food aid: the challenge and the opportunity. Oxford.

Sharpley, Richard; Telfer David J.. 2002. Tourism and development: concepts and issues. Clevedon.

Sherman, Neal. 2003. Refugee Resettlement in Uganda: 11. NIRP Research for Policy. Amsterdam.

Snyder, Margaret. 2004. Women Determine Development: The Unfinished Revolution. Signs. Vol. 29, 2.

Snyder, R. Claire. 2008. What Is Third-Wave Feminism? A New Directions Essay. Signs. Vol. 34, 1.

Solow, Robert M.. 1993. Sustainability: an economist's perspective. In: Dorfman, R., Dorfman, N.S (eds). Economics of the Environment. New York.

Soretz, Susanne. 2009. Entwicklungsökonomie. Entwicklungspolitische Ziele. (http://www.rsf.uni-greifswald.de/fileadmin/mediapool/lehrstuehle/soretz/dokumente/folien_dev2.pdf; 12.12.2009).

Stein, Barry N., Clark, D. Lance. 1985. Older Refugee Settlement in Africa: Final Report. Refugee Policy Group. Washington DC.

Stiglitz, Joseph. 1998. Towards a New Paradigm for Development: Strategies, Policies, and Processes. (http://web.worldbank.org/WBSITE/EXTERNAL/TOPICS/TRADE/0,,contentMDK:2002

5537~menuPK:167371~pagePK:64020865~piPK:149114~theSitePK:239071,00.html, 13.11.2009).
Svensson, Jakob. 2005. Eight Questions about Corruption. The Journal of Economic Perspectives. Vol. 19, 3.
Sylvester, Christine. 1987. Some Dangers in Merging Feminist and Peace Projects. Alternatives 1987. Vol. 12.
Sylvester, Christine. 1994a. Feminist Theory and International Relations in a Postmodern Era. Cambridge.
Sylvester, Christine. 1994b. Empathetic Cooperation: A feminist Method for IR. Millennium: Journal of International Studies. Vol. 23, 2.
Sylvester, Christine. 1998. Homeless in International Relations? 'Women's' Place in Canonical Texts and Feminist Reimaginings. In: Phillips, Anne (ed.). Feminism & Politics. Oxford.
Sylvester, Christine. 2002. Feminist International Relations. An Unfinished Journey. Cambridge.
Tamale, Sylvia. 2004. Gender Trauma in Africa: Enhancing Women's Links to Resources CODESRIA (ed.). Gender, Economies and Entitlements in Africa. CODESRIA Gender Series. Vol. 2. Dakar, Senegal.
Terrill, Roman. 1999. Globalization in the 1990s. In: Carrasco, Enrique R.; Berg, Kirsten J. (ed.). The E-Book on International Finance and Development. Revised edition. (http://www.uiowa.edu/ifdebook/ebook2/contents/contents.shtml, 09.11.2009)
Tejani, Bahadur. 1974. Farewell Uganda. Transition. Vol. 42.
The National Archives. 2009. Cabinet Papers 1915 – 1978. Protectorate and trusteeship. (http://www.nationalarchives.gov.uk/cabinetpapers/themes/protectorate-trusteeship.htm, 29.11.2009).
Thielemann, Eiko R.. 2006. Burden Sharing: The International Politics of Refugee Protection. The Center for Comparative Immigration Studies. Working Papers 134. University of Texas, Austin.
Tickner, J. Ann. 1995. Re-visioning Security. In: Booth, Ken/Smith, Steve (ed.): International Relations Theory Today. Cambridge.
Tickner, J. Ann. 2005. Gendering a Discipline: Some Feminist Methodological Contributions to International Relations. Signs. Vol. 30, 4.
Tickner, J. Ann. 2002. Feminist Perspectives on 9/11. In: International Studies Perspectives 2002. Vol. 3.
Tickner, J. Ann. 1994. A Feminist Critique of Political Realism. In: Beckman, Peter R.; D'Amico, Francine (ed.). Women, Gender, and World Politics. London.
Tickner, J. Ann. 1997. You Just Don't Understand: Troubled Engagements Between Feminists and IR Theorists. International Studies Quarterly 1997. Vol. 41.
Tickner, J. Ann. 1999. Why Women can't run the World: International Politics according to Francis Fukuyama. International Studies Review. Vol. 1, 3.
Tickner, J. Ann. 2005b. What is your Research Program? Some Feminist Answers to International Relations Methodological Questions. International Studies Quarterly 49.
Tickner, J. Ann. 2001. Ann. Gendering World Politics. Issues and approaches in the post-Cold War Era. New York.
Tiessen, Rebecca. 2007. Everywhere/Nowhere. Gender Mainstreaming in Development agencies. Bloomfield.
Truman, Harry S.. 1949. Truman's Inaugural Address, January 20, 1949. (http://www.trumanlibrary.org/whistlestop/50yr_archive/inagural20jan1949.htm, 29.11.2009).
Tuyizere, Alice Peace. 2007. Gender and Development. The Role of Religion and Culture. Kampala.

Ünay, Sadik. 2006. Neoliberal Globalization and Institutional Reform *the* Political Economy of Development and Planning in Turkey. Hauppauge, NY.
UN. 1995. Beijing Platform for Action.
UN. 2002. Women, Peace and Security. Study submitted by the Secretary-General pursuant to Security Council Res. 1325 (2000). New York.
UN. 2006. High Level Dialogue on International Migration and Development. (http://www.un.org/esa/population/migration/hld/index.html, 12.12.2009).
UN. 2008. News Center. UN refugee agency restores dozens of schools across Northern Uganda. (http://www.un.org/apps/news/story.asp?NewsID=27124&Cr=uganda&Cr1=, 23.12.2008).
UN. 2009. International Migration. (http://www.un.org/esa/population/migration/index.html, 13.12.2009).
UNDG. 2004. Guidance Note on Durable Solutions for Displaced Persons (refugees, internally displaced persons, and returnees). (http://www.unhcr.org/refworld/docid/4a54bbf4d.html, 29.01.2010).
UNDP. 2005. Uganda Human Development Report 2005. Linking Environment to Human Development: A Deliberate Choice. New York.
UNDP. 2008. Empowered and Equal Gender Equality Strategy 2008-2011. New York.
UNDP. 2009a. Human Development Report 2009. Uganda. The Human Development Index - going beyond income. Fact Sheet. (http://hdrstats.undp.org/en/countries/country_fact_sheets/cty_fs_UGA.html, 15.02.2010).
UNDP. 2009b. Human Development Report 2009. Uganda. The Human Development Index - going beyond income. Data Sheet. (http://hdrstats.undp.org/en/countries/data_sheets/cty_ds_UGA.html, 15.02.2010).
UNDP. 2010. EC-UN Joint Migration & Development Initiative. (http://www.undp.org/eu/ec-un_joint_migration_and_development_initiative.shtml, 29.01.2010).
UN DPKO. 2004. Gender Resource Package. New York.
UNHCR. 1987. Refugee Children, 12 October 1987, No. 47 (XXXVIII). (http://www.unhcr.org/refworld/docid/3ae68c432c.html, 10.09.2008)
UNHCR. 1990. Policy on Refugee Women. Geneva.
UNHCR. 1991. Guidelines on the Protection of Refugee Women. Geneva.
UNHCR. 1992. A Framework for People oriented Planning in Refugee Situations taking Account of Women, Men and Children. Geneva.
UNHCR. 1993. Interpreting in a Refugee Context. Geneva. (www.unhcr.org/refworld/pdfid/3cce9bbb4.pdf, 22.09.2009).
UNHCR. 1994. Returnee Aid and Development. (www.unhcr.org/print/3bd40fb24.html).
UNHCR. 1995. Sexual Violence against Refugees: Guidelines on Prevention and Response. Geneva.
UNHCR. 1996. Environmental Guidelines. Geneva.
UNHCR. 1997. Policy on Harmful Traditional Practices. Geneva.
UNHCR. 1999a. Handbook for Emergencies. 2. edition. Geneva.
UNHCR. 2001a. Project Planning in UNHCR. A Practical Guide on the Use of Objectives, Outputs and Indicators for UNHCR Staff and Implementing Partners. Geneva.
UNHCR. 2001b. UNHCR's Commitments to Refugee Women. Geneva.
UNHCR. 2001c. Learning for a Future: Refugee Education in Developing Countries. Jeff Crisp, Christopher Talbot and Daiana B. Cipollone (eds.). Geneva.
UNHCR. 2002. UNHCR Gender Training Kit on Refugee Protection and Resource Handbook. Geneva.
UNHCR. 2003a. Sexual and Gender-Based Violence Against Refugees, Returnees and Internally Displaced Persons. Guidelines for Prevention and Response. Geneva.
UNHCR. 2003b. Partnership. An Operations Management Handbook for UNHCR's Partners.

Revised edition. Geneva.
UNHCR. 2003c. Agenda for Protection. 3. edition. Geneva.
UNHCR. 2003d. Framework for Durable Solutions For Refugees and Persons of Concern. Geneva.
UNHCR. 2003e. Handbook for Registration. Procedures and Standards for Registration, Population Data Management and Documentation. Geneva.
UNHCR. 2003f. Global Report. Uganda. Geneva.
UNHCR. 2004a. Operational Protection in Camps and Settlements. A reference guide of good practices in the protection of refugees and other persons of concern. Geneva.
UNHCR. 2004b. Handbook for Repatriation and Reintegration Activities. Geneva.
UNHCR. 2005a. Ensuring Gender Sensitivity in the context of Refugee Status Determination and Resettlement. Geneva.
UNHCR. 2005c. Handbook For Planning And Implementing Development Assistance for Refugees (DAR) Programmes. Geneva.
UNHCR. 2005e. Global Appeal. Geneva.
UNHCR. 2006a. UNHCR and International Protection. A Protection Induction Programme. Geneva.
UNHCR. 2006b. The State of The World's Refugees 2006: Human Displacement in the New Millennium. Geneva.
UNHCR. 2006c. Global Appeal 2006. Finding durable solutions. Geneva.
UNHCR. 2006d. Operational Protection in Camps and Settlements. A Reference Guide of Good Practices in the Protection of Refugees and Other Persons of Concern. Geneva.
UNHCR. 2006f. Global Appeal. Geneva.
UNHCR. 2006g. High Level Dialogue on International Migration and Development. (http://www.unhcr.org/45799d762.html, 12.12.2009).
UNHCR. 2007a. Protecting Refugees and the role of UNHCR. Geneva.
UNHCR. 2007b. Statute of the office of the United Nations High Commissioner for Refugees. Geneva.
UNHCR. 2007c. Safe Schools and Learning Environment. How to Prevent and Respond to Violence in Refugee Schools. A Guide. Geneva.
UNHCR. 2007d. Global Appeal. Geneva.
UNHCR. 2008a. Handbook for the Protection of Women and Girls. Geneva.
UNHCR. 2008b. A Community-based Approach in UNHCR Operations. Geneva.
UNHCR. 2008c. Global Appeal 2008-2009. Uganda. Geneva.
UNHCR. 2008d. A Guidance for UNHCR Field Operations on Water and Sanitation Services. Geneva.
UNHCR. 2009. Frame Toolkit. Framework for Assessing, Monitoring and Evaluating the environment in refugee-related operations. Geneva.
UNHCR. 2009a. Refugee Women. (http://www.unhcr.org/cgi-bin/texis/vtx/protect?id=3b83a48d4, 27.01.2009).
UNHCR. 2009c. Publications. (http://www.unhcr.org/pages/49c3646c4b8.html, 06.09.2009).
UNHCR. 2009d. Women and Gender Equality. (http://www.unhcr.org/refworld/women.html, 09.12.2009).
UNHCR. 2010. Country operations profile – Uganda. (www.unhcr.org/pages/49e483c06.html; 15.05.2010).
UNHCR RefWorld. 2009. Women and Gender Equality. http://www.unhcr.org/refworld/women.html, 09.12.2009)
UNICEF. Uganda. Newsline. UNICEF-developed computer kiosk aims to provide information access to isolated communities in Uganda. (http://www.unicef.org/infobycountry/uganda_60096.html, 22.01.2012).
UNIFEM. 2004. Pathway to Gender Equality: CEDAW, Beijing and the MDGs. New York.

UN OCHA. 2004. Regional Support Office for Central and East Africa; Integrated Regional Information Networks. "when the sun sets, we start to worry...". An Accort of Life in Northern Uganda. Nairobi.
UN OCHA. 2010. Uganda clusters. Peace Recovery and Development Plan for Northern Uganda (PRDP). (http://www.ugandaclusters.ug/prdp.htm, 23.05.2010).
UN OSAGI. 2009. About the Office of the Special Adviser to the Secretary-General on Gender Issues and Advancement of Women. (http://www.un.org/womenwatch/osagi/aboutosagi.htm, 10.11.2009).
UN Secretary-General's Bulletin. 2003. Special Measures for Protection from Sexual Exploitation and Sexual Abuse. ST/SGB/2003/13. New York 09.10.2003.
van Heuven Goedhart, Gerrit Jan. 1953. Statement at the Meeting of the Third Committee of the United Nations General Assembly, 13 October 1953.
Vüllers, Johannes. 2008. Friedensprozess Norduganda. Zum Stand der Friedensverhandlungen. Länderbericht der KAS. Kampala. (http://www.kas.de/proj/home/pub/36/1/dokument_id-13255/index.html, 20.08.08).
Walby, Sylvia. 2007. Gender Mainstreaming: Productive Tensions in Theory and Practice. (http://sp.oxfordjournals.org/cgi/content/full/12/3/321?ijkey=yFk0XdpzrxyGm8C&keytype=ref, 14.08.2007).
Warkalla, Lutz. 2008. Lernen für den Wiederaufbau. Uganda. In: Bonner General-Anzeiger. 07.01.2008.
Weber, Cynthia. 1994. Good Girls, Little Girls, and Bad Girls: Male Paranoia in Robert Keohane's Critique of Feminist International Relations. Millennium. Journal of International Studies. Vol. 23, 2.
Whitworth, Sandra. 1994. Feminism and International Relations. Towards a Political Economy of Gender in Interstate and Non-Governmental Institutions. Houndmills.
Whitworth, Sandra. 1989. Gender in the Inter-Paradigm Debate. Millennium. Journal of International Studies. Vol. 18, 2.
Wisotzki, Simone. 2005. Gender und Frieden. In: Jahn, Egbert; Fischer, Sabine; Sahm Astrid (eds.). Die Zukunft des Friedens. Die Friedens- und Konfliktforschung aus der Perspektive der jüngeren Generationen. Vol. 2. Wiesbaden.
WCRWC. 2004. Emergency Contraception for Conflict-Affected Settings. A Reproductive Health Response in Conflict Consortium Distance Learning Module. New York.
WCRWC. 2007. Engaging Men and Boys in Refugee Settings to Address Sexual and Gender Based Violence. New York.
WCRWC. 2008. Rebuilding Lives Refugee Economic Opportunities in a New Land. A report from a workshop held in Cape Town, South Africa, 22-25 September, 2008. New York.
Weiss Fagen, Patricia. 2003. Post-Conflict Reintegration and Reconstruction. Doing it right takes a while. In: Steiner, Niklaus; Gibney, Mark; Loescher, Gil. Problems of Protection. The UNHCR, Refugees and Human Rights. New York.
World Bank. 2008. Uganda at a glance. (http://devdata.worldbank.org/AAG/uga_aag.pdf; 15.02.2010).
World Bank. 2009. IDA at Work. Uganda. (http://siteresources.worldbank.org/IDA/Resources/IDA-Uganda.pdf; 25.03.2010).
World Bank. 2010a. Data Profile. Uganda. (http://ddp-ext.worldbank.org/ext/ddpreports/ViewSharedReport?REPORT_ID=9147&REQUEST_TYPE=VIEWADVANCED&DIMENSIONS=213; 15.02.2010).
World Bank. 2010b. County Snapshot. Education. Uganda. (http://web.worldbank.org/WBSITE/EXTERNAL/TOPICS/EXTEDUCATION/EXTDATASTATISTICS/EXTEDSTATS/0,,menuPK:3232818~pagePK:64168427; 15.02.2010).
Zalewski, Marysia. 1994. The Women/'Women' Question in International Relations. In: Millennium: Journal of International Studies. Vol. 23, 2.

Annex

List of Figures with Bibliography

List of Tables with Bibliography

Refugee Population Statistics in Rhino Camp

Table 7. Details on the refugee statistics at Rhino Camp.

Year	Overall	Female	Male	Children (5-17)	Children (<5)	Source (DED report)	Page
1997	28571	5188	6108	11831	5444	*97/AP/UGA/LS403*	*2*
1998	27677	4969	5866	11364	5478	*98/AP/UGA/LS403*	*2*
1999	30817	6031	7024	13647	4115	*99/AP/UGA/LS403*	*2*
2000	35333	8650	7341	14291	5051	*00/AB/UGA/LS403*	*2*
2001	24727	4511	4344	11352	4520	*01/AB/UGA/LS403*	*4*
2002	25453					*02/AB/UGA/LS403*	*4*
2003	25836					*03/AB/UGA/LS403*	*5*
2004	26418					*04/AB/UGA/LS403*	*5*
2005	25157					*05/AB/UGA/LS403*	*4*
2006	20231					*06/AB/UGA/LS/403*	*4*

Gaps in the table above are due to missing data in the respective annual reports of the DED Refugee/IDP Programme. The sum of the data in the table above is represented in the table 6 below with the refugee population statistics in Rhino Camp.

Table 4. Annual refugee population statistics from 1997 until 2006 in Rhino Camp

1997	1998	1999	2000	2001	2002	2003	2004	2005	2006
28,571	27,677	30,817	35,333	24,727	25,453	25,836	26,418	25,157	20,231

Research Approach

1. Theoretical Framing

As J. Ann Tickner, in accordance with Harding (Harding 1987: 2-3), states in *What is your research program?*, "I [also] distinguish between the term "methodology," a theory and analysis of how research does or should proceed, and "method," a technique for gathering and analyzing evidence" (Tickner 2005b: 3).

1.1. Feminist Research of International Relations

Integrating the gender perspective within research on refugee assistance means to me to analyze procedures in a gender-sensitive way and thus embrace roles, relations and statuses of women and men. In order to do so, the feminist research of International Relations is applied.

International Relations (IR) as part of political sciences emerged centuries ago. Platon, Aristotle, Cicero, Thomas von Aquin, Machiavelli, Erasmus von Rotterdam, Thomas Hobbes, John Locke, Immanuel Kant and Karl von Clausewitz are only few pioneers who shaped today's political science discipline of IR. Some scholars argue that the Peace of Westphalia of 1648 indicates the birth of IR as the study of foreign affairs. It certainly reveals a cornerstone in terms of the understanding of state sovereignty. However, the aforementioned persons facilitated the development of IR through their documented ideas, visions and thoughts about states and international affairs including concepts of war and peace. The First World War and the 1920s, nevertheless, mark a time in which IR became recognized as an academic discipline. Theories such as idealism, realism, positivism, structuralism, and constructivism were developed and changed the study of IR.

Feminism emerged in the framework of the feminist movement claiming equal rights and opportunities for women and men. The three waves of the political feminist movement started in the nineteenth century (Krolokke/Sorensen 2005). In addition to the political waves, feminism is also to be understood as a research methodology of IR. It entered the discipline in the 1980s and was led by the recognition of androcentric views within IR. Men seemed to lead the world while not acknowledging and integrating women with their views and needs.

IR-trained feminist scholars such as J. Ann Tickner, Cynthia Enloe, Carol Cohn, Felicity Hill, Vanessa Farr, and Sandra Whitworth[69] have broadened the IR horizon and contributed to academic emancipation concerning the emphasis of the lack of equal opportunities for women and men in the global context. Feminism in IR grew throughout the past three decades and gained recognition. It influenced global political, social, societal and related structures. Yet, it still remains on the margins of the IR discipline. Nonetheless, IR feminists continue to pursue

69 The names of IR feminists are mainly from the USA and constitute only a small list which is by far not complete. These scholars in addition to Birgit Sauer, Barbara Holland-Cunz, Nira Yuval-Davis, Eva Kreisky (and many more), have influenced my research.

progressive aims with their research; they focus on and integrate women's lives, experiences, and relations to the other sex within the context of global affairs and research.

But what is feminism in IR about? What are goals, features and contents of research? As said by Tickner, "feminists are motivated by emancipatory goals — investigating the often disadvantaged lives of women within states or international institutions and structures in order to change them" (Tickner 2005a: 2178). Feminist research focuses on women and their experiences, roles, and statuses within societies. IR feminists also view and analyze human beings — men and women — as well as their relations and stand in social contexts, hierarchies and dynamics. Nevertheless,

> [...] feminism is more than a study of gender relations — it is a critical politics of those relations. All feminists agree that in every facet of life, women have been and continue to be oppressed as a sex because of our sex, by and for the benefit of men. All feminists are united in seeking to end the subordination of women [...]. Beyond that core, the rubric of feminism encompasses an enormous diversity of views on the primary sources and manifestations of women's oppression and strategies of overcoming that oppression (Greschner 1989 in Klinger 1994: 140).

Although feminists focus on gender relations, they do so within the context of further thematic areas. Feminist research is always led by the feminist curiosity to develop new relevant questions about the real world. Feminist approaches utilize different ontologies and epistemological stances. Harding points out clearly that

> feminist epistemologists criticize criteria used in the sciences to evaluate beliefs because they think these criteria are themselves infused, mostly unintentionally, with androcentric and antidemocratic commitments. Feminists intend to substitute feminist values and interests not for value-neutral criteria but for those criteria or aspects of them that are androcentric and antidemocratic and that block the growth of knowledge. This is why feminism needs "an epistemology of its own" (Walby, in this issue, 504): the nonfeminist ones are androcentric and thus incompetent (Harding 2001: 520).

Feminist research is conducted through feminist lenses to overcome the gender-blindness within IR as an academic political discipline as, well as real world politics and global affairs (Fonow/Cook 2005: 2212; Fierke 2001: 115-135; Tickner 2005b: 1; Zalewski 1994: 412).

With the feminist perspective of "the personal is international" (Enloe 1989: 194), IR feminists attempt to deconstruct imaginary boundaries.[70] "The dichotomy between the private and the public is central to almost two centuries of feminist writing and political struggle; it is ultimately, what the feminist movement is about" (Pateman 1989: 118). Feminists abrogate and neutralize constructed boundaries between private and public, political and apolitical, high and low politics. They integrate differentiated and different scopes of individual experiences into their research. Through that, feminists analyze the real world and circumvent an unwanted

70 I intentionally termed the boundaries between the public and personal spaces 'imaginary'. Although deconstructing these borders constitutes a key element of feminist IR research, I agree with Nouria Ali-Tani (2006: 17 ff) and further feminists. Public and personal spaces only exist in human imaginations. They are abstract and philosophical constructs. Thus, definitions of both terms remain unclear and wide. The public space is generally understood as the foundation of legitimized political acting while the private one is often used as a "synonym for the silence of women". (translated: Ali-Tani 2006: 18)

"pseudo-objectivity" (Tickner 2005b: 8-9). "Feminists in IR are linking the everyday lived experiences of women with the constitution and exercise of political and economic power at state and global levels" (Tickner 2005a: 2178).

By means of deconstructing boundaries between the public and the private, the political and the apolitical, feminists make those visible who are normally invisible within research. Reinharz points out that

> [m]aking the invisible visible, bringing the margin to the center, rendering the trivial important, putting the spotlight on women as competent actors, understanding women as subjects in their own right rather than objects for men – all continue to be elements of feminist research (Reinharz 1992: 248).

Hence, feminists focus on women, as well as on adding more information to a topic by means of integrating both sexes and their relations into research.

IR feminists highlight and address "issues of research as it was lived at a particular moment in time" (Fonow/Cook 2005: 2212). According to the authors, feminist research is historically and geographically focused and thus committed and connected to specific contexts. The bond to contexts exposes a clear orientation towards post-positivism (Peterson/Runyan 1999: 22ff; Locher-Dodge 1998: 432f).

Gender is generally understood as the socially constructed identity of a woman or man in contrast to sex. Sex represents the biological, anatomic category of a person. Gender has become a central analytical category for IR feminists. This means more than merely examining gender-related differences in social milieus. IR feminists do not understand gender as an independent variable. It is analyzed in interaction with social factors such as classes and ethnic identities as well as in dependence on social procedures (Reiman 2003: 11).

Due to a broad repertoire of methods used by IR feminists, they not only pursue the goal of analyzing gender-related topics. Feminists moreover target to reach objectivity by plural and gender equality-oriented thinking (Tickner 1997: 622; Tickner 2005b: 8-10, 15).

1.1.1. Feminist Sub-Categories within IR

In general, feminist research classifies several sub-categories. Since the feminist movements emerged, diverse sub-categories, waves, and generations occurred, developed, and changed. All sub-categories define specific demands.[71] For example, the liberal feminism particularly claims political rights and access to education for women (Roth 2004: 41). "The desideratum of liberal feminism is to bring women into sociality as individual agents with rights equal to those that individual white and privileged adult men enjoy on principle in liberal societies [...]" (Sylvester 1994a: 37). Liberal feminists therefore deal with traditional role allocations and relations of men and women, which comprise the unequal representation of women in occupational and political fields. According to liberal feminists, freedom, equality, and access to resources can be given by the state (Tickner 2001: 12-13; Locher-Dodge 1998: 429; Sylvester 1994a: 37).

Radical feminists observe women in oppressed roles within patriarchal societies. They criticize the private oppression and submission, and the public isolation of women in the male dominated hierarchies. Radical feminism analyzes phenomena of war, military, and

71 I do not aim and claim to demonstrate a complete list of all feminist sub-categories.

androcentric aggression. It contrasts these phenomena with the stereotypical soft, peaceable, and cooperative features of women to reason how durable peace can be achieved through the involvement of the 'weaker' sex. Changing the social and political arrangements to move towards gender equality requires a transformation of the societal contexts and structures. Radical feminists are often criticized because of the naturalization of stereotypical gender (relations) models and their clichéd features as well as the production and construction of a positive femininity as an alternative to the dominating masculinity (Holland-Cunz 2003: 97, 116ff; Tickner 2001: 13-14; Locher 2000: 339; Whitworth 1994: 20, 30).

Critical feminism rather constitutes a discourse on why it matters to differentiate between women and men. Zalewski asks about women in IR. „Now the question about women is not just 'who and where are women in IR?' but 'who are "women" (or what are "women", or even how are "women"), what is the difference and why does it matter?'" (Zalewski 1994: 408) It is therefore crucial to deconstruct stereotypes on masculinity and femininity (Whitworth 1994: 24 ff; Hedinger 2002: 46).

Many feminists believe that the 'bridging approaches' between diverse feminist perspectives and thematic areas of IR facilitate research with new or revised synergies. Looking at issues through feminist lenses helps to absorb the complexity of reality and contemplate the marginalization of collectives or individuals (Harding 1986: 243; Tickner 2005b: 14; Weber 1994: 439).

1.1.2. Post-Modern Feminism

Within this study, post-modern feminism deserves its own explanation since it is partly applied within the research. In dependence on the post-modern feminism, the focus of my research is not on women's biologically determined roles or women's experience and stories within multifaceted social nets. Post-modern feminists rather concentrate on both sexes and their relations. These gender-specific relations are "culture specific, historical variable, social constructs" (translated: Brabandt/Locher/Prügl 2002: 11).

Sex-specific roles shall be clarified in order to deconstruct gender stereotyping. Post-modern feminists believe that stereotypes are counterproductive because in androcentric international politics, men are perceived as leaders and women as victims who are to be protected. Male stereotypes of strong masculinity, power and bravery are listed next to the soft female features of peacefulness and helpfulness (Hedinger 2002: 46; Herrmann 2005: 45; Apelt/Dittmer 2008: 65-66).

Post-modern feminists disagree with particular identities and role specifics of the sexes. This is why they attempt to highlight how diverse and culturally dissimilar roles of women and men are per se (Wisotzki 2005: 113).

The aim of post-modern feminism therefore is to deconstruct these gender-specific roles in order to observe both sexes as equally able to progress. If men are continued to be seen as active and women as passive, gender equality becomes even more complicated to be achieved.

A necessary post-modern factor is language because it shapes realities and helps to deconstruct roles. Frug states the following:

> The postmodern position locating human experience as inescapably within language suggests that feminists should not overlook the constructive function of legal language as a critical frontier for feminist reforms. To put this "principle" more bluntly, legal discourse should be recognized as a site of political struggle over sex differences (Frug 1995: 8).

Although Frug refers to the legal context, I adopt her idea and use language in my research.

Post-modern feminists criticize that older feminist sub-categories analyzed conditions from a western point of view only. By doing so, they ignored specific historical and social structures in non-western countries and societies (Krell 1996: 157). Post-modern feminism is criticized for its strong focus on complete deconstruction of gender. Through that, women as such disappear. This is seen as problematic within the context of emancipatory development (Tickner 2001: 20). The scenario of the "disappearing women" (translated: Finke 2003: 494) seems to dread the feminist ability to act and react.

1.2. Applied Post-Modern Feminism of IR

In spite of several critical aspects, the post-modern feminist research of IR is applied within my research. The aim is to deconstruct gender roles. Thus involving both sexes is essential.

My research on development-oriented refugee assistance is based on a threefold analysis concept: 1. theoretic-programmatic examination of the previous working approaches to produce features; 2. field studies at Rhino Camp to scan programmatic realization; 3. linking results of the first two fractions to draw up the conclusion. Subsequently, research is to be characterized by a strong theory-practice linkage.

By means of the post-modern feminism, I take both sexes within the refugee settlements into consideration. In order to see how efficient and sustainable operations are, I investigate how lasting activities are implemented and how the refugee communities and national population are able to profit from activities. Since I believe that the processes towards gender equality and development go hand in hand, the pillars are inseparably connected. While feminist analysis is often bottom-up rather than top-down, I conduct research from a meta-level at the refugee settlement in the context of the case study. That is, analyzing the operations of the refugee working approach as an entirety and examining the pillars. The factor of language is taken into account, particularly through reports; it is examined if gender plays a role and is part of the holistic programming. The differentiation between private and public spheres is captured through public descriptions of conditions and progressions as well as identified facts; i.e.: Are findings of official statements and reports consistent with findings through other sources such as interviews? What methods are used to achieve research findings? How findings are reviewed and assessed is explained hereafter. It is also explained how the three pillars of sustainability, efficiency and gender sensitivity are operationalized throughout the research.

2. Operationalizing the Pillars

The pillars were operationalized based on the definitions stated in Chapter II.

As noted above, this research on development-oriented refugee assistance is based on three pillars: sustainability, efficiency and gender sensitivity. The previous section already defined the terms and revealed its linkages. In order to be able to examine in research later on, how these pillars are to be included in the to be elaborated features of development-oriented refugee assistance and whether they were achieved in operations at Rhino Camp, the pillars are to be operationalized.

Sustainability is understood in the context of sustainable development. It is used as type of development assistance that strives for identifying durable solutions that betters lives of current and future generations by intentionally respecting and protecting the limited natural resources, supporting economic growth and promoting just social relations between the genders. To operationalize that, specific contents of this definition are to be considered. It is thus to be analyzed and eventually concluded if and how the features of development-oriented refugee assistance per se are applied against the operations at Rhino Camp target to:

- be of durable use,
- increase livelihood conditions,
- protect natural resources,
- support the process towards economic growth, and
- promote the process towards just social relations between the genders.

Efficiency, or rather dynamic efficiency, is understood as the most appropriate concept in this context. It is understood that innovative inputs are necessary to achieve best outputs within monopolies. The innovative input is constituted by an optimal use of resources and the mix of adequate approaches and methods to ensure refugee protection. In the refugee context, financial, political, natural and social costs need to be considered. To operationalize this understanding, again, specific contents are to be considered. It is thus to be analyzed and eventually concluded if and how the features of development-oriented refugee assistance per se are applied against the operations at Rhino Camp target to:

- be innovative per se and by creating a suitable mix of approaches and methods,
- involve political actors, and
- have an optimum use and protection of natural resources.

Since budgets of the DED Refugee/IDP Programme cannot be accessed, financial aspects cannot be analyzed and are not included.

Gender sensitivity is understood to obtain a dual imperative in the context of development-oriented refugee assistance; adequate refugee assistance can support the psychological transitional process in promoting equality aims for reaching gender parity, and development aid can only be performed sustainably and efficiently if both men and women are involved in the process. Gender sensitivity is defined as an integral part of operations of development-oriented refugee assistance through psychological support to refugees, integration and participation of both sexes of refugee and local communities and therewith provision of equal opportunities. Gender-sensitive planning and implementation should moreover be a cross-cutting theme.

One way to measure gender sensitivity would be to ask if the psychological transitional process was promoted and therewith gender equality achieved. To assess the actual extent of revised gender roles, research would have to be based on refugee identities and how specific roles changed over a scope of time from before refuge, while in the settlement and potentially also after repatriation. Thus, the ideal typical procedure would include three timeframes for analyses: before refuge, during encampment (assuming operations are gender-sensitive) and after repatriation. Only by means of that would a comprehensive analysis of the revision of the gender images and roles towards gender equality through development-oriented refugee assistance be possible. However, this would imply that the refuge is predictable and research was done on the tribe that flees in the near future or the local communities that will host refugees. Since refugee waves are understood to be unpredictable, it would imply that research was done on the tribe without knowing that they may flee or would host refugees. Either way, the traditional gender constellations of the refugees and locals would have to be known to measure and conclude if they were revised due to operations of development-oriented refugee assistance. My research project, however, is limited towards the above ideal typical procedure due to regional and time settings as well as the research focus. My research project is about the holistic development-oriented refugee assistance concept and the case. Refugee identities are not part of my research. How (much) traditional gender roles were revised through operations of refugee assistance is therefore barely traceable since historical, political, cultural and social constellations of the tribes in South Sudan and Uganda are not analyzed. Therefore, I cannot operationalize gender sensitivity by asking the most obvious questions: Have and if so to what extent have gender images and roles been revised toward gender equality? For that, I would have needed comparison attributes.

Since my research focuses on the holistic development-oriented refugee assistance concept and therefore looks at programmatic operations, manners of operationalizing gender sensitivity are to be on the same, somewhat interim level. Therefore, the process towards gender equality and empowerment is to be analyzed through programmatic inclusion of both men and women in operations in general terms. The already explained dual imperative captures the refugee and development assistance side with respective beneficiaries; hence, refugees and locals. Strongly simplified, the psychological transitional process can be analyzed by the means of support provided, while the development especially needs the involvement and participation of men and women to reach sustainability and efficiency.

Based on that, in the context of this research, gender sensitivity is operationalized through analyses of if and how the features of development-oriented refugee assistance are applied against the operations at Rhino Camp target to:

- psychologically support both sexes and especially women,
- integrate women and men and promote their participation in activities, and
- mainstream gender in planning and implementation processes.

On a more basic level, the post-modern feminist factor of language is to be taken into account as well. This is operationalized particularly through DED's annual reports. It is screened if gender plays a role in the reports and therefore is part of programming. Hence, the factor of language is primarily operationalized by the reference to gender in DED reports. The way of referring to gender is to be analyzed; i.e., in terms of women only or both sexes.

3. Methods

Methods of IR feminists are diverse. While political schools normally apply specific methods, "feminists have drawn upon a variety of methods [...]" (Tickner 2005b: 3).

In general, feminists tend to use qualitative rather than quantitative methods mainly because the 'realities' demonstrated through the empirical data directly depends on generated indicators. What was asked? Who asked whom and how? How many different sources were accessed? Question like these are to be considered before using data and drawing assumptions and conclusions from them. IR feminists came to the conclusion that numeric data often reflects a biased gendered picture. Thus, it "does not adequately reflect the reality of women's lives and the unequal structures of power within which they are situated" (Tickner 2005b: 5).

Feminists use a broad selection of research methods (Fonow/Cook 2005: 2214) to pursue objectivity. Feminists "rely on hermeneutic, historical, narrative, and case study methodological orientations rather than on causal analysis of unproblematically defined entities and social relations" (Tickner 2005b: 6).

Jacobsen and Landau outlined possible difficulties. They pointed point out while researching such delicate topics as refugee and humanitarian assistance they face a "*dual imperative*: both to satisfy the demands of the academy and to ensure that the knowledge and understanding our work generates are used to protect refugees, influence governments, and improve the ways institutions like the United Nations or Non-Governmental Organizations do their work" (Jacobsen/Landau 2003: 1). Thus, methods and approaches should be chosen carefully and fitted to the respective research topic. Scholars are recommended to provide sufficient background information and conceptual clarity on how the research was conducted. Revealing the research design clearly helps readers to follow the argumentation cycles and eventually judge if the findings are valid. Jacobsen and Landau moreover stress the necessity of ethical sensitivity while researching in the field (Jacobsen/Landau 2003: 2, 6, 9-10).

In this research, the above mentioned critical aspects are taken into account. A "multi-method approach" (Kohlbach 2006: 23) is used to accumulate and utilize data. The exact methods applied in this approach are explained hereafter.

3.1. Data Collection and Analyses

Data was collected through qualitative methods. Research was carried out in the framework of a desk-based review of the existing research literature. For the case study, methods of document review, field studies with participatory observation, semi-structured and structured interviews, and ero-epic dialogues were applied.

Data collection for the theoretic-programmatic examination of refugee assistance related developments and of the new working approach was done by consulting subject-specific and research literature. Research literature was to satisfy scientific demands. Publications of researchers comprised of, among others, monographs, articles in scientific journals, papers in volumes. Subject-specific literature primarily constitutes publications of organizations, institutions and authors that are about relevant topics. Policy-related publications of UNHCR's Evaluation and Policy Analysis Unit were considered. UNHCR's manuals and guidelines on various topics regarding refugee aid were consulted.

For the case study in Uganda, primary data collection was done through the annual reports about program implementation. DED provided access to annual reports from 1997 to 2006. Having access to the annual reports of the LS 403 program of the DED Refugee/IDP Programme enabled me to follow the programmatic progress and operations throughout the research period. The LS 403 program is the Local Settlement program. The annual report of 2005 was not accessible; instead, the bi-annual report was provided. In addition to the LS 403 annual reports, the annual report of the Voluntary Repatriation program (sub-project code: RP 331) of 2006 and the annual report of the Community Based Environment Management (sub-project code: LS 453) of 2006 were made available.

The documents were examined by means of systematic content analyses to find out what activities constituted the implementation processes throughout the research period. The annual reports of the DED Refugee/IDP Programme constituted the main source of information in order to trace and comprehend what sector-specific activities were conducted to what extend with which targeted group of beneficiaries.

These reports were the basis of field visits and studies not only because the subject focus within my dissertation is on the operational level rather than individual perceptions. Hence, reports were the foundation of field studies in order to grasp the complexity at Rhino Camp and ask relevant questions during ero-epic dialogues and interviews.

In addition, DED provided access to an internal database on infrastructure. The database reveals the broad scale of infrastructural developments at Rhino Camp. In 2007 and 2008, it was developed to assess the functionality and usability of and access to infrastructure for beneficiaries of refugee and local communities. The entire database contains information of the four settlements Rhino Camp, Ikafe, Madi Okollo and Imvepi managed by DED (DED 2008). However, only the information about Rhino Camp was screened and used. The database provided insights on the sustainability aspects of the operations.

During field studies, data was collected through participatory and unstructured observation, expert interviews and ero-epic dialogues. Participatory and unstructured observation is a research method that is originally used by ethnological studies. In the ideal-typical sense, it allows the observer to attend situations fully. Since the observer does not examine conditions according to a systematic plan, s/he is able to have the flexibility to capture complex settings. Observations can be participatory; then the observer can raise questions and participate in conversations with the persons present (Girtler 2001: 62-69). In the context of this project, observations were carried out at Rhino Camp. Due to the focus of the research project on operations, observations were not participatory in the original sense. They were unstructured and focused on the overall set up of Rhino Camp. Personal observations during field studies were written down and, if suitable in the context of the thesis, used with a note about when and where incidences were observed. Accessing the abovementioned database on infrastructure provided the opportunity to me to not merely observe aspects but also verify them through the database, which I understand as a more objective source than personal observation.

Expert interviews and ero-epic dialogues were held. An expert interview is a social science method in accordance with Meuser and Nagel. Expert interviews can applied in structured and semi-structured manners. Experts are understood to be representatives of organizations or institutions who have a voice in finding problem solutions and decision making. Furthermore, experts are persons who have privileged access to information about collectives and decision structures (Meuser/Nagel 2005: 74-75). Subject matter of interviews is not the interviewee with personal history and experiences, but rather the organizational and institutional context (Meuser/Nagel 2005: 72-73). Thus, interviewed persons are to be part of decision-making structures or to have in-depth experience and relevant knowledge about the field of analysis. All expert interviews were held with former or current DED staff that had in-depth experiences working in refugee assistance. All interviews were offered to be treated anonymously. They were conducted and oriented towards a guideline of questions. Prepared lists of questions were followed during the interviews. Questions were adjusted to the background of the interviewees. The interviews were written down to eliminate technical obstacles; afterwards I presented the document to the respective interviewee for revision. In case interviewees were not in Uganda and therefore not available for a personal interview, the list of questions was sent via email and returned to me. Interviewees agreed to be cited with their names for quotation. Information provided was used for the analysis. They were quoted in an exact phrase with reference to details of the interview including names and dates. The table below states an overview of samples taken.

Table 8. Sample Set based on interviews.

Data Set	Data Content
Number of interviews	15
Number of interviewees	8
Rank of interviewees	3 management positions (2 female, 1 male) 5 program staff (1 female, 4 male)
Sex	3 female; 5 male
Nationality	3 Ugandan; 5 German

The ero-epic dialogues are an interpretative social science method. These dialogues are constructed as a conversation without a prepared list of questions. The 'interviewer' rather takes time and develops a comforting environment to find out more background information, stories, and habits of a culture. It is important that the interviewee feels secure in order to talk freely (Girtler 2001: 147-154). In this research, ero-epic dialogues took place at Rhino Camp with DED staff. Each counterpart was asked if I was allowed to use the information for my research. Twelve dialogues with lower ranking local staff of DED were conducted. Dialogues were summarized at the end and written down. All dialogues were treated anonymously. When information from ero-epic dialogues was used in the analysis, the source of information was indicated by writing ero-epic dialogue with the respective date in brackets. It is to note that only one dialogue was eventually rated as containing useful information. The other dialogues were seen to not contain new or useful information.

Interviews and dialogues were analyzed by means of systematic content analyses according to Meuser and Nagel (2005). While interviews were cited with the exact phrasing or used through paraphrased structures, the aim was to learn about the shared knowledge among the interviewees. An adjusted concept of Meuser and Nagel was applied: after holding the interviews, they were transcribed. As a second step, they were paraphrased with my wording in order to then add headlines for the respective information sections. Finally, the information was compared in order to identify which knowledge and ideas were shared or if interviewees had different opinions.[72]

3.2. Elaboration of Features

The main objectives of the research project are to develop general features necessary to realize development-oriented refugee assistance and to apply the features on the case study.

A catalogue of features is elaborated by taking research findings of previous operational approaches and methods of and research findings about refugee aid and development assistance into account. Hence, the elaboration of features is based on the accumulated information gathered from four parameters:

1. The research community has given little attention to development-oriented refugee assistance. Nevertheless, there were related academic debates. The leading research in the field is Betts. His ingredients ((Betts 2009a: 13-18) are integrated in the elaboration of the features.

2. The four previously conceptualized operational approaches are analyzed and used to build the features through a kind of lessons learned process in a way to discern what was done and what was rated as factors of failure or success.

3. Development assistance is an important aspect to consider when looking at refugee aid not only as being part of emergency assistance. The elaboration of the features of development-oriented refugee assistance therefore also take into account the latest conceptual progress of development assistance.

4. Common sense and personal work experience in the field in Uganda is also integrated. Common sense is to be understood as a weighing up process while elaborating the features. Through work experience, I particularly aim to develop features that are practice-oriented instead of being located on a meta-level far from operational realities. I therefore strive for producing features that are relevant for and applicable in refugee protection.

The abovementioned four parameters are the foundation of the elaboration of the features. The features are distinguished from Betts' ingredients due to several aspects. Betts predominantly looks at the Northern donor states and Southern refugee hosting states and thus bases his argumentation on the 'high' decision making level. While these levels are certainly significant, I extend the scope and integrate the 'low' level or grass-roots level of the beneficiaries' sides. Beneficiaries are refugees and local communities. By that, I accept the important roles communities have in achieving sustainable, efficient and gender-sensitive outcomes. This is an innovative approach since it is known that the focus has mainly been on the decision making level in research (Loescher et al. 2008; Crisp 2001, 2003; Gorman 1993).

72 Meuser and Nagel additionally create conceptions to then generalize shared knowledge. Since my focus was not on the share knowledge per se, there was no need to conduct the final steps of conceptualizing and generalizing.

Hence, the features aim to capture a broader scope. The features I propose are practice-oriented and understood to be most fundamental, required in order to execute development-oriented refugee assistance successfully and to achieve durable solutions. Since development-oriented refugee assistance is understood to incorporate the three pillars of sustainability, efficiency, and gender sensitivity, the specific hints are stated within the explanation of the features. They encompass situational, timely, and actors' dimensions, and are thus multi-dimensional.

In Chapter V, operations implemented at Rhino Camp are assessed against the features. Applications of the features are done by taking all collected data through document review and interviews into account. It targets to eventually conclude, how sustainable, efficient, and gender-sensitive assistance was provided in Rhino Camp which is stated in Chapter VI.

4. *Thematic Focus*

4.1. Regional and Timely Dimensions of the Case Study

Based on the gaps in scientific literature, it is necessary to undertake research not only on the general development of development-oriented refugee assistance, but also with particular regional focus. The West Nile region of Uganda has been a refugee hosting region, but received little attention in research. To reflect on and demonstrate a real world picture of development-oriented refugee assistance, it is crucial to use a refugee settlement to perform a case study. Rhino Camp is therefore used for the case study in the context of the research project.

Rhino Camp is a local settlement. The Government of Uganda allocated approximately 225 square kilometer to be used for refugee settlements (DED LS/403 2001: 2). The local settlement type differentiates from camps in several ways. It is to highlight that it gives the "opportunity to legally reside in the host country [of the beneficiaries] and to enjoy civil and economic rights comparable to the local population, activities in this category help refugees become self-supporting in the country of first asylum, and to integrate into the economic and social life of the new community" (UNHCR 2003: 38-39).

Rhino Camp was established in 1992 and has been managed by DED since 1996. The actors play significant roles in the planning and implementation processes. UNHCR provides the implementing partner with programmatic concepts and guidelines; while the Office of the Prime Minister holds a supervisory function ensuring that operations proceed in accordance with agreements between UNHCR and the Government of Uganda. The implementation is done by the DED Refugee/IDP Programme.

Although DED managed further refugee settlements, the research of the case study merely focuses on Rhino Camp. DED allowed to conduct the case study in Rhino Camp and provided me with annual reports. The time focus is from 1997 up to 2006. This long timeframe appears to be crucial to follow developments and analyze whether planning and implementation procedures were performed in a gender-sensitive, sustainable, and efficient manner.

4.2. Thematic Containment

The aim of this project is not to develop a systematic comparison between old and new refugee aid approaches which include development initiatives. Neither does this study intend to research nor present broad-scaled pictures of historical developments of refugees worldwide. The study is about linking refugee assistance with development initiatives to prevent long-term encampment in protracted refugee situations. Even in the context of development-oriented refugee assistance, each programmatic attempt of UNHCR to implement refugee aid that includes development projects is not considered. Global changes of development-oriented refugee assistance are rather examined from a meta-level.

It is important to note that the term gender, although in colloquial usage often referring to women only, is understood to consider both men and women. In the context of my research, both sexes are taken into consideration. The research project is not about how refugee women are perceived or feel in their roles as refugees, or to grasp the type of assistance provided to them. Neither is the project only about women's rights or the rights of refugee women per se. Gender sensitivity is understood as the guiding pillar that may contain opportunities to support the process towards gender equality within the context of development-oriented refugee assistance. In addition, through post-modern feminism, as the applied research approach, I focus on both men and women. Furthermore, it is important to note that I initially elaborated on the hypothesis that gender-sensitive operations in development-oriented refugee assistance have the potential to revise obsolete and discriminatory stereotypes of gender. I assumed that gender sensitivity entails a dual imperative in the context of development-oriented refugee assistance. This means that on the one hand, adequate refugee assistance would support the psychological transitional process in promoting equality aims for reaching gender parity. On the other hand, it means that development aid can only be performed sustainably and efficiently if both men and women are involved in the process. During the research process, I faced two unexpected obstacles, which created challenges in examining this hypothesis. Voluntary repatriation of refugees was increasingly pursued in operations. By the time I conducted field research, most of the refugees had repatriated and the few remaining were residing in different locations within the camp, which did not constitute the original setting. Therefore, I was unable to conduct focal group discussions with refugees. Since the hypothesis still appeared to be of central meaning, I decided to draw information from expert interviews as well as DED's annual reports. Although certain data was collected, first-hand information from refugees about stereotypical gender relations and whether or not operations helped to overcome obsolete gender images, remain to be missing. Hence, the hypothesis of empowering impact through development-oriented refugee assistance towards gender leaves the window for further research on the ground.

This study neither intends to document and analyze individual experiences of refugees nor their identity perceptions. I am aware that many researchers working on refugee assistance direct their attention rather to psychological impacts of refugee lives or socio-economic misery while they are residing in camps and settlements. Nevertheless, the research goal is to examine entire processes of the working model from a meta-level. Moreover, my research focuses on refugees although Uganda obtains not only numerous refugees but also IDPs. It should be noted that IDPs are not part of the research project.

At Rhino Camp and in regard to relevant actors, it is to note that although WFP ensures food security in the camp, it does not give any further support. The German Federal Ministry for Economic Cooperation and Development is neither actively nor passively present. Thus, both WFP and the federal ministry are not included in the analysis as actors. The focus remains on the following three actors: UNHCR, OPM, and DED.

It may be noted that there are limitations in the access to documentation. DED provided me with annual reports about the implementations at Rhino Camp. However, neither proposals submitted to receive funds from donors nor annual budgets were accessible. It was not be traceable to see what kind of additional activities DED proposed to realize in comparison to those eventually implemented and stated in the annual reports. Efficiency could not be analyzed against financially efficient implementation. In addition, DED allowed me to access their database on infrastructures at Rhino Camp. The database was developed by external experts to screen the functionality, usability, and access of infrastructures for beneficiaries of refugee and local communities. Due to a lack of indication when particular infrastructures were constructed, data could only be used in general terms.

Finally, I do not claim to conduct research that is all-encompassing or fully comprehensive in its coverage. Moreover, as criticized by Jacobs and Landau, I also do not pursue "'advocacy research', where a researcher already knows what she wants to see and say, and comes away from the research having 'proved' it" (Jacobsen/Landau 2003: 2).

4.3. Final Limitations Faced

The voluntary repatriation of refugees to South Sudan was slowly launched in 2006. More than 40,000 refugees were in West Nile region in 2007 (DED LS/400 2007: 5). When the research project was designed, it was not expected that refugees would return to South Sudan because it was assumed that refugees would await the referendum that took place in January 2011. This assumption was based on security and safety concerns which caused the flight of refugees almost two decades ago. In 2009, however, about 5,000 refugees remained in the West Nile region (DED LS/400 2009: 4) which is why the initial design of methods was adjusted. In the design phase of the research project, it was initially planned to apply focal group discussions, ero-epic dialogues, unstructured observation, and expert interviews during field studies. Focal group discussions with refugees were impossible to conduct due to repatriation. Discussions would have been essential if I had intended to analyze refugee identities and personal histories. Since I aimed at grasping the holistic development-oriented refugee assistance approach, it was reasoned and decided that focal group discussion can be left out because sufficient data could be collected through the other methods. Ero-epic dialogues were conducted through unstructured conversations in which the counterparts released information. It was summarized and written down after the dialogue. Only one ero-epic dialogue appeared to contain useful information for the research, which is why only one was eventually referred to. Unstructured observations aimed at capturing the complexity of settings at Rhino Camp. These were conducted. Since the DED provided access to the infrastructure database, little new information was observed in comparison with insights gained through the database. The database was used as a more comprehensive and objective source for analyses. Expert interviews were done in a structured manner with DED staff through a previously prepared list of questions. Not all planned interviews with DED staff were eventually conducted because meetings were cancelled or rejected. Inquiries for interviews with staff of OPM and UNHCR remained unanswered or were cancelled.

In addition to that, a lack of data prevented me from drawing a fully comprehensive picture. Little to no information was accessible, for example, on psychological counseling and the loan scheme. The lack of information posed obstacles in responding to questions about the process towards gender equality.

The lack of certain information furthermore caused obstacles for the research methodology. I used the post-modern feminism approach of IR in my analyses. Thereby, the aim was to grasp and deconstruct gender stereotypes by involving both sexes. While gender-related aspects were taken into consideration, I was unable to collect first-hand data in the field at Rhino Camp about gender relations. Data about traditional gender roles and relations was therefore predominantly drawn from the research of Mulumba, a Ugandan researcher. In spite of some shortcomings, it was possible to draw upon a conclusion.